THE
BISHOP'S
PALACE

A VOLUME IN THE SERIES
Conjunctions of Religion & Power in the Medieval Past

EDITED BY *Barbara H. Rosenwein*

THE BISHOP'S PALACE

ARCHITECTURE
AND AUTHORITY IN
MEDIEVAL ITALY

MAUREEN C. MILLER

Cornell University Press

Ithaca and London

First published 2000 by Cornell University Press

Printed in the United States of America

Cornell University Press strives to use environ-
mentally responsible suppliers and materials to the
fullest extent possible in the publishing of its books.
Such materials include vegetable-based, low-voc
inks and acid-free papers that are recycled, totally
chlorine-free, or partly composed of nonwood
fibers. Books that bear the logo of the FSC (Forest
Stewardship Council) use paper taken from forests
that have been inspected and certified as meeting
the highest standards for environmental and social
responsibility. For further information, visit our
website at www.cornellpress.cornell.edu.

Cloth printing   10 9 8 7 6 5 4 3 2 1

Library of Congress Cataloging-in-Publication Data

Miller, Maureen C. (Maureen Catherine), 1959–
    The bishop's palace : architecture and authority in
medieval Italy / Maureen C. Miller.
        p. cm. — (Conjunctions of religion and power
    in the medieval past)
    Includes bibliographical references and index.
    ISBN: 0-8014-3535-8 (cloth)
    1. Bishops—Dwellings—Italy. 2. Italy—Church
history—476–1400. 3. Palaces—Italy. I. Title. II.
Series.

BR874.M55 2000
262'.12245'0902—dc21

                                        00-022380

For my parents
Archie and Catherine,
and for my friends
Nancy and Peter

CONTENTS

Acknowledgments *ix*
Abbreviations *xi*

Introduction *1*
I. OFFICE / SPACE
    The Architectural Expression of Episcopal Authority, 300–1300 *13*

Chapter One
    The Episcopal Residence in Late Antiquity: *The Episcopium 16*
Chapter Two
    The Episcopal Residence in the Early Middle Ages: *The Domus Sancte Ecclesie 54*
Chapter Three
    The Episcopal Residence in the Central Middle Ages: *The Bishop's Palace 86*

II. CULTURE / POWER
    The Character of Space and the Meaning of Actions *123*

Chapter Four
    Urban Space and Sacred Authority *125*
Chapter Five
    What Kind of Lord? *The Bishop in His Hall 170*
Chapter Six
    Spiritual Space, Interiority, and Charismatic Authority: *The Bishop's Chapel 216*

Conclusion *253*
Appendix *261*
Selected Bibliography *277*
Index/Glossary *303*

ACKNOWLEDGMENTS

To acknowledge adequately the dense genealogy of generosities underlying every page in this book would require the creation of a new mode of annotation, some capacious referential system to register scholarly kindness in its many and varied forms. Lacking such software at present, I must limit myself to these prefatory pages.

This project was generously supported from start to finish by Hamilton College. Two deans of the faculty — Eugene M. Tobin, now president, and Bobby Fong — funded various trips to Italy and granted me several leaves to bring the book to completion. My colleagues — in my department and in the wider college community — offered wise commentary and cheerful support. Christine R. Ingersoll produced all of the line drawings. Her gifts as an artist brought visual legibility to my imprecise paste-ups; the grace and clarity in these figures reflect hers. Marianita J. Amodio developed and printed all of my photographs in addition to rectifying some disasters of my own creation.

The Trinity Barbieri Prize, awarded by the Society for Italian Historical Studies and funded by the Trinity Barbieri Foundation, made possible an extended archival tour of northern Italy in the spring of 1994, and a Travel to Collections Grant from the National Endowment for the Humanities also supported this research. This book was written, in large part, in the genial setting of the Stanford Humanities Center. My fellowship at the center enriched this study and my life beyond words. Its director, Keith Baker, associate director, Susan E. Dunn, and all my fellow fellows from 1996 to 1997 provided stimulation and support in just the right measures. I would also like to thank Susan Sebbard, Susan Dambrau, and Gwen Lorraine, who do so much more than make the place run.

Two historians deserve special thanks for their unflagging support of both this project and me: William M. Bowsky and Barbara H. Rosenwein. Barbara's careful and critical reading of the manuscript in draft form led to numerous substantial improvements, and Bill's bibliographical suggestions and forthright commentary enlarged and focused my thinking on key points. Their friendship and support have been of incalculable value. Giles Constable, Philippe Buc, Paula Findlen, Lisa Rothrauf, Laura Smoller, and William L. North read individual chapters and offered helpful suggestions. I also thank participants in the University of California Medieval Seminar, the University of California, Berkeley Medieval Studies program, and the European History Workshop at Stanford University for their commentary and questions. Several art and architectural historians have generously tutored me in the mysteries of their discipline: Virginia

Jansen, Barbara Abou-el-haj, Juergen Schulz, and Gary Radke (who read the entire manuscript in draft form). The second reader for Cornell University Press, Steven Epstein, also offered very helpful suggestions for revision.

Archivists and colleagues throughout Italy made this study possible. I would like to thank, in particular, prof. Giancarlo Andenna in Novara, don Guido Agosti of the Archivio Capitolare in Reggio Emilia, don Bianchi at the Curia in Parma, dott. Giulio Orazio Bravi of the Biblioteca Civica Angelo Mai in Bergamo, don Bruno Caccia of the Ufficio dei Beni Culturali Ecclesiastici della Curia di Bergamo, dott. Piero Castignoli of the Archivio di Stato in Piacenza, dott. Adriano Franceschine in Ferrara, don Giovanni Montanari of the Archivio Arcivescovile in Ravenna, mons. Alberto Piazzi and don Giuseppe Zivelonghi at the Biblioteca e Archivio Capitolare di Verona, ing. Natale Rauty in Pistoia, prof. Antonio Rigon of the Università degli Studi at Padua, and don Saverio Xeres of the Archivio Diocesano in Como.

At Cornell University Press, John G. Ackerman supported this project from its infancy, and his editorial wisdom has much improved it as it has matured. If there are still qualities of awkward adolescence, they are a measure of my own authorial willfulness.

Finally, this book is dedicated to two couples. My parents, Archie and Catherine Miller, have taught me more about endurance and change than any medieval palace could. They remain incredibly supportive of my passion for history, even with all the mobility and distance it entails, and I am deeply grateful for both their example and their love. The other couple has transformed my understanding of friendship. So I also dedicate this book to Peter and Nancy Rabinowitz, with all my love and with profound gratitude.

ABBREVIATIONS

AALucca
  Archivio Arcivescovile di Lucca
AARavenna
  Archivio Storico Arcivescovile di Ravenna
ACAFerrara
  Archivio della Curia Arcivescovile di Ferrara
ACCReggio
  Archivio del Capitolo della Cattedrale di Reggio Emilia
ACFaenza
  Archivio Capitolare del Duomo di San Pietro, Faenza
ACPiacenza
  Archivio della Cattedrale di Piacenza
ACPistoia
  Archivio Capitolare di Pistoia
ACRimini
  Archivio Capitolare di Rimini
ACTreviso
  Archivio Capitolare di Treviso
ACVerona
  Archivio Capitolare di Verona
ADComo
  Archivio Diocesano di Como
ADPavia
  Archivio Diocesano di Pavia
ASBologna
  Archivio di Stato, Bologna
ASFerrara
  Archivio di Stato, Ferrara
ASModena
  Archivio di Stato, Modena

ASPiacenza
> Archivio di Stato, Piacenza

ASReggio
> Archivio di Stato, Reggio Emilia

ASVerona
> Archivio di Stato, Verona

AVBergamo
> Archivio Vescovile di Bergamo

BCFaenza
> Biblioteca Comunale di Faenza

BCFerrara
> Biblioteca Comunale "Ariosto" di Ferrara

BCRimini
> Biblioteca Civica Gambalunga di Rimini

FREQUENTLY CITED WORKS

AASS
> *Acta sanctorum quotquot toto orbe coluntur*, ed. Jean Bolland et al., Editio nova (Paris and Rome: Victor Palmé, 1863–).

Agnellus, *LP*
> *Agnelli et Andreas Liber Pontificalis Ecclesiae Ravennatis*, ed. O. Holder Egger in *Monumenta Germaniae historica, Scriptores Rerum Langobardicarum et Italicarum saec. VI–IX* (Hannover: Hahn, 1878), 265–391.

Arezzo-Documenti
> *Documenti per la storia della città di Arezzo nel medio evo*, ed. Ubaldo Pasqui, 2 vols. (Florence: G. P. Vieusseaux/R. Deputazione di Storia Patria, 1899).

Carte Cremonesi
> *Le carte cremonesi dei secoli VIII–XII*, ed. Ettore Falconi, 4 vols., Ministero per i beni culturali e ambientali, Biblioteca statale di Cremona, Fonti e sussidi I/1–4 (Cremona: Linograf S. N. C., 1979–88).

Carte Reggio
> *Le carte degli archivi reggiani fino al 1050*, ed. Pietro Torelli (Reggio Emilia: Cooperativa Lavoranti Tipografi, 1921).

CC
> *Corpus Christianorum*. Series Latina (Turnhout: Brepols, 1953–).

CC Cont. Med.
> *Corpus Christianorum*. Continuatio Mediaevalis (Turnhout: Brepols, 1966–).

CDL
> *Codice diplomatico langobardo*, ed. Luigi Schiaparelli (vols. 1–2), Carlrichard Brühl (vol. 3), 3 vols., Fonti per la storia d'Italia 62, 63, 64 (Rome: Istituto storico italiano, 1929–73).

CDP

    Codice diplomatico padovano, ed. Andrea Gloria, 3 vols. (Venice: Deputazione di storia patria per le Venezie, 1877–81).

CDV

    Codice diplomatico veronese, ed. Vittorio Fainelli, 2 vols. (Venice: Deputazione di storia patria per le Venezie, 1940–63).

DDC

    Dictionnaire de droit canonique, 7 vols. (Paris: Librarie Letouzey et Ané, 1935–65).

DMA

    Dictionary of the Middle Ages, ed. Joseph R. Strayer, 13 vols. (New York: Scribner, 1982).

Duchesne, *LP*

    Le Liber Pontificalis, ed. Louis Duchesne, 2 vols. (Paris: Ernest Thorin/École française D'Athènes et de Rome, 1886–92). Reprinted with a third volume of commentary and indices, ed. Cyrille Vogel (Paris: Boccard, 1955– 57). English translation by Raymond Davis, *The Book of Pontiffs (Liber Pontificalis)* (Liverpool: University Press, 1989); *The Lives of the Eighth-Century Popes (Liber Pontificalis)* (Liverpool: University Press, 1992); *The Lives of the Ninth-Century Popes (Liber Pontificalis)* (Liverpool: University Press, 1995).

EAM

    Enciclopedia dell'arte medievale (Rome: Istituto della Enciclopedia Italiana, 1991–).

Fantuzzi, *Mon. rav.*

    M. Fantuzzi, *Monumenti ravennati de' secoli di mezzo per la maggior parte inediti*, 6 vols. (Venice: Francesco Andreola, 1801–4).

Gregory the Great, *Dialogues*

    Gregory the Great, *Dialogues*, ed. Adalbert de Vogüé, Sources chrétiennes 260 (Paris: Cerf, 1979); trans. Odo John Zimmerman OSB, *Fathers of the Church* 39 (New York: Fathers of the Church, 1959).

Jaffé, *Regesta*

    Regesta Pontificum Romanorum, ed. Philipp Jaffé, 2nd ed. Corrected W. Wattenbach, ed. S. Loewenfeld, F. Kaltenbrunner, P. Ewald, 2 vols. (Leipzig: Veit, 1885–88).

Lauer, *Latran*

    Philippe Lauer, *Le Palais de Latran. Étude historique et archéologique* (Paris: Ernest Leroux, 1911).

Manaresi, *Placiti*

    I placiti del «regnum Italiae», ed. Cesare Manaresi, 3 vols., Fonti per la storia d'Italia 92, 96, 97 (Rome: Tipografia del Senato, 1955–60).

Mansi

    Sacrorum conciliorum nova et amplissima collectio, ed. J. D. Mansi, 53 vols. (Florence and Venice: Antonius Zata, 1759–98).

MEFR

    Mélanges de l'École française de Rome—moyen âge.

Mem. e doc.

 Memorie e documenti per servire alla storia di Lucca, 16 vols. (Lucca: 1813–1933).

MGH Auct. Ant.

 Monumenta Germaniae historica, Auctorum antiquissimorum (Berlin: Weidmannsche Verlagsbuchhandlung, 1879–1919).

MGH Concilia

 Monumenta Germaniae historica, Legum sectio III: Concilia (Hannover and Leipzig: Bibliopolius Hahnianus, 1893–).

MGH DD

 Monumenta Germaniae historica, Diplomatum regum et imperatorum Germaniae (Berlin: Weidmannsche Verlagsbuchhandlung, 1879–).

MGH Epist.

 Monumenta Germaniae historica, Epistolae, 8 vols. (Berlin: Weidmannsche Verlagsbuchhandlung, 1887–1939).

MGH SRM

 Monumenta Germaniae historica, Scriptorum rerum Merovingicarum, tomus I (Hannover: Hahn, 1885).

MGH SS

 Monumenta Germaniae historica, Scriptorum (Hannover: Bibliopolius Hahnianius, 1826–; reprinted, Stuttgart: Anton Hiersemann, New York: Kraus, 1903-).

MGH SSRL

 Monumenta Germaniae historica, Scriptores rerum Langobardicarum et Italicarum saec. VI–IX (Hannover: Hahn, 1878).

Miller, *Formation*

 Maureen C. Miller, *The Formation of a Medieval Church: Ecclesiastical Change in Verona, 950–1150* (Ithaca: Cornell University Press, 1993).

Miller, "Ravenna"

 Maureen C. Miller, "The Development of the Archiepiscopal Residence in Ravenna, 300–1300," *Felix Ravenna* 141–44 (1991–92): 145–73.

Niermeyer, *MLLM*

 J. F. Niermeyer, *Mediae Latinitatis Lexicon Minus* (Leiden: E. J. Brill, 1976).

Parma IX

 Codice diplomatico parmense. Volume primo, secolo VIIII, ed. Umberto Benassi (Parma: R. Deputazione di storia patria per le province parmensi, 1910).

Parma X

 "Le carte degli archivi parmensi dei secoli X-XI," ed. Giovanni Drei, *Archivio storico per le province parmensi* ns. 22bis (1922): 535–612; 23 (1923): 225–353; 24 (1924): 221–95.

Parma XI

 "Le carte degli archivi parmensi dei secoli X–XI," ed. Giovanni Drei, *Archivio storico per le province parmensi* ns. 25 (1925): 227–334; 26 (1926): 135–239; 28 (1928): 109–273.

Parma XII

    Le carte degli archivi parmensi del sec. XII, ed. Giovanni Drei (Parma: L'Archivio di Stato, 1950).

Perg. Bergamo

    Le pergamene degli archivi di Bergamo, a. 740–1000, ed. Mariarosa Cortesi, 2 vols., (Bergamo: Bolis, 1988).

PL

    Patrologiae cursus completus, Ser. Lat., ed. J. P. Migne, 221 vols. (Paris: Garnier, 1844–64).

Rauty, *Palazzo*

    Natale Rauty, *L'antico palazzo dei vescovi a Pistoia. I, Storia e restauro* and *II.1, Indagini archeologici* and *II.2, I documenti archeologici*, ed. Guido Vannini (Florence: Leo S. Olschki Editore, 1981–85).

Reg. Mantua

    Regesto mantovano, ed. Pietro Torelli, Regesta chartarum Italiae 12 (Rome: Ermanno Loescher, 1914).

Reg. Modena

    Regesto della chiesa cattedrale di Modena, ed. Emilio Paolo Vicini, 2 vols., Regesta chartarum Italia 16 and 21 (Rome: Maglione, 1931–36).

Reg. Volterra

    Regestum Volterranum. Regesten der Urkunden von Volterra (778–1303), ed. Fedor Schneider (Rome: Ermanno Loescher, 1907).

RIS

    Rerum Italicarum scriptores, ed. Lodovico Antonio Muratori, 25 vols. (Milan typographia Societatis palatinae, 1723-51).

RSCI

    Rivista di storia della chiesa in Italia

Salimbene, *Cronica*

    Salimbene de Adam, *Cronica*, ed. Giuseppe Scalia, 2 vols. (Bari: Laterza, 1966); trans. Joseph L. Baird (Binghamton, N.Y.: Medieval & Renaissance Texts & Studies, 1986).

Ughelli, *IS*

    Italia sacra, ed. Ferdinando Ughelli, 2nd ed., 9 vols. (Venice: Sebastianus Coleti, 1717–22).

THE
BISHOP'S
PALACE

INTRODUCTION

Enter just about any Italian city today. Wend your way to its center and you will find yourself in a broad piazza dominated by the communal palace. In Gubbio it's the crenelated gray mass of the Palazzo dei Consoli. In Siena the fan-shaped *campo* is raked so that gravity (if not knowledge of Duccio, Martini, and Lorenzetti) pulls you down into the Palazzo Pubblico. In Bologna the splash of the Neptune fountain focuses your senses, but it is the rising mass of the communal palace behind you that offers shade. Go up the old Via Emilia and in Modena, Parma, and Piacenza, the cafes at the heart of downtown spill out from the porticos of a communal palace or take in the view of its facade. Similarly pleasurable configurations are offered in cities all along the northern edge of the Po valley: Como, Bergamo, Brescia, Padua, and Treviso. This scenic characteristic of urban northern Italy feels quite venerable. And it is. These monuments to civic consciousness were built at the very end of the twelfth century or, more often, in the thirteenth. The ideals they visualized then — autonomy, collaborative government, civic pride — have lived on in varied forms into the modern era. And thus their reordering of urban space has endured.

But a very different topography of power preceded them. In the eleventh and twelfth centuries a visitor to any of these cities would also have found a "palace" at its center: its tower located it from afar and its massive walls bespoke wealth, military power, and public authority. This palace was the bishop's. It flanked the city's central sacred space, the cathedral, and like the communal palace that de-centered it in the urban fabric, it too represented lofty ideals: those of civic unity, individual and collective salvation, good lordship, and a right ordering of society.

Today's visitor would be hard pressed to locate this palace in the modern Italian city; the bishop's palace is generally not part of the "itinerario turistico." And an intrepid seeker who manages to discover it most likely would be disappointed. In most cases, these are no longer elegant structures: renovated repeatedly over the centuries, most present a motley mix of styles to the viewer and an ungainly imbalance of additions and truncations. Mainly for this reason, architectural historians have not been much interested in them.[1] One goal of this book is to recover some sense of these structures that

1. A few individual palaces in Italy have been the subject of local studies: Nestore Pelicelli, *Il vescovado di Parma* (Parma, 1922); R. Zanocco, "Luogo e vicende del palazzo vescovile di Padova

were so central to the medieval city. Another is to use them as a vantage point to reexamine two important historical transformations: the birth of the communes and the reform of the medieval church.

The emergence of communal government is the central narrative in Italian medieval history. During the early Middle Ages, northern and central Italy constituted a kingdom. Ruled by Lombard kings in the sixth through eighth centuries, then incorporated into the Frankish empire by Charlemagne, the *regnum Italiae* devolved in the tenth and eleventh centuries to the German emperors who had revived royal authority in the eastern lands of the fractured Carolingian state. These rulers came over the Alps only intermittently and depended on local functionaries — counts and bishops — to govern their Italian territories. This system was fatally disrupted in the late eleventh century when imperial authority was in abeyance during the long contest between Pope Gregory VII and Emperor Henry IV over the lay investiture of bishops. During this period of political instability, oath-bound associations of citizens (the "communes") formed to preserve peace and order in their cities. Slowly, and usually through cooperation with their bishop, they began to acquire and exercise governing powers. By the late twelfth century, they had become the officially recognized governments of their towns. Historians usually characterize the commune's rise to power as a heroic, meteoric victory of popular self-determination. The role of bishops in the process is generally minimized, their collaboration with the citizens portrayed as grudging and temporary.[2] The vantage point of the bishop's palace suggests otherwise. As we shall see, the bishop's use of the word *palace* to describe his residence was a response to the first stirrings of these citizen aspirations. And this palace was the place where the leaders of the early commune learned about governance: the early officials of the commune often met in the bishop's palace, and they were among the local notables who attended his court there. The

---

nel medioevo," *Bollettino diocesano di Padova* 12 (1927): 593–603;Federico Frigerio and Giovanni Baserga, "Il palazzo vescovile di Como," *Rivista archeologica dell'antica provincia e diocesi di Como* 125–26 (1944): 9–104; Giuseppe Pistoni, *Il palazzo arcivescovile di Modena*, Deputazione di storia patria per le antiche provincie modenesi, Biblioteca n.s. 33 (Modena, 1976); Maria Ortensia Banzola, "Il palazzo del vescovado," *Parma nell'arte* 14 (1982): 25–51; Rauty, *Palazzo;* Emanuele Barletti, *Il palazzo arcivescovile di Firenze vicende architettoniche dal 1533 al 1895* (Florence, 1989). In the 1960s Wolfgang Braunfels raised a series of questions relating to the position of bishops in their cities, in passing mentioning their palaces, but there has been little response to his "Tre domande a proposito del problema «vescovo e città» nell'alto medioevo," *Il romanico pistoiese nei suoi rapporti con l'arte romanica dell'occidente*, Atti del I Convegno internazionale di studi medioevali di storia e d'arte (Pistoia, 1966), 117–42. Michael Thompson's *Medieval Bishops' Houses in England and Wales* (Aldershot, 1998) catalogues buildings with some commentary and includes useful plans and photos, but having been written for a popular audience of architectural enthusiasts, it is of little interpretive value.

2. A recent example of this characterization is Philip Jones, *The Italian City-State: From Commune to Signoria* (Oxford, 1997), 136–41. He acknowledges the cooperation or alliance between bishops and communes, but concludes "condominium, where attested, was a mask for revolution, an expedient or subterfuge" (141) on the part of early communal leaders. More examples are found later in Chapter 4. The best introduction for students and nonspecialists to the emergence and character of the Italian communes is Daniel Waley, *The Italian City-Republics*, 3rd ed. (New York, 1988).

FIGURE 1. *Cities of northern and central Italy. (C. Ingersoll.)*

buildings these leaders of the commune later devised show its influence. I argue here that the episcopal lordship exercised from this palace was more than a brief transitory phase in the political life of the medieval Italian city.

The bishop's palace also illuminates the mixed heritage of the great ecclesiastical reform movement of the eleventh and early twelfth centuries. Usually called the Gregorian reform after the vociferous pontiff Gregory VII (1073–85), this movement originated earlier and with lay, not papal, initiatives. Local attempts to reintroduce rigor into monastic life and institutions in the tenth century escalated in the eleventh to calls for a general reform of the church. Particularly targeted were the secular (or diocesan) clergy. Lay people wanted their clergy to be celibate (and therefore pure to celebrate the eucharist) and demanded an end to simony (the custom of giving gifts in exchange for clerical offices that often devolved into outright purchase of ecclesiastical positions). Overall, a greater separation of the sacred from the profane, of the church from the world, was the reformers' aim. This goal was usually expressed in calls for the "freedom of the church" (*libertas ecclesiae*), and it had its most dramatic expression in the investiture contest. This struggle between popes and emperors over the practice of monarchs investing bishops with the symbols of their office divided Europe for close to a half century and led to fundamental changes in the organization of the medieval church and in its relationship to society.

In evaluating the impact of the reform movement, historians emphasize the growth of papal monarchy as its most important result.[3] Here too the bishop's palace offers a different perspective. It reveals a world of collective clerical creativity that had little to do with the papacy. The architecture and decor of episcopal residences in the twelfth and thirteenth centuries were aspects of a distinctive clerical culture emerging in response to reform. By "clerical culture" I mean the particular way of life of the clergy; their institutions; their values, beliefs, and customs; their use of objects; and their material life.[4] One of the chief complaints of reformers in the eleventh century was that the clergy had become indistinct from the laity — they wore lay clothing, carried arms, and lived with women — and other sources verify this blurring of social and sacred boundaries. Here we will look at only an elite subset of the clergy, bishops, but these

3. Generally, on the reform and investiture conflict, see Uta-Renate Blumenthal, *The Investiture Controversy: Church and Monarchy from the Ninth to the Twelfth Century* (Philadelphia, 1988); Gerd Tellenbach, *The Church in Western Europe from the Tenth to the Early Twelfth Century*, trans. Timothy Reuter (Cambridge, 1993); Giles Constable, *The Reformation of the Twelfth Century* (Cambridge, 1996). Raoul Manselli, summarizing "The Historical Significance of the Reform Movement," concluded that the Concordat of Worms constituted another element in the slow but progressive formation and juridical constitution of the temporal power of the papacy: "Egemonia imperiale, autonomia comunale, potenza politica dell chiesa," in *Storia d'Italia*, ed. Giuseppe Galasso, vol. 4: Ovidio Capitani, et al., *Comuni e signorie: istituzioni, società e lotte per l'egemonia* (Turin, 1981), 91.

4. A definition of culture I have borrowed from John Clarke, Stuart Hall, Tony Jefferson, and Brian Roberts, "Subcultures, cultures and class," *Cultural Studies* 7 / 8 (1975): 10. Medievalists traditionally have treated culture as synonymous with intellectual life. Thus, in Louis John Paetow's *A Guide to the Study of Medieval History* (1917; reprinted, Millwood, N.Y., 1980), topics such as the development of the Latin language, the classical heritage, medieval schools and the rise of the universities, books and libraries, and the history of philosophy constitute medieval "culture." Since literacy was largely the domain of the clergy, intellectual life or "culture" has been described as "clerical." It is in this sense that Jacques Le Goff, in an article entitled "Culture cléricale et traditions folkloriques dans la civilisation mérovingienne," *Annales* 22 (1967): 780–91, used the phrase "clerical culture": it stood in contrast to "traditions folkloriques" or popular culture. More recently, this sense of clerical culture has taken on more ominous overtones. In David Noble's *A World without Women: The Christian Clerical Culture of Western Science* (Oxford, 1992), the phrase "clerical culture" is generally a shorthand for learned or literate culture but also, more pointedly, for misogynist, exclusive, and repressive ecclesiastical culture. Influenced by more recent work in cultural studies, I will use the term "clerical culture" in a more capacious fashion to include not only the intellectual life of the clergy, but also their material life and their popular beliefs and practices. Like lay or secular culture, in my view, clerical culture has positive as well as negative aspects.

clerics were highly influential: they were the leaders of the local church and superiors of its clergy. Through this exploration of episcopal residences and the actions that took place within them, we will see how the culture of these clerical elites differed from that of their secular counterparts. We will also see that it differed from the papacy's.

This reassertion of cultural difference, moreover, was part of a complex and highly significant shift in power. Basically, bishops lost temporal authority in their cities, and this loss was a final legacy of the investiture conflict. They had achieved temporal powers within their cities in the ninth and tenth centuries by becoming imperial functionaries, and the great contest between Pope Gregory VII and Emperor Henry IV had fatally undermined this relationship. It created the uncertain political conditions that gave birth to the communes and theorized the separation of the sacred and temporal that was ultimately valorized in the communal takeover of civil powers formerly exercised by bishops. Yet ecclesiastical leaders were not willing to abandon claims on civil society; they believed that the church should influence, if not control, public life and sought new means to accomplish this. By necessity, the strategies of power they developed were less direct than the political authority they had previously enjoyed. Bishops sought to retain power within their communities by placing new emphasis on cultural and spiritual presence.

Much of this transformation was relatively benign. For example, bishops compensated architecturally for their loss of authority, doubling or tripling the size of their palaces and competing directly with the commune for visual dominance in the urban landscape. They reoriented their palaces in relation to the public space of the piazza and used this space to heighten awareness of their presence and social connections. But not all of the new episcopal strategies of power were unobjectionable. They increasingly relied on the coercive use of spiritual authority to retain status and public influence. These new methods were a major factor in the emergence of a significantly more oppressive climate within the western church and European society as a whole.

Understanding the causes of growing intolerance and repression in western Europe over these centuries has been a preoccupation in scholarly discourse on the Middle Ages since the publication in 1987 of R. I. Moore's *The Formation of a Persecuting Society*. Moore describes a pattern of increasing persecution of heretics, Jews, and lepers across the eleventh and twelfth centuries. He pinpoints the late twelfth century as the period in which "a comprehensive apparatus of persecution was worked out"; by the middle of the thirteenth century it had been perfected.[5] Moore attributes the definition of aberrants and their systematic persecution to the emergence of the bureaucratic state: "the suspicion and accusation of heresy among the population at large was used as a means of suppressing resistance to the exercise of power over it, and of legitimizing the new regime in church and state."[6] The view we get from the vantage point of the bishop's palace complicates this picture considerably. It suggests at least two modifications to

5. R. I. Moore, *The Formation of a Persecuting Society: Power and Deviance in Western Europe, 950–1250* (Oxford, 1987), 66.
6. Ibid., 144.

Moore's explanation. First, although Moore was right to locate the rise of intolerance in political rivalry, his identification of new regimes as the persecutors is too simple. Close analysis of political rivalry and the use of oppressive tactics in northern Italian cities in the twelfth and early thirteenth centuries suggests that those consolidating bureaucratic power, the communes, were not necessarily the oppressors. Those whose power was slipping away, the bishops, used persecution to maintain influence and a sphere of authority. This realization points directly to the second problem with Moore's thesis: he conflates all authorities — "emerging nation states," "nascent papal monarchy," "municipal government" — into one "new order" that was the source of systematic intolerance. Moore sees "a single regime" in these various powers.[7] But as will become clear, distinctions, particularly those between secular and ecclesiastical authorities, are crucial in understanding how political rivalry produced oppression.

We will see, moreover, that material culture has much to offer the ecclesiastical historian.[8] The study of Christianity has long been a subfield of intellectual history, emphasizing the development of doctrine, law, theology, and spirituality. Social and economic historians since the 1950s have grounded this intellectual history in the institutional realities of religious life, making manifest its economic underpinnings and deep connections with the social worlds of local communities.[9] But this grounding is still insufficient. The practice of Christianity in Late Antiquity and the Middle Ages produced an extraordinarily rich material culture. Liturgical structures — churches, chapels, oratories, baptisteries, and shrines — were ubiquitous in local landscapes and highly significant in everyday life. Liturgical objects — vestments, reliquaries, books, altar vessels, processional crosses, croziers, and censers — were familiar but highly charged symbols invested with precious decoration and sacred power. Although architectural and art historians have studied these structures and objects, their work has not challenged the general narrative of Christian history, and ecclesiastical historians still tend to see art and architecture as ornamentation and illustration. Some very recent

7. Ibid., 136.

8. Interest in material and visual culture — interpretive approaches influenced by cultural studies and critical theory — has been much stronger among scholars of the eras before and after the Middle Ages; medievalists have been slow to make use of these methods. For antiquity, note John R. Clarke, *The Houses of Roman Italy, 100 BC–AD 250: Ritual, Space, and Decoration* (Berkeley, 1991); Andrew Wallace-Hadrill, *Houses and Society in Pompeii and Herculaneum* (Princeton, 1994); and Jas Elsner, *The Roman Viewer: The Transformation of Roman Art from the Pagan World to Christianity* (Cambridge, 1995). For the Renaissance, see Michael Baxandall, *Painting and Experience in Fifteenth-Century Italy* (Oxford, 1974; 2nd ed., 1988); Paula Findlen, *Possessing Nature: Museums, Collecting, and Scientific Culture in Early Modern Italy* (Berkeley, 1994); *Reframing the Renaissance: Visual Culture in Europe and Latin America 1450–1650*, ed. Claire Farago (New Haven, Conn., 1995); and Lisa Jardine, *Worldly Goods* (London, 1996).

9. I would place my first book, *The Formation of a Medieval Church: Ecclesiastical Change in Verona, 950–1150* (Ithaca, 1993), squarely in this tradition. Other good examples are Barbara H. Rosenwein, *To Be the Neighbor of Saint Peter: The Social Meaning of Cluny's Property, 909–1049* (Ithaca, 1989); and Constance Brittain Bouchard, *Holy Entrepreneurs: Cistercians, Knights, and Economic Exchange in Twelfth-Century Burgundy* (Ithaca, 1991).

work by art historians begins to bring the evidence of material and visual culture to bear more forcefully on our general understanding of medieval civilization.[10] This study of the bishop's palace will demonstrate how the evidence of visual and material culture can help us rethink traditional narratives of the development of western Christianity.

Because this approach to the medieval church through its visual and material culture is novel, a body of well-documented evidence of the clergy's material life has not yet been achieved. Indeed, when I began writing this book, I realized that a good portion of it would have to be devoted to a presentation and synthesis of the evidence available. Thus, the entire first part provides an overview of the development of episcopal residences in Italy from Late Antiquity to the thirteenth century. The second part focuses on the central Middle Ages and uses the evidence of the bishop's palace to question traditional narratives of political and religious change in this period. In proffering both a developmental narrative of the episcopal residence and a close reading of its significance in one era, I am aware of the fragmentary, frustrating, and at many points inadequate character of the evidence at hand. Often those cities with the richest documentary heritage offer no medieval remains of the bishop's palace. Well-studied physical remains of entire medieval palaces are rare (the best being at Pistoia, Parma, and Como), but partial remains from other cities and documentary descriptions do present provocative evidence. Only more archeological work will prove or disprove some of the interpretations essayed here. If they provoke further research and debate, I will rest contented even if proved wrong.

Wherever possible, I have considered evidence from other parts of Europe, and readers will find citations to this work in my annotation. But I have focused my inquiry on northern and central Italy for two reasons. First, this geographical area shared certain political structures and transformations during the central Middle Ages. Although its southern bounds varied with the ambition of different kings, the lands between the Alps and Rome were part of the Kingdom of Italy and experienced the rule of Ottonian and Salian emperors in the tenth and eleventh centuries. Over the twelfth century, communes emerged in cities throughout this area. There is strong regional variation within this geographical zone, but in each and every one of these cities, the bishop came to call his residence a "palace" (*palatium*), and this fact in and of itself called for a broad inquiry. The appendix sets out in detail regional variations in the linguistic evidence, but one geographical distinction is perhaps most important for the general reader: the patterns described here are strongest in the Po valley and northern Tuscany. This area was the heart of the Italian kingdom. Commerce along the Po fostered cultural and po-

10. Michael Camille, *The Gothic Idol: Ideology and Image-Making in Medieval Art* (New York, 1989) and *Image on the Edge: The Margins of Medieval Art* (Cambridge, Mass., 1992); Jeffrey P. Hamburger, *Nuns as Artists: The Visual Culture of a Medieval Convent* (Berkeley, 1997); Roberta Gilchrist, *Gender and Material Culture: The Archaeology of Religious Women* (New York, 1997). Although focused on the Renaissance, Richard A. Goldthwaite's *Wealth and the Demand for Art in Italy 1300–1600* (Baltimore and London, 1993), 70–148, is the best discussion to date of the significance of the material culture of western Christianity.

litical contacts among these cities, and imperial rule was most concerted in this economically vibrant zone. Communal development also was most precocious here.

The second reason to focus on northern and central Italy is more pragmatic. Southern Italy has a very different history. Arab dominion over Sicily and Byzantine control over Apulia lasted into the eleventh century; then the Normans arrived and established a kingdom. These different historical circumstances and, certainly, scholarly prejudices, have led to the development of different historiographies and research communities. My own training and background have been in one, that of northern and central Italy, and since my knowledge of the other is weak, I thought it more prudent to leave the history of episcopal palaces in southern Italy to those better qualified to do it justice. Communes did emerge in some southern cities, and these may provide a salutary test of the interpretations offered here.

The ongoing reevaluation of medieval political history provides another reason to focus on developments in northern and central Italy. This area is usually absent from traditional accounts of medieval politics, which narrate the rise of strong monarchies in both church and state. Even when present, the political landscape of northern and central Italy is often included only to illustrate the "failure" of effective centralization in the German empire. Such traditional narratives, however, are now being radically revised, and the focus of inquiry shifted from governance and the state to the diverse ways in which power was exercised, experienced, and represented in medieval Europe. Medieval Italy has much to offer this new historical discourse. Its long notarial tradition produced an immensely rich documentary record, and its urban chroniclers offer us quite sophisticated reflections on the uses and abuses of power in their societies. The city state, that lively joining of "power and imagination" (in the felicitous description of Lauro Martines) that was the dominant political construct in medieval Italy, never came to dominate subsequent European politics. But the transformations of power I will narrate here were as much part of the political landscape of medieval Europe as were the writs of Henry II and the territorial conquests of Philip Augustus. There is much to be gained by stepping back from the pursuit of a "developmental history of power" to appreciate fully the meaning and practice of power in this society. As T. N. Bisson succinctly reminds us, "[p]eople in the twelfth century did not know they were inventing the state."[11] Recovering the manifold and sinuous workings of power in medieval society requires looking at cultural capital as well as government bureaucracies, losers as well as winners. This sort of recovery is the aim of the present book.

Finally, in resurrecting the medieval bishop's palace, I am participating in a uniquely twentieth-century endeavor. Until this century, episcopal palaces were renovated rather than restored. From the Middle Ages on, their current occupants brought them up-to-date, periodically redecorating them in the latest fashion, making them more comfortable and more "modern." This process has continued but it has been joined since the opening decades of this century by efforts to "restore" the bishop's palace.

11. *Cultures of Power: Lordship, Status, and Process in Twelfth-Century Europe*, ed. Thomas N. Bisson (Philadelphia, 1995), 8.

Contemporaries began to view these buildings as historical artifacts to be preserved, and they attempted to return them at least in part to their medieval appearance. Much of this work is problematic by today's standards of archeological inquiry and architectural restoration, but we still owe much to the enthusiasm of the local clerics, architects, engineers, and historians who articulated the first arguments for the significance of these buildings and who passionately worked for their preservation. They understood much about the meanings of place. They felt a deep sense of connectedness with those who had come before them in their city. The past was not just history; it was *their* history, narrowly focused on the streets and buildings around them. I admire and have learned from these enthusiasts, but my aims are different from theirs. Italy is not my "patria," nor that of my ancestors. A brief glance at the restoration of the episcopal palace in Parma will serve to distinguish my own interest in these buildings from previous enthusiasms for them.

Like most all of the buildings considered here, the bishop's palace in Parma was renovated repeatedly over the centuries after its foundation just after the millennium: in the late twelfth, early thirteenth, sixteenth, and eighteenth centuries, additions and "improvements" were made. Efforts to restore the palace began in 1920 and continued into the 1930s, and they were the project, chiefly, of Nestore Pelicelli. A priest born and raised just outside Parma, Pelicelli taught in the city's seminary and became an enthusiast for local history. It was said of Pelicelli that "he knew the history of every stone in Parma." From 1900 he served as "Honorary Inspector of Monuments of the City."[12]

The one that concerned him most was the bishop's palace. Pelicelli spearheaded a campaign to recover its thirteenth-century facade, which had been "veiled over by the ugliness of an eighteenth-century reconstruction." Distaste for the facade of the age of the Enlightenment dominates accounts: these Settecento renovations were deemed "injuries to art" and a "disfigurement of the original."[13] The rationale for recovering the thirteenth-century palace was a desire to harmonize the piazza, but repeated insistence that this restoration had not only local but also national significance begs a look at the context in which it was undertaken.

The *Gazzetta di Parma* publicized and praised Pelicelli's campaign; it also advocated support for the "blocco d'ordine," the fascists.[14] An obituary for Pelicelli published just after his death in 1937 reveals that the paper's political stance and the priest's restoration activities were not entirely unrelated.

12. P. Placido da Pavullo, *Don Nestore Pelicelli: «Genius loci»* (Parma, 1937), 5–6.

13. *Gazzetta di Parma* July 20, 1920, page 2 and August 14, 1920, page 2. Pelicelli himself published the first study of the structure: *Il vescovado di Parma* (Parma, 1922).

14. The lead article in the October 26, 1920 edition of the *Gazzetta* was entitled "I blocchi d'ordine" and advocated their support "contra gli estremisti del partito socialista che hanno nella nostra città la prevalenza." Its coverage in the November 9, 1920 edition of a melee that had occurred between socialists and fascists differed entirely from the account in the socialist paper, *L'Idea*. The *Gazzetta* reported that a socialist insulted a fascist trying to put up a manifesto and that this insult led to the violence. *L'Idea*, in an article published on November 13, blamed the violence on "un gruppo di studenti, di liberali e di fascisti."

His patriotism made him welcome in all circles. With passion he followed the affairs of our Fatherland and with interest he followed its events. All of us remember when recently in the Square he commented on the news of our glorious Ethiopian undertaking and we remember with great pleasure when with radiant joy he listened to the speech on the foundation of the Empire given by our great Leader.[15]

The revival and restoration of the cultural and artistic patrimony of the fatherland, the *patria*, were strong elements in fascist ideology and don Pelicelli participated in these enthusiasms.[16] A 1935 article on the restoration of the bishop's palace in the journal of the commune of Parma places it in its context. The restored thirteenth-century facade of the building graces the opening page of the piece with a headline celebrating "A Jewel of Romanesque Art," but on the opposite page are different faces. Here are the "Children of the Kindergarten of A. San Vitale Elementary School" being congratulated for collecting scrap metal to help arm the forces of the fatherland. A strange class picture it is, the solemn faces of about two-dozen five-year-olds clutching odd pieces of discarded metal while the text below them celebrates "the faith Il Duce cultivates in the souls and hearts of the new generation." More telling is the fact that this edition of the communal journal contained articles on the restoration of two medieval palaces. In addition to the piece on the bishop's palace there was one on the renovation of a communal palace, the palace of the *podestà*, as the new seat of the fascist "squadri" (Federazione dei Fasci di Combattimento). The latter explicitly connected the history of the medieval palace to its modern appropriation. Just as the "popolo" rose up to form the commune and maintain the city's independence from papal and imperial rule, so in 1935 the people of Parma fulfill their destiny in the struggle against foreign domination. This renovation of the medieval palace of the *podestà* equated the fascist party with "the heroic forces of the past," the medieval commune.[17]

Like all highly politicized invocations of history, the fascists' depiction of the medieval commune is somewhat fanciful. But in supporting the restoration of the medieval form of the bishop's palace, did they intuit some of the historical and architectural messages in the structure that have become clear to me only after a decade of study? These medieval episcopal residences were about power, about governance, about a certain vision of order. Their rounded Romanesque portals represented an authority that resorted increasingly to repressive measures. It seems not entirely casual that fascist enthusiasm for "Storia Patria" stripped the bishop's palace of its Enlightenment facade and returned it to its early-thirteenth-century incarnation.

15. Placido da Pavullo, *Don Nestore*, 7.

16. Pelicelli's political ties were certainly the reason why the socialist paper *L'Idea* published on June 3, 1911 (page 4) a devastating attack on his scholarship.

17. *Crisopoli. Rassegna del comune di Parma*, anno 3, no. 6 (1935): the article on the bishop's palace ("Il Vescovado di Parma dopo gli utlimi restauri") is on pages 553–60, with the "bimbi del Giardino d'Infanzia del R. Ist. Magistrale «A. San Vitale»" and their "ferro alla Patria" on page 552. The piece on "La nuova sede della Federazione dei Fasci di Combattimento. Il Palazzo del Governatore" occupies pages 535–41.

My own recovery of the medieval bishop's palace has a different relationship to the repressive aspects of structures of power. In the course of writing my first book, a study of ecclesiastical change in Verona, I was struck by a marked change in tone toward the end of the twelfth century: the growth, vitality, and openness to novelty and experimentation that so characterized the church of the eleventh and early twelfth centuries seemed to evaporate. In the documentation of the period, rancorous litigation over rights and boundaries replaced the celebration and affirmation of new initiatives. Ecclesiastical authorities appeared more concerned about exercising control than about fostering spiritual life. Novelty began to be viewed with suspicion and measures against "heresy" invoked. This present book on episcopal palaces has grown out of my own struggle to understand these changes: Why did the church become more rigid, more controlling, and in many ways more oppressive, from the late twelfth century? This is but a partial answer, but it is motivated by a desire to understand a complex heritage rather than by a political agenda or desire for power.

PART I
OFFICE / SPACE
The Architectural Expression of Episcopal Authority, 300–1300

To appreciate the novelty and significance of the bishop's palace of the central Middle Ages, we must trace its genealogy. It is a rather long trek, taking us all the way back to the formative development of the episcopal office in the early church. I have chosen this long view to emphasize function and its relationship to form. Function, indeed, informs form: it inhabits, molds, expresses, and visualizes itself in the local currency of wood, stone, and mortar. Bishops made use of contemporary forms of domestic architecture, and both the ideals and challenges of their office were made visible in the spaces they inhabited. And form, in turn, communicates and generates meaning, affecting those who stand outside the building as well as those who live within it. The most basic theme of this first part is this relationship between office and space, between the values and demands of the bishop's role and the character of the domestic space he inhabited.

In exploring this fundamental relationship, we will be preoccupied by change, for the differences in the spaces inhabited by our prelates are more striking than the similarities that function might mandate. Yes, all these residences afforded a place to sleep and a place to gather with others and conduct the business — both spiritual and temporal — of the church. But these spaces with similar purposes had very different characters over the millennium that spans our first evidence of episcopal abodes and the full flowering of the bishop's palace. This, I believe, is valuable to ponder: it forces us to acknowledge important changes in the episcopal office. Too often this fundamental position of leadership in the church is portrayed as timeless, and although this depiction emphasizes real and important continuities in the duties of prelates, it does not allow us to appreciate the many difficult challenges these men faced. Such historical empathy is fostered here.

Four interrelated changes will be traced in the chapters that follow: changes in the language used to describe the residence, in its structure, in its relationship to the cathedral, and in its ecclesiastical character.

First, there is linguistic change; it provides the organizing framework of this overview. In Late Antiquity (circa 300–750), the episcopal residence was called an *episcopium* — a term derived from the very title of the bishop's office and used only to designate his residence and his see. This unique word emphasized the special leadership role of the bishop in Christian society and an essential unity between his person, power, and place. This unity was attenuated in the Middle Ages, and the terms used to designate his residence reflect this change. During the early Middle Ages (circa 750–1050), the episcopal residence was usually called the "house of the holy church" (*domus sancte ecclesie*). The generic quality of the term *domus* ("house"; also *domus* in the nominative plural) and the need for modifying possessive language are significant. The bishop, the "holy church," had a *domus* just as others aspiring to power in this era had a *domus*, and one needed to specify to which contender's "house" one was referring. This pattern continued into the central Middle Ages, circa 1050–1300, when bishops came to call their residences "palaces." No longer the "holy church's," these palaces were very much the bishop's. But the invocation of the imperial term *palatium* presaged new claims to power while it borrowed secular nomenclature. The abandonment of a distinctively ecclesiastical term (*episcopium*) to adopt and adapt secular nomenclature (*domus*, *palatium*) suggests a crucial divide between Late Antiquity and the Middle Ages.

Changes in form underscore this break. The *episcopium* was a peculiarly episcopal variant of the classical Roman house. It used the vocabulary of Roman domestic architecture — the *aule* (halls), *cubicula* (bedrooms), *triclinia* (dining rooms), and *atria* (open courtyards) of classical social life — to articulate a new set of ideas about power and its origins. The early-medieval episcopal *domus*, however, was a radically different, decidedly and simplistically medieval, structure: a fortified sanctuary, it consisted of a tower and a two-story rectangular building with storage areas on the ground floor and living quarters above. This structure was very different in form and organization from the Roman house. Like the *episcopium*, it enunciated ideas about power, but there was nothing distinctively ecclesiastical about this architectural form: it was just like the domiciles of secular elites. However, a new and distinctive religious character was articulated in the episcopal architecture of the central Middle Ages. As the *domus* became *palatia*, they expanded, lost their forbidding fortified appearances, opened their walls with windows and porticos, and enunciated a new architecture of civic domination based on charismatic authority rather than force. These changes were also related to developments in secular domestic architecture, but religious meanings reappear strongly in decorative and architectural choices. In each of these periods, form reflects and reveals changes in the episcopal office. But there is greater continuity in form between the early and central Middle Ages than there is between the early church and what came after.

These linguistic and structural changes coincide with a fundamental transformation of the bishop's relationship with his primary sacred space: the cathedral. Just as one word, *episcopium*, identified the bishop's residence in Late Antiquity, there was an organic unity between his living and liturgical space. Conceptually, spatially, and legally, the bishop's see was one. It included his church, ancillary liturgical structures (baptisteries; *chrismaria*, places for anointment with chrism, used particularly for confirmation; *xenodochia*, hospices), and his residence. This unity began to break down in the early Middle Ages. The cathedral clergy moved out of the bishop's household to form "chapters"; their institutional and spatial autonomy complicated the space of the cathedral. It was still the bishop's see, but it was officiated on a day-to-day basis by the chapter. Most episcopal residences remained architecturally attached to the cathedral in this period, and the term *domus sancte ecclesie*, or "house of the holy church," still identified the bishop with his church. But one can discern the beginnings of change. Some residences were spatially detached from the cathedral. In the central Middle Ages, this distance was enlarged and emphasized, as episcopal residences turned away from the church and addressed the piazza. Many stood opposite rather than next to the church. And their ties to the cathedral were further attenuated by the claims of lay people: the commune and its guilds met in the cathedral and rebuilt it. They made it largely their own, the symbol of their community. The bishop's particular space became his palace, and to compensate for the loss of undisputed claim to the sacred space of the cathedral, he added his own sacred space to his residence in the form of a private chapel.

The fourth and final change is in the ecclesiastical character of the bishop's residence. My evidence suggests that the episcopal residence had a distinctively ecclesiastical character in both Late Antiquity and the central Middle Ages. In the early Middle Ages, however, the clerical character of the residence was occluded. It seems — whether because of circumstances or the paucity of our sources — to have been exactly like the domiciles of elite lay persons. This finding matches Gregorian rhetoric; the reformers railed that bishops had become royal creatures, abandoning their priestly responsibilities to become courtiers. Although their domestic architecture lends some credence to these critiques, my own interpretation is less harsh. To protect their churches and their people, bishops entered an alliance with power; to do so meant taking on some of its trappings. It was the reform movement of the eleventh and twelfth centuries, however, that led to the architectural articulation of a new, distinctively clerical culture. The bishop's palace forcefully enunciated these new values, articulating a new image of power that was rooted in local traditions but looking toward Rome, insistent on temporal concerns but emphasizing spiritual authority. In the cities of central and northern Italy, this new image of power did not ensure that bishops retained power. By the end of the thirteenth century, Italian bishops had lost their temporal prerogatives to lay communal governments. But their articulation of new modes of dominance — a new ecclesiastical vision of lordly authority — influenced the lay governments that replaced episcopal lordship.

CHAPTER ONE:
THE EPISCOPAL RESIDENCE
IN LATE ANTIQUITY
The Episcopium

The abundant writings of Pope Gregory the Great (590–604) offer us different views into the late-antique episcopal residence. In his *Dialogues*, a collection of stories about saints and their miracles, Gregory gives lively portraits of several holy bishops defending their sees in an Italian peninsula ravaged by Germanic armies. The *episcopium* in these accounts is depicted as a center of episcopal charity. During the Vandal invasion of Campania, Bishop Paulinus of Nola distributed all the goods and furnishings of his *episcopium* to redeem captives and alleviate the misery of his people. When he had nothing left to give, he offered himself as a slave to redeem the captive son of a widow. In another story, the poor and destitute knock at the door of the bishop's house begging alms. The *episcopium* was also a place of sanctuary in these troubled times, as when Bishop Cerbonius of Populonia offered hospitality to several Roman soldiers to hide them from roving Gothic bands.[1]

Gregory's correspondence, however, reveals the *episcopium* in a somewhat less idyllic fashion. In 599, he wrote to a certain Scholasticus, the son of a deceased bishop. According to the pontiff's informant, this disgruntled heir had taken over the *episcopium* after his father's death, claiming "clothes or other things" found there. "If this is so," wrote Gregory sternly, "we order you to withdraw without delay from the *episcopium* . . . since no one but the church alone may accede to these things which the bishop acquired during the tenure of his office."[2] This reprimand offers us a brief glimpse of episcopal domestic life in late-antique Italy, which seems, both emotionally and fiscally, to have been rather complex. If only we could know more about the relationship between this father and son! But the pope's prose, focusing narrowly on the defense of property, does not invite speculation. Despite the pontiff's legal preoccupations, the property central to this dispute — the *episcopium* — is revealed in its personal as well as official aspects. The son's claim is couched in references to possessions — clothes and other things — reminding us that the bishop lived in this place.

1. Gregory the Great, *Dialogues*, I.9.10–13; III.1.1–8; III.11.1; trans. Zimmerman, 38.
2. *CC*, 140, IX.195; VI.42 and XII.10 are other letters concerning the invasion or unlawful detention of *episcopia*.

What kind of place was this episcopal residence? Whether as a site of beatific charity or of quite earthly contention, the *episcopium* in these narrative accounts is never described with architectural precision. Collections of episcopal biographies and deeds (*gesta*), however, do reveal at least parts of these residences with greater solidity and form.[3] Some physical remains of these late Roman structures, preserved within subsequent buildings or unearthed by archeologists, also allow us to explore late-antique *episcopia*. After describing some of the features of these residences, I want to establish two things. First, in this early period, the bishop's residence cannot be understood separately from the cathedral and its ancillary liturgical spaces. All of these structures together constituted a unity, the bishop's see, and the spaces within them offered differing degrees of access to the bishop just as the late Roman *domus* of the secular aristocracy offered a subtle gradient of access to the *patronus* (patron, householder). Second, although late-antique bishops drew on a secular tradition of domestic architecture, their residences took distinctive forms that had religious meaning. The *episcopium* was an expression of episcopal self-understanding, and the theological underpinnings of the office, with its own aesthetic.

LOCATION

Let us then, like so many modern seekers of episcopal alms, first locate the *episcopium* in the landscape of late-antique Italy. To do this, we must go to the city. The ecclesiastical geography of the early church, like the administration of the late Roman state, was focused on urban centers: only cities had bishops. The bishop's residence was adjacent to the church housing his *cathedra*, the throne that represented his pastoral and teaching authority and the very real seat from which he presided over the liturgy. This episcopal church, or cathedral, was usually within the walls of the old Roman city.[4]

3. First among these is the Roman *Liber Pontificalis*, consisting of a series of lives of the popes compiled in the sixth century and then additions to this corpus continuing the work down to 870. Raymond Davis, in the introduction to his translation of the work (1989, xxxvi–xxxvii), provides a good overview of the arguments concerning its composition. A work patterned on the Roman *Liber Pontificalis* was compiled for the see of Ravenna circa 830 by a cleric named Andreas Agnellus. Josquín Martínez Pizarro, *Writing Ravenna: The Liber Pontificalis of Andreas Agnellus* (Ann Arbor, 1995), 1–6, gives a summary of the text's transmission and difficulties; see also Ruggero Benericetti, *Il pontificale di Ravenna. Studio critico* (Faenza, 1994). A new critical edition of Agnellus's *Liber* is being prepared by Deborah Mauskopf Deliyannis, and her article "Agnellus of Ravenna and Iconoclasm: Theology and Politics in a Ninth-Century Historical Text," *Speculum* 71 (1996): 559–76 provides references to the extensive literature on the work. In the late eighth or early ninth century, a similar, although much less original, compilation was produced for the see of Naples. It interpolates details of the careers of Neapolitan bishops with material from the Roman *Liber Pontificalis* and other sources. See G. Waitz's introduction in *MGH SSRL*, 398–402, and his edition of the text, 402–36. A similar sort of source for the patriarchate of Grado is published in the same volume (392–97), but it provides no significant details concerning the *episcopium*. On the genre generally, see Michel Sot, *Gesta episcoporum Gesta abbatum*, Typologie des sources du moyen âge occidental, fasc. 37 (Turnhout, 1981).

4. Archeological work in this century has radically revised our understanding of the location of

In some cities — such as Sarsina, Faenza, Trieste, Ivrea, and Pavia — the bishop's *cathedra* was at the very heart of the Roman center, on or near the *forum*.[5] More often the episcopal complex was perched on the edge of the late Roman city. The Lateran, the papal residence in Rome, grew up just within the walls at the Porta Asinaria, and the *episcopium* in Ravenna nestled against the old city walls, incorporating one of its towers into the residence. The episcopal complexes at Pesaro, Florence, Rimini, Trent, and Novara were also just within the oldest urban walls.[6] Others, if not directly associated with a city gate, were located in relation to major arteries. The cathedral and episcopal residence in Parma were at the edge of the Roman city but on an important late-antique thoroughfare leading to Brescello, a crossing on the Po river that was already a significant communications center in the time of Augustus.[7] Turin's complex was located just off the *cardo maximus*, which continued through the Porta Romana linking the city and its northeastern suburbs.[8] Rivers could also influence location: Verona's cathedral and residence were right on the bank of the river Adige, and the episcopal centers in both Piacenza and Cremona were on canals connecting to the Po.[9]

This tendency for the episcopal complex to be perched on the very edge of the city was not just an accident of Christianity's late arrival on the grid of Roman urban design. Not just chance located the bishop's house at a gate looking out of the "civilized" urban center to the world beyond the walls, or on a road, canal, or river wending its way deep

---

these *cathedrae* in the urban landscape. Formerly, a shift from a peripheral site, usually associated with suburban cemeteries, to a location within the city center was taken as the norm. See Cinzio Violante and Cosimo Damiano Fonseca, "Ubicazione e dedicazione delle cattedrali dalle origini al periodo romanico nelle città dell'Italia centro-settentrionale," in *Il romanico pistoiese nei suoi rapporti con l'arte romanica dell'occidente*, Atti del I Convegno internazionale di studi medioevali di storia e d'arte (Pistoia, 1966), 314–17, 344–45. But recent scholarship has established that continuity on an urban site was the most common pattern for Italian sees. P. Testini, G. Cantino Wataghin, and L. Pani Ermini, "La cattedrale in Italia," in *Actes du XIe Congrès international d'archéologie chrétienne — Lyon, Vienne, Grenoble, Genève et Aoste (21–28 septembre 1986)*, 3 vols. (Rome, 1989), 1: 5–229, especially 11–13. See also Cosimo Damiano Fonseca and Cinzio Violante, "Cattedrale e città in Italia dall'VIII al XIII secolo," in *Chiesa e città: Contributi della Commissione italiana di storia ecclesiastica comparata aderente alla Commission internationale d'histoire ecclésiastique comparée al XVII Congresso internazionale di scienze storiche (Madrid, 26 agosto-2 settembre 1990)* (Galatina, 1990), 8–9.

5. Testini, et al., "La cattedrale," 119, 148, 181, 214, 224; later evidence also suggests that the episcopal complexes of Bergamo and Como were located on the old *forum* (211, 213), but for many cities the plan of the ancient Roman center is poorly known.

6. Ibid., 117, 124, 144, 203, 122; Lauer, *Latran*, 17; a brief overview of the development of the Lateran residence before Sixtus V's sixteenth-century demolition of its late-antique and medieval structures is Mariano Delle Rose, "Il Patriarchio: Note storico-topografiche," in *Il palazzo apostolico lateranense*, ed. Carlo Pietrangeli (Florence, 1991), 19–35.

7. *Il palazzo apostolico*, 156; Reinhold Schumann, *Authority and the Commune, Parma 833–1133* (Impero e comune, Parma 833–1133) (Parma, 1973), 22.

8. Testini, et al., "La cattedrale," 225; Silvana Casartelli Novelli, "Le fabbriche della cattedrale di Torino dall'età paleocristiana all'alto medioevo," *Studi medievali* ser. 3, 11 / 2 (1970): 617–658.

9. Cinzia Fiorio Tedone, Silvia Lusuardi Siena, and Paolo Piva, "Il complesso paleocristiano e altomedioevale," in *La cattedrale di Verona nelle sue vicende edilizie dal secolo VI al secolo XVI* (Verona, 1987), 19–21; Testini, et al., "La cattedrale," 205, 193–94, 159.

into the countryside. His urban flock certainly claimed the bishop's attention: Augustine's sermons imply a contentious and willful congregation whose grasp of basic Christian principles seems to need constant reinforcement.[10] But early Christian narratives reveal a passionate interest in the world beyond the walls, in the missionary territory of the late-antique countryside. In a reversal of the visual emphasis in Lorenzetti's lyrical depiction of late-medieval Siena — in which the crowded and lively city speaks more loudly than the placid countryside in its somber hues — a late-antique bishop's view depicted the countryside in vivid and energetic strokes. This landscape — or at least the Christian imagination of it — was the terrain of saintly adventures and holy deeds. Saint Martin turned a pagan band of rustics "rigid as rocks" to impede superstitious rites and in villages throughout the countryside demolished ancient temples and destroyed idols. Sermons and letters reveal less drama and less success: Bishop Maximus of Turin decried the idolatry and fertility rites practiced in the countryside, and Bishop Vigilius of Trent reported the martyrdom of three of his priests at the hands of pagans.[11] This was where the bishop's real work lay, and his abode looked out on this less-hallowed ground.

This site held a complex of structures that, together, constituted the bishop's seat. The origins and character of these early Christian cult sites have long intrigued scholars. Scriptural passages depict the earliest Christians meeting in private homes, and archeological evidence (Dura-Europos in Syria, San Clemente in Rome) from the third century demonstrates that the earliest Christian churches were renovated houses. Often there were several reworkings or expansions of this piece of domestic architecture adapted to religious needs before a new "church" was built on the site. The construction of buildings specifically for congregational meeting and worship began in the second half of the third century. Remains from San Crisogono in Rome show a large open hall with a portico around the exterior. Note that this is not quite a "basilica." This distinctive early Christian church form, based on the Roman *basilica* or audience hall, became dominant as a direct result of Constantinian policy: the newly converted emperor wanted a monumental ecclesiastical architecture consonant with the elevated status he granted the church. Thus, the Christian basilica was not an evolution of earlier church structures but a design imposed from above. However, it did not immediately supersede earlier forms: its dissemination began in the early fourth century, but it was not dominant until the sixth century.

By this time, the basilica was the most imposing building in the episcopal complex. Most bishops had only one basilica, but in several cities (Aquileia, discussed later, Milan, Pavia, and others) the episcopal center had two coordinated churches.[12] Another

10. Augustine, *Sermones*, 61, 111, 177 (*PL*, 38: 409–14, 641–43, 953–60); Peter Brown, *Augustine of Hippo: A Biography* (Berkeley and Los Angeles, 1967), 194–97, 244–58.

11. Sulpicius Severus, *Vita sancti Martini*, ed. Jacques Fontaine, Sources chrétienne 130 (Paris, 1967), Chap. 5, 12–15; trans. F. R. Hoare, *The Western Fathers* (New York, 1954); Rita Lizzi, "Ambrose's Contemporaries and the Christianization of Northern Italy," *Journal of Roman Studies* 80 (1990): 156–73.

12. Good introductions to the long and complex debate over the form and function of these double-cathedral structures are Paolo L. Zovatto, "Il significato della basilica doppia: L'esempio di

key structure was the baptistery, often free-standing and, in double-cathedral groups, between the two basilicas. It was sometimes flanked by a *consignatorium* or *chrismarium*, a special room in which the newly baptized received confirmation, were anointed with chrism, and were blessed by the bishop. Then, there was the episcopal residence. It originally may have been just a house already on the site, perhaps even the house that served as the cult site before a church was built. L. Michael White suggests that the church edifice at Cirta, in plan still resembling a house in the early fourth century, "also served as the bishop's residence, or maybe it had been his own house before." Augustine's church at Hippo Regius grew from "what was originally an adjacent peristyle house and then served as an episcopal residence."[13] By the sixth century, however, the *episcopium* was itself a collection of several buildings and spaces.

The spatial relations of these different parts of the episcopal complex — the *episcopium*, the cathedral, and the baptistery — were varied. In the Italian peninsula, remains of late-antique *episcopia* survive at Aquileia, Florence, Grado, Naples, Parenzo, and Ravenna. These examples reveal several ways in which the episcopal residence related to the liturgical structures (Figure 2). The *episcopium* at Grado — occupied by the patriarchs of Aquileia briefly in the fifth century when Attila visited the peninsula, and then for a longer exile in the sixth and seventh centuries during the Lombard invasions — was situated along the southern flank of the basilica of Sant'Eufemia. The restricted space within this episcopal fortress certainly influenced this arrangement.[14] The fourth-century residence at Ravenna was also on one side of the cathedral, but off and extending around its apse.[15] This seems also to have been the arrangement at Naples.[16] *Episcopia*, however, could also be in front of the cathedral. At Florence the episcopal residence faced the facade of the church of Santa Reparata, separated from it by a plaza and the baptistery. The *episcopium* at Parenzo radiated off the north portico of the atrium in front of the basilica.[17]

Aquileia," *RSCI* 18 (1964): 357–93; Paolo Piva, *Le cattedrali lombarde: Ricerche sulle "cattedrali doppie" da Sant'Ambrogio all'età romanica* (Quistello, 1990); and Paolo Piva, *La cattedrale doppia* (Bologna, 1990).

13. Richard Krautheimer, *Early Christian and Byzantine Architecture* (Baltimore, 1965), 1–8, 14–27; L. Michael White, *Building God's House in the Roman World: Architectural Adaptation among Pagans, Jews, and Christians* (Baltimore, 1990), 126 — the reconstruction of the development of Christian architecture I give here is based on Chapters 1, 2, and 5. Delle Rose, "Il patriarchio," in *Il palazzo apostolico*, 19–20, suggests on the basis of recent archeological work that the papal residence at the Lateran developed from a house-church.

14. Carlo Guido Mor, "La fortuna di Grado nell'altomedioevo," in *Aquileia e l'alto Adriatico 1: Aquileia e Grado*, Antichità altoadriatiche 1 (Udine, 1972), 299–315; Paola Lopreato, "Lo scavo dell'episcopio di Grado," in *Aquileia e le Venezie nell'alto medioevo*, Antichità altoadriatiche 32 (Udine, 1988), 326, 332–33.

15. Miller, "Ravenna," 149–50.

16. Raffaella Farioli, *Aggiornamento dell'opera di Émile Bertaux sotto la direzione di Adriano Prandi* appended to Émile Bertaux, *L'Art dans l'Italie méridionale*, as volume 4 (Rome and Paris, 1978), 159.

17. Luisa Bertacchi, "Contributo allo studio dei palazzi episcopali paleocristiani: I casi di Aquileia, Parenzo e Salona," *Aquileia nostra* 56 (1985): 386. The *Testamentum Domini*, in its most

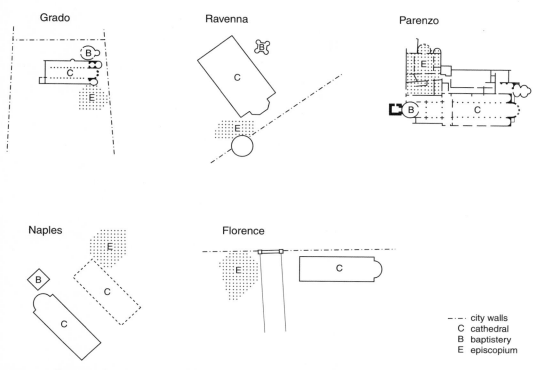

FIGURE 2. *Location of* episcopia *in relation to cult buildings at Grado, Ravenna, Parenzo, Naples, and Florence.* (*C. Ingersoll.*)

These various positions may have developed and shifted over time. Archeological remains at Aquileia reveal three different structurings of the episcopal residence from the early fourth to the late fifth century (Figure 3). The earliest was embraced by the liturgical buildings. This ancient see had a double-cathedral, two parallel basilicas usually called the "aule teodoriane" after Bishop Theodore (308–320?). Between these two churches were the bishop's audience hall, the baptistery, a hallway connecting all these spaces, and a portico leading to the bishop's living quarters. In the second half of the fourth century, the north basilica was enlarged and the *episcopium* reconstructed on a new site, off the north portico of the atrium extending in front of the church. The old episcopal audience hall was refashioned into a larger baptistery, and the remaining parts of the old *episcopium* devoted to other uses. In the middle of the fifth century, the new residence extending off the atrium was destroyed during Attila's invasion. It was rebuilt on the same site, but its orientation to the cathedral changed once again. The entrance off the atrium was abandoned, and access to the *episcopium* was provided by a

ancient form a fifth-century Syriac text (later translated into Latin), stated that the episcopal residence should be off the atrium of the church as it is here at Parenzo. See Mariella Malaspina, "Gli episcopia e le residenze ecclesiastiche nella 'pars orientalis' dell'impero romano," in *Contributi dell'Istituto di archeologia* 5, ed. Michelangelo Cagiano de Azevedo (Milan, 1975), 37.

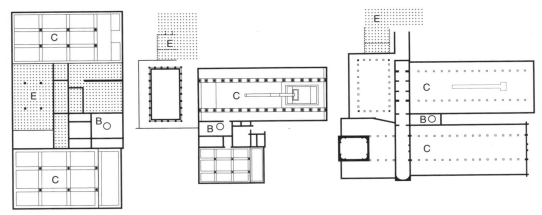

FIGURE 3. *Aquileia, changes in the location of the* episcopium *over the fourth and fifth centuries. C = cathedral; B = baptistry; E = episcopium. (C. Ingersoll.)*

long corridor paved with mosaics, paralleling the cathedral's facade and extending beyond the edge of the old atrium.[18]

All this evidence suggests that local site exigencies strongly influenced the relationship of the episcopal residence to the cathedral. No one placement was normative, and the location of the *episcopium*, as at Aquileia, could change over time to accommodate the expansion of cult structures. The residence always retained some close relation to the cathedral and, through a door or covered passageway, allowed the bishop direct access to his church.

RAVENNA

Our best evidence — documentary and physical — for a late-antique *episcopium* in Italy comes from Ravenna. An important naval center on the Adriatic Sea from the first century B.C., Ravenna enjoyed significant imperial patronage when it became home to the Augustan fleet for the eastern Mediterranean. It became head of a province from the third century A.D. and an imperial residence when the emperor Honorius (395–423) took refuge there from the Visigoths. It remained an imperial residence even after the invaders became emperors: the Ostrogothic emperor Theodoric (490–526) lived in the city and contributed greatly to its architectural splendor. Even after the region's return to direct Byzantine rule with the conclusion of Justinian's Gothic wars, Ravenna was the seat of the exarch and center of Byzantine administration. The bishops of Ravenna came to enjoy significant wealth and power as their city's fortunes rose. The see was raised to metropolitan status in 546, joining Milan and Aquileia as the peninsula's most venerable Christian centers (after Rome, of course).

The early history of the see and its bishops survives in the *Liber Pontificalis* of Andreas Agnellus, a ninth-century Ravennate cleric. Agnellus describes the *episcopium* at

18. Bertacchi, "Contributo," 366–73.

Ravenna as unified by a set of exterior walls; within were several related buildings and courtyards constructed in different periods. But even at Ravenna, these walls were not necessarily sharp delimitations of the bishop's space — the episcopal baths were located outside the walls, and the relationship of these walls to the cathedral and its other subordinate structures is unclear. Old boundaries probably were transgressed with regularity because *episcopia* seem only rarely to have been designed and built at a single moment. Instead they tended to grow organically, various bishops modifying and adding to the structures inherited from their predecessors. This development often took place on an oddly shaped site, with parameters determined by the placement of the cathedral, fixed streets, and preexisting structures.

The oldest core of the episcopal residence at Ravenna, however, seems to have antedated the cathedral basilica built by Bishop Ursus in the second half of the fourth century. Indeed, Agnellus mentions the *episcopium* in the context of describing the choice of site for the Ursian basilica.[19] It is possible — as Cirta and Hippo Regius suggest — that the cult structure replaced by the Ursian basilica originally grew out of the episcopal residence. The exact relationship of the fourth-century residence at Ravenna and the Ursian basilica, however, is impossible to reconstruct. All our sources — archeological as well as documentary — are mute on the character of this house in which "the most holy man" Ursus lived. Luckily they are more loquacious about the additions to this earliest residence, and those additions were substantial.

The first major addition described by Agnellus was the work of Bishop Neon (458). More famous for his reconstruction of the baptistery[20] — still today a marvel of design and rich mosaic decor — Neon added a building housing a formal dining room or *triclinium* to the residence. Agnellus refers to it as the "house called the five couches" (*domus quae vocatur Quinque agubitas*, i.e., *accubita*) from the traditional reclining dining couches (*accubita*) that furnished a Roman *triclinium*. It had five niches to accommodate the dining couches, two along each side wall and a slightly larger one for the bishop opposite the entrance.[21] This form is typical of late-antique *triclinia*. Earlier classical *triclinia* had been rectangular and furnished with three rectangular couches arranged in the shape of a "U". But a new form of dining couch, the semicircular *stibadium* or *sigma*, became fashionable in the second century A.D. and dominant in the late antique.[22] The

19. Agnellus, *LP*, Chap. 23; see also F. W. Deichmann, *Ravenna Hauptstadt des spätantiken Abendlandes*, 3 vols. (Wiesbaden, 1969–89) 2 / 1: 194.

20. See Annabel Jane Wharton, "Ritual and Reconstructed Meaning: The Neonian Baptistery in Ravenna," *Art Bulletin* 69 (1987): 358–75, and *Refiguring the Post Classical City: Dura Europos, Jerash, Jerusalem and Ravenna* (Cambridge, 1995), 105–31. Wharton's reading of Neon's baptistery as a representation of episcopal authority, one performed for catechumens at the Easter vigil, is compelling and resonates with the interpretation of his dining room I offer below. The discussion of the episcopal center (108–9), however, is marked by inappropriate, even nonsensical, uses of "episcopate" that undermine confidence in the author's understanding of the larger complex.

21. Agnellus, *LP*, Chap. 29; the description that follows is based on this chapter.

22. Lise Bek, "*Questiones Convivales*: The Idea of the Triclinium and the Staging of Convivial Ceremony from Rome to Byzantium," *Analecta Romana Instituti Danici* 12 (1983): 83–84; see also

curvaceous niches of Bishop Neon's dining room presuppose and architecturally mimic the arrangement of these semicircular reclining dining couches. The earliest multiniched *triclinia* — such as those of the Villa of Hadrian at Tivoli and Piazza Armerina — were *triconch* halls, retaining the traditional number of couches arranged in three semicircular niches. The number of niches tended to multiply with ambition over time: the Great Palace at Constantinople boasted the Triclinium of Nineteen Couches, and the dining room Pope Leo III (795–816) added to the Lateran had eleven. While there are secular precedents for a *triclinium* with five apses — notably the Triclinium of the Five Niches in the Great Palace in Constantinople — Bishop Neon's decision to build the "quinque accubita" was surely also scripturally informed: Jesus multiplied five loaves to feed his followers in the Gospels.[23]

Agnellus describes in detail not only the form but also the decor of Bishop Neon's five-niched dining room. It had a window on either side to admit natural light, and its floor was "ornamented with different stones." This was probably *opus sectile*, paving of colored marble tiles. An extensive mosaic and inscriptional program, complex in its iconography and redolent with meaning, decorated the walls.[24] This decor mixed allusions to food and eating with scriptural references to articulate a powerful conception of episcopal authority.

Along the outer long wall was a depiction of Jesus multiplying the loaves and fishes, miraculously feeding the crowds near Bethsaida. Opposite, on the other long wall facing the cathedral, were two related sets of images: one celebrating God's creation, and the other depicting the great flood he used to purify it in the time of Noah. The creation imagery, Agnellus informs us, was based on Psalm 148, sung every morning at Lauds. It offered rich material for the bishop's artist:

> Praise the Lord from the earth,
> ye dragons and all deeps:
> Fire, and hail; snow, and vapors;
> stormy wind fulfilling his word:
> Mountains, and all hills;
> fruitful trees, and all cedars:

Katherine M. D. Dunbabin, "Triclinium and Stibadium," and Jeremy Rossiter, "Convivium and Villa in Late Antiquity," in *Dining in a Classical Context*, ed. William J. Slater (Ann Arbor, 1991), 121–48, 199–214.

23. Bek, "*Questiones Convivales*" 91–97; Duchesne, *LP*, Chap. 98: 39; Guglielmo De Angelis D'Ossat, "Sulla distrutta aula dei *quinque accubita* a Ravenna," *Corsi di cultura sull'arte ravennate e bizantina* 20 (1973): 265.

24. My own reading of Agnellus's description of the pictorial cycle accords with Deichmann's, *Ravenna*, 2 / 1: 194–97. D'Ossat's reconstruction ("Sulla distrutta aula," 266–68) is not warranted by the Latin text of Agnellus's description, which clearly places both the *mundi fabricam* and the *istoria Petri apostoli* in the "front" of the room (*Ex una autem parte frontis . . . et in alia fronte . . .*) — Agnellus, *LP*, Chap. 29.

Beasts, and all cattle;
creeping things, and flying fowl:
Kings of the earth, and all people;
princes, and all judges of the earth
Both young men, and maidens;
old men, and children:
Let them praise the name of the Lord:
for his name alone is excellent;
his glory is above the earth and heaven.
   [Ps. 148: 7–13]

The images of the flood were surely linked to the psalm through some visual allusion to Genesis (9: 1–3):

God blessed Noah and his sons, and said unto them, Be fruitful, and multiply, and replenish the earth. And the fear of you and the dread of you shall be upon every beast of the earth, and upon every fowl of the air, upon all that moveth upon the earth, and upon all the fishes of the sea; into your hand are they delivered. Every moving thing that liveth shall be meat for you: even as the green herb have I given you all things.

The front wall continued and developed this theme, pairing a depiction of God's creation of the world with an image of Saint Peter's vision at Joppa. This story from the Acts of the Apostles (10: 9–16) tells of Saint Peter praying by himself for several hours and feeling hungry afterward. He then received a vision of a vessel descending from heaven and a "great linen" in which "all quadrupeds, all serpents of the earth, and all birds of the sky" were gathered, and the voice of the Lord saying, "Rise up, Peter, kill and eat." When Peter responds that he never eats things common and impure, he is admonished, "What God purifies, you should not call common." This rejoinder to traditional Jewish dietary prohibitions at least suggests that the bishop's table took advantage of the bounty of God's creation![25]

But it suggests, in fact, much more. The inscription below this image forcefully linked this divine meal offered to the apostle to a robust interpretation of Peter's special place in the church:

Do not doubt those pure things the omnipotent Creator,
supreme Lord of all things, created.
Praise to you, Simon Peter, Apostolic light,
whom Christ's golden mind delights to embellish
all through the ages:
In you the holy prevailing church of God shines forth,
In you the Son of heaven, brilliant through the ages,
placed the firm foundations of His house

25. Deichmann, *Ravenna*, 2 / 1: 196–97.

Radiant virtue is yours in everything, and censure and faith.
Given first place among the twelve brothers
New laws are given to you from on high,
You who tames the wild hearts of men, who soothes the soul
And teaches all the worshipers of Christ throughout the world.
Already Christ's glory prepares the kingdom through your works.[26]

This inscription and the images accompanying it were the backdrop for the bishop's place at table — a not so subtle identification of the bishop with the Prince of the Apostles. Facing the bishop, probably over the door, was a more somber image of Peter and Paul at the foot of the cross. Below it was an inscription reminding him of his predecessor: *Domnus Neon episcopus senescat nobis* (probably best translated, "May Lord Bishop Neon be long remembered among us").[27]

Both the form and decorative ensemble of this late-antique episcopal *triclinium* reveal significant similarities and differences with elite lay dining rooms. While the multiniche form was typical of late-antique official residences, the bishop's choice of five niches infused the structure with Christian meaning that was also inscribed in the wall decor. Christ multiplied five loaves and two fishes to feed the throngs who came to hear him teach. This image in the room faced the guests reclining at the traditional place of honor in a Roman *triclinium*, those at the places just on the right as one entered the room. Reclining on their left elbows, they would have a comfortable view of both the bishop and this depiction of Christ miraculously feeding his flock. That their host no longer reclined at their side but took a place at the center of the room was another shift in traditional Roman dining practice shared with secular notables in Late Antiquity. The rise of an imperial aesthetic had prompted this shift in the position of the host, and the development of the niched form emphasizing this position. The new ideology of sovereignty entailed an important concomitant change in the character of the activities taking place within the dining room: the convivial meal became less an entertainment of participants than a performance of lordly authority. With the intensification of the imperial cult, these performances and the spaces staging them took on a quasi-mystical dimension.[28]

26. "In nullis dubitare licet, quae munda creavit / Omnipotens genitor, rerum cui summa potestas. / Euge, Simon Petre, quem gaudet mens aurea Christi / Lumen apostolicum cunctos ornare per annos: / In te sancta Dei pollens ecclesia fulgit, / In te firma suae domus fundamenta locavit / Principis aetherei clarus per secula natus. / Cunctis clara tibi est virtus, censura fidisque. / Bis senos inter fratres in principe sistis / Ipse loco, legisque novae tibi dantur ab alto, / Quis fera corda domas hominum, [quis] pectora mulces / Christicolasque doces tu omnes esse per orbem. / Iamque tuis meritis Christi parat gloria regnum." Agnellus, *LP*, Chap. 29. This includes the more accurate Testi Rasponi readings (*RIS*, 2.2: 82, notes 8 and 14).

27. Such inscribed acclamations were common in secular decor; Deichmann, *Ravenna*, 2 / 1: 196–97.

28. Bek, "*Quaestiones Convivales*," 89–98, 102–5; on interpreting Roman domestic decor generally, see John R. Clarke, *The Houses of Roman Italy, 100 B.C.–A.D. 250* (Berkeley and Los Angeles, 1991). This episcopal borrowing of secular, particularly imperial, practices has other instantiations

Our bishop of Ravenna took these meanings imbedded in the borrowed secular architectural forms and gave them an ecclesiastical twist. He took the emperor's place at table, framed by the crowning apse of the room. He surrounded himself with different images — Christian symbols and stories rather than Dionysian episodes — but they imbued the bishop with a mystical aura akin to that cultivated by the emperors in their decor. As Christ miraculously provided a meal for the crowd at Bethsaida, the bishop gave his guests repast. The images framing the bishop also associated him with the Prince of the Apostles, Christ's representative on earth, the visionary Peter fed directly by the Almighty. At his disposal is all the bounty of God's creation, spilling in rich mosaic splendor around the bishop.

But this vision had an even stronger message: in patristic commentary on this passage, the beasts that Saint Peter is urged to kill and eat are pagan peoples; his consumption of them is their conversion. The selection of this image as the backdrop to the bishop's place at table casts him as an apostolic missionary. The equation of eating with conversion was surely also a reminder to those at table to bring their hearts into more perfect accord with the Gospels. It was also an allegory of the legitimate exercise of power. The allusion to Noah on the wall to the bishop's left was glossed in a fashion similar to the vision at Joppa. The dominion God gave the sons of Noah over all the animals represented the bishop's authority over the people, enslaved since the Fall to their bestial human natures, the "wild hearts" of Neon's inscription. Eating here was the mark of superiority, the symbol of the prelate's special status. All these images — Jesus feeding the crowds, Peter's vision, the creation, and the flood — emphasized the bishop's charismatic authority and its wide dominion over a fallen people.[29] Neon's dining room took a powerful secular aesthetic and used it to articulate a powerful vision of the episcopal office, one performed for important visitors to the *episcopium* of Ravenna.

The residence continued to grow under Neon's successors, those bishops addressed by the inscription above the door of his richly decorated dining room. Bishop Peter II (494–520) added a three-story brick building off the Salustra Tower (Figures 4, 5). This tower, once part of a gate in the oldest Roman walls of the city, had been incorporated into the very earliest episcopal residence. From at least the time of Peter II's additions, it probably functioned as a stairwell linking the various buildings joined to it. The building Bishop Peter attached to its northeast side created several significant spaces,

in Late Antiquity; see Sabine G. MacCormack, *Art and Ceremony in Late Antiquity* (Berkeley and Los Angeles, 1981), especially 21, 64, 130.

29. I thank Philippe Buc for calling my attention to these scriptural commentaries; see his *L'Ambiguïté du livre: Prince, puvoir, et peuple dans les commentaires de la Bible au moyen âge* (Paris, 1994), 208–17; on the relationship generally between images and Christian scripture, see Jas Elsner, *Art and the Roman Viewer: The Transformation of Art from the Pagan World to Christianity* (Cambridge, 1995). Elsner's attempt to appreciate the shift from naturalism to abstraction in late-antique art as transition rather than decline is salutary, but at points is undermined by assertions that this new link between imagery and a canonic text in Christian art constituted a narrower, more exclusive, range of meanings and implied subjectivity than the elite naturalistic art of the classical era.

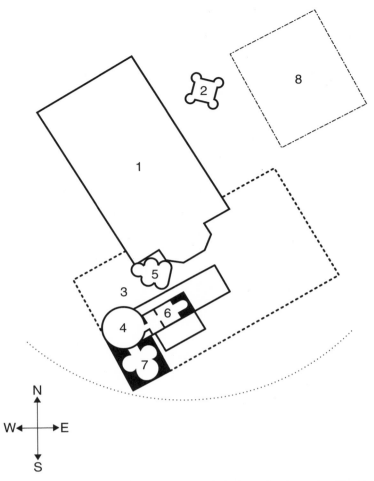

FIGURE 4. *Ravenna, the late-antique* episcopium. *1 = cathedral; 2 = baptistery; 3 = location of fourth-century episcopal residence?; 4 = Salustra Tower; 5 = Bishop Neon's* triclinium, *the "Quinque Accubita"; 6 = chapel of Sant'Andrea; 7 = triconch hall, the "Domus Tricoli"; 8 = baths. (C. Ingersoll.)*

the most stunning being a mosaic-embellished chapel on the uppermost floor. Still extant, and restored in the 1930s, the chapel could be entered from a hallway within the building (the entrance today's visitor takes) or from the Salustra Tower. Both entrances bring one into a barrel-vaulted entryway culminating in an image of Christ as Victor — the savior dressed in military attire, a cross on his shoulder, an open gospel in his hand. The chapel proper, a cross-vaulted structure with an apse extending off the northeast arm, feels even more intimate than its five-meter (sixteen-foot) diameter might suggest: Glistening mosaics press in on the viewer from every arch and rib. Medallion images of the twelve apostles and an equal number of male and female martyrs gaze down from the four central arches with the haunting intensity of rough mosaic Fayum portraits. Looming up along the ribs of the central vault are four angels holding aloft a *chrismon*

FIGURE 5. *Ravenna, Palazzo Arcivescovile, Salustra Tower, chapel building, and partial remains of the* vivarium. *(M. Miller.)*

(a symbol of Christ), and nestled beneath their wings and robes are symbols of the evangelists with their gospels. One feels dwarfed and overwhelmed by these intense images; this is probably what Bishop Peter had in mind.[30]

The hallway leading out of the chapel deposited one in a large room, today the main hall of the Museo Arcivescovile. Well into the Middle Ages this room was the site of important gatherings, such as judicial hearings and the investiture of vassals. Its late-antique uses are not enunciated by any source. The spaces on the floor below had lower ceilings (3.3 meters, or eleven feet, high, compared to the five-meter [sixteen-foot] ceilings above), suggesting more common uses (Figure 6). The bishop's *mensa* (literally, "table"), where he and his clergy regularly took their meals, was here. The ground level, today inaccessible and half flooded, had an elevation similar to that of the second floor. No documentary sources explicitly discuss the uses of these spaces, but the proximity of Neon's formal dining room, the location of the *mensa* on the floor above, and the later construction of a *vivarium* off this ground floor suggest that at least parts of it were probably devoted to kitchen and food storage areas. The *vivarium* was a structure consisting in a series of arches and niches used to house various species — animals, fish, and fowl — destined for the archbishop's table.[31] It faced out on what is today the pontiff's garden, and such horticultural enclosures seem to have been common elements within late-antique *episcopia*. As one of Gregory the Great's *Dialogues* relates, Bishop Boniface of Ferentino one day found his garden infested with caterpillars:

> Seeing all his vegetables going to ruin, he turned to the caterpillars and said, 'I adjure you in the name of our Lord God, Jesus Christ, depart from here and stop eating these vegetables.' In obedience to his voice all the caterpillars, down to the very last one, disappeared from the garden.[32]

Beyond the demonstration of saintly pest control, this story suggests that episcopal gardens were not purely ornamental, but contributed to provisioning the bishop's table.

In addition to the chapel building, Peter II also began construction of another *domus* that took the efforts of five successors over three decades to bring to completion. Agnellus calls it the *domus quae dicitur tricoli* ("the house which is called three-necked"), and this odd title has elicited some fanciful theories as to its character. Most likely, the building extended to the southeast off the Salustra Tower and housed a *triconchos*, a large hall with three apses (see Figure 4). Attested in several *episcopia* in the eastern Mediterranean, a triconch hall was in keeping with the self-assured flair Bishop Peter's mosaic-encrusted chapel reveals, not to mention Neon's dining room with multiple apses. Peter only lived to complete its "bulwark with great piers inspiring wonder," but

30. Miller, "Ravenna," 153–54; Agnellus, *LP*, Chap. 50; Deichmann, *Ravenna*, 2 / 1: 198–204; Giuseppe Gerola, "Il ripristino della cappella di S. Andrea nel palazzo vescovile di Ravenna," *Felix Ravenna* 41 (1932): 71–132; Luisa Ottolenghi, "La cappella arcivescovile in Ravenna," *Felix Ravenna* 72 (1956): 5–32.

31. Gerola, "Il ripristino," 75–78, 121–32; Agnellus, *LP*, Chap. 163; Deichmann, *Ravenna*, 2 / 1: 206–7; C. Ricci, "Il vivaio dell'arcivescovado di Ravenna," *Bollettino d'arte* 13 (1919): 33–36.

32. Gregory the Great, *Dialogues*, I.9.15; trans. Zimmerman, 39.

FIGURE 6. *Ravenna, Palazzo Arcivescovile, elevation of chapel building. (C. Ingersoll.)*

clearly his plan for two substantial new structures radiating off the Salustra Tower guided development of the Ravennate *episcopium* for the next generation.[33] Archbishop Maximian completed the Domus Tricoli, decorating its hall with an image of himself and all his predecessors in the see. This representation of the series of the see's bishops is still today the standard decorative program of episcopal audience halls.[34]

As the Domus Tricoli was nearing completion, Bishop Victor (537–544) restored the bath complex associated with the residence. Located just outside the northeast wall of the *episcopium*, next to the baptistery, the baths were built in the late fourth or early fifth century. Victor added "most precious marbles" to the walls, "diverse figures in

33. Miller, "Ravenna," 152–53; Irving Lavin, "The House of the Lord: Aspects of the Role of Palace Triclinia in the Architecture of Late Antiquity and the Early Middle Ages," *Art Bulletin* 44 (1962): 1–27.

34. Agnellus, *LP*, Chap. 75; Jean-Charles Picard, *Le Souvenir des évêques: Sépultures, listes épisco-pales et culte des évêques en Italie du Nord des origines au Xe siècle* (Rome, 1988), 505–20. Extant examples may be seen in the episcopal palaces of Verona, Padua, and Como and in the Castello di Buon Consiglio in Trent.

golden tesserae," and an inscription recording his generosity in allowing the clergy of the city to bathe for free twice a week. The remains of these baths, discovered during an excavation in 1980, accord well with a smaller, privately owned *balnea*, appropriate to a bishop's residence, as opposed to a large, state-run *therma*. The three semicircular and rectangular basins retrieved from the site, now displayed at the Museo Nazionale in Ravenna, are roughly three meters, or nine feet, wide, comparable to baths in Pompeiian houses and rustic villas.[35]

The location of the bishop's baths outside the walls of the *episcopium* may have been determined by water supply: they were next to the baptistery, which also required running water.[36] But it may also signal that the bishop and his clergy were not its only patrons. Many smaller privately owned baths were open to public use for a small fee. Bishop Victor's pride in his own largesse for allowing the clergy to bathe for free on Tuesdays and Fridays, indeed, suggests that the episcopal baths had paying customers.[37] One can easily imagine that clerical and lay use of the baths could have been regulated through different times of use, which was the way that male and female bathing was accommodated in most public facilities (morning hours reserved for women and afternoons for men). Many Christian moralists did have grave reservations about the baths. When Epiphanius became bishop of Pavia in 467, "the holy bishop drew up for himself laws by which to regulate his daily life." "First," his biographer Ennodius assures us, "he determined not to bathe lest by frequentation of the public baths, haunts especially attractive to the unclean, he might dim the luster of his soul and dissipate the strength of the inner man."[38] But bathing "for the needs of the body" was widely recognized as a necessary activity, and many of the holy men appearing in Gregory the Great's *Dialogues* went to the baths without compromising their sanctity. Bishop Germanus of Capua went "at his doctor's advice" to the baths of Angulus, and a "saintly priest" in the diocese of Centum Cellae frequented the baths of Tauriana "whenever his health required."[39] Indeed, Victor's license for clerical bathing twice a week shows a moderation unknown to the average Roman accustomed to bathing daily.[40] There is no reason to

35. G. Bermond Montanari, "Ravenna — 1980 — Lo scavo della Banca Popolare: Relazione preliminare," *Felix Ravenna* 127–30 (1984–85): 21–24; Maria Grazia Maioli, "Ravenna, lo scavo della Banca Popolare I «Bagni del clero»," in *Flumen Aquaeductus. Nuove scoperte archeologiche dagli scavi per l'acquedotto della Romagna*, ed. Luciana Prati (Bologna, 1988), 76–80; Fikret Yegül, *Baths and Bathing in Classical Antiquity* (New York and Cambridge, Mass., 1992), 52–54.

36. On the exigencies of the early Christian baptismal liturgy and the Ravennate baptistery, see Wharton, "Ritual and Reconstructed Meaning," 358–64.

37. Bryan Ward-Perkins's assumption of the decline of privately owned baths open to public use for fee ignores this evidence. His reading of clerical baths is presaged on the idea that they were quite different and distinct from secular public baths. *From Classical Antiquity to the Middle Ages: Urban Public Building in Northern and Central Italy AD 300–850* (Oxford, 1984), 140, 148. I see no evidence to support such an interpretation.

38. Ennodius, *The Life of Saint Epiphanius*, ed. and trans. Genevieve Marie Cook (Washington, D.C., 1942), 50–51 (Chap. 47).

39. Gregory the Great, *Dialogues*, IV.42.3, IV.57.3; trans. Zimmerman, 250, 266.

40. Yegül, *Baths*, 315–20.

think, however, that the relaxed sociability that was the main appeal of bathing to the Romans was absent from the gatherings of clergy in the episcopal baths. In fact, it seems that these special days for clerical bathing probably fostered solidarity and fellowship among the city's clerics.

All this construction and decoration in the first half of the sixth century presaged Ravenna's promotion to metropolitan status: Maximian (546), who completed the Domus Tricoli, was the first to hold the title of archbishop.[41] Whatever the character of the original Ursian residence, these fifth- and sixth-century additions certainly suggest the cultivation of a graceful style of living. Private baths, an elaborately decorated *triclinium*, a triconch audience hall, a *vivarium* — all these were characteristic of elite households in late-antique Italy. Evidence from other *episcopia* suggests that the bishops of Ravenna were not the only prelates on the peninsula aspiring to gracious living.

REMAINS OF OTHER *EPISCOPIA*

The Lateran residence in Rome, for example, had a private bath complex. Its precise age and location are impossible to fix with any certainty, but the *Liber Pontificalis* mentions it in the late seventh century: Emperor Constans II bathed here when he was the guest of Pope Vitalian (657–672). Other popes built baths at ecclesiastical sites around Rome. Pope Hilary (461–468) built both an enclosed bath and an open-air pool at the monastery of San Lorenzo. Early in the sixth century, Pope Symmachus built baths at the urban churches of San Pancrazio and San Paulo. Such baths, as Fikret Yegül points out, were intended for the use not only of the clergy but also of the poor.[42]

Ravenna was also not alone in having a *triclinium*. Three other *episcopia* — at Rome, Naples, and Grado — had formal dining rooms. The evidence for the Lateran is surprisingly late. Only in the mid-eighth century does the *Liber Pontificalis* report that Pope Zacharias built two new *triclinia* within the papal residence. Perhaps the author's description of these two dining rooms as "new" suggests the existence of one or more "old" *triclinia*. But we do know that when Emperor Constans II came to dine with Pope Vitalian (657–672), the meal was served in one of the papal halls, the "basilica of Vigilius."[43] If there was an old *triclinium* in the residence, it was clearly too small to accom-

---

41. As Von Simson has argued, the promotion of the see to full metropolitan status may well have been the work of Emperor Justinian. But the bishops of the see had long been positioning themselves for this promotion, and as early as the fifth century the papacy had acknowledged the see's metropolitan jurisdiction over Aemilia. Otto G. Von Simson, *Sacred Fortress: Byzantine Art and Statecraft in Ravenna* (Chicago, 1948), 11, 15.

42. Duchesne, *LP*, Chaps. 78, 48, 53; Yegül, *Baths*, 319; Lauer, *Latran*, 101, suggests two possible locations of the Lateran baths in the Carolingian era, the most likely one near the Constantinian baptistery.

43. Duchesne, *LP*, Chap. 78.

modate the imperial entourage. Both of Zacharias's *triclinia* were highly ornamented. One was "adorned with varieties of marble, glass, metal, mosaic, and painting," and the other, located in a tower the same pontiff built, had brass railings and "a representation of the world" and various verses painted on its walls.[44] The latter decor recalls the images of creation and the inscriptions in the Ravennate *triclinium*. Evidence of a dining room in the Neapolitan *episcopium* comes earlier. The *Gesta episcoporum neapolitanorum* tells us that Bishop Vincentius of Naples (554–578) "built the baptistery of the minor font within the *episcopium* and the *accubitum* next to it decorated with great care." Remains of this "accubitum" or dining hall were discovered during nineteenth-century excavations in the sacristy of the Neapolitan cathedral. The mosaic paving of the central niche of the hall reveals a motif appropriate to a dining room: a *cantharus*, a drinking vessel with handles. Below is an inscription: VINC(enti)VS VOTUM SOLBIT ("[Bishop] Vincentius fulfilled a vow").[45] Only the central niche of the *triclinium* is legible in the remains, so the overall form of this Neapolitan hall is unknown. In Grado, however, the design of the *triclinium* is more clear. The dining room was situated, like Bishop Neon's in Ravenna, next to the cathedral, and its door opened onto a courtyard linking the *episcopium* to the church. A later enlargement of the basilica expanded over part of the *triclinium*, but what remains indicates that it had five niches arranged just like those in the Neonian dining room (Figure 7).[46]

The *episcopium* at Grado also had a large central hall (roughly a ten-meter, or thirty-four-foot, square) with a hypocaust heating system. This ingenious Roman method of radiant heating used spaces created below a suspended floor and within walls to circulate air heated by an adjacent furnace. Developed and diffused from the late second century B.C., this technology was most commonly used not only in baths but also in elite domestic architecture in the cooler climates of Roman Britain and northern Roman Europe. Located on a peninsula jutting out into the northernmost reaches of the Adriatic Sea (roughly eighty kilometers, or fifty miles, northeast of Venice), Grado had a chilly, damp, winter climate in which the heat radiating from the patriarch's marble floors would have been appreciated.[47]

The floors of the late fourth- and fifth-century (post-Attila) *episcopium* at Aquileia were carpeted with mosaics. Fish-scale patterns pull the eye along a passageway; bold geometric patterns carpet another (Figure 8). More complex patterns are also found: curvaceous swirls, undulating waves, and Solomon's knots. These tapestries of tesserae, however, are not continuous. Sections paved in ceramic tile and in "cocciopesto" (red

44. Duchesne, *LP*, Chap. 93.18; Lauer, *Latran*, 91–92; Marina Di Berardo, "Le aule di rappresentanza," in *Il palazzo apostolico*, 37–49, and Delle Rose, "Il patriarchio," in the same volume, 24–25.

45. *Gesta episcoporum neapolitanorum*, Chap. 23, *MGH SSRL*, 412; Farioli, *Aggiornamento*, 159, tav. X.b.

46. D'Ossat, "Sulla distrutta aula," 269–72.

47. Pieces of the *suspensura* (hanging floor) survive on the remains of the furnace (*praefurnium*) located in the middle of the east wall. Lopreato, "Lo scavo," 327–29.

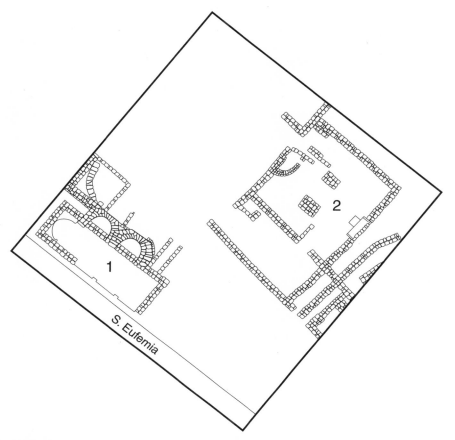

FIGURE 7. *Grado, remains of* episcopium. *1 = five-niched* triclinium?; *2 = hall with hypocaust heating system. (C. Ingersoll, based on Paola Lopreato, "Lo scavo dell'episcopio di Grado,"* Aquileia e le venezie nell'alto medioevo, Antichità altoadriatiche *32 [Udine, 1988]: 329, by permission of the author.)*

cement flooring made with crushed terra-cotta, also called *opus signinum*) are interspersed.[48] This could be the articulation of different functional areas within the residence. John Clarke, for example, has delineated a hierarchy of mosaic styles — plain white coverage, simple all-over patterns, more complex patterns with axial emphases — that differentiated common spaces (corridors, service areas) from more important social spaces used to display status.[49] None of the mosaics discovered within the *episcopium* match in quality the delightful figural mosaics within the basilica at Aquileia. This is a point to which we will return.

The skewed nature of our evidence, indeed, probably gives a much more luxurious image of late-antique *episcopia* than was the norm. The best archeological remains and

48. Bertacchi, "Contributo," 373–82.
49. Clarke, *Houses of Roman Italy*, 273–78.

FIGURE 8. *Aquileia, designs of pavement mosaics within* episcopium. *(C. Ingersoll, based on Luisa Bertacchi, "Contributo allo studio dei palazzi episcopali paleocristiani," Aquileia Nostra 56 (1985): 382, by permission of the author.)*

documentary sources illuminate the wealthiest and most prestigious sees: Rome, the metropolitan sees of Aquileia-Grado and Ravenna, and the ancient and populous see of Naples. These were in no way "typical" episcopal residences. Some evidence within the Roman *Liber Pontificalis* suggests, in fact, that an *episcopium* could be simply a few rooms attached to the church. Pope John VII (705–707) built an *episcopium* "above" the church of Santa Maria Antiqua in Rome "for his own use, and there his life and the time of his pontificate came to an end."

The see of Parenzo on the eastern Adriatic offers some corrective here. A moderately prosperous diocese on the Istrian coast within the patriarchate of Aquileia, Parenzo's *episcopium* has been occupied continuously since the sixth century. The late-antique structure was two-storied, with a large audience hall, approached through an atrium and vestibule, at its center. This hall took the form of an apsed basilica; it was flanked by two narrower consonant wings, each concluding in a semicircular apse. As the entire center of the structure was given over to the great hall, other elements — dining rooms, bedrooms, storage areas, and offices — would have been relegated to the more circumscribed spaces of the wings (one roughly four meters, or fourteen feet, wide, the other about 3.5 meters, [twelve feet]; both about thirteen meters, or forty-two feet, long)(Figure 9).[50] This is still an impressive late-antique building, but the entire structure occupied an area of roughly 1,700 square meters, or 5,600 square feet. The additions that Bishop Peter II annexed to the Ravennate residence exceed the area of the entire *episcopium* at Parenzo.

The commonly shared element in all the residences was a sizable audience hall. Indeed, at Parenzo, the remains of which best reveal an overall plan of an *episcopium*, the

50. Bertacchi, "Contributo," 384–88.

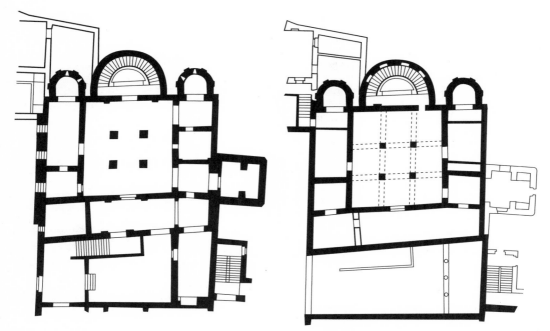

FIGURE 9. *Parenzo, plan of* episcopium, *ground and upper floors. (C. Ingersoll, based on Luisa Bertacchi, "Contributo allo studio dei palazzi episcopali paleocristiani,"* Aquileia Nostra *56 (1985): 386, by permission of the author.)*

hall is the central element and focal point of the architectural ensemble. The late-antique *episcopium* might even be conceived as an audience hall with ancillary rooms. Surely, by necessity, all would have had rooms that would serve as bedrooms, although mention of these is quite rare. In saints' lives, only the death of a bishop reveals him in a bedroom: when Bishop Paulinus of Nola passed into eternal life "the room (*cubiculum*) in which he lay shook with an earthquake, while the rest of the house stood firm."[51] We only know of a papal bedroom in the Lateran because in the late seventh century a terrified imperial official, the *spatharius* Zacharias, sought refuge *in cubiculo pontificis* (in the papal bedroom). The *Liber Pontificalis* reports that when troops from Ravenna surrounded the Lateran, "in extreme terror and despair for his survival Zacharias the *spatharius* got under the pontiff's bed so that he went out of his mind and lost his senses."[52] Storage areas, kitchens, and dining rooms of an ordinary sort — like the Ravennate *mensa* — also were probably common elements. Beyond these essentials, it is difficult to define norms. We know that baths were part of episcopal complexes at the Lateran and Ravenna, and that several of our *episcopia* had elaborately decorated *triclinia*. Chapels are found within the residences at Rome and Ravenna. But the "average" *episcopium* is impossible to define in this period. Even for the eastern Mediter-

51. Gregory the Great, *Dialogues*, III.1.9; trans. Zimmerman, 115.
52. Duchesne, *LP*, Chap. 86; trans. Davis, 1989, 85; Lauer, *Latran*, 90.

ranean, where archeological remains of episcopal complexes are more numerous, better preserved, and more systematically studied, Wolfgang Müller-Wiener was forced to conclude that discernment of an architectural "type" is impossible.

Indeed, Müller-Wiener and other scholars who have studied late-antique episcopal residences express both some frustration and disappointment with their findings.[53] The sources of their frustration and disappointment are highly significant and merit our attention.

SPATIAL UNITY AND ROMAN DOMESTIC ARCHITECTURE

A major frustration is difficulty in determining which structures were part of the *episcopium*, or residence proper, and which were spaces attached to the cathedral supporting the liturgy. As noted earlier, the residence itself was attached or adjacent to the early Christian basilica, but so too were other structures: sacristies, vestries, treasuries, archives, libraries, *scrinia* (writing offices), *salutatoria* (reception halls), and *diaconia* (hospices or almshouses where deacons ministered to the poor).[54] In an archeological site, where indicators of use or function are often lacking, it is difficult to distinguish

53. Mariella Malaspina's "Gli episcopia" (see above note 17) is the earliest systematic survey of archeological evidence. Although she contends that the episcopal residence was distinct from surrounding structures, her evidence better supports her assertion of the complexity and unity of the episcopal group. Several figures (19, 23, 25, 30) do not even attempt to label the residence (by implication relegating all structures except the basilica itself to residential functions) and several areas labeled as part of a residence (Figures 2, 14) could as easily be rooms with other functions. Malaspina admits great variation in form and plan of ecclesiastical residences, making it difficult to articulate their general characteristics (136–38). Wolfgang Müller-Weiner, focusing exclusively on episcopal residences, does distinguish common elements but sees no "Typus" or regular plan and emphasizes their lack of symmetrical or axial organization: "Riflessioni sulle caratteristiche dei palazzi episcopali," *Felix Ravenna* 125–26 (1984): 144–45; "Bischofsresidenzen des 4.-7. Jhs. im östlichen Mittelmeer-Raum," *Actes du XIe Congrès international d'archéologie chrétienne — Lyon, Vienne, Grenoble, Genève et Aoste (21–28 septembre 1986)* 1: 653–57, 697–709. Similar conclusions have been reached by Noël Duval, Paul-Albert Février, and Jean Lassus, "Groupes épiscopaux de Syrie et d'Afrique du Nord," in *Apamée de Syrie: Bilan des recherches archéologiques*, ed. Janine and Jean Ch. Balty (Brussels, 1972), 233–44; and Noël Duval, "L'évêque et la cathédrale en Afrique du Nord," *Actes du XIe Congrès international d'archéologie chrétienne* 1: 391. Moreover, Duval in 1985 delivered a forthright critique of the idea of a "système palatial" that has guided research and interpretation of palatial sites in the twentieth century: "Existe-t-il une «structure palatiale» propre à l'antiquité tardive?" in *Le Système palatial en orient, en Grèce et à Rome*, Actes du Colloque de Strasbourg 19–22 juin 1985, ed. E. Lévy (Strasbourg, 1987), 463–90.

54. Sible de Blaauw, "Architecture and Liturgy in Late Antiquity and the Middle Ages," *Archiv für Liturgiewissenschaft* 33 (1991): 15–17; *Dictionnaire d'archéologie chrétienne et de liturgie* (Paris, 1907–53) s.v. "diaconicum," "offertoire," "sacristie"; Janet Charlotte Smith, "The Side Chambers of San Giovanni Evangelista in Ravenna: Church Libraries of the Fifth Century," *Gesta* 29 (1990): 86–97.

among the many spaces abutting the basilica: is a rectangular space on the cathedral's flank, with access both to the church and to other structures, part of the liturgical complex or part of the bishop's residence?

F. W. Deichmann, for example, discusses the *secretarium* and the *sacrarium* (both terms can denote a sacristy) with the cathedral of Ravenna, but includes the archive, the treasury (*cimeliarchium*), and the *salutatorium* in his discussion of the *episcopium*.[55] In light of the sources, the division especially between the *secretarium* and the *salutatorium* seems arbitrary. Both these spaces are mentioned by Pope Gregory the Great in letters to the archbishops of Ravenna correcting their practices in wearing the pallium (a woolen liturgical scarf bestowed on high-ranking sees as a mark of special connection to Rome). The pope's concern in both letters is to restrict the wearing of the pallium to the archbishop's celebration of the mass. He forbids wearing it in open public areas (*in plateis*) and expresses concern about Archbishop John's wearing of it to receive the faithful *in secretarium*. Several years later, writing to John's successor Marinianus and referring back to this earlier warning, Gregory cautions that the pallium was conceded

> for use in no other manner, you will remember, except within your own church of your city, having already dismissed the faithful, proceeding from the *salutatorium* to the sacred celebration of the solemnities of the mass; indeed, the mass having been performed, back in the *salutatorium* you will take care to lay it aside.[56]

Both the *secretarium* and *salutatorium* were obviously places where the bishop received the faithful before and after mass; why should we place one in the cathedral complex and the other within the bishop's residence?

Indeed, Jean-Charles Picard has recently pointed out that the words *salutatorium* and *secretarium* are used interchangeably in ecclesiastical sources. Moreover, he demonstrates that the *secretarium* was a place for many kinds of episcopal actions. The bishop held councils there, received the faithful before or after mass, and bestowed there the veil on those entering a religious profession. All of these presume, and many mention, the bishop garbed in sacred vestments and seated on a throne surrounded by his clergy. This association with vestments is probably what gave *secretarium* the sense of sacristy or vestry. In classical usage, the *salutatorium* was where the patron received the *salutationes* of his clients. Rooms called *salutatoria* came to be attached to early Christian basilicas to provide a space for the bishop to receive members of his flock. Such encounters, as Picard notes, also are described as taking place in *secretaria*.[57]

55. Deichmann, *Ravenna*, 2 / 1: 12–13, 205–8.

56. *CC*, 140, III.54.70–5; V.61.5–8; Deichmann asserts that Agnellus distinguishes between these two spaces, but the chronicler never discusses them together and I see no evidence of such clarity, Deichmann, *Ravenna*, 2 / 1: 12–13, 207–8.

57. Jean-Charles Picard, "La Fonction des salles de réception dans le groupe épiscopal de Genève," *Rivista di archeologia cristiana* 65 (1989): 87–104. Judicial cases brought to the bishop were among these encounters: John C. Lamoreaux, "Episcopal Courts in Late Antiquity," *Journal of Early Christian Studies* 3 (1995): 143–67.

The evidence of the *Liber Pontificalis* on the Lateran complex is no more clear. The church of San Giovanni, for example, is described as being surrounded by many chambers, and some of these, which are clearly used as meeting halls, are called *basilicae*. When the *episcopium* was surrounded by a threatening mob of soldiers clamoring for the *spatharius* Zacharias (who was, you may remember, cowering under the pope's bed), "the pontiff went outside to the basilica named after the lord pope Theodore; opening the doors and sitting on a seat beneath the Apostles, he honorably received the common soldiers and the people who had come to see him."[58] Roughly forty years later, when Pope Zacharias built one of his new *triclinia* "in front of the basilica of pope Theodore of blessed memory," the structures are described as being within the Lateran residence. Also confusing is the description of the Lateran *episcopium* as having "inner" and "outer" parts. When a schism erupted upon the death of Pope Conon in 687, one contender (Theodore) got to the residence first with his supporters and "occupied its inner areas," while the other contender (Paschal) "held the outer parts, from the oratory of St. Silvester and the basilica of the house of Julius."[59]

In sum, the effort on the part of archeologists and historians to demarcate the early Christian church and structures relating to it from the episcopal residence seems futile — and beside the point. The very ambiguity in the relationship of these structures calls for a different interpretation of episcopal space. That ambiguity suggests that there were often no clear and distinct boundaries conceptually or architecturally between the *episcopium*, the liturgical structures of the see, and other spaces supporting the bishop's ministry. A unity and fluidity of space were intended.

Lay Christian Romans and pagan Romans conceived of their domestic spaces in a similar fashion. Even in the classic Roman *domus*, "public" and "less public" spaces were intermingled. As Andrew Wallace-Hadrill points out, spaces that we think of as "private" — bedrooms, for example — were used by Romans for the reception of friends and conduct of business. There was an articulation of space. The most public was the route the clients took from the vestibule of the house, through the central great hall (atrium) to the framed space (tablinum) in which the master of the house received their *salutationes* (Figure 10). The less public spaces were the dining rooms (*triclinia*), bedrooms (*cubicula*), and alcoves (*exedrae*) reserved for more intimate friends and associates. The contrast, Wallace-Hadrill writes, was "not between public and private in our terms but between degrees of access to outsiders."[60] In the plans of Roman *domus*, highly public and less public spaces are commingled. Bedrooms are attached to the tablinum and

58. Duchesne, *LP*, Chap. 86; trans. Davis, 1989, 86; Lauer, *Latran*, 90.

59. Duchesne, *LP*, Chaps. 93.18, 86. Lauer interprets this passage as the first evidence of the two sections (one fronting Piazza San Giovanni and the other off the atrium of the basilica) that constitute the Lateran in the later Middle Ages and into the sixteenth century. I'm less confident that this is exactly the division of space meant here; the passage is too brief and ambiguous to bear the weight of Lauer's interpretation. Lauer, *Latran*, 90.

60. Andrew Wallace-Hadrill, *Houses and Society in Pompeii and Herculaneum* (Princeton, 1994), 44. A good introduction to Roman houses is A. G. McKay's *Houses, Villas and Palaces in the Roman World* (Ithaca, N.Y., 1975), especially Chapters 2 and 3.

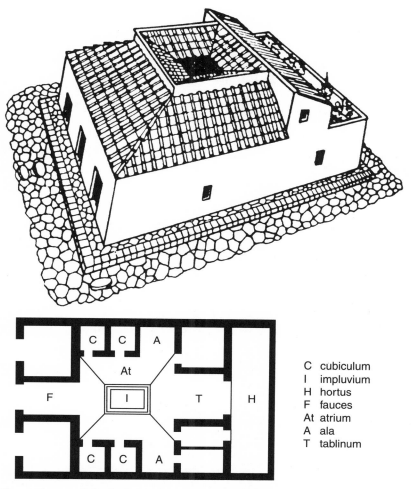

FIGURE 10. *Roman domus of the third century* B.C. *(C. Ingersoll, based on John R. Clarke,* Houses of Roman Italy, 100 B.C.–A.D. 250: Ritual, Space, and Decoration *(Berkeley and Los Angeles, University of California Press, 1991), 3, copyright © 1991 The Regents of the University of California; reprinted by permission of the University of California Press.)*

the ornately decorated *triclinium* in the House of the Prince of Naples in Pompeii. Several similar couplings are found in the Villa of the Mysteries (Pompeii) and at the Villa of Settefinestre. The House of the Smith at Pompeii has three bedrooms opening off the atrium (Figure 11). Moreover, motifs from monumental public and sacral architecture — columns, apses, and *festigia* (triangular pediments usually found on temples and palaces) — were used both to reinforce highly public spaces and to inscribe grandeur and sacrality on *triclinia* and *cubicula*.[61] Both decoratively and architecturally, there was no sharp distinction between public and less public spaces in the Roman house, but a gradient registering many different shades of intimacy.

61. Wallace-Hadrill, *Houses and Society*, 17–37, 47–50, 53, 56.

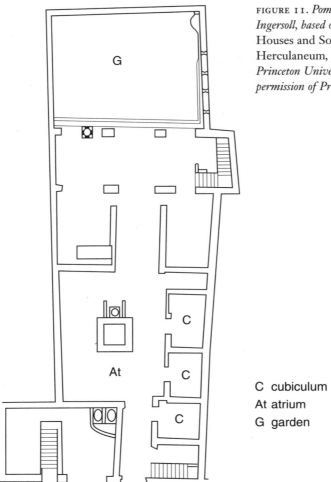

FIGURE 11. *Pompeii, House of the Smith. (C. Ingersoll, based on Andrew Wallace-Hadrill,* Houses and Society in Pompeii and Herculaneum, *56, copyright © 1994 by Princeton University Press; reprinted by permission of Princeton University Press.)*

C cubiculum
At atrium
G garden

    This lack of sharp demarcation grew more marked in the imperial era. Two developments fostered it: the breakdown of the vestibule-atrium-tablinum axis in favor of a more complex arrangement of spaces around a peristyle (surrounded by columns) courtyard, and the multiplication of spaces for receiving and entertaining guests within the house. In houses dating from the early Empire at Pompeii and Herculaneum, the decay of the traditional atrium-tablinum vista is already evident: the House of the Vettii lacks a tablinum altogether, and the House of the Stag's atrium is dark and deemphasized. In the fourth-century houses of Ostia, the strong axial inscription of the *salutationes* route on the house plan that was typical of the classical *domus* becomes much rarer. In the House of Diana, a courtyard with a cistern has replaced the atrium, and the entrance to this area is indirect due to the incorporation of several ground-floor shops at the front of the house. An even greater loss of axiality is evident in the House of the Painted Vaults and the House of the Graffito (Fig-

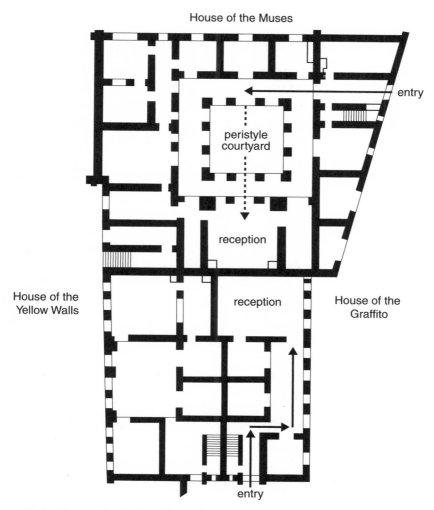

House of the Muses

peristyle courtyard

entry

reception

House of the
Yellow Walls

reception

House of the
Graffito

entry

FIGURE 12. *Ostia, House of the Graffito, House of the Muses.* (C. Ingersoll, based on John R. Clarke, Houses of Roman Italy, 100 B.C.–A.D. 250: Ritual, Space, and Decoration *(Berkeley and Los Angeles, University of California Press, 1992), 307, copyright © 1992 The Regents of the University of California; reprinted by permission of the University of California Press.)*

ure 12). In even these smaller Ostian houses, however, one room is still marked off — usually through size and a more complex and ornamental floor mosaic — as the more public part of the house meant for the reception of guests and clients. In grand homes, such as the House of the Muses, it is usually off the peristyle courtyard and on an axis horizontal to the entry vista. With the abandonment of the traditional atrium-tablinum axis, these later reception halls became more deeply imbedded in the less accessible spaces. This suggests, as Wallace-Hadrill remarks, "an attempt to impose greater control on the exposure of the master to the public." At the same time, however, the number of significant spaces for entertaining increases. The Casa del Menandro at Pompeii, for example, had five major reception rooms of various sizes.[62]

The House of the Hunt at Bulla Regia in north Africa provides an important example in this regard (Figure 13). In the mid-fourth century, a wealthy individual combined several smaller properties and some of their preexisting structures on this site to create a large urban residence. It combines several peristyle courtyards and several large reception areas — most notably a basilica — with numerous smaller rooms. Private baths and latrines also were incorporated into the residence. This elite *domus* reads as a group of larger formal spaces surrounded by smaller, more intimate, ones.[63] Its incorporation of a basilica seems particularly significant in tracing precedents for the indistinct boundary between the early Christian basilica and the episcopal residence that scholars have found so frustrating. The wealthy homeowner in Bulla Regia had some things in common with Bishop Ursus of Ravenna. He had a residence. He acquired more property and built a basilica on it. There were rooms along the flanks of the basilica and on either side of its apse. He added a set of baths. If the basilica in Bulla Regia were a Christian church, it would be impossible to trace a clear boundary between the spaces servicing the church and the living spaces of the bishop and his clergy. This is, indeed, the same difficulty scholars have encountered in studying *episcopia*. The fate of late-antique *domus* in Rome, moreover, supports this reading of Bulla Regia as a model for reading episcopal complexes. Early saints' lives and the *Liber Pontificalis* record how members of the Christian elite often donated their houses to the church. Saint Melania and the Roman matron Lucina, for example, gave their *domus* to establish churches and, indeed, many late-antique churches in Rome (Santa Balbina, Santi Quattro Coronati, San Saba, Sant'Andrea Catabarbara) were established by renovating the private basilicas these donated residences included.[64] And, as we have already seen, the renovation of private domestic spaces for religious purposes had a long history in the Roman world.[65]

All of these patterns in Roman domestic architecture suggest that we view the entire episcopal complex as an elite *domus*. Indeed, within this "house," the Christian basilica — with its atrium, nave, and apse — inscribed an axial route for Christian clients seek-

---

62. Wallace-Hadrill, *Houses and Society*, 54; Clarke, *Houses of Roman Italy*, 269–73; Russell Meiggs, *Roman Ostia* (Oxford, 1973), 235–62; Giovanni Becatti, *Case ostiensi del tardo impero* (Rome, 1949), 10–15 (Domus del Ninfeo), 23–25 (Domus della Fortuna Annonaria), 26 (Domus su via degli Augustali).

63. Yvon Thébert, "Private Life and Domestic Architecture in Roman Africa," in *A History of Private Life from Pagan Rome to Byzantium*, ed. Paul Veyne, trans. Arthur Goldhammer, volume 1 of *A History of Private Life*, ed. Philippe Ariès and Georges Duby (Cambridge, Mass., 1987), 337, 343–44.

64. Federico Guidobaldi, "L'edilizia abitativa unifamiliare nella Roma tardoantica," in *Società romana e impero tardoantico, vol. II: Roma politica economia paesaggio urbano*, ed. Andrea Giardina (Rome and Bari, 1986), 228–36.

65. See above pages 19–20 and White, *Building God's House*.

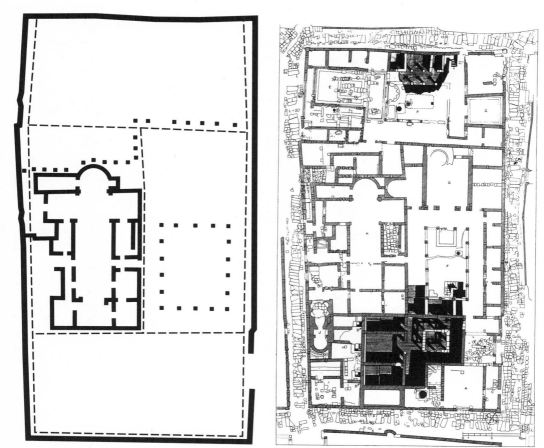

FIGURE 13. *Bulla Regia, the House of the Hunt. A = courtyard; B = vestibule; C = stairway leading to upper stories; D = bedroom; E = triclinium; F = peristyle; G = exedra for reception; H = private basilica; I = latrines; J = baths. (From Azedine Beschaouch, Roger Hanoune, and Yvon Thébert,* Les Ruines de Bulla Regia, *Collection de l'École française de Rome 28 (1977), by permission of the l'École française de Rome.)*

ing their divine patron. Vestries, *secretaria*, the bishop's hall, his dining room, and other more intimate spaces were off to the sides. And like the spaces within a late Roman house, the spaces within the episcopal center were distinguished through decoration. In the Roman house it was the *tablinum* or other large room in which the patron met his clients and usually one of the *triclinia* that were decorated with the most complex mosaic floor patterns and wall paintings. Within the episcopal see, the church and the baptistery were marked off through decoration as the most important parts of the complex. The floor mosaics within the basilica at Aquileia, for example, with their delightful figural representations — of Jonah being gobbled by a sea monster, of the good shepherd surrounded by muscular sheep, of fish and crustaceans set out in poses to prompt culinary fantasies — are far superior in quality to the geometric patterns carpeting the residential areas (Figure 14). Similarly, the descriptions within both the Ravennate and the

FIGURE 14. *Aquileia, south basilica: Jonah, the whale, sea creatures. (Scala / Art Resource, N.Y.)*

Roman *Liber Pontificalis* of the building and decorating activities of bishops leave no doubt that churches and baptisteries were far more embellished than other spaces.

Functional hierarchies of decor also were deployed in these other spaces, but our knowledge of them is more partial. The *salutatoria* where the bishop received the faithful before and after mass could be highly decorated. At Grado, a *salutatoria* added to the south wall of the church by Patriarch Elia (571–587) has a carved stone throne (which also served as a reliquary) and a floor mosaic decorated with the patriarch's monogram (Figures 15, 16). This monogram is centered in the floor mosaic, and the names of seven of the patriarch's clerics (a deacon, a *cubicularius*, four notaries, and a lector), each followed by the phrase "votum solvit" ("fulfill a vow"), are inscribed within it. These patriarchal servants, notes Guglielmo De Angelis D'Ossat, "inscribed in this pavement a memorial to their oblations and seem to render homage to and wrap themselves ideally around the bishop Elia, just as their names circle his monogram in tesserae of gold."[66] Spaces such as Neon's dining room and Bishop Peter's chapel at Ravenna were

66. " . . . hanno concentrato in questo pavimento il ricordo delle loro oblazioni e sembrano rendere omaggio e muoversi idealmente intorno al vescovo Elia, così come i loro nomi ruotano intorno al suo monogramma in tessere d'oro," D'Ossat, "Sulla distrutta aula," 272; Farioli, *Aggiornamento*, 159, note 38.

also distinguished by their elaborate decor. Only more complete archeological work, however, would allow us within one site to understand the hierarchies of space inscribed within an episcopal complex through decor.

In sum, if we stop trying to treat the late-antique *episcopium* in isolation from liturgical structures, these episcopal centers become much more legible. Like a late Roman house, the bishop's see exhibited no sharply defined boundaries between "public" and "private," between the liturgical spaces and the living spaces of the bishop and his clergy. Instead, there was a fluidity of space along a gradient of access to outsiders. The basilica in the episcopal complex, as in that of the lay patron, was the most open — here large crowds of believers attended the bishop, heard him preach, and received the sacraments at his hands. An array of more intimate spaces of various sizes accommodated smaller groups. At the Lateran, these were the smaller "basilicae" such as the one in which Pope Sergius met with the soldiers in pursuit of the *spatharius* cowering under his bed. In other sees, the *salutatorium*, *secretarium*, or sacristy was used to allow the faithful to approach their bishop in a more intimate setting. Further along the gradient of access were halls spatially associated with the bishop's household: the triconch hall at Ravenna, the large room next to Bishop Peter's chapel, or the heated aula of the *episcopium* in Grado. More intimate still were spaces such as Bishop Neon's formal dining room and the *cubiculum pontificalis* where a frightened official sought the protection of his pastor.

That he sought asylum within the episcopal residence further demonstrates the unity of space constituted by the entire complex. From the late fourth century, Christian bishops began to claim for their sacred places the rights of sanctuary once accorded Roman temples. The Council of Sardica as early as 347 decreed that the clergy should assist and ask clemency for all those who "seek refuge in the mercy of the church" (*ad misericordiam ecclesiae confugiant*). The idea that those fleeing oppression should be safe in the church was emphatically asserted in saints' lives. In Paulinus of Milan's *Life of St. Ambrose* (425), a man named Cresconius, "guilty of the gravest crimes," had sought refuge in the church. Soldiers sent by Count Stilicho entered and forcibly removed the man, "and the bishop long lay prostrate before the altar of the Lord, shedding tears over the deed." The soldiers who violated the sanctuary, however, soon suffered divine retribution: leopards released at the amphitheater leapt into the crowd and severely mauled the offenders. Count Stilicho repented, made amends to the bishop, and released Cresconius, sending him into exile.[67]

With or without the help of divinely inspired leopards, episcopal insistence on the right of sanctuary in their churches eventually gained the force of law. Imperial edicts in the early fifth century recognized the inviolability of Christian churches, and Theodosius's edict of 431 (later included in the Justinianic code) defined the topography of this sanctuary as including

---

67. Paulinus of Milan, *Vita sancti Ambrosii*, Chap. 34, ed. A. Bastiaensen, *Vita di Cipriani. Vita di Ambrogio. Vita di Agostino* (Milan, 1975); trans., F. R. Hoare, *The Western Fathers*, 175; Anne Ducloux, *Ad ecclesiam confugere: Naissance du droit d'asile dans les églises (IVe–milieu Ve s.)* (Paris, 1995), 26–34, 85–91.

FIGURE 15. *Grado, patriarchal throne from* salutatorium. *(Museo Diocesano d'Arte Sacra di Venezia, photograph by Osvaldo Böhm.)*

FIGURE 16. *Grado, pavement mosaic in* salutatorium *with monogram of the Patriarch Elia. (Sovrintendenza per i Beni Ambientali Architettonici Archeologici Artistici e Storici del Friuli-Venezia-Giulia.)*

not only the altars and enclosed prayer space of the temple, which encompasses the church within its four walls, but all the way to the outermost doors of the church . . . so that whoever shall have been in the space between the temple's girding of walls and the first doors of the church after the public places — whether in storage areas, or houses, gardens, baths, open areas, or porticos — shall be protected as if having fled into the interior of the temple.[68]

These storage areas, houses, gardens, baths, and porticos are clearly the *episcopium* and, legally, it is considered one with the church proper. A story related in Jordanes's *Romana* (mid-sixth century) confirms that the episcopal residence was considered part of the sacred space accorded asylum: Empress Ariadne fled to the *episcopium* of Bishop Acacius when she discovered that a high court official was plotting against her.[69]

There are even more important theological reasons for late-antique bishops to collapse distinctions between their residences and their churches. While the elite Roman residence had only one lord, the episcopal complex really had two. It was a space devoted to the Lord, of course, but dominated and administered by His local earthly representative, the bishop. This duality of proprietorship complicated spatial relations within the complex and the terminology deployed to designate spaces. In the third century, the church was called the *domus Dei*, *domus ecclesiae*, or *domus orationis*. From the fourth century, the terms *ecclesia* and *basilica* became the more common designations for the cult building.[70] But the earlier term *domus Dei* (1 Tim. 3:15), the "house of God," expresses an important concept that strongly influenced the terminology applied to early episcopal residences. God was the *patronus* of this "house" and its *familia*, the faithful gathered within it. Its natural partner to designate the bishop's residence would have been *domus episcopi*, and indeed, some fourth-century sources employed this term (see Appendix). But late-antique bishops did not choose to embrace this highly dichotomized terminology and its concomitant delimitation of space. They chose to use the term *episcopium*, a word emphasizing the office and person of the bishop (*episcopus*), to refer to the entire complex. One reason for the preference for the term *episcopium* over *domus episcopi* may have been the social pretensions attached in Roman culture to the *domus*. As Richard Saller and others point out, status within Roman society was asserted through real estate: the size, character, and location of an elite *domus* made claims of rank and importance.[71] Christian bishops, indeed, may not have wanted to invoke these associations by calling their residences *domus*. But their preference for the

---

68. Ducloux, *Ad ecclesiam confugere*, 207–36, 284–85. I thank Barbara Rosenwein for this reference and allowing me to read her work on early forms of immunities.

69. Jordanes, *Romana et Getica*, 351, *MGH Auct. Ant.*, 5, part 1, 45.

70. Franz Joseph Dölger, " 'Kirche' als Name für den christlichen Kultbau," *Antike und Chrisentum*, Kultur-und religionsgeschichtliche Studien, 6 (Münster, 1976), 161–95; Victor Saxer, "Domus ecclesiae — οικος Της Εκκλησιας in den frühchristlichen literarischen Texten," *Römische Quartalschrift für christliche Altertumskunde und Kirchengeschichte* 83 (1988): 167–79.

71. Richard P. Saller, "*Familia, Domus*, and the Roman Conception of the Family," *Phoenix* 37 (1984): 336–55.

term *episcopium* surely is also rooted in their relation to the sacred space of the *domus Dei* and the dual patronage, celestial and earthly, of the see. Constructing their sees to blur the boundaries between God's spaces and their own was a more appropriate way for the bishop to enhance his authority and place in the community.

This was theologically appropriate. Bishops were conceived of as Christ's representatives on earth, spiritual descendants of the Apostles. Their claims to authority were grounded in a sacred genealogy reaching back through the Apostles, Christ's chosen "brothers" on earth, and through the son-hood of Christ to God the Father. Liturgically, the bishop stood in the place of Christ among the faithful. He was their "pastor" just as Christ was Good Shepherd to all the faithful. He processed in the place of Christ on Palm Sunday, reenacting Jesus' entry into Jerusalem, he washed the feet of the twelve "apostles" on Holy Thursday, and he held the bread aloft saying Christ's words: "This is my body."[72]

Late-antique bishops consciously refused a clear delimitation of space between their residences and the liturgical structures of their sees because such a distinction was neither theologically appropriate nor politically useful. Although some bishops came from elite Roman families, many, like Augustine, had more humble social origins. Only by wrapping themselves in the carefully constructed mantle of episcopal authority could these men effectively preach their beliefs to a largely pagan elite within late Roman cities and defend their followers and their churches within the imperial state. The topography of the Theodosian law of asylum has already demonstrated how this blurring of space helped bishops protect their flocks. Their physical settings — the collection of buildings and spaces that constituted the bishop's see in a late-antique city — were important semiotic elements in the construction of episcopal authority, and the identification of the bishop with the Lord was an essential underlying premise of this construction. Thus, the desire of scholars to distinguish clearly the episcopal residence from the house of God is frustrated by the desire of episcopal residents to impede such clarity.

THE LOGIC OF "ANARCHIC" ORGANIZATION

The other distinguishing characteristic of modern scholarship on late-antique *episcopia* is similarly significant. Müller-Weiner was notably disappointed that episcopal residences in the eastern Mediterranean followed no discernible "plan." It was impossi-

---

72. In 1 Peter 1: 25, Christ is called shepherd and bishop (episcopus) of souls, and Christ the Good Shepherd was invoked as the exemplar of episcopal duty from the earliest Christian writings. Moreover, Paul's first letter to Timothy, which sets out the qualifications and qualities of a bishop, depicts him as a sober *patronus* who rules his house well. The church in this letter is explicitly called the "house of God" (1 Tim. 3: 1–15). In the second century, Irenaeus wrote of bishops as "successors of the Apostles" and asserted that it was through this succession that bishops received the same sure knowledge of truth imparted to the Apostles by the Holy Spirit on Pentecost. *Dictionnaire de spiritualité ascétique et mystique, doctrine et histoire* (Paris, 1937–95) s.v. "épiscopat"; MacCormack, *Art and Ceremony*, 64, 130.

ble, he discovered, to discern any *Typus* in the remains of *episcopia*. This should hardly surprise us, however, since church structures themselves show great variation down to the sixth century. Local fashions in domestic architecture produced differing types, and this variety was not immediately eclipsed with the advent of the Constantinian basilica form in Rome. Müller-Weiner's findings, in fact, support the close relationship I am arguing between episcopal residences and cult structures. Both early church buildings and episcopal residences resist conformity to an architectural "type" for the same reason: they were agglomerate structures, with sections added and reworked constantly over time, rather than being conceived and built at a particular juncture.[73] Christian cult buildings lost this character with the adoption of the Constantinian basilica as the dominant church plan — and this uniformity of plan, scholarship suggests, was not an organic development but an imposition from above for political purposes. Constantine desired not only doctrinal but also aesthetic uniformity in the new imperial church.[74]

But episcopal residences retained their agglomerate character long after the basilica brought a uniformity of plan to Christian liturgical architecture. This agglomerate character is amply born out in the Ravennate *episcopium* and in the Lateran. Why was this so? Some of the lack of symmetry and order that Müller-Weiner and other scholars are discerning may simply be general characteristics of the development of elite domestic architecture in Late Antiquity. Our knowledge of late Roman private structures is still quite incomplete, but preliminary work does delineate several changes that intersect with aspects of episcopal residences: for example, the general absence of peristyles, a predilection for curvilinear structures (apsed halls, *trichora*) that create nonorthogonal spaces, and the constraints of building on long-developed sites with preexisting edifices.[75] But the additive character of episcopal residences, to which scholars attribute their "anarchic" organization, does seem particularly pronounced in these ecclesiastical structures. Late Roman private residences, even if their plans differ substantially from the elegant symmetry of the classical *domus*, do not seem to have developed in the accretionary fashion that characterizes *episcopia*.

Perhaps one could view this character as a peculiarity deriving wholly from the sequence of inhabitants of the *episcopium*. But elite Roman houses also were inhabited by generations of different owners without resulting in the relatively "planless," agglomerate composition of episcopal residences. Rather than bemoaning the disorderly architectural aesthetics of late-antique episcopal residences, I think we need to inquire into the logic of their agglomerate character. Four factors in particular seem to have produced this character.

The first is readily apparent both in the Roman and Ravennate *Liber Pontificalis* and in the *Gesta episcoporum neapolitanorum*: building is a praiseworthy activity. Episcopal biographies, like those of secular rulers, are careful to enumerate the edifices and ameni-

73. Müller-Wiener, "Bischofsresidenzen," 701; Duval, Février, and Lassus found some residences with "plans réguliers" but more with what they called "plans anarchiques" (meaning "plans par adjonctions successives"), "Groupes Épiscopaux," 233.

74. White, *Building God's House*, 18.

75. Guidobaldi, "L'edilizia abitativa," 209–13, 219–22.

ties contributed to the locale by bishops. And the builders themselves advertised their contributions in inscriptions. The building patronage of bishops, however, had to be exercised within a more constricted landscape than that enjoyed by rulers. This is the second factor influencing the architecture of the *episcopium*: the topography of the holy. Episcopal building programs had to articulate or restore the local geography of the sacred through the construction of churches or the addition of fountains, rooms, or baths to holy sites. This meant that the bishop's options for improving his own residence were limited. An emperor or imperial functionary dissatisfied with a preexisting residence could simply build a new one at a different site.[76] Elite Romans built, bought, and sold houses to suit their personal preferences and were not as emotionally attached to properties as the aristocracies of later times.[77] But a late-antique bishop's residence, as we have seen, was intimately related to the sacred spaces, which were the guarantors of his power. Addition and renovation to the structures adjacent to the cathedral were the bishop's only architectural choice.

Another factor contributing to the agglomerate character of the *episcopium* was the development of the episcopal office itself. Over the centuries we call Late Antiquity, the bishop's social role in the city changed considerably. Once the leader of only a marginalized sect, the bishop increasingly became a civic patron and a leader of the entire urban community as Christianity became dominant and the late Roman state declined. This more prominent episcopal role in late-antique society certainly fueled the addition of formal dining rooms and different kinds of audience halls to episcopal residences. During this same period, by contrast, the social roles and rituals of elite lay Romans remained relatively stable. Although the arrangement of space within the Roman *domus* was modified, and the number of spaces for entertaining guests rose, the kinds of spaces required by the social conventions of elite life were not altered radically.

Finally, it seems the agglomerate character of episcopal residences was not only unobjectionable to their inhabitants, but also a positive virtue worthy of preservation. Surely, a bishop imbued with renovating fervor could have chosen to rationalize the architecture of the *episcopium*, to impose a pleasing symmetry on its many parts. But late-antique bishops seem not to have chosen this path. Indeed, the tendency to commemorate additions to the *episcopium* in inscriptions and to record these building campaigns carefully in episcopal histories suggests a different aesthetic at work. Visually, the different sections of the residence that seem disordered to modern eyes — lacking in symmetry, axial organization, and rational plan — constituted *memoria* of predecessors. Victor's inscription at his renovated bath complex, the inscription recalling Bishop Neon within his dining room, Vincentius of Naple's assertion in tesserae that he had "fulfilled a vow" in building his *triclinium*, and the mosaic monogram of Patriarch Elia in the floor of his *salutatorium* in Grado: all these signs imbedded in additions to *epis-*

76. McKay, *Houses, Villas and Palaces*, 73–77.

77. Elizabeth Rawson, "The Ciceronian Aristocracy and Its Properties," in *Studies in Roman Property*, ed. M. I. Finley (Cambridge, 1976), 85–102; Susan Treggiari tempered Rawson's interpretation in "Sentiment and Property: Some Attitudes," in *Theories of Property: Aristotle to the Present*, eds. Anthony Parel and Thomas Flanagan (Waterloo, Ont., 1979), 53–85.

copia commemorate their builders. A history of the see, an architectural genealogy of one's episcopal forefathers, was preserved in the different parts of the residence. Let us take this constellation of meaning seriously. Rather than assuming bishops had impoverished architectural taste or a defective sense of residential propriety, let us suppose that these bishops chose to preserve and further articulate their houses in ways that had meaning for them. If we embrace this supposition, then these agglomerate structures become the visual histories of the see. As such, they articulate the power of the episcopal office, for that power was grounded in a sacred lineage reaching back to the Savior. As we have already seen, the bishops of Ravenna visually traced such a lineage in the pictorial decoration of their triconch hall. Similar impulses to articulate and represent a sacred episcopal lineage found expression in the compilation of episcopal lists (such as the Roman and Ravennate *Liber Pontificalis*) and in the veneration of episcopal forebears.[78] Architecturally, the many parts of the *episcopium* spelled out that same genealogy of power. It visually represented the see's claims to sacred authority, solidified in stone, brick, and mortar claims that defined the men that exercised the office and lived within their confines.

Although using a late Roman architectural vocabulary and drawing on ideas about space that informed contemporary domestic architecture, Christian bishops created new forms and new meanings. They added *triclinia*, baths, and triconch halls to their homes. But these decidedly Roman elements meandered and sprawled over sites next to their churches, eschewing the symmetrical angularity that announced secular ambitions in order to articulate a genealogy of priestly succession. Bishops also borrowed the powerful ideology of Roman patronage, and notions of how it was exhibited and deployed in domestic architecture, in order to enhance their own authority and that of their office. By keeping the lines fluid and indistinct between God's house and their own, bishops mobilized deeply ingrained habits of deference and awe.

78. Picard, *Le Souvenir des évêques*, 502–35, 713–19.

CHAPTER TWO:
THE EPISCOPAL RESIDENCE
IN THE EARLY MIDDLE AGES
The Domus Sancte Ecclesie

On the octave of Easter in 968, the people of Verona heard their bishop preach. His sermon — really, an invective-ladened harangue — was on themes familiar to the Veronese: their lies, wickedness, and impious persecution of their bishop. Their abuse of his house, however, tops this particular list of complaints. Bishop Ratherius lamented,

> For though in these three years I have spent almost forty pounds (according to those who were in charge of the work) on the restoration of this episcopal *domus*, I have been expelled from it by them, and the house has remained without a tenant. Yet the same people who are upbraiding me for this do not stop looting it, while those visiting there keep violently wrecking it, as the evidence shows, while I, to be sure, am not strong enough to resist either group, either the thieves because I am at a distance, or those visiting there because I am absent and seem far inferior in power, since they are known to be returning from the imperial army or on their way to it. Hiring inspectors, they lyingly accuse *me* of destroying it — as though it could be credible that I myself would destroy or willingly allow to be destroyed what I have built at such expense of my own! Lodging there, they abuse it, with such show of authority that if any of my staff, whose business it is, come there to inspect it, they at once seize him, beat him savagely, and lock him up.[1]

The curious subject of this sermon may well cause the reader to wonder: Why was this bishop expelled from his house? Why were individuals, particularly imperial officials or soldiers, looting and wrecking it? Why was the bishop powerless to stop this destruction? Obviously, we are at some distance here from the self-confident articulation of spiritual power that characterized the late-antique bishops' architectural demeanor. Ratherius also introduces us to the new terminology used to denote the episcopal residence: he abandons the late-antique term *episcopium* and simply calls his residence the episcopal house or *domus*. Moreover, its character as well as its name was different. The

---

1. *CC Cont. Med.*, 46: 171–72 (*De octavis paschae*, Chap. 1, lines 35–51); trans. Peter L. D. Reid, *The Complete Works of Rather of Verona* (Binghamton, 1991), 509, with modifications. Reid translates "domus episcopalis" as "episcopal palace."

domus that was the subject of Ratherius's concern lacked the heated *aule* and baths, the mosaic-ladened chapels and *triclinia*, and the quiet gardens and porticos of the late-antique *episcopium*. Indeed, much had changed. To understand Bishop Ratherius's predicament, we need to explore two particular sets of changes in early-medieval Italy: changes in domestic architecture and changes in the bishop's office.

The early Middle Ages constitutes a period of profound transformation and rupture in the history of Italian domestic architecture generally, and in the development of episcopal residences in particular. The key rupture was the end of the classical *domus* and the emergence of new, decidedly medieval, forms of domestic architecture. The first part of this chapter will elucidate the continuity and change in the structures that constituted the bishop's residence. In brief, some late-antique buildings did survive into the Middle Ages, but additions to the ancient *episcopia* — particularly towers — began to change their character. Moreover, the new episcopal residences built in the early Middle Ages were quite different from the sprawling complexes typical of Late Antiquity. They were simple structures: two-story rectangular buildings attached to towers. They were heavily fortified. In composition, construction, and appearance they seem exactly like the residences of lay notables; nothing distinctively ecclesiastical marks their architecture.

The changed character of the buildings in which bishops lived was related to changes in the episcopal office. Just as late-antique episcopal residences articulated an ideology of sacred authority, the bishop's house in the early Middle Ages registers changes in his profile and role. I believe that several changes in the episcopal office are particularly important to the new form and character of the bishop's *domus*.

The first is the bishop's new relation to power. Although late-antique bishops assumed many public responsibilities in their cities, early-medieval bishops became much more deeply implicated in governance. Invoking, and probably exaggerating, the instability of their times, bishops throughout Italy claimed and were granted numerous rights and power normally wielded by secular rulers (kings, counts). They obtained, for example, imperial grants that provided the means and authority to build fortifications against the attacks of "pagani" and the depredations of powerful lords. With those royal gifts and concessions, however, came new duties to serve kings as advisers, messengers, judges, and warlords. Indeed, these new demands tended to make bishops more like counts, and by the end of the tenth century many of the bishops of northern Italy actually were counts. Bishops became, for better or worse, local functionaries of royal government.[2] This alliance with power that bishops entered (in their view) in or-

2. Good overviews of the changing character of the episcopal office in this period are Giovanni Tabacco, "Il volto ecclesiastico del potere nell'età carolingia," and Giuseppe Sergi, "Vescovi, monasteri, aristocrazia militare," both in *Storia d'Italia. Annali 9: La chiesa e il potere politico dal medioevo al'età contemporanea*, ed. Giorgio Chittolini and Giovanni Miccoli (Turin, 1986), 7–41, 74–98; Enzo Petrucci, "Attraverso i poteri civili dei vescovi nel medioevo," *RSCI* 34 (1980): 518–45; Paolo Golinelli, "Strutture organizzative e vita religiosa nell'età del particolarismo," in *Storia dell'Italia religiosa, I: L'antichità e il medioevo*, ed. André Vauchez (Rome and Bari, 1993), 155–92 but especially 155–62; in English, Giovanni Tabacco, *The Struggle for Power in Medieval Italy: Structures of Political Rule*, trans. Rosalind Brown Jensen (Cambridge, 1989), 125–36, 166–76.

der to serve Christian communities strongly influenced the character of their residences in the early Middle Ages.

The alliance with power also influenced their relation to both the clergy and the laity of their dioceses. This represents another important change in the episcopal office, one that is much more amorphous and difficult to gauge. Several manifestations of it will concern us here. The first is the transformation of the bishop's household. The new royal duties of bishops — attendance at court, the exercise of judicial rights, the management of larger estates — led to the development of an episcopal household that was more worldly, including vassals and lay servants as well as clerics. Another is the increasing independence and power of the cathedral clergy. No longer part of the bishop's immediate household, these clerics became institutionalized as the cathedral chapter — with their own buildings and endowments — and assumed the major responsibility for the day-to-day liturgy of the bishop's church. This altered, in turn, the bishop's relationship to the sacred space of the cathedral and to the urban populace gathered within it.

The transformation of the episcopal office and residence was part of a much broader evolution of Christianity as it both accommodated itself to and attempted to change the new conditions in Western Europe that we call "medieval." Many were alarmed at this evolution, or specific aspects of it. Ratherius was one. But to understand his perspective and to form our own, we need to return to late Late Antiquity and see what happened to the *episcopia*. With his lament not too far out of mind, let us follow the episcopal residence into the Middle Ages.

THE EVOLUTION OF LATE-ANTIQUE SITES

In all three of our best-documented *episcopia* — Ravenna, Naples, and Rome — late-antique buildings survived into the central Middle Ages. These complexes continued to evolve: at all three sites, there is evidence of new building in the eighth and ninth centuries. Some of this construction, particularly at the Lateran in Rome, appears to be reconstruction and restoration necessitated by the dilapidation of ancient buildings. Some new construction, however, suggests additions of a very different character. A new vocabulary of medieval architectural elements begins to appear in the descriptions of these eighth- and ninth-century additions to the oldest episcopal residences. These new elements — particularly towers — suggest a changing architectural character as the episcopal residence entered the Middle Ages.

The residence at Ravenna shows the strongest continuity over this period. References in medieval sources to most of the buildings that comprised the late-antique Ravennate *episcopium*, for example, indicate their continued use. The sixth-century "Domus Tricoli" was the site in 1079 where a group of the archbishop's vassals put a petition to their lord, and an investiture of vassals was held in the same triconch hall in 1213. Bishop Neon's formal dining room was probably where Charlemagne dined with Archbishop Gratiosus in 787: Agnellus portrays the kindly prelate urging the king to eat using the motherly phrases of his native Romagnole dialect. There are many attestations as well to Peter II's building with its chapel, hall, and mensa. Two imperial judicial sessions, or *placita*, were held here in the 1030s in the upper room next to the chapel of Sant'Andrea.[3]

In addition to this substantial late-classical inheritance at Ravenna, significant new construction occurred in the eighth and early ninth centuries. The "Domus Felicis," a building that initially may have provided new living quarters for the archbishop, was added on the northeast side of the cathedral behind the baptistery in the early eighth century. By the early twelfth century it was used as a hall for synods and seems to have continued to serve this function until it was demolished in the thirteenth century.[4] A more enduring addition to the residence was made by Archbishop Valerianus of Ravenna (789–810). He demolished the residences of his vanquished Arian rivals in the city and used the materials to build a new *domus*. This structure, which Agnellus in the ninth century called the "new house" or "the Domus Valeriana," stood on the location of the present Arcivescovado, and remains of its foundation survive within it (Figure 17).[5] During the central Middle Ages, in fact, this building became the most important part of the residence and has remained so to the present. Note, however, that it was built from *spolia*, the scavenged remains of earlier structures. Although there were clearly ideological reasons for using the materials of the Arian *episcopia* to enhance the archbishop's residence, one also suspects that economy factored in. No other additions to the residence in the ninth and tenth centuries are noted after the Domus Valeriana, but Agnellus's *Liber Pontificalis* ends with the death of Archbishop George in 846, and our sources then become much more fragmentary.

The development of the episcopal residence in Naples follows a similar pattern: significant additions were made in the late eighth and early ninth centuries. Bishop Stephen II (766–794) added an apse to some structure within the residence, erected two towers "to a noble height," and built a chapel dedicated to Saint Peter. This chapel, "embellished with wonderful works," had a depiction of the "six councils of the holy fathers" on its facade. Adjacent to the chapel, Bishop Stephen also added an extensive *solarium* (a balcony or terrace). His successor, Paul III (794–819), secured relics for the altar of the new chapel, painted Stephen's two towers, and built a large granary somewhere near the entrance of the residence.[6] These are the last additions noted in the *Gesta episcoporum neapolitanorum*, but like the Ravennate *Liber Pontificalis* this episcopal chronicle breaks off in the late ninth century.

3. Fantuzzi, *Mon. rav.*, 2, no. 4; 5, no. 55; Agnellus, *LP*, Chap. 165; Manaresi, *Placiti*, 3 / 1 nos. 331, 334; Miller, "Ravenna," 161–64.

4. Miller, "Ravenna," 154, 162; Deichmann, *Ravenna* II / 1: 207; *AARavenna*, perg. nr. 2809 (July 26, 1123).

5. Agnellus, *LP*, Chap. 70; Miller, "Ravenna," 165–66.

6. *Gesta episcoporum neapolitanorum*, Chaps. 42, 46, in *MGH SSRL*, 425–27.

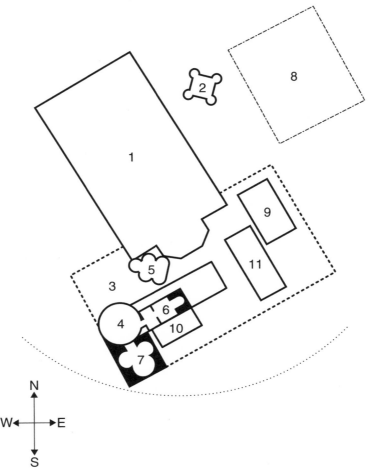

FIGURE 17. *Ravenna, the early-medieval* domus. *1 = cathedral; 2 = baptistery; 3 = location of fourth-century residence?; 4 = Salustra Tower; 5 = Bishop Neon's* triclinium, *the "Quinque Accubita"; 6 = chapel of Sant'Andrea; 7 = triconch hall, the "Domus Tricoli"; 8 = baths; 9 = "Domus Felicis"; 10 = vivarium; 11 = "Domus Valeriana." (C. Ingersoll.)*

Additions to the Lateran also continued in the late eighth and ninth centuries, but increasingly the dilapidation of the residence is cited as the reason for new building and renovation. Hadrian I (772–795)

> newly constructed and built there a tower adorned with wondrous beauty, adjoining the portico which goes down to the bath; and there he had a gallery, a veranda that is, built very beautifully, with bronze railings. He also rebuilt the portico itself, which had been destroyed by age, as was much needed; and adorned that tower and all his new constructions with painting and marble.[7]

7. Duchesne, *LP*, Chap. 97.56; trans. Davis, 1992, 151; Lauer, *Latran*, 100.

As Davis notes, these buildings are mentioned in no other source and their location is impossible to fix. Hadrian also restored the Claudian aqueduct, which "had been demolished for a period of years" and provided water for the Lateran baths and the Constantinian baptistery.[8]

Hadrian's successor, Leo III (795–816), made even more significant renovations to the residence. He added two large *triclinia*, one a triconch hall in the east wing of the residence (near the chapel of San Lorenzo, also called the Sancta Sanctorum) and the other a massive structure with eleven niches decorated with representations of the apostles preaching to the nations. This impressive *triclinium* was on the north side of the basilica of San Giovanni facing the piazza (or "campus") and was used into the central Middle Ages for holding councils (Figure 18). Leo also added a new chapel dedicated to the archangel Michael and decorated with mosaics and marble. Finally, he restored what the *Liber Pontificalis* author calls the "macrona" or extension, probably the north portico of the western part of the Lateran. "[A]bout to collapse from great age," the pontiff "freshly restored it from its foundations along with its roofing and veranda from bottom to top and improved it by laying it with solid marble."[9]

Gregory IV (828–844) added another *triclinium*, a triconch hall just to the east of Leo III's (Figure 18). The *Liber Pontificalis* indicates that it had mosaics in one apse, and that the other two were "painted with various representations." In the same area near the chapel of San Lorenzo / Sancta Sanctorum, Gregory built "a quite suitable dwelling." The main reason for the construction of this suite of apartments seems to have been access to the chapel: "there too the stillness is excellent, and the pontiff can emerge from it with his clerics and perform the praises due to the Lord almighty." The *Liber* also credits Gregory with the restoration of older buildings within the Lateran that were "now destroyed and almost on the point of collapse from great age." He remodeled the stairs leading to the cellar and "from this place to St. Laurence's oratory he restored all that was old and added other things new, amongst which he ordered the building of 3 parlours."[10]

These descriptions of additions to episcopal residences in the late eighth and early ninth centuries reveal an important change: the beginnings of a new — and decidedly medieval — vocabulary of domestic architecture. Some of the classical vocabulary — words such as *aula* (hall), *triclinium* (dining room), *cubiculum* (bedroom) — remains in use. But these traditional Roman terms are joined by new ones. The word *solarium* — terrace or balcony — is used for the first time in the *Liber Pontificalis* when describing Hadrian's addition in the late eighth century of an open-air gallery or veranda (*deambulatorium, scilicet solarium*). At about the same time, Bishop Stephen II of Naples added a

8. Duchesne, *LP*, Chap. 97.62; trans. Davis, 1992, 154.

9. Duchesne, *LP*, Chaps. 98.9, 98.27, 98.39, 98.92; trans. Davis, 1992, 183–84, 193, 198, 223, and note 181; Lauer, *Latran*, 103–18.

10. Duchesne, *LP*, Chaps. 103.15, 103.35–36; trans. Davis, 1995, 57, 66–67; Lauer, *Latran*, 121–22; Delle Rose, "Il patriarchio," in *Il palazzo apostolico*, 24–25.

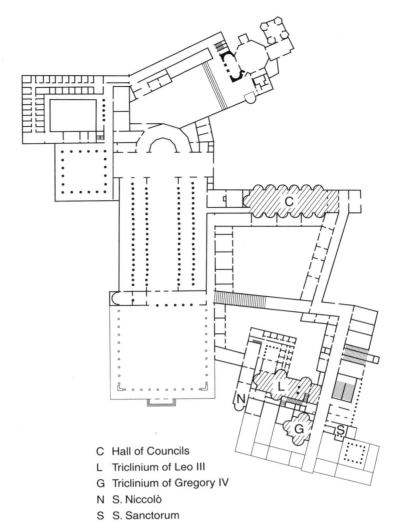

C Hall of Councils
L Triclinium of Leo III
G Triclinium of Gregory IV
N S. Niccolò
S S. Sanctorum

FIGURE 18. *Rome, Lateran residence. (C. Ingersoll.)*

wide *solarium* to his residence. This is one of the most frequently mentioned architectural elements in elite domestic architecture of the Middle Ages. Another term, *caminata*, is used in the life of Pope Gregory (828–844) to describe three "parlours" added to the Lateran. Unlike *solarium*, the word *caminata* does not occur in classical Latin. It is, however, quite common in medieval Latin and denotes a heated room, a room with a *caminus* or fireplace.[11] Finally, in the late eighth century, both Bishop Stephen II of Naples and Pope Hadrian I added towers (*turres*) to their residences. In Antiquity, such

11. Duchesne, *LP*, Chaps. 97.56, 103.36; *Gesta episcoporum neapolitanorum*, Chap. 42, *MGH SSRL*, 426; Niermeyer, *MLLM*, "solarium" (1), "caminata."

fortified spaces were not characteristic of domestic architecture, but in the Middle Ages towers were among the most important elements defining elite residences.[12]

The incorporation of fortifications into episcopal residences was partially a response to insecure times. War and invasion troubled the peninsula sporadically from the eighth through the tenth centuries. In the late eighth century, repeated Lombard incursions into papal territory resulted in the Carolingian intervention in Italy. This intervention brought its own destruction: the Veronese episcopal residence, for example, was burned during the Frankish conquest of the city. In Rome in this era, Pope Hadrian "renewed the walls and towers" of the city. The chief concerns motivating this refortification were Saracen raids, which intensified in the early ninth century, leading Pope Gregory IV (828–844) to fortify and rebuild Ostia as a bulwark of Roman defense. Leo IV's contributions in the mid-ninth century to the defense of the city and its holy places were even more substantial. He restored the walls, rebuilding their gates and towers. "This was done," the *Liber* reports frankly, "because of the coming danger of the Saracens and for the city of Rome's safety." From 848 to 852, Leo had a circuit of walls built around Saint Peter's, conscripting labor from papal cities, estates, and monasteries to accomplish the construction of what would be called the "Leonine city."[13] In the mid-ninth century, Sicopolis, the hilltop fortress to which Capua had been evacuated to escape Saracen raids, burned to the ground ("perhaps by divine judgement," the chronicler adds). The devastation was so complete that "not even one house remained, the episcopal aula even having been burned."[14] And, as we shall see, Saracen raids caused the bishop of Genoa to abandon his residence at the cathedral of San Lorenzo and to build a new, highly fortified one on a walled promontory overlooking the port. The Saracen raids of the ninth century gave way to Magyar invasions in the tenth. These too directly affected episcopal residences. After Magyars sacked Reggio in 899, its bishop built a new residence and cathedral within an already fortified part of the city.[15]

12. Towers were sometimes incorporated into provincial villas to facilitate estate supervision: McKay, *Houses, Villas and Palaces*, 219–20, note 418. On the development and significance of towers in the Middle Ages, Aldo A. Settia, "Lo sviluppo di un modello: origine e funzioni delle torri private urbane nell'Italia centrosettentrionale," in *Paesaggi urbani dell'Italia padana nei secoli VIII–XIV* (Bologna, 1988), 157–71; Loris Macci and Valeria Orgera, *Architettura e civiltà delle torri. Torri e familie nella Firenze medievale* (Florence, 1994).

13. Duchesne, *LP*, Chaps. 97.52, 103.39, 105.38–39, 105.68–74; trans. Davis, 1995, 68, 126–27, 139–44; Bernhard Schimmelpfennig, *The Papacy*, trans. James Sievert (New York, 1992), 103; on invasions and castle building generally, Pierre Toubert, *Les Structures du Latium médiéval; Le Latium méridional et la Sabine du IX a siècle à la fine du XIIe siècle*, 2 vols. (Rome, 1973), and Aldo Settia, *Castelli e villaggi nell'Italia padana: Popolamento, potere, e sicurezza fra IX e XII secolo* (Naples, 1984).

14. *CDV*, 1 no. 71; Erchempertus, *Historia Langobardorum Beneventanarum*, Chap. 24 in *MGH SSRL*, 243.

15. Archeological work at the episcopal fortress of San Cassiano provides eloquent testimony of the devastating impact these raids had on some episcopal residences: levels 4 and 5 reveal that the site was burned (ninth to tenth centuries) and then a ditch was dug in an attempt to fortify it. Sauro

It is impossible to know exactly how many episcopal residences were destroyed as a result of war and invasion. Our curiosity about the development of these *domus* is frustrated by the cessation of episcopal chronicles: Agnellus's narrative draws to a close in 846, the *Gesta episcoporum neapolitanorum* breaks off around 872, and the Roman *Liber Pontificalis* ends in 870. The few later continuators of the latter source are not in any way comparable to the *Liber*. This break in the chronicles leaves us to ponder the changing configuration of episcopal residences in very different, and much more terse, sources: notarial charters and archeological finds. These sources are difficult and their evidence is fragmentary, at best. Considered in relation to one another, however, they do allow us to piece together some picture of the new kinds of residences bishops were building in medieval Italy.

Let us start with the evidence of notarial charters. The redaction clauses of these sources (specifying where and when the charter was drawn up) reveal many of the spaces within episcopal residences and allow us to define at least their most common architectural elements in the early Middle Ages. As at Naples and Rome, towers are frequently mentioned. A charter of 935 was redacted "in the *domus* of the holy church of Parma, in the tower newly built by lord Sigifredus, venerable bishop of this holy church."[16] Bishop Lando of Cremona in 902 got Emperor Louis III to grant him two of the city's towers that are described as "next to his [the bishop's] small fortress (*municiuculam suam*)" along with the right to exercise all public jurisdictions within that fortified center.[17] The episcopal residence in Cremona, it seems, was more what we might call a castle.

The linkage evident in this gift between the fortification of the episcopal residence and the bishop's acquisition of public authority is highly significant. Fortifications were useful for defense but they were, more importantly, articulations of power. Towers, for example, were not merely functional. Throughout the Middle Ages they were significant markers of status: only the elite had towers. Not only were these fortified structures expensive and difficult to build, but also visually they made a huge impression. A tower gave its owner a powerful visual prominence in the urban center. Although towers became common in Italian cities in the central Middle Ages, before the millennium only a few would have announced themselves on the skyline of town. Thick walls would have been enough to protect the bishop, his household, and its wealth. The addition of towers to episcopal residences must be read more as an assertion of status than as a defensive gesture.

The tower of the bishop of Piacenza's *domus* reveals another common feature of medieval episcopal residences. In 990, a judicial hearing was held "in the city of Piacenza

---

Gelichi, "Castelli vescovili ed episcopi fortificati in Emilia-Romagna: Il castello di Gotefredo presso Cittanova e il *castrum S. Cassiani* a Imola," *Archeologia medievale* 16 (1989): 184; for Reggio, see note 25.

16. *Parma X*, no. 42.
17. *Carte Cremonesi*, no. 35.

in the archbishop's own tower of the holy Piacentine church, in the great loggia (*laubia magiore*) of this tower."[18] The loggia — a covered room open on at least one side affording a view and a place to take the air — is a familiar and ubiquitous element in Italian architecture, and it has its origins in the early Middle Ages. The word *laubia*, in fact, is a new term in medieval Latin, its earliest appearances in ninth-century imperial pleas (the first reference in Milan dated 865). The word has its root in Old High German *louba*, meaning "porch," and this suggests that its incorporation in the medieval Latin lexicon arose either from the encounter of Frankish imperial notaries with Italian architecture or from the adoption of Germanic elements in elite architecture generally.[19] Medieval episcopal residences seem to have been studded with loggias. The specification of the loggia in the Bishop of Piacenza's tower as "magiore" implies the existence of one or more "minor" loggias. Additionally, this residence had a "laubia maiore" off a solarium and a loggia described as being "in front of the church of Saints Cosmas and Damian." Reggio Emilia's episcopal residence had at least two loggias off the bishop's *sala*, a room described as located along the flank of the cathedral.[20] Another kind of open space incorporated into episcopal residences in this era was the *solarium*, a sort of sun deck or terrace on an upper story (in a general sense, the term also can mean a second floor). As we have seen, Bishop Stephen II added one to the Neapolitan residence in the eighth century. *Solaria* are also found at the episcopal residences in Pavia and Piacenza.

The most fundamental element in episcopal *domus* of this era, however, was a large room where the bishop held court. It is designated in several ways. Sometimes it is simply called the "room of the house" (*camera domui* or *sala propria domui*) or the "great room" (*camara majore*).[21] *Sala* was another Germanic (*Saal*) loan word that begins to appear in Latin charters in the eighth century to describe a hall.[22] In describing episcopal halls, notaries more frequently use the specific medieval term for a room with a hearth — *caminata*. A judicial hearing in 1001, for example, was held "in the great hearth room" of the *domus* of the bishop of Cremona. Another document recording imperial

18. Manaresi, *Placiti*, no. 212.

19. Niermeyer, *MLLM*, s.v. "laubia"; *Dizionario enciclopedico di architettura e urbanistica*, ed. Paolo Portoghesi (Rome, 1968–69), s.v. "loggia"; Michelangelo Cagiano de Azevedo, "Laubia," *Studi medievali* 10 / 2 (1969): 431–63.

20. The episcopal *domus* at Cremona, Lucca, Milan, Padua, and Pavia also had loggias. Manaresi, *Placiti*, nos. 213, 273 (Piacenza), 142, 143, 146 (Reggio); *Carte Cremonesi*, no. 109; *Mem. e doc.*, 4 supp., app. no. 52; Manaresi, *Placiti*, no. 101 (Milan); *CDP*, no. 98; Manaresi, *Placiti*, no. 383 (Pavia).

21. *Carte Cremonesi*, no. 32; Manaresi, *Placiti*, no. 347; *AARavenna*, perg. no. 2190, doc. 2.

22. Niermeyer, *MLLM*, s.v. "sala"; see also the discussion following Gian Piero Bognetti's "Problemi di metodo e oggetti di studio nella storia delle città italiane dell'alto medioevo," in *La città nell'alto medioevo*, Settimane di studio del Centro italiano di studi sull'alto medioevo 6 (Spoleto, 1959), 195, 219–20; D. A. Bullough, "Urban Change in Medieval Italy: The Example of Pavia," *Papers of the British School at Rome* 34 (1966): 106; Michelangelo Cagiano de Azevedo, "Le case descritte dal Codex traditionum ecclesiae Ravennatis," *Rendiconti dell'Accademia nazionale dei Lincei. Classe di scienze morali, storiche e filologiche* 27 (1972): 168.

pleas informs us that the bishop of Pavia's "caminata maoris sale" was located just behind the apse of the cathedral of San Siro. That large room flanking the cathedral in
the episcopal residence at Reggio Emilia was called either the *sala* or the *caminata
maior*. An early-eleventh-century reference to the "great hearth room" in the archiepiscopal residence in Milan locates it "near the bath called the stove" (*prope baneum dicitur
stuva*), suggesting that heated areas within the residence were clustered together.[23]

The language of one tenth-century charter, moreover, suggests that this great room
was considered the key constituent element of the bishop's *domus*. In Pavia in 967, a notary specified that the plea he was recording was heard "in the hearth room of the great
hall, namely in the house of the bishop of the holy church of Pavia" (*in caminata maioris
sale, scilicet domus episcopi sancte Ticinensis ecclesie*).[24] The use of *scilicet* (namely, that is)
clearly equates this large room or hall with the episcopal *domus*, and indeed this was
probably where most visitors to the bishop's house were received. Thus, when charters
simply indicate that they were redacted "in domo ipsius sancte ecclesie" or "in domum
episcopi ipsius civitatis," the actions they describe most likely took place in the bishop's
"great room."

The spatial arrangement of the various elements mentioned in charters is difficult to
discern. A series of imperial judicial pleas held in the episcopal residence in Reggio
Emilia over the tenth century, however, provides us some clues. The century had
started out poorly for the see. In 899, after defeating the forces of Berengar I at the river
Brenta (Veneto), Magyar bands sacked Reggio. Bishop Azzo was killed in the attack, and
his successor Peter moved the see from the extramural church of San Prospero to a site
within the section of old Roman Regium that had been fortified by the Lombards.
Bishop Peter quickly obtained a *diploma* from Louis III, Berengar's opponent for the
crown, granting him license to fortify his church and permission to alter plazas and
streets within the city to accomplish this. Louis also gave the bishop considerable properties (the island of Suzzara in the Po and the manor of Mercoriatico being the most
significant) to finance these new fortifications.[25] Note that it was his church (*ecclesiam
suam*), not the city, that the bishop was to fortify. Indeed, later documentation suggests
that Peter built a *castrum* enclosing the area around his residence and the new cathedral
of Santa Maria. In 944, for example, a plea was redacted "at the *domus* of the holy church
of Reggiò, within the *castrum* of this *domus*, in the hall (*sala*) which is next to that mother
church, in the loggia of the hall." This hall — also described as "in latere ipsius ecclesie"
— flanked the northeast wall of the basilica, the entrance to the residence probably
opening on the street still called today Stradone Vescovado.[26] Adjacent to the crypt of
the cathedral, some remains of the early-medieval walls of the residence were discov-

23. *Carte Cremonesi*, no. 106; Manaresi, *Placiti*, nos. 158 (Pavia), 142, 143, 146 (Reggio), 301
(Milan).

24. Manaresi, *Placiti*, no. 158.

25. Paolo Golinelli, *Città e culto dei santi nel medioevo italiano*, 2nd ed. (Bologna, 1996), 154; *Carte
Reggio*, no. 32.

26. Manaresi, *Placiti*, nos. 142, 143, 145.

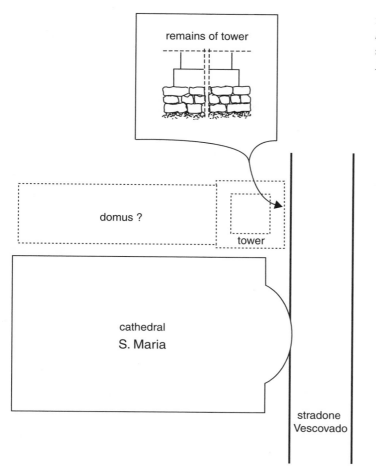

FIGURE 19. *Reggio, location of* domus *and remains of tower. (C. Ingersoll.)*

ered in 1960 (Figure 19). They reveal, not surprisingly, heavy fortification: the base of the wall, constructed from large paving stones of basalt and granite scavenged from Roman roads, was topped by walls two meters (seven feet) thick that narrow slightly about a meter, or a yard, up.[27] That these dense walls survive to a height reaching the second story of the present Vescovado suggests an imposing tower attached to the east end of the bishop's hall. Also opening off the bishop's hall was another, probably smaller, room with a fireplace where the bishop slept (*camminata dormitorio*).[28]

Archeologically investigated remains of tenth- and eleventh-century episcopal residences confirm and elaborate the impressions gleaned from Reggio and the evidence of charters. Our earliest example is an episcopal residence established in the late

27. Gianni Baldini, "Reggio nell'Emilia: Duomo, vescovado, S. Michele e battistero. Ricerche e testimonianze," *Atti e memorie della Deputazione di storia patria per le antiche provincie modenesi*, ser. 11, 9 (1987): 71–72. At the base the walls are 2.20 meters thick, narrowing about a meter up to 1.80 meters, or roughly 6 feet.

28. Manaresi, *Placiti*, no. 143.

tenth century within the ancient *castrum* of the city of Genoa located on a promontory at the southeast end of the old port. This *oppidum*, constructed perhaps as early as the fifth century B.C., was probably the same fortification rebuilt by the Romans in 205 B.C. During the imperial era, however, the hilltop was at least partially abandoned in favor of lower ground closer to the port, where the grid of a typical Roman town developed. Here, indeed, the cathedral of San Lorenzo was established as early as the fifth century A.D.[29] Although the cathedral was just within the early-medieval walls of the city, in the late tenth century the bishop moved his residence to the hilltop *castrum*. He did not build a new cathedral in this location, accomplishing a curious separation of residence and cathedral encountered in no other Italian city. Since the late ninth century, however, Genoa had experienced recurrent Saracen attacks. The city was sacked in 935. Luitprand of Cremona reported that the Saracens "with a huge fleet arrived there, and taking the people by surprise burst into the city, massacred everyone except the children and women, and putting on board ship all the treasures belonging to the city and to God's churches sailed back to Africa."[30] Only in the second half of the tenth century did the Genoese begin to score victories against the invaders. It was in the context of this military *risorgimento* that the bishop of Genoa moved his residence up to the *castrum*, and the development of this complex reflects these circumstances. The residence established circa 980 was an immense stone tower (*casa-torre*). This house-tower was built right against the east wall of the fortress, next to and controlling its only gate (Figure 20). Its walls were thick, but they enclosed a sizable internal living area (eleven by eleven meters, or thirty-six feet by thirty-six feet). On the house-tower's north face, an external stone staircase led to a balcony leading to a second-story entrance. A buttress at the extreme east end of this wall indicates that the tower was connected to another building that extended to the northeast (roughly in the location of an east wing of the palace rebuilt in the early fifteenth century).[31]

The remains of the early-eleventh-century episcopal *domus* at Como are complementary. Here the tower does not survive, but the building attached to it does. Before the millennium, the cathedral of Como and the bishops of the see were at the church of Sant'Eufemia (today San Fedele) located near the center of the Roman city.[32] Bishop

29. Chiara Lambert and Luigi Gambaro, "Lo scavo della cattedrale di San Lorenzo a Genova e i centri episcopali della Liguria," *Archeologia medievale* 14 (1987): 200–202.

30. *Antapodosis*, 4.5; trans. F. A. Wright, *Luidprand of Cremona: The Embassy to Constantinople and Other Writings*, ed. John Julius Norwich (London and Rutland, Vt., 1993), 102.

31. David Andrews and Denys Pringle, "Lo scavo dell'area sud del Convento di San Silvestro a Genova," *Archeologia medievale* 4 (1977): 56–60, 85–90. The walls of the tower were 0.8 meter thick (roughly 2.5 feet); its internal measurements are 11 by 11 meters. The balcony was roughly four meters, or 13 feet, long and its second-story entrance to the tower was at the west end.

32. The local tradition has been that the earliest seat of the see was outside the city at the basilica of the Apostles, later the monastery of Sant'Abbondio, but no documentary or material evidence supports this theory. Excavations within Sant'Eufemia, however, have demonstrated its paleo-Christian origins and early-medieval documentation locates the see here. Testini, et al., "La cattedrale," 1: 211–13.

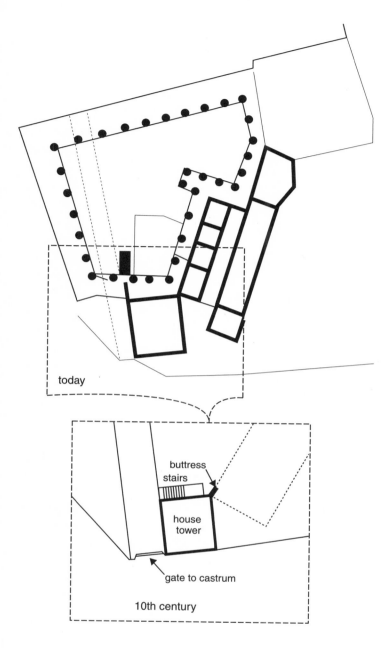

FIGURE 20. *Genoa, episcopal house-tower. (C. Ingersoll.)*

today

buttress

stairs

house
tower

gate to castrum

10th century

Alberic (1010–28), or one of his immediate predecessors,[33] moved the see north, closer to the lake, building a new cathedral (Santa Maria) and a new residence. Ultimately the see had its own "darsena" — a center for building and outfitting ships — behind the residence on the lake. The new residence incorporated a very thick (two-meter, or seven-foot) early-medieval wall into the south face of the ground floor. Excavations in

33. The identification of Alberic as the bishop who moved the see seems based on the now disproved theory that the see was originally at Sant'Abbondio. Thus, Alberic's 1013 donation of

front of this wall reveal remains of more stone fortifications, and a document of 1031 confirms these impressions. The charter of Bishop Litigerius describes the residence as "our house with a solarium near the lake, girded about with an embankment and palisade" (*in ipsa nostra domo solariata, vicina lacui, leva et palam roborata*). The probable base of the tower at the east end — a section of wall similar in width and composition to the south face wall — also dates from before the millennium.[34]

To these substantial early-medieval fortifications, a portico framed by enclosed spaces was built on the ground level, and an upper floor with a *solarium* was added on top of this base. The resultant structure formed a two-story rectangular block (roughly 36 by 6 meters, or 118 feet by 20 feet). On the east end of the building, three arched portals pierce the north face at ground level creating the portico. The two columns supporting the arches were mismatched: one a reused Roman column, the other wider and cut from different stone. The blockish capitals were of rough manufacture, perhaps also recycled from a late Roman building. Subsequent modifications within the portico make it impossible to determine how the ceiling of the passage was constructed, but the space to be covered was not great. The dense outer fortifications occupied close to half of this section of the ground floor, leaving a passageway roughly three meters (nine feet) wide. Two wider enclosed spaces seem to have occupied the west end of the structure where the outer south wall narrows considerably. The second story in the eleventh century contained four rooms: a long narrow central hall flanked by an open *solarium* and then three roughly square rooms, one on the east end and two on the west. The outer partial wall of the *solarium* rose only to the bottom ledge of the windows that now offer a view of the courtyard, and most likely an exterior staircase engaged (on the west end?) this open patio, offering access to the great hall (Figure 21).[35]

An episcopal residence built in the late eleventh century in Pistoia was similar. As it still exists today and systematic archeological work elucidated it during the 1970s, its evidence is particularly compelling.[36] The first element built in the complex was a tower. It rises to a height of twenty-four meters, or seventy-nine feet, and the thickness of its walls approximate the remains of fortifications at Reggio and Como. A two-story rectangular building was joined to it with a thick (1.20 meters, or four feet wide)

---

substantial lands and rights to the monastery of Sant'Abbondio is usually interpreted as his provision for the property of the old see once he had moved into the city. Some scholars even assert that he donated the old episcopal residence to the monks (see Pietro Gini, "La diocesi di Como nel patriarcato di Aquileia (607–1751)," *Archivio storico della diocesi di Como* 1 (1987): 264), but in fact there is no mention of the residence in the donation charter: *ADComo*, Fondo curiale antico, pergamene, no. 2; transcription published in *Rivista archeologica della provincia di Como* 5 (1874): 15–21.

34. Ughelli, *IS*, 5:287; for the archeological finds, see Frigerio and Baserga, "Il palazzo vescovile," 20, 42.

35. Frigerio and Baserga, "Il palazzo vescovile," 21, 27–30, tav. I–II. The hall measured roughly 20 meters by 4 meters (66 feet by 13 feet) and the open *solarium* was the same length but about 1.5 meters (5 feet) wide. Of the three roughly square rooms, two measured 5.5 meters by 5 meters (18 feet by 16 feet 6 inches), and one was slightly smaller at 5 meters by 4 meters (18 feet by 13 feet).

36. Rauty, *Palazzo*, 1: 83–96; 2.2: 27, 95, 169, and Figure 7.

FIGURE 21. *Como, Palazzo Vescovile, north facade of eleventh-century* domus. *The ground level has risen, obscuring most of the columned portico. The eleventh-century wall rose only to the bottom of the windows.* (M. Miller.)

perimeter wall that continued and attached to the southwest corner of the cathedral to create an enclosed courtyard. An entrance to the ground floor opened off the piazza in front of the cathedral, and another connected the residence to structures along the south flank of the church (among them the cloister and canonry). The visitor entering this way into the courtyard had access, via a stairway along the north wall of the tower, to both the tower and the second floor of the residence (Figure 22). At the top of this stairway was an open wooden deck, a *solarium*, bridging the space between the tower and the east wall of the two-story edifice. Here, *in solario eiusdem Pistoriensis episcopi* ("on the balcony of the bishop of Pistoia"), Bishop Peter dictated a document in 1091 founding and endowing the monastery of San Pier Maggiore.[37] Wood was used extensively in this Pistoian *domus*: the roof, the floor creating the second level, the ground-

37. The tower enclosed an internal space 3 to 3.5 meters by 8 meters (roughly 11 feet by 26 feet) and was not evenly squared (the south wall just under 2 meters, or roughly 6 feet longer than the north wall). Its walls varied in thickness, being about 1.5 meters, or 5 feet, thick on the side facing the courtyard and 2 meters, or 6 feet 6 inches on the sides facing the street. The building attached to it enclosed an interior space 31 meters (102 feet) long, 7 meters (23 feet) wide on its narrow end, and a little over 9 meters (29.5 feet) on the wider end facing the tower. My reconstruction of the *solarium* differs from Rauty's: Rauty, *Palazzo*, 1: 283 (app. doc. no. 11). He takes the word *solarium* to mean simply the second story. The odd space left between the top of the stairway and the east end of the building, and the penchant evident in other cases (Genoa, Como) for providing a transitional open space between an exterior stairway and the edifice, lead me to posit this reconstruction.

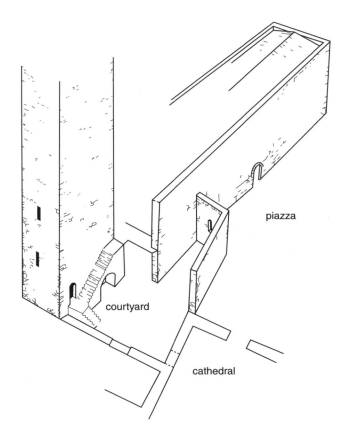

FIGURE 22. *Pistoia, Palazzo dei Vescovi, reconstruction of eleventh-century residence. (C. Ingersoll, based on Rauty, Palazzo, 89, by permission of the Cassa di Risparmio di Pistoia e Pescia.)*

piazza

courtyard

cathedral

floor supports for the spine of this floor, and any internal divisions of space, were all constructed of wood (see Figure 30). Probably for this reason, the building had no hearth. However, heat could have been provided through the use of braziers.

The excavations at Pistoia also afford us a rare glimpse of how a building of this sort was constructed. Note that this episcopal residence, in contrast to the bishop's house at Como, did not incorporate significant amounts of late Roman *spolia*. This seems mainly due to the catastrophic devastation the city suffered during the incursion of the Ostrogoths under Radagaiso in November of 406. Archeological data from different sites in Pistoia all record evidence of massive destruction in this era. On the site of our bishop's residence, for example, this chronological level in the dig indicates the total destruction of preexistent buildings, "often with traces of burning." Recovery was a long time coming. An extended war between the Byzantines and Lombards for this region in the sixth century inhibited recovery and brought new destruction.[38] The site of the episcopal *domus* shows no evidence of habitation again until the ninth century, and then only very rudimentary structures were erected. Sometime in the second half of the eleventh century, construction of the bishop's tower began. Its siting may have been determined by

38. Natale Rauty, *Storia di Pistoia I: Dall'alto medioevo all'età precomunale, 406–1105* (Florence, 1988), 25–30, 68–75; Rauty, *Palazzo,* 2.2: 53.

the desire to incorporate an early-medieval well, the remains of which are located roughly at its center against the north wall. After the construction of the tower was underway, the area chosen for the main building was cleared of the few ninth- and tenth-century structures that had sprung up there. A furnace was constructed in the western half of the site chosen for the building, roughly equidistant from the three main perimeter walls. It was used to heat limestone to yield the desiccated lime necessary to mix mortar in significant quantities. All the eleventh-century walls were built using rocks culled from local streams layered with mortar in fairly regular rows (Figure 23). There is no evidence that these rough walls were finished, either on the interior or on the exterior, with any smoothing or beautifying facing. The builders dug down to a compact strata of clay to provide a stable base for the foundation of the walls, and they interrupted this foundation at several points with arches, following natural water conduits, to facilitate drainage on the site. Only narrow arrow-slit windows were constructed on the ground level, but slightly larger arched windows admitted light to the second story. These windows — one of which survives on the south face of the building — were bordered with large bricks, skillfully aligned and joined with the rock layers of the walling (Figure 24). Stone brackets were fixed in the walls to support the flooring of the second story and the roof.[39]

This was, clearly, a more primitive and less commodious structure than the episcopal residence built earlier at Como, which was more sophisticated in design and richer in materials (greater use of stone, incorporation of reused Roman elements). This underscores a certain range of variance in episcopal dwellings. At the higher end were sees like Ravenna and Rome, which were wealthy and had inherited a substantial complex of Roman buildings through the good fortune of not having suffered directly the ravages of war and invasion. At the lower end were smaller sees like Pistoia, which did experience the devastation of barbarian incursions and had limited resources to rebuild. The bishops of Reggio and Como were somewhat better endowed, mainly through the resources of their dioceses and their ability to tap into imperial wealth. Some of the variation in building materials (rough stream stones versus cut stone or brick) and techniques among sees like Pistoia, Como, and Genoa was probably the product of local building traditions. But our evidence is far too meager to posit "regional types" in episcopal architecture.

More striking, in fact, are the similarities suggested by both the notarial and the archeological evidence. In the sees that built new residences during the early Middle Ages, there is a great consistency in form and primary characteristics. A tower and a two-story rectangular stone edifice, containing a large hall on the second floor and one or more smaller rooms, were the basic components of the early-medieval episcopal residence. Features such as *solaria*, hearths, and loggias were also common elements. The character of these structures suggests a sharp decline in episcopal standards of living from Late Antiquity. Fortification was the main cause. Thick, heavy stone walls and small windows yielded dark and poorly ventilated interior spaces. Since heat was pro-

39. Rauty, *Palazzo*, 2.2: 54, 57, 27 (note 73), 62; 1: 86–87, 93–95.

FIGURE 23. *Pistoia, Palazzo dei Vescovi, late-eleventh-century walls. (M. Miller.)*

vided only by hearths or braziers, these interiors would have been suffused with smoke in the cooler seasons. The popularity of both *solaria* and loggias was surely the result of these conditions: they provided lighter and airier spaces where the bishop and those in his company could pass time or conduct business. These early-medieval buildings offered their residents fewer living spaces than did the late-antique *episcopia*. Whereas a sixth-century bishop of Ravenna had at least two halls, a formal dining room, an everyday dining room or *mensa*, a chapel, and other spaces to choose from, the bishop of Pistoia at the end of the eleventh century in his brand new house had one hall, a solarium, and one or two rooms within his tower (where he slept). Functional articulation of space within the early-medieval residence was markedly reduced.

THE DOMESTIC ARCHITECTURE OF SECULAR ELITES

But was this decline in the quality of residential space solely an ecclesiastical phenomenon? Were these episcopal residences very different from examples of secular domestic architecture? Extant comparative material suggests not, but our knowledge of secular domestic architecture in the early Middle Ages is quite limited and scholarly work has not addressed this particular issue. It has focused on the highly significant question of when and why the traditional Roman *domus* disappeared. Before the emergence of postclassical archeology as an active field of research, the Roman *domus* was seen, like the empire itself, as a victim of the multiple disasters that plagued the west in the fifth and sixth centuries.[40] Archeological work in the 1970s and early 1980s, however, has given rise to a new consensus that socioeconomic causes were behind the disappearance of the *domus*. Depopulation, the "ruralization" of urban centers, and the gradual impoverishment of the Roman upper classes now seem most to blame.[41] Accord

40. Simon P. Ellis, "The End of the Roman House," *American Journal of Archeology* 92 (1988): 565–66.

41. Bryan Ward-Perkins, "La città altomedievale," *Archeologia medievale* 10 (1983): 123 R. De Marinis, U. Tochetti Pollini, and G. P. Brogiolo, "La città in Lombardia. La sua nascita e la sua evoluzione," in *Archeologia urbana in Lombardia. Valutazione dei depositi archeologici dei vincoli* (Mod-

FIGURE 24. *Pistoia, Palazzo dei Vescovi, eleventh-century window on south face of residence. (M. Miller.)*

on the chronology of these changes, however, requires much more data. Some scholars see the sixth century as the real divide, whereas others emphasize evidence of continuity until the late eighth and early ninth centuries.[42] A great deal of variability is likely, given the differing experiences of Italian cities in this age of upheaval.

---

ena, [1985]), 49–53; Guidobaldi, "L'edilizia abitativa," 228–37; *EAM*, sv. "casa"; Bernard Bavant, "Cadre de vie et habitat urbain en italie centrale byzantine (VIe — VIIe siècles)," *MEFR* 101 (1989): 465–532.

42. Bavant, "Cadre de vie," is the strongest recent voice arguing for the sixth century, but see also Andre Guillou, "L'Habitat nell'Italia bizantine: Esarcato, Sicilia, Catepanato (VI–XI secolo)," in *Atti del Colloquio internazionale di archeologia medievale (Palermo-Erice, 20–22 settembre 1974* (Palermo, 1976), 140–54; Peter J. Hudson, "La dinamica dell'insediamento urbano nell'area del cortile del tribunale di Verona. L'età medievale," *Archeologia medievale* 12 (1985): 284–85; De Marinis, et al., "La città in Lombardia," 50. Some archeological and architectural evidence supports a later and more gradual chronology: Gian Pietro Brogiolo, "Brescia," in *Archeologia urbana in Lombardia. Valutazione dei depositi archeologici dei vincoli* (Modena, [1985]), 88; D. A. Bullough, "Urban Change," 104–5.

Material for a description of the early-medieval domestic architecture that replaced the Roman *domus* is accruing, and here chronological variance in the evidence has led to a lively debate over the origins of this new style. Using mainly the evidence of the *Codice Bavaro*, a collection of early-medieval leases from the region around Ravenna that contains extraordinarily detailed descriptions of houses, Michelangelo Cagiano de Azevedo argued that the characteristic early-medieval house in Italy was Lombard in origin.[43] Other scholars, citing archeological evidence, characterized it as the product of Byzantine influence.[44] More recently, however, these theories of foreign origins are losing ground to interpretations stressing change within Italy, namely the transference of rural architectural forms into the urban centers.[45]

The character of this new early-medieval Italian house, however, is not controversial. Written sources and archeological remains, in fact, have yielded a remarkably consistent picture. The new domestic architectural unit consisted of a main building, usually having two stories, and then dependent structures organized around a courtyard. The main building, whether *pedeplana* (single story) or *solariata* (two story), was rectangular with walls of uncut stone, or recycled stone and brick, set in mortar. Reuse of scavenged Roman materials was substantial. Sometimes stone was used only on the ground floor, and the upper story was constructed of wood or clay, but Ravennate leases suggest that stone walling "to the ceiling tiles" in a two-storied structure was not uncommon. Roofing was in clay tiles or wooden shingles, and floors were usually of beaten earth or wood. The simpler *pedeplana* house had little functional division of space, but the two-storied *solariata* was more articulated. The ground floor often contained a portico opening onto a courtyard; the house was oriented toward this internal space with few windows addressing the street. Most of the ground floor was devoted to a *canafa*, a space for storing provisions and equipment. Sometimes it also contained a *balneum* or *calidarium*, meaning a tub for bathing with some provision for heating water. Corner hearths are evident in some archeological sites. A kitchen, or *coquina*, might also be located on the ground floor, but leases suggest these were often separate dependent structures. The second floor contained the main living areas and usually was reached through an exterior stairway. The largest room was a space for gathering and eating, called variously the *sala*, *cenaculum*, or *triclinium*. One or more smaller rooms for sleeping, described as *camere* or *cubiculi*, opened off the main space. The dependent structures or annexes might provide, as noted earlier, a kitchen, a shop or work area, or stables. Most seem to have had gardens for growing vegetables and fruits. Access to a well

43. Cagiano de Azevedo, "Le case," 159–81.

44. Guillou, "L'habitat nell'Italia bizantina," 151–54; De Marinis, et al., "La città in Lombardia," 51.

45. Ward-Perkins, "La città altomedievale," 123; Bavant, "Cadre de vie," 129–30; Gian Pietro Brogiolo, "Brescia: Building Transformations in a Lombard City," in *The Birth of Europe: Archaeology and Social Development in the First Millennium AD*, ed. Klaus Randsborg, Analecta Romana Instituti Danici Supplementum XVI (Rome, 1989), 160–61.

was often specified in leases, but only the largest and most complex houses seem to have had their own wells.[46]

The stone dwellings described earlier — even with variations in size and complexity — were all residences of people with some means. More impoverished structures have been revealed in archeological work. At Luni in Liguria, simple houses were built over the old Roman forum in the sixth century. These structures had stone footings but a timber superstructure with posts supporting the roof. Similar sorts of houses also have been discovered in Lombardy. Excavations at Siena have brought to light a crude seventh-century hut of clay and wood using the remains of an old Roman wall as its support.[47] This reuse of the ruins dotting urban landscapes is ubiquitous; indeed, the picture one gets from both charters and archeological finds is of an early-medieval populace of squatters, camped out amidst the former glories of their town's past. The remains of Roman structures were subdivided, usually with wooden partitions, into tiny apartments.[48] There is yet no scholarly consensus, nor the evidence to construct it, on the extent to which wooden structures housed the population of medieval Italy. Sharp regional variation is revealed in the research accomplished: in Lazio there is no evidence of buildings in wood, whereas in Lombardy, Emilia-Romagna, and Tuscany compelling examples have survived.[49] Thus, at this point it is impossible to link social groups with any precision to particular types of housing or to estimate how wealthy one needed to have been to live within stone walls. A rough hierarchy of possibilities, however, is discernible: at the low end, small structures of wood or clay incorporating the ruins of Roman buildings; somewhere in the middle, one-level (*pedeplana*) stone structures; at the high end, two-story stone structures with some functional articulation of space. What is clear is that at the upper end of the spectrum there is strong formal consistency. Very elaborate *solariata* may have more bedrooms and more outbuildings, but they are arranged in the same general patterns as are simpler ones.

It is surely obvious at this point that there are many similarities between examples of this high end of the secular domestic architectural spectrum and our episcopal residences. As our examples of Como and Pistoia best illustrate, they were two-storied

46. *EAM*, s.v. "casa"; Bavant, "Cadre de vie," 513–28; Cagiano de Azevedo, "Le case," 164ff.

47. Bryan Ward-Perkins, "Two Byzantine Houses at Luni," *Papers of the British School at Rome* 49 (1981): 91–98; *Santa Maria della Scala. Archeologia e edilizia sulla piazza dello Spedale*, ed. Enrica Boldrini and Roberto Parenti (Florence, 1991): 15, 17 (Fig. A), 188–91; *EAM*, s.v. "casa," 353.

48. Brogiolo, "Brescia: Building Transformations," 156–65. Cristina La Rocca has strenuously contested this bleak appraisal. Although her arguments against assuming radical depopulation and contraction of urban centers have merit, La Rocca's positive depiction of the reuse of Roman ruins does not convince me that early-medieval domestic architecture offered a standard of living that was not radically inferior to what preceded it. Cristina La Rocca, " 'Dark Ages' a Verona. Edilizia privata, aree aperte e strutture pubbliche in una città dell'Italia settentrionale," *Archeologia medievale* 13 (1986): 31–78, reprinted with updated addenda in *Paesaggi urbani dell'Italia padana nei secoli VIII–XIV* (Bologna, 1988), 71–122.

49. David Andrews, "Medieval Domestic Architecture in Northern Lazio," in *Medieval Lazio: Studies in Architecture, Painting and Ceramics*, BAR International Series 125 (Oxford, 1982), 2–3; Brogiolo, "Brescia: Building Transformations," 160–62.

stone structures in which the living space occupied the second floor and was divided into a large room suitable for gatherings and one or more smaller rooms for sleeping. All of the building materials and construction techniques encountered in episcopal *domus* are evident in secular residences: walls were of uncut stone and mortar or of recycled Roman *spolia*, floors and internal divisions of space were often of wood, and roofs were constructed with wooden shingles or clay tiles. Courtyards, porticos, and external staircases were common to both.

The main feature setting off our episcopal residences from the average elite lay house was their towers. Only once in the *Codice Bavaro* is a *domus* described as having a tower. The lease, dating from the episcopate of Archbishop Sergius of Ravenna (744–769), was of

> an entire house with its upper and lower parts, having on the upper floor a *triclinium* and five bedrooms, along with its tower, and on the lower level a *canapha* [storage area] and a shop on either side. The walls extend all the way to the rafters, the roof having clay tiles and gutters. There is also a kitchen with an upper level constructed of posts and covered with shingles, together with a courtyard, a vegetable garden, and a well.

This *domus* was located on one corner of the "public forum" of Rimini and abutted a garden of the church of Santa Maria in Curte, believed to be the chapel associated with the ducal residence of Rimini. Thus, this leased *domus* was in the vicinity of the center of public authority in early-medieval Rimini, the Court of the Duke. This seat of local Byzantine (later papal) rule was highly fortified and located just north of the "public forum" against the city walls near the Porta San Petri. Given the location of our *domus*, right on the public forum in the shadow of the ducal residence, and its composition of both a sizable rectangular building and a tower, the reader will not be surprised at the identity of the person leasing it. It was rented by "Mauricius, glorious Master of the Army."[50]

Towers and fortifications characterized the residences of those few individuals in early-medieval society who held public authority.[51] By the twelfth and thirteenth centuries, the urban skylines of Italy were a forest of towers: most wealthy families had one.[52] But this was not the case before the millennium. Mentions of towers are few and they are associated with a more restricted elite wielding public authority: counts, dukes, kings. Unfortunately, Bryan Ward-Perkins in 1981 was able to lament that "we know next to nothing" archeologically of the houses of the secular aristocracy in the early Middle Ages: "Not a single ducal, comital, or royal palace has been excavated. . . ."[53]

50. *Codice Bavaro. Codex traditionum ecclesiae Ravennatis*, ed. Ettore Baldetti and Alberto Poverari, Deputazione di storia patria per le Marche, Studi e testi 13 (Ancona, 1983) no. 71 (61); Grazia Gobbi and Paolo Sica, *Rimini* (Rome and Bari, 1982), 33.

51. As Settia's examples indicate, those elites holding public authority were the earliest and most consistent owners of towers, but elites without specially defined legal rights were quick to mimic them: Settia, "Lo sviluppo di un modello . . . " in *Paesaggi urbani*, 159ff.

52. See Carol Lansing, *The Florentine Magnates: Lineage and Faction in a Medieval Commune* (Princeton, 1991), 84–105.

53. Ward-Perkins, "La città altomedievale," 121. We know something of an eleventh-century *domus* in the countryside east of Bergamo near Lake Iseo that is believed to be a comital residence. Like our episcopal residences, it was a two-story rectangular structure with thick stone walls and

Little has changed since then. Lacking archeological evidence, we can only turn back to our documents. Luckily, elite lay residences do appear frequently in notarial charters, and these descriptions reveal strong similarities to episcopal residences. Marquis Milo of Verona, for example, when he dictated his will in 955, left several residences to his heir, his brother Count Mainfredus. Milo's "castle which is called Ronco," with its tower and its chapel dedicated to the Blessed Virgin, was left to Mainfredus and, continued Milo, "another castle of mine with a *solariata* house with a *sala* and hearth room and loggia and lower floor and chapel built in honor of Saint Boniface" (*alio castro meo cum casa solariata cum sala et caminata atque labia uel subtessorar atque capella inibi constructa in honore Sancti Bonifatii*).[54] Comital, ducal, and even royal residences also appear very much like episcopal residences in imperial *placita*. The ducal residence in Lucca had a *caminata* and the one in Milan had a "great hearth room which is next to the loggia of this court." Count Adelbert in 981 hosted a judicial hearing *in castro Gunsaga in caminata maiore sala*. The upper room of Marquis Ugo's residence was called his *sala* as was that of the "castro Basilica Duci" where Count Lanfranc and his brother Adelbert heard pleas in 1021. Loggias are mentioned frequently. Pleas heard at the ducal residence in Milan consistently took place *in laubia eiusdem curtis* and one held in 1055 in Mantua took place "in the Marquis Boniface's loggia *solariata*". At "Sprino Lanberti" this same Boniface had a "lordly loggia" (*laubia domnicata*) overlooking the river Scultine. Count Giselbert's residence in Pavia had a *solarium*.[55] Finally, although its architectural features are not described, the comital residence in the city of Verona appears in the writings of Bishop Ratherius as a highly fortified place. When the bishop was being harassed at his own residence, Count Bucco (who was living in the royal palace within the more heavily fortified *castrum* of the city) urged Ratherius to live at the ducal residence within the city at Cortalta, "because it was more protected." "I believed him, I did so," Ratherius wrote, "from fortified, I made it very fortified."[56]

Even the glimpses we get in the *placita* of the royal palace at Pavia suggest a building with features similar to episcopal, comital, and ducal residences. It had a "lesser hearth room" (*caminata minore*), implying the existence of a "greater" (*maggiore*) one, and several loggias: one described as *maggiore* in the early tenth century, one off the garden, another described as "newly built" in 985, one located "in front of the chapel of San Mauritius," and still another called "the public loggia newly built next to the royal palace on its south side." The "heated bedroom" (*caminata dormitoria*) of the palace was the site of several judicial hearings, and one of these indicates that there was a hearth room "in front of" this bedroom. The palace's stairway (*scala*) is also mentioned. Other

---

small windows. But the site has not been fully excavated. Gian Piero Brogiolo and Andrea Zonca, "Residenze medievali (XI-XII secc.) nel territorio lombardo," *Storia della città* 52 (1989): 37–38.

54. *CDV*, 2, no. 255.

55. Manaresi, *Placiti*, nos. 73, 139, 194 (camminate); 230, 307 (sale); 10, 110, 112, 129, 400, 389 (loggias); 133 (solarium).

56. *CC Cont. Med.*, 46: 128–29 (*Qualitatis coniectura*, Chap. 14, lines 495–500); trans. Reid, *Rather*, 439.

royal residences are described as having *solaria*, loggias, aulas, *sale*, and porticos.[57] Certainly royal residences were larger and more elaborately decorated than were comital and ducal residences. Our Ravennate chronicler Agnellus, for example, who visited the royal palace in Pavia in the early ninth century, described a beautiful mosaic image of Emperor Theodoric on horseback on one of its vaulted ceilings.[58] But the elements revealed in the *placita* suggest that they had a similar composition. That a duke's house was not so far from a king's is also suggested by Luitprand of Cremona's famous description of Duke Adelbert of Ivrea's "palace" at Lucca. When King Louis visited and "saw whole companies of well equipped soldiers standing about in Adelbert's palace (*domo Adelberti*), and noticed the expenses that his display of power involved, he was seized with jealous envy and said privately to his followers: 'This fellow might well be called no marquess but king; in nothing but the name is he my inferior.' "[59]

The similarities between episcopal residences and those of counts and dukes certainly parallel changes in the juridical status of bishops that made them more like these secular office holders. In Late Antiquity, through Constantinian constitutions and the later Theodosian code, bishops had exercised special jurisdiction over the clergy and in litigation brought to them by Christians. This jurisdiction, however, was concurrent with that of secular judges. De facto, when the secular apparatus of justice broke down in the late-antique west, episcopal tribunals offered the most accessible and sure justice. Similarly, the maintenance of urban amenities increasingly fell to bishops as the only public figures with the resources to repair aqueducts and walls.[60] This de facto sphere of activity and power expanded in the early Middle Ages. The Carolingian era began the incorporation of bishops into the administration of the *regnum* through grants of specific public rights and through the creation of ecclesiastical immunities. By the late ninth and early tenth centuries, many Italian bishops had acquired comital or other public powers.[61]

The building of new episcopal residences of the sort we have been describing, in fact, coincides quite directly with the acquisition of these powers. In some cases, the devastation of their sees allowed bishops to assume governance of their cities. The building of a new fortified residence occurred as they assumed this role. Reggio Emilia well illustrates this scenario. After the Magyars overran Reggio in 899, destroying the see and killing Bishop Azzo, the new bishop built a new fortified residence within the

---

57. Manaresi, *Placiti*, nos. 122, 126, 206, 266, 283 (loggias); 136, 144, 153, 225 (camminate); 226 (stairs); 141, 169, 268, 358 (other residences).

58. Agnellus, *LP*, Chap. 94.

59. *Antapodosis*, 2.39; trans. Wright, *Luidprand*, 52.

60. Giulio Vismara, "La giurisdizione civile dei vescovi nel mondo antico," in *La giustizia nell'alto medioevo (secoli V–VIII)*, Settimane di studio del Centro italiano di studi sull'alto medioevo (Spoleto, 1995), 225–57; John C. Lamoreaux, "Episcopal Courts in Late Antiquity," *Journal of Early Christian Studies* 3 (1995): 146–50; Ward-Perkins, *From Classical Antiquity*, 119–54, 191–99.

61. Tabacco, *The Struggle for Power*, 100–105, 125–36; Vito Fumagalli, "Il potere civile dei vescovi italiani al tempo di Ottone I," in *I poteri temporali dei vescovi in Italia e in Germania nel medioevo*, ed. Carlo Guido Mor and Heinrich Schmidinger (Bologna, 1979), 77–86; Golinelli, "Strutture organizzative," 157–58; Jones, *The Italian City-State*, 70–71.

city. He did not legally hold public authority at this time, but in the absence of secular challenges he assumed leadership. His chancery began forging *diplomata* claiming the delegation of comital powers, and when Otto I brought an army over the Alps in 962, the Bishop of Reggio presented one of these forged diplomas and received an authentic charter confirming his exercise of all public functions in the city and up to three miles beyond its walls.[62]

In cities that did not so directly suffer crises of rulership as the result of disorder, the building of a fortified episcopal *domus* is still associated with a significant enhancement of the bishop's powers. At Como and Pistoia the building of new fortified episcopal residences coincided with the bishop's acquisition of comital authority. At Como, the bishops started acquiring public rights — such as market rights and tolls — under Charlemagne. Its ninth- and early-tenth-century bishops attended imperial coronations and participated in imperial elections; Bishop Angilbert served as arch-chancellor to Louis the German. Not until the beginning of the eleventh century, however, did the see gain comital rights. In 1002 King Arduin granted the see comital authority in Chiavenna — a key mountain pass at the confluence of the rivers Mira and Liro, north of Lake Como — and in 1006 Henry II added half the viscounty of Valtellina. The new episcopal *domus* in the city was built in the early eleventh century, no later than 1031.[63] At Pistoia also the bishops began acquiring significant public authority with the advent of Carolingian rule. Under the Byzantines, the bishop of Pistoia had a role in the election of the local judge (*iudex*); in ninth-century pleas he was actually exercising judicial functions. The city's first Frankish bishop, Oschiso (850–877), even led the Pistoian military contingent on Louis II's campaign against the Arabs at Amantea (868–869). By the late tenth century, the see had acquired an immunity on its own lands and significant market rights, but it lacked full public authority. After 1006, however, the counts of Pistoia ceased exercising their rights in the city, and documentation from the mid-eleventh century reveals the bishop with a group of leading citizens (*boni homines*) governing the urban center. The bishop built his new *domus* in the second half of the eleventh century.[64]

---

62. *Carte Reggio*, nos. 32, 35, 37, 39, 41, 42; forged diplomata, nos. 5, 6, 7, 14, 50. This last is the most important and effective forgery. The document purportedly granted the bishops of Reggio 1) all royal lands in the city and up to 3 miles beyond the walls; 2) the city's walls and defensive ditches; 3) tolls (*theloneo, stradatico*); 4) "all public functions"; 5) the right to have advocates, notaries, and other ministers; 6) immunity; 7) imperial protection. Otto's confirmation of these privileges is no. 60. The bishop of Reggio was not the only one to use false privileges to acquire real ones: see Cesare Manaresi, "Alle origini del potere dei vescovi sul territorio esterno delle città," *Bullettino dell'Istituto storico italiano per il medio evo e Archivio muratoriano* 58 (1944): 249–59, on Reggio, and 325–34 on the larger pattern of deception.

63. Pietro Pensa, "Dall'età carolingia all'affermarsi delle signorie," in *Diocesi d Como* (Brescia, 1986), 46–53; Giustino Renato Orsini, "La giurisdizione spirituale e temporale del vescovo di Como," *Archivio storico lombardo* 81–82 (1954–55): 157–59, 168–71; *MGH DD*, 3: 138–39 (Henry III, no. 113, to Bishop Eberhard of Como, 1006), 702–3 (Arduin, no. 3, to Bishop Peter of Como, 1002).

64. Rauty, *Palazzo*, 1: 20–35, 41–44; and Rauty, *Storia di Pistoia I*, 175–83 (on Oschiso).

As bishops became like counts through their acquisition of public rights, and then in some cities officially became counts through imperial ratification of these powers, their residences became like comital castles. Just as *incastellamento* (castle building) was the most decisive change affecting settlement generally in early-medieval Italy, the fortification of the bishop's *domus* most altered the character of the episcopal residence. The new character of this *domus* both represented the bishop's new relation to power and was the culmination of the complex accommodation of the episcopal office to the political realities of the early Middle Ages. This evolution of the episcopal office and residence entailed changes in the bishop's relationship to his clergy and his people. Some of these are discernible in the relationship of the bishop and his house to the cathedral.

THE BISHOP AND HIS CHURCH

In Late Antiquity, as I have argued, there was a fluidity and unity of space between the bishop's residence and the liturgical structures of his see. Most sees retained this coherence into the eleventh century. At Ravenna, even with the additions of the eighth and ninth centuries, the residence remained wrapped around the end of the Ursian basilica. Newer residences built in the early Middle Ages were also usually linked to the bishop's church. The new residence at Pistoia was directly adjacent to the cathedral, and the only access to the bishop's hall was from this side. At Reggio too the new episcopal *domus* flanked the new cathedral, and this entire cluster of ecclesiastical structures was enclosed in walls. In some sees, however, a greater spatial detachment of the bishop's house and his cathedral begins to appear. In Como, a broad piazza separated the bishop's new *domus* from his new cathedral. This was probably motivated by the bishop's desire for access to the lake, where his ships dominated trade and navigation. But this plaza separating the bishop from his church was exploited later by groups contesting his lordship, so this initial separation of episcopal domestic and liturgical space in the early eleventh century was not without consequence. More radical still — and quite anomalous — was the bishop of Genoa's abandonment of the cathedral precinct entirely in order to build his new fortified residence in the city's *castrum*. But even in most sees where the bishop's residence remained integrated with the cathedral, changes in the episcopal household in this period began to attenuate his dominance of the see's liturgical center. The separation of the cathedral clergy from the episcopal residence and their institutionalization as the cathedral's "chapter" effected this change.

Most scholars believe that the cathedral clergy in Late Antiquity lived with their bishop. The model of Saint Augustine has been taken as paradigmatic in this regard. As bishop of Hippo, Augustine had demanded that his priests share a monastic life in common with him in the episcopal residence. Possidius, one of his priests, remembered fondly how he "and other brothers and fellow servants who were living with that holy man" would be gathered at the dinner table and hear his teaching. "Clerics were always with him," Possidius reported, "together in one house and at one table, fed and clothed at the expense of the community."[65] Augustine, however, seems a rather high standard from which to generalize about other dioceses. Some clerics surely did live in the *epis-copium*. The story of Bishop Boniface of Ferentino in Gregory the Great's *Dialogues*, for example, depicts the bishop's nephew Constantius as a resident of his household. When the pious bishop gave his nephew's gold to some poor people begging alms at the *epis-copium*, Constantius exclaimed, "All others can live here quietly . . . but for me there is no peace in your house!" The exasperated nephew's outburst suggests that other clerics also lived with his overgenerous uncle.[66] The Ravennate chronicler Agnellus tended to depict the archbishops as surrounded by clerics, and his story of Archbishop John VI at table (*mensa*) implies that at least a small group of his clergy gathered there.[67]

Over the early Middle Ages, however, the cathedral clergy came to have their own corporate identity and they no longer lived with the bishop. In this development, the impact of Carolingian reforming legislation was key — although not in the tidy fashion that historians have assumed. In 816 Louis the Pious convened a council at Aachen to address an array of ecclesiastical concerns. One of the canons promulgated by this council, *De institutione canonicorum*, aimed to reform and more uniformly institutional-ize the living arrangements of clerics serving cathedral churches. It envisioned these clerics forming their own community and living together near the cathedral within a very specific architectural complex: a cloister surrounded by walls (having only one en-trance), and containing a refectory, dormitory, and a storeroom.[68] Historians of me-dieval Italy have been too quick to leap from some evidence of the existence of a cathe-dral chapter to the existence of this prescribed architectural complex and the quasi-monastic life the rule of Carolingian reformer Chrodegang of Metz defined within in it. But this Carolingian reform ideal did begin to transform, in highly signifi-cant ways, the organization of cathedral clergy and their relationships to both their bishop and their church.

Let us first consider a "best-case" scenario for the implementation of this Carolin-gian reform in Italy. In May of 897 Bishop Adalbert of Bergamo held a synod in his *do-mus*. In attendance were all his priests, the entire clergy of his church, and some nobles. While discussing the state of the church, the charter reports, "[T]hese priests and cler-ics with one voice beseeched their lord bishop — out of his love for Saints Vincent and Alexander, martyrs in Christ — to institute a canonry (*canonicam*) for the restoration of

65. Possidius, *Vita Augustini*, 25.1, 22.6, 15.1 in A. A. R. Bastiaensen, *Vita di Cipriano, Vita di Ambrogio, Vita di Agostino*, 2nd ed. (Milan, 1981), 194, 186–88, 166; Peter Brown, *Augustine of Hippo: A Biography* (Berkeley and Los Angeles, 1967), 142-44, 198-200.

66. Gregory the Great, *Dialogues*, I.9.11; trans. Zimmerman, 38.

67. Agnellus, *LP*, Chap. 163.

68. *MGH Concilia*, 2 / 1: 398 (Concilium Aquisgranense 816, can. 117). Most of the Italian man-uscripts of these canons date from the eleventh century or later (one Pisan and one Vatican manu-script date from the tenth century). Ibid., 310–11. Generally, on the slow diffusion of Carolingian reform legislation, see Rosamond McKitterick, *The Frankish Church and the Carolingian Reforms, 789–895* (London, 1977), 21ff.

the priests and clerics serving in this holy church of God." Bishop Adalbert, "considering their petition and deeming it just that those serving the altar share in its bounty, inquired of them: at what place close to the church, and under the control of the see, would it be agreeable to the church and canonical to establish their refuge?" Not surprisingly, this enterprising group of clerics had a plan: "All together, they chose and requested that cloister next to the church of Saint Vincent so that they might complete the office in due time, receive restorative food and drink, and, sleeping there at night, rise more easily to say the night offices." Responding to their plea, the bishop gave them the cloister they requested and "the hall (*sala*) and other buildings there, with their courtyard and garden." He also donated several other properties to provide a patrimony to support this newly established *canonica*.[69] Note that what the cathedral clergy of Bergamo have at this point is a cloister, a *sala*, and some dependent structures. This is not exactly what canon 117 of the Council of Aachen prescribed.

Subsequent charters demonstrate that the cathedral clergy had from this point an independent organization: they are identified in documents as clergy "of the order of the holy church of Bergamo," they had their own provost and rector, and they controlled their own patrimony — leasing and exchanging its lands and receiving donations enlarging it. But all of them did not live in the canonry. The will of one of these priests, redacted in 952, reveals that he lived in his own house within the city. A lease of 996 demonstrates that even the provost of the chapter had his own residence (*casa abitacionis vestre in vestra civitate Bergamo*) in the city. Indeed, it would appear from the language of another tenth-century charter that the members of the *canonica* — perhaps those who actually lived there — constituted a subset of the entire cathedral clergy: the deacon Adelbert is described as provost "of the canonry" and "of the order of the holy church of Bergamo."[70] Not until the early eleventh century did the seat of the cathedral clergy begin to approximate the architectural complex set out at Aachen. A necrology records that Bishop Reginfrid (996–1012) "built the dormitory, refectory, and cellar of this city." Charters redacted in the 1020s and 1030s suggest a greater architectural unity, describing the location of the act as "in casa que dicitur canonica" or "intus casa Sancti Alexandri" and donating goods to support "the communal life of the canons there ordained."[71] The same pattern of development is evident in other sees.[72]

The actual fulfillment of the vision of canonical life set out in the Council of Aachen was a centuries-long and piecemeal process in northern Italian dioceses. But the important point here is that from the ninth century, the clergy serving the cathedral had their own institutional identity distinct from that of the bishop. They constituted a "chapter" with their own patrimony and officials. They were the cathedral's clergy, not the bishop's household. Wherever they lived, it was not in the episcopal residence. The

69. *Perg. Bergamo*, no. 34.

70. Ibid., nos. 91, 173, 84.

71. "V Kal. Januarii [1011] obiit Reginfredus Episcopus Pergamensis qui dedit decimam & fecit dormitorium, & refectorium, & cellarium hujus civitatis." Mario Lupo, *Codex Diplomaticus civitatis et ecclesiae Bergomatis*, 2 vols. (Bergamo, 1784–1799) 2, cols. 462, 555–56, 567–68, 581.

72. Parma and Verona are good examples: *Parma IX*, AC no. 13; *Parma X*, nos. 23, 37, 45, 46, 56, 82, 79; Miller, *Formation*, 43–44, 57–58.

formation of the cathedral clergy into chapters had two important and interrelated ramifications.

First, the episcopal *domus* was more purely the bishop's space than was the late-antique *episcopium*. Not surprisingly, the character of the household of the *domus* reflected the new duties of the episcopal office. Bishops in the early Middle Ages still had clerics in their households, but by the millennium they were a long way from the monastic character of Augustine's dinner table. Imperial service required bishops to offer hospitality to royal officials, and such visitors constituted a significant lay presence. They also might be destructive of more than the clerical ambiance of the episcopal household: Bishop Ratherius of Verona accused these guests of abusing both the house itself and its servants. Moreover, episcopal wills from this era reveal that the bishop's intimates were as likely to be knights as clerics. The cathedral clergy, and those of other urban churches and *xenodochia* (hospices caring for the poor), did receive benefactions in these documents. Bishop Elbunco of Parma, when he drew up his last will and testament in the spring of 913, left an amazing list of liturgical objects and vestments to his church; lands and other immovables also were granted to the clergy. But even these endowments, before they were to devolve to cathedral chapters, were entrusted for life to those one senses were the bishop's "friends." Billongus, Verona's bishop in the mid-ninth century, left all his goods in usufruct for life to his vassals Fulchernus and Gerard. The latter is also described as his *cubicularius*, or chamber attendant. For Notker, Billongus's early-tenth-century successor, these intimates meriting special bequests were Bernard Bishop of Trent; his vassal Odelbert "who is called Ocio"; Odelbert's son Ingelbald; Adelelmus, son of Count Adelmus; and finally John, acolyte of the Veronese church.[73] The bishop's household in this period appears less clerical in character just as his residence seems less distinct from secular houses.

Second, the new corporate identity of the cathedral clergy made the cathedral itself a more complicated space. It was, to be sure, still the bishop's church. He was the prime celebrant in the great feasts that inscribed Christian time in early-medieval communities. His *cathedra* was still there. But the day-to-day liturgy of this church became the province of the chapter. The canons sang the offices there; maintained the lighted candles, the *luminaria*, that seem so important to medieval testators; protected the relics of the city's saints; and said masses, particularly for the souls of their predecessors in the service of the cathedral. Singular a case as it is, the bishop of Genoa's relocation of his residence at a distance from the cathedral in the tenth century was only possible because of this new relationship of the chapter to the cathedral.

Several exigencies of the early-medieval episcopate fostered this development. One was the acquisition of manors and regalian rights in the countryside. As monarchs endowed sees with more of these resources, bishops appear to spend more time in the countryside administering their estates and rights. Many of the administrative documents the bishops of Modena issued in this period were redacted in their castles at Vignola and Savignano. Bishop Fredulfus of Reggio leased some lands from his castle at

73. *CDV,* 1 no. 182, 2 no. 109.

Novi in 923, and the bishops of Cremona regularly administered their property from their castle at Genivolta in the late tenth and early eleventh centuries.[74] A more important factor fostering the absence of bishops from their cathedrals was a by-product of their duties toward the king. In return for royal grants of lands and rights, bishops increasingly owed their monarchs *servitium*: attendance at court, counsel, judicial duties, and even armed contingents. This aspect of the episcopal office in the early Middle Ages helps explain why bishops Billongus and Notker were so close to their vassals. It also kept them outside their dioceses with enough regularity that many bishops appointed a special officer — the *vicedominus* — to administer the see in the absence of its pastor. Such officials are evident at Bergamo, Verona, Lucca, and other sees from the early ninth century.[75]

This changing relationship between the bishop and his church is manifest (nearly caricatured) in the woes of the querulous bishop who opened this chapter, Ratherius of Verona. He is, to be certain, an extreme case, but nonetheless instructive. Like many prelates in this period, he received his see from the king, and the hardball politics of the *regnum* interrupted his tenure in the see more than once: he was bishop of Verona from 931 to 934, 946 to 947, and 961 to 968. His first fall from grace, occasioned by his reception in Verona of King Hugh's rival, Arnold of Bavaria, left him imprisoned in Pavia. His last restoration to the see was also the result of imperial politics: when Otto I descended into Italy with a sizable army in 961, Ratherius regained the city as his faithful follower. He clearly both benefited and suffered from the new episcopal alliance with power. As a conflicted participant-observer, Ratherius had much to say of the effects of this new alliance on the episcopal office. He excoriated his fellow bishops for abandoning their flocks and the decorum of the priesthood to take on the habits and vices of the court: hunting with dogs and falcons, drinking, gambling, playing at sports, consuming extravagant feasts, and enjoying bawdy musicians, tumblers, and dancers.

Ratherius's critique certainly should not taint every bishop, but again episcopal wills give some credence to his words. "They would rather," he complained,

> embrace actors than priests, players than clerics, drunken spouters than theologians, scoundrels than men of true worth, men of shame than men of modesty, mimics than monks. They yearn for Greek glories, Babylonian show, exotic decoration. They commission golden goblets, silver salvers, cups of even greater value, bowls, or rather conches of greater weight of a size unseen in any age.[76]

74. *Reg. Modena*, nos. 46, 54, 67, 72, 112, 123, 124, 126, 133, 170–172, 188, 190–193 (Vignola) and nos. 23, 116, 145, 230, 232, 233, 236, 252 (Savignano); *Carte Reggio*, no. 46; *Carte Cremonesi*, nos. 86, 47, 66, 100, 102, 137, 138, 177, 204, 215, 223.

75. *Perg. Bergamo*, no. 7 (April 805); Miller, *Formation*, 148 and note 32; Raffaele Savigni, "La signoria vescovile lucchese tra XI e XII secolo: Consolidamento patrimoniale e primi rapporti con la classe dirigente cittadina," *Aevum* 66 (1993): 364; *Regesto di Farfa compilato da Gregorio di Catino*, eds. I. Giorgi and U. Balzani, 5 vols. (Rome, 1879–1914), 2: no. 97 (776).

76. *CC Cont. Med.*, 46A: 146–47 (*Praeloquia* V.6, lines 201–7).

Indeed, *vascula*, or vessels, are the most prominent type of movable property distributed in some episcopal wills. That of John of Pavia left vessels "of wood, of stone, of bronze or copper, of *stannea* (an alloy of lead and silver), and of silver," and Bishop Billongus's will gave a similar list that also included gold. None of the couches inlaid with gold and upholstered in silk and tapestry that Ratherius decried show up in wills, but cloth — usually linen and wool, but silk too — does in abundance.[77] As much as these hints of wealth in some wills suggest a more secular mode of living within the episcopal residences of the early Middle Ages, other testaments suggest that Ratherius was not alone in trying to uphold a more pious standard. There were also episcopal bequests to found or endow hospices for the poor, to restore churches, and to free slaves.[78]

Whether pious or not, to be a bishop in the early Middle Ages one had to enter the alliance with royal power. Ratherius was only bishop of Verona when he courted royal favor and performed service for his king. As bishops increasingly became the king's men in the towns of northern Italy, cathedral chapters came to represent the local church. Its members were drawn from well-to-do families of the city, from the lower nobility and the families of judges and notaries. Their bishops, however, were commonly from beyond the Alps. Ratherius was from Liège, and many of the prelates appointed to Italian sees in the early Middle Ages were from Bavaria and other northern territories of the empire.[79] With their bishops foreigners, deposited and removed nearly like so much baggage as the king's entourage visited and revisited their cities, local communities protected their traditions of worship, asserting their claim to their churches through these chapters. As Ratherius discovered, some chapters could be very assertive. A faction within the cathedral chapter of Verona constituted his most violent opposition in the city. These canons had suffered the biting scorn of their bishop, who criticized not only their lax morals but also the local customs of the church, particularly those concerning the distribution of wealth among the clergy. Ratherius's critique of local custom was not unfounded, but we should not accept his portrayal of the struggle as one of good against evil, God against Satan, the church against the world. This was also a war between insiders and outsiders, between local tradition and foreign interference. The unspecified forces who attacked Ratherius and drove him from the episcopal residence were these threatened elements in the chapter; he was saved only by the grudging intervention of another outsider, Count Bucco. The spatial dynamics of this struggle are not insignificant. The canons not only drove the bishop from his house, but also drove him away from his church. The cathedral chapter's claims to this sacred space were powerful and could change, literally and figuratively, the bishop's place in the community. These claims would be joined by others as the eleventh century progressed.

77. *CDV*, 2 no. 86, 1 no. 182.
78. *Carte di San Fedele in Como*, ed. D. Santo Monti (Como, 1913), 4–9 (no. 2); *CDL*, no. 114; *CDV*, 1 no. 219; *CDP*, no. 11.
79. Miller, *Formation*, 144–46, especially footnote 8.

CHAPTER THREE:
THE EPISCOPAL RESIDENCE
IN THE CENTRAL MIDDLE AGES
The Bishop's Palace

The beautiful Romanesque cathedral of Parma (Figure 25) enters time and again into the narrative of the chronicler Salimbene de Adam. Writing in 1283, the chatty Franciscan is particularly informative about the city of Parma, for Salimbene was born and raised there. His family's house was on a corner of the great piazza where the cathedral of Santa Maria stood; the majestic church was, so to speak, in his backyard. This easy familiarity with the city's central sacred space shapes its presence in the friar's narrative: we get a very native view of the cathedral in the urban landscape. Salimbene tells us of an old man's affectionate protection of the building, punishing little boys who threw rocks at its sculptured facade. He mentions it repeatedly in passing as a landmark that locates myriad other sites. The addition of carved lions to its front entrance is recounted among the "public works" accomplished by his fellow citizens. And he carefully names the citizens, especially those who fell in battle defending Parma, who were buried within the cathedral. In describing the burial site of one, Salimbene locates quite precisely the storage place of the city's *carroccio* — the war-wagon representing the town's honor and carrying its standards that every Italian commune took into battle. For much of the historical period narrated by Salimbene, this spot in the cathedral was conspicuously empty; the Cremonese had captured Parma's *carroccio* in 1250, and the citizens of Parma did not regain this fetish of communal identity until 1280.[1]

Cathedrals had always been sites central to their communities, but in the eleventh century they began to take on new meanings. As prosperity refashioned the urban centers of northern Italy, a self-confident urban middle class began redefining the sense of community: they began envisioning themselves as less a flock to be protected and led, and more as a corporation with rights and interests. In the eleventh and early twelfth centuries, these urban dwellers formed oath-bound societies to defend these rights and advance their interests. They slowly took over public functions, particularly during the tumultuous years of the investiture crisis, and by the end of the twelfth century these

---

1. Salimbene, *Cronica*, 47, 76, 887–88, 759–60, 85, 487, 739; trans. Baird, 8, 30, 616, 529, 37, 334–35, 516. On the *carroccio*, see Hannelore Zug Tucci, "Il carroccio nella vita comunale," *Quellen und Forschungen aus italienischen Archiven und Bibliotheken* 65 (1985): 1–104.

FIGURE 25. *Parma, cathedral. (M. Miller.)*

"communes" were the recognized governments of their cities.[2] Some of the earliest and most solemn acts of these nascent citizen governments took place at the cathedral. Loyalty oaths from both individuals and outlying communities were taken by the leaders of the commune in Modena over the 1170s, always in or next to that city's cathedral.[3] The consuls and other officials of the commune of Piacenza received oaths in the cathedral but also settled judicial matters and significant debts: on February 20, 1191 "in maiori ecclesia" they paid the imperial treasurer Rodolf of Sibenech eight hundred pounds for the regalia, or rights, Henry VI had ceded to the commune.[4]

As many of these citizens had helped build these churches, we should not be surprised that they felt entitled to use them for communal assemblies. In the eleventh and twelfth centuries, most of these northern Italian towns, like Parma, rebuilt their cathedrals. Although church building was, traditionally, the bishop's responsibility, the new climate of assertive civic-mindedness led to a spirited involvement in the Romanesque remaking of these cathedrals. Salimbene's father, as construction of Parma's baptistery was begun, "placed stones in its foundation as a memorial," and the guilds of Piacenza contributing the massive piers of that city's new cathedral had their gifts commemorated in bas-relief plaques. Thus do images of shoemakers, cloth merchants, dyers, stone carvers, tanners, and bakers mingle with those of the saints in the new cathedral.[5] Usually, a body called the *opera* (literally, "the works") emerged to oversee the long, complex, and costly project of erecting the church. At first a branch of episcopal administration, the *opera* became a joint venture with representatives of the commune and the bishop's officials cooperating to raise and embellish the city's new cathedral.[6]

In this regard, the cathedral was a microcosm of the larger urban political transformation: the emergence of the commune was usually accomplished through an alliance between bishop and *cives* to protect the city's independence. This cooperative sharing of power was more or less cordial depending on the local history of the see. In cities like Cremona and Parma whose bishops were very rich, very powerful, and ultra-com-

2. Good overviews in English of the rise of the communes are Waley, *The Italian City-Republics;* the early chapters of Lauro Martines, *Power and Imagination: City-States in Renaissance Italy* (New York, 1979); and Tabacco, *The Struggle for Power,* Chaps. 5 and 6. A good selection of more recent work on these issues is *L'evoluzione delle città italiane nell'XI secolo,* ed. Renato Bordone and Jörg Jarnut, Annali dell'Istituto storico italo-germanico Quaderno 25 (Bologna, 1988).

3. *Registrum privilegiorum comunis Mutinae,* ed. L. Simeoni and E. P. Vicini (Reggio-Emilia, 1940), nos. 10, 15, 17, 20, 21, 39, 42.

4. *Il registrum magnum del comune di Piacenza,* ed. Ettore Falconi and Roberta Peveri, 4 vols. (Milan, 1984) nos. 55, 136, 139, 180, 188, 196, 211 (payment to imperial treasurer), 247, 250, 256, 259.

5. Salimbene, *Cronica,* 849–50, trans. Baird, 590; Angiola Maria Romanini, "Per una 'interpretazione' della cattedrale di Piacenza," *Il duomo di Piacenza (1122–1972)* (Piacenza, 1975), 31.

6. Arthur Kingsley Porter, *Lombard Architecture,* 4 vols. (New Haven, 1917), 1: 21–27; in some cities — like Florence, Orvieto, Pisa, Siena, Lucca, and Naples — it passed totally under the management of the commune by the late thirteenth century: George Dameron, *Episcopal Power and Florentine Society, 1000–1320* (Cambridge, Mass., 1991), 118–20; Robert Brentano, *Two Churches: England and Italy in the Thirteenth Century* (Berkeley and Los Angeles, 1968), 98–99.

plicitous imperial servants, power sharing was only accomplished either by the violent overthrow of a bishop (Landulfus of Cremona's fate circa 1031) or by going over to the reform party during the investiture crisis. The *cives maiores* of Parma took the latter route, electing the papal legate Bernard of the Uberti as bishop in 1104 after the convenient demise of the imperial bishop Vido.[7] In other towns, where bishops had never been so dominantly powerful that they could ignore local sentiments, an alliance was initiated more discretely. This was the more common pattern. When imperial rule weakened, bishops hedged their bets by cultivating stronger ties with other powerful men in the city. The bishop's goal was to hold onto what power he had; if the emperor could not be depended on to guarantee that power, then the bishop needed to develop an understanding with those best positioned to challenge his authority. The men forming the commune, for their part, were interested in allying themselves because the bishop gave them legitimacy. As the long-standing urban lord, the bishop was, in most cities, the dominant partner in this relationship into the second half of the twelfth century.[8] But after the communes emerged victorious in their resistance to the emperor Frederick Barbarossa's attempt to reassert imperial rule in Italy, the balance of power shifted. The Peace of Constance (1183) recognized the communes as the legitimate governments of the Italian cities and bishops had to redefine their roles in the new political order.

Writing a century later, Salimbene gives us a good view of their new place in the community. Bishops abound in his chronicle; a good portion of the first part of his book is a treatise on how prelates should behave, and episcopal anecdotes are frequent throughout the text. They were clearly a forceful presence in this Franciscan friar's world. That presence was surely manifest in the cathedral, but this is not where bishops are found in Salimbene's narrative. Bishops are found in their palaces.[9]

A NEW DESCRIPTION

The bishop of Parma's "palace" was directly across the piazza from the cathedral of Santa Maria and it was built before the new Romanesque church. The construction of this new episcopal residence followed the deployment of new language to describe the bishop's house. The see of Parma was the earliest to call the bishop's residence a "palace." This lexical shift was first recorded on a late September day in 1020 when a group of men gathered in their bishop's residence to transact some business. The sub-

---

7. For Cremona, see below; on Parma, Schumann, *Authority*, 211–13.

8. Good examples are Modena, discussed below, Bologna, Ferrara, Pavia, and Verona: Gina Fasoli, "Sui vescovi bolognesi fino al sec. XII: Possessi e rapporti con i cittadini," *Atti e memorie della R. Deputazione di storia patria per le provincie di Romagna*, ser. 4, 25 (1934–35): 13–23; Andrea Castagnetti, *Società e politica a Ferrara dall'età postcarolingia alla signoria estense (secoli X-XIII)* (Bologna, 1985), 42–44, 57–78; Pietro Vaccari, *Pavia nell'alto medioevo e nell'età comunale* (Pavia, 1956), 51–57; Miller, *Formation*, 151, note 43, 163–74.

9. Just a few examples are Salimbene, *Cronica*, 383–84, 461, 469–70, 562–63, 580, 621; trans. Baird, 260, 316, 322–23, 391, 403, 435.

deacon Peter, provost of the cathedral chapter and acting with its consent, leased some of the canons' property in Poviglio to a priest named Liuzo. Five men witnessed the act and the notary Benzo recorded that it was done "within the city of Parma, in the aforesaid house of the see of Parma, in the palace of lord Henry the bishop" (*infra suprascripta civitate Parma in predicto domum episcopio Parmensis in palatio domni Einrici episcopus*).[10] This burst of locative prose combines familiar terms — *domus, episcopium* — with a radically new and ambitious description: *palatium*. This is an imperial word, a powerfully resonant arrogation of spatial status. Before Benzo put quill to parchment on this fall day in Parma, this was a word usually reserved to indicate the emperor's abode or the court and institutions that exercised his will from that place. The emperors, all from beyond the Alps, had *palatia* throughout northern Italy. The only other individual on the peninsula using it was the pope.[11]

So what did it mean for a bishop to call his residence a palace? One by one, across the eleventh and twelfth centuries, every bishop in northern Italy began calling his residence a palace (see Appendix). By the late twelfth century, the change in terminology was complete and permanent: to this day, the bishop's residence in every one of these towns is called his palace, *il palazzo vescovile*. Benzo's first deployment of the term was hyperdescriptive, layering old and new language to make sure contemporaries knew exactly where they were. But most of the notarial flourishes introducing this new word into episcopal formulary were either more vaguely furtive or casually nonchalant. In the latter mode, episcopal residences in Bergamo, Piacenza, and Ravenna seem to pass easily from being *domus sancte ecclesie* or *domus episcopalis* to *palatia episcopi* without a great deal of notarial indecision or verbal fuss. But often an extended period of lexical experimentation preceded the establishment of a stable locative formula in a see's documents. This experimentation offers us some clues to the meaning of this change.

The invocation of a specific bishop's name is one. Just as Benzo identified the palace at Parma with the name of his particular bishop (Henry), the first reference to the episcopal palace in Vicenza attributes it to "lord John by the grace of God Bishop of Vicenza" and the first at Lucca to "lord Bishop Peter."[12] In Pistoia's first use of the term, the notary redacting a lease for Bishop Ildebrand specified that he was "in *your* palace, the above-named Ildebrand bishop."[13] While there is good evidence to attribute the

10. *Parma XI*, no. 26.

11. Wilhelm Albert Diepenbach, *"Palatium" in spätrömischer und fränkischer Zeit*. Phil. diss. Hessischen Ludwigs-Universität, Gießen (Mainz, 1921), 9–30. Carlrichard Brühl's *Palatium und Civitas: Studien zur Profantopographie spätantiker Civitates vom 3. bis zum 13. Jahrhundert*, 3 vols. (Köln and Vienna, 1975–90) analyzes the documentary evidence for the existence and locations of *palatia* in thirty-one cities. For Italian usage in the early Middle Ages, see Bognetti, "Problemi di metodo," 79 and the discussion following 196–200, 218–20. On the papacy's use of the term, see the Appendix and also Walter Ullmann, *The Growth of Papal Government in the Middle Ages* (London, 1955; reprinted 1965), 148, 326–27; Karl Jordan, "Die Entstehung der römischen Kurie," *Zeitschrift der Savigny-Stiftung für Rechtsgeschichte, Kanonistische Abteilung* 28 (1939): 100ff.

12. Tommaso Riccardi, *Storia dei vescovi vicentini* (Vicenza, 1786), 58; *Mem. e doc.*, IV no. 109.

13. *Regesta chartarum Pistoriensium. Vescovado, secoli XI e XII*, ed. Natale Rauty (Pistoia, 1974), no. 18: "in palatio tuo qui supra Ildebrando episcopo."

building of this new palace at Pistoia to Bishop Ildebrand, one should not immediately leap from grammatical possessiveness to architectural instigation. The episcopal palace at Modena is described as "of Bishop Eribert" in 1071, "of Bishop Ribald" in 1148, and "of lord Bishop Henry" in 1157.[14] The palace was that of its resident, it seems, not necessarily that of its builder. This is important: the invocation of this imperial word was an official change, not a whim of personal aggrandizement.

Sometimes the new word described a new place. In two cases a change in language was definitely accompanied by the construction of a new building. The archeological work done at Pistoia allows us to date the construction of the new episcopal residence there to the late eleventh century, and this is exactly when the language describing the building changes. In 1067 the residence is the *domus sancti Zenonis*, and the next direct reference to it in 1112, after the building of the new structure, calls it a *palatium*.[15] At Verona, Bishop Tebaldus built himself a new episcopal residence as soon as he was elevated to the see in 1135. A document of 1136 already mentions the "new house of Lord Tebaldus" and in 1145 a notary informs us that he is writing "in palatio episcopi Tebaldi." Thereafter the episcopal residence is called a palace.[16] In several other cases (Padua, Modena, and Mantua) there is some evidence to suggest that construction or reconstruction occurred around the time of the shift in terms.[17] But for several other cities (Como, Parma, Pavia, Ravenna, and Piacenza) none of the evidence of construction and reconstruction corresponds with this change of language.[18] In Piacenza, for ex-

14. Pistoni, *Il palazzo arcivescovile di Modena,*" 13.

15. Rauty, *Palazzo*, 1: 83–85, 282–83; 2.1: 53–65.

16. *ACVerona*, III-7–8r (BC 36 m4 n14): "in civitate Verone in casa nova domni Tebaldi venerabilis episcopi"; Giuseppe Muselli, in *Memorie, istoriche, cronologiche, diplomatiche, canoniche, e critiche del capitolo e canonici della cattedrale di Verona*, busta DCCCXXXVI at 1145. An edition of these charters was just published: *Le carte del capitolo della cattedrale di Verona I (1101–1151)*, ed. Emanuela Lanza (Rome, 1998). For the documents cited above, see nos. 71, 120.

17. *Padua*: The episcopal residence is definitely a "palace" from 1116 and the earliest remains on the present site of the episcopal palace date from the twelfth century, R. Zanocco, "Il palazzo vescovile attuale nella storia e nell'arte (1309–1567)," *Bollettino diocesano di Padova* 13 (1928): 175, note 4. *Modena*: The only scholar to have studied the bishop's palace believes that it was built or rebuilt under Bishop Eribert (1056–95), during whose episcopate the terminological shift occurs. However, the evidence he cites (that the building is called "palacii Heriberti") is not entirely conclusive when compared with patterns in other cities. Pistoni, *Il palazzo arcivescovile di Modena*, 13. *Mantua*: The episcopal residence is a palace in 1021; this structure was located near the old cathedral, San Paolo (now obliterated by the diocesan seminary). During demolition work within the seminary, however, evidence was discovered of San Paolo and a number of adjacent buildings — all having been reconstructed "poco dopo il mille," Ercolano Marani, "L'antico centro episcopale di Mantova e il battistero urbano," *Civiltà mantovana* ns 1 (1983): 25.

18. *Como*: The residence within the walls was built in the early eleventh century, but it was not called a palace until the early twelfth century. Frigerio and Baserga, "Il palazzo vescovile," 75. *Ravenna*: There is evidence of rebuilding in the mid-eleventh century under Archbishop Gebeardus and in the early thirteenth under Simon. Alessandro Testi Rasponi, "Un'antica cronaca episcopale ravennate," *Felix Ravenna* 3 (1911): 123–25; Alessandro Torre, "Lavori fatti dall'Arcivescovo Simone nell'arcivescovado (1223)," *Felix Ravenna* 36 (1930): 15–17.

ample, the episcopal residence is called *palatium*, and then about a half-century later a new building is raised.[19] Parma offers the most compelling evidence: in 1020 the episcopal residence is called a *palatium* for the first time; then either Bishop Ugo or Cadalus, sometime in the middle of the century, abandoned this residence and built a new one just outside the city walls (also called a palace).[20] In sum, the use of this word "palace" may be accompanied by new construction, but it seems it could also provoke or lead to a new building rather than merely reflect one.

Some of our earliest references to episcopal palaces might suggest that the palace was at first conceived as a part or section of the *domus*. Benzo's use first of *domo* and then, perhaps more specifically, *in palatio* could be read this way. The earliest reference in Padua locates us "in the palace of Padua's house" (*in palatio domi Patavi*) and the first use in Florence *in palatio de domui*. . . . Como's earliest reference, however, suggests the exact opposite — it locates an act of Bishop Wido "in the house of his palace" (*in domo palacii eius*) — and an 1146 document from Faenza treats both terms as synonyms (*in domo sive palatio domini episcopi faventini*).[21] Such juxtapositions of "house" and "palace," moreover, disappear rapidly, leaving *palatium* as the only identifying term.

More interesting — and ultimately more meaningful — is the tendency in early references to describe the palace as belonging not to the bishop, but to a saint or, more generally, to the city.[22] A residence once identified as the "house of the holy church," the "house of the bishop," or "the episcopal house" suddenly became the "palace of Saint Peter," the "palace of Saint Donatus," or the "palace of Saint John" (San Giovanni). In all these cases — Bologna, Arezzo, and Florence — the saints invoked were those to whom the cathedral was dedicated. The case of Florence is particularly interesting because the bishops had been promoting the cult of Saint John for some time.

19. *Palatium* is used by 1121 — *ACPiacenza*, Cass. 12 — Permute no. 74, May 14, 1121 — but we know that the bishop had built a new palace by 1171: *ASPiacenza*, Archivio Diplomatico degli Ospizi Civili di Piacenza — Atti Privati, cartella 4, perg. 6. This new palace was built in conjunction with the second phase of construction on the cathedral and attached to it.

20. *Parma XI*, no. 26; Schumann, *Authority*, 292–93; Nestore Pelicelli, *I vescovi della chiesa parmense* (Parma, 1936), 118–19.

21. *CDP*, nos. 150 and 151, both dated Nov. 10, 1048, but redacted by different notaries; Manaresi, *Placiti*, no. 353 and also no. 373 from Arezzo, "infra palatium domus sancti donati"; *Carte di San Fedele in Como*, no. 11; Johanne-Benedicto Mitarelli and Anselmo Costadoni, *Annales camaldulenses ordinis Sancti Benedicti*, 9 vols. (Venice, 1755–73) 3: 293 (app. no. 426).

22. Some precedents for these *palatium* forms may be found earlier, but they reveal particular tensions. At Verona, for example, the episcopal residence from the eighth century was called the *domus sancti zenonis*. But this was because the body of the town's patron saint — Saint Zeno — was located not at the bishop's cathedral of Santa Maria Matricularis but at the wealthy and powerful Benedictine monastery of San Zeno outside the city walls — where, significantly, an imperial palace was built. The bishops claimed the patron for themselves by identifying their residence in this fashion. By the time Bishop Tebaldus built his "palace," however, the monastery of San Zeno was firmly under the bishop's control and its imperial guests were no longer the arbiters of the see. The palace, as a result, was never identified as Saint Zeno's; it was always the bishop's. Miller, *Formation*, 122–4, 163–7; *La Torre e il palazzo abbaziale di San Zeno: Il recupero degli spazi e degli affreschi* (Verona, 1992).

Saint John originally was patron only of the baptistery, but in the ninth century the bishops began invoking his name to identify the cathedral and the see as a whole. By the eleventh century, the bishops were using the patron to reinforce their lordship in the countryside, having episcopal tenants pay their rents on the saint's feast day (June 24). Leaseholders were required to come to the episcopal palace, the *palatium sancti Iohannis*, and in a ceremony of submission to the authority of both bishop and saint, offer the annual payments for the lands they held from the see. At about the same time, as its patrimony was growing, the cathedral chapter began invoking a different patron, Saint Reparata.[23] The claims to lordship in the bishop's invocation of Saint John were not lost on the canons.

Spatial contiguity with a church and its relics also clearly figures in this nomenclature. The episcopal residence in Florence was behind the baptistery of San Giovanni and was connected to it. At Ferrara, the seat of the bishops moved several times, and the residence took the name of the saint of the church to which it was attached: when the see was outside the walls at San Giorgio there are references to the *palatium sancti Georgii*, and then when it was at the urban church of Santo Stefano, we read of a *palatium sancti Stefani*. In Brescia, a chapel dedicated to Saint Martin and later incorporated into the residence lent its saint's name to first parts of, then the entire, episcopal palace.[24]

The urge to identify the palace at first as a saint's perhaps stemmed from an awareness that the use of this regal word *palatium* by mere bishops might be viewed as presumptuous. But the other vague identification favored in early references to the bishop's palace suggests not a camouflaging of lordly claims to power but their bold assertion. In Modena and Cremona, the palace is first identified as that "of the city," and only later references clarify that this urban palace is the residence of the bishop.[25] So

23. *palatium sancti Petri* (Bologna): *S. Giorgio Maggiore*, ed. Luigi Lanfranchi, 4 vols. (Venice, 1968) 2: 165–67 (no. 68); *ASBologna*, Demaniale, Abbazia di S. Stefano 8 / 944 no. 22, 9 / 945 no. 5 and S. Giovanni in Monte 1 / 1341 nos. 25, 42, 43. *palatium sancti Donati* (Arezzo) and *palatium sancti Iohanni* (Florence): Manaresi, *Placiti*, nos. 373, 353, 372, 413, 424, 430, 434, 480. On the relationship between the cathedral and baptistery, see Dameron, *Episcopal Power*, 62–63, 67, 149; and Anna Benvenuti, "Stratigrafie della memoria: Scritture agiografiche e mutamenti architettonici nella vicenda del 'Complesso cattedrale' fiorentino," in *Il bel San Giovanni e Santa Maria del Fiore: Il centro religioso di Firenze dal tardo antico al rinascimento* (Florence, 1996), 95–127, especially 118–22.

24. *Le carte ferraresi più importanti anteriori al 1117*, ed. Italo Marzola (Città del Vaticano, 1983), nos. 44, 62, 72; *ASFerrara*, Archivio Estense-Tassoni, busta 1, nos. 8, 9; *ASModena*, Archivio Estense, Giurisdizione Sovrana Vescovado Ferrara, busta 251, nos. 10, 11; *ACAFerrara*, Reparto Pergamene, sec. XII, no. 11; on the movement of the see, Adriano Franceschini, "Il duomo e la piazza nella città medievale," *Storia illustrata di Ferrara*, ed. Francesca Bocchi (San Marino, 1987), 82–86; Maureen C. Miller, "Vescovi, palazzi e lo sviluppo dei centri civici nelle città dell'Italia settentrionale, 1000–1250," in *Albertano da Brescia: Alle origini del razionalismo economico, dell'umanesimo civile, della grande Europa*, ed. Franco Spinelli (Brescia, 1996), 32–33.

25. This convention also is found sporadically in other cities. The episcopal residence in Brescia is called the *palatio Brixiano* in 1176, Federico Odorici, *Storie bresciane*, 11 vols. (Brescia, 1953–65) 5: 139; in Piacenza it is once the *palacio placentino*, *AAPiacenza*, Atti Publici, perg. 27; in Ivrea, "palace of the bishop" and "palace of Ivrea" (*palacio yporiensi*) are used interchangeably over the first half of the thirteenth century, *Le carte dello archivio vescovile d'Ivrea fino al 1313*, ed. Ferdi-

ambiguous is the identification in Modena that scholars since the nineteenth century have mistaken this "palace of the city" for the first communal palace. I think the ambiguity was purposeful. In both Modena and Cremona the bishops were, by imperial grant of regalian rights, lords of their cities. Both bishops from the tenth century held full comital authority within the walls. But when they first started calling their residences the palace of the city, both were facing challenges to their authority from a new and powerful noble family: the Canossa.

Adalbert Azzo, founder of the house of Canossa, appeared with the title "Count of Reggio and Modena" in the late tenth century, and the family's claims in the region mounted in the early eleventh. This clearly unsettled the bishop of Modena, whose power was centered in the city but whose patrimony lay in the countryside where the Canossa were exercising power. The bishop appealed to Emperor Conrad I in 1026 for confirmation of his rights. In the 1030s, a series of *diplomata* were forged in Modena that claimed to grant the bishop comital authority throughout the entire countryside surrounding the city. The bishop had reason to feel threatened: the Marquis Boniface of Canossa had taken over several episcopal castles in the decade before the mysterious "palace of the city" appears in 1046. The Canossan challenge to the bishop's lordship seems to have prompted his invocation of the imperial word "palace" and his identification of it as the "palace of Modena." The bishop's identification of his lordship with the city also went beyond this renaming of his residence. In the second half of the century the bishops of Modena entered into an alliance with the nascent urban commune to stave off the external threat of the expanding Canossan lordship (which was so powerful by the early twelfth century under Countess Matilda that historians have taken to calling it a "state").[26]

The power of the Canossan "state" also forced a rapprochement between the bishops of Cremona and that city's commune. Here, however, there was a long history of animosity to overcome, and the truce was temporary. Cremona's movement for urban autonomy had been particularly precocious. Already in the late tenth century, the Cremonese were chafing under the lordship of their count-bishop, invading his properties and disputing his rights (particularly those of collecting tolls on the Po). Having "suffered many injuries at the hands of wicked men," the bishop of Cremona had to appeal for imperial protection in 992, and a group of citizens in 998 made so bold as to challenge the bishop's lucrative rights on the Po in an imperial tribunal. In 1031, as a charter laconically explains, these tensions came to a head:

> . . . the citizens of Cremona conspired and swore [an oath] against the holy Cremonese church, their spiritual mother, and against the now deceased Landulfus, bishop of this see and their spiritual patron and lord. The result of this conspiracy was that the citizens threw the bishop out of the city with grave ignomy and shame,

nando Gabotto, 2 vols., Biblioteca della Società storica subalpina 5–6 (Pinerolo, 1900), nos. 48, 55, 77, 81, 83, 84, 93, 101, 109, 110, 123, 154, 159, 160; for Modena and Cremona, see below.

26. Maureen C. Miller, "Il «Palazzo della Città di Modena»: Di chi era questo 'palazzo'?" *Atti e memorie della Deputazione di storia patria per le antiche provincie modenesi* ser. XI, 21 (1999): 3–12.

and pillaged his goods and destroyed a tower with a castle with double walls and seven towers built around it.[27]

But the same Canossan threat that allowed the commune of Modena to emerge in alliance with the city's bishop led the Cremonese to reconsider their hostility toward their "spiritual patron and lord" in the late eleventh century. In 1098, for example, Countess Matilda invested a group of men from the city with an enormous property (Isola Fulcheria), and they received it "on behalf of the church of Santa Maria of Cremona and for the commune of this city of Cremona." As the dominion of the countess weakened and then collapsed in the second decade of the twelfth century, however, the commune renewed its more aggressive posture. In 1114 an imperial concession confirmed to the citizens of Cremona not only control of lands previously held by the bishops but also rights on the Po. In 1123 the bishop first called his residence a *palatium*, and from this point until virtually the eve of the Peace of Constance (the imperial pact of 1183 that officially recognized the governance of the northern Italian communes), he alternately characterized his residence as the "palacio Cremone" or the more accurate but restricted "palacio episcopi Cremone."[28]

Since many of these bishops began invoking the term *palatium* in the general period of the great contest between the papacy and empire, one might object that the sudden adoption of this language had more than local sources. Indeed, there is one reference at Parma in 1081 to the "Parmesan palace of the lord king and of the see of Parma which is near the house of the holy church of Parma."[29] Since bishops were royal vassals, they were often expected to offer hospitality to the king and his entourage, and when, as at Parma in the eleventh century, the monarch did not have his own palace, he usually lodged with the bishop. But imperial use of episcopal residences does not seem to explain why many came to be called palaces. Even in cities where the emperor had *palatia* (Pavia, Milan, and Ravenna), bishops began applying this term to their residences, and in many cities the episcopal residence became a "palace" when the emperors were least in Italy. Nor does the chronology or geography of this change bear any relation to the politics of the investiture conflict. Mantua and Parma were the earliest to adopt the new language: one was a stronghold of the reform movement and the other a seat of an imperial antipope.

Only the more resolutely local fluctuations in power seem to coincide with this change in language, this apparently sudden transformation of episcopal *domus* into *palatia*. Local challenges to the bishop's authority, usually linked to the emergence of the commune, seem to prompt the change in city after city. Through the invocation of this powerful word, bishops seem to be reasserting a central place for themselves in their

27. *Carte Cremonesi*, no. 169.

28. The documentation for the nomenclature applied to the episcopal residence is in Miller, "Il «Palazzo della Città di Modena»," note 42; for the emergence of the commune in the city, see Alessandro Groppali and Francesco Bartoli, *Le origini del comune di Cremona* (Cremona, 1898); the 1098 and 1114 documents are *Carte Cremonesi*, nos. 242, 264.

29. Manaresi, *Placiti*, "Compositiones," no. 9.

communities. This bid for centrality and the primacy of local concerns is evident in the ambiguous proffering of the residence as the palace of the city, or the palace of the town's patron saint. Although the language of sonorous imperial or papal tones is novel, the sentiment driving it seems nostalgic. For, as we have seen, in the early Middle Ages the bishop had been central to the city — to its survival and defense in the face of repeated invasions, to the maintenance of its basic institutions and services, to its relations with myriad *potentes* beyond its walls, to its physical and moral unity, and to its identity as a collectivity. All of these roles were challenged, and by the end of the twelfth century largely subsumed, by new citizen governments.

The episcopal use of the term *palatium* was nostalgic in that it tried to reassert a definition of the bishop's place that was fast becoming obsolete. But the gesture was not just wishful thinking. The rise of the communes has for us an aura of inevitability; we know how the story came out. Too often, moreover, we succumb to the temptation to import the overdetermined and anachronistic language of the "rise of the nation state" into the narrative of communal ascent. These histories do run parallel. The rise of the communes became a central theme in Italian historiography as a modern Italian "nation state" was emerging. But if we abandon our bird's-eye historian's view and look at local politics as the communes were forming from somewhere on the ground — from a castle in the *contado*, from a market in the piazza, or even from the bishop's palace — the certainty of these transformations of power begins to give way to doubt. Particularly in the late eleventh and early twelfth centuries — when most of our bishops began calling their houses *palatia* — the character and extent of the commune's role in local governance were not at all fixed and determined. Most communes emerged through some sort of alliance — more or less prickly or polite, depending on local circumstances — with their bishops. The commune emerged, at least in part, out of the bishop's court, where his vassals (both rural and urban elites) and administrators gathered to give him counsel. Serving the bishop acquainted these men with the bishop's rights and dues: what they entailed, how they were exercised, and how they generated income. They attended him as he administered justice and as he heard and acted on petitions. Their service to the bishop also gave them the detailed knowledge of the countryside — the juridical status of different communities, the resources available in them, and the leading families in different areas — that later aided the commune in extending its rule here. In sum, as the new alliance of elites we call the "commune" was organizing, many of its members were already schooled at the episcopal court in ways of exercising local power. The period of collaborative rule continued and probably intensified the transfer of practical knowledge (of resources, of communities, of customs) and techniques of administration. But no formula defined this collaboration or "condominium"; how powers were shared or divided up was continually negotiated, and little of this surfaces explicitly into the sources.

It was during these sometimes quite-extended periods of local power sharing that bishops refashioned their houses as palaces, and these places were extremely significant in the gestation of the communes. Most basically, the bishop's palace was one of the first meeting places of the early commune. These new urban governments did not build their own palaces until the late twelfth or early thirteenth century. This means that often for more than a century they conducted their business in a variety of places: in private homes, in public squares, in monasteries, in churches — particularly, as we have seen, the cathedral. But the bishop's palace figures prominently and consistently among these early gathering places. In Como the first time the commune's elected leaders, or consuls, appear in 1109, they are gathered within the bishop's palace, and at Lucca too their first appearance (1119) is in their bishop's hall. The first appearance of the consuls of Verona is also documented as they met in Bishop Tebaldus's new palace, and one of the earliest references to the consuls of Modena is in a charter redacted in the bishop's palace.[30] In the long inchoate period of the commune's gestation, the space in which the bishop exercised power offered a formative example of lordly practice. It should not surprise us, then, that when these communes built their own palaces they had much in common with episcopal seats. This is a point to which we will return.

THE CHANGING "PALACE"

At this juncture, however, we need to look at the buildings. When bishops began calling their houses *palatia*, the houses themselves differed hardly at all from the simple, heavily fortified structures that characterized the tenth and early eleventh centuries. Remember that this shift in language did not necessarily indicate a new building, and even when it did, the building was highly traditional. In the twelfth and thirteenth centuries, however, bishops did modify their towered fortresses in significant ways. Let us return to Parma to consider what kind of building contemporaries deemed a "palace" in the middle of the eleventh century and how that structure changed over the twelfth and thirteenth centuries.

Just after first deploying the term *palatium*, the bishop of Parma built a new residence just outside the city walls directly opposite the site chosen for the new cathedral. A long debate over exactly which bishop built the new palace has animated local scholarship for decades, some scholars attributing it to Bishop Ugo (1027–44) and others to

---

30. *ACVerona*, II-7–4r (AC 37 m2 n1) and I-6–5v (BC 44 m4 n4)[now also Lanza, *Le carte del capitolo*, nos. 130, 131]; see also Maureen C. Miller, "From Episcopal to Communal Palaces: Places and Power in Northern Italy (1000–1250)," *Journal of the Society of Architectural Historians* 54:2 (1995): 178. The first evidence of consuls in Modena is in a letter of Pope Innocent II in 1135: Paul F. Kehr, *Regesta pontificum romanorum: Italia Pontificia*, 10 vols. (Berlin, 1906–) 5: 302–3; Emilio Paolo Vicini, "Serie dei consoli modenesi," *Atti e memorie della reale Accademia di scienze lettere ed arti di Modena* ser. 4, 4 (1933–34): 64–65, 69ff. When they next appear in a document of 1142, they are in the bishop's palace: "adesset Domnus Ribaldus, Dei gratia Mutinensis Ecclesiae Episcopus, in Palatio Domnicato et cum eo assidentibus septem sibi Consulibus Urbis Mutinae . . . " Lodovico Muratori, *Antiquitates Italicae medii aevi*, 6 vols. (Milan, 1738–42) 4: 51. For Lucca, see *AALucca*, Diplomatico, ++ N 99; Thomas W. Blomquist and Duane J. Osheim, "The First Consuls at Lucca: July 10, 1119," *Actum Luce* 7 (1978): 37–39. Pierre Racine has also noticed the tendency for the consuls of the early commune to meet in their bishop's palace: "Les Palais publics dans les communes italiennes (XII–XIIIe siècles)," in *Le Paysage urbaine au moyen-âge*, Actes du XIe Congrès des historiens médiévistes de l'enseignement supérieur (Lyon, 1981), 135.

Bishop Cadalus (1045–71).[31] Both men were trusted imperial servants. Ugo was chancellor and chaplain to Emperor Conrad before his elevation to the see of Parma, and he continued his duties as chancellor while bishop. Cadalus became an imperial antipope as Honorius II in 1061. The remains of this palace, which constitute the northwest angle of the present structure, cannot be dated more precisely than to the mid-eleventh century, so either bishop could have effected the move.

Like other eleventh-century episcopal residences, the bishop of Parma's new palace was highly fortified. It was surrounded by a moat and had an imposing tower (Figure 26). Attached to the tower, extending eastward toward the site of the new cathedral was a rectangular building of two stories. On the ground floor, it had a broad arched entrance on the north face (Figure 27); the entrance to the second floor was either on the south face or at the east end facing the cathedral. The tower had only narrow, arrow-slit windows, but the second floor of the main building had several small bifores, arched windows each subdivided with a slender column in the center supporting two arches of white stone alternating with dark brick (Figure 28). Unlike the residences at Pistoia and Como, the bishop of Parma's palace was built entirely of brick and the tops of its walls were crowned with Romanesque battlements (Figure 29). The exterior brick walls were also finished with red-lead paint (*minio pictum*).[32]

Although built of more sophisticated materials and incorporating more decorative elements, this "palace" at Parma was structurally quite traditional: it was a tower with a two-story rectangular building attached. Its walls were thick and its windows small, giving it the fortress-like character of its tenth-century predecessors. Like other episcopal seats, the palace at Parma underwent expansion and renovation over the twelfth and thirteenth centuries, and in this process the character of the building changed significantly.

First, episcopal palaces expanded: some doubled or tripled in size. To appreciate the significance of this prodigious expansion, we must look briefly at its economic context. Everything that we know about episcopal patrimonies in this period suggests that these were not financially easy times. Sees were losing revenue-generating rights (tolls, market and judicial fees) to the communes. By the 1190s the commune of Como, for example, was collecting tolls within the city and exercising jurisdiction over several communities formerly controlled by the bishop. Some prelates in the early thirteenth century elicited compensation from communes for the rights communal officials had arrogated, while others engaged in lengthy legal battles trying to defend or reclaim lost prerogatives.[33] Bishops were also losing castles, vassals, fiefs, and feudal dues as the

31. Pelicelli, *Vescovado*, 10–13, attributed the new palace to Ugo; Banzola, "Palazzo," 28–29, argued that an attribution to Cadalus is more plausible and in note 9 outlined local debate over the issue.

32. Pelicelli, *Vescovado*, 13–16; Banzola, "Palazzo," 30.

33. Cesare Cantù, *Storia della città e diocesi di Como*, 2 vols. (Florence, 1856) 1: 221; after years of litigation with the commune, Bishop Tiso of Treviso in 1218 formally ceded the collection of mercantile rights and tolls in the city and countryside known as the *muda* or *muta* and received a sum in return: Augusto Lizier, *Storia del comune di Treviso* (Treviso, 1979), 61–65; *Storia di Treviso*, ed. Ernesto Brunetta, 4 vols. (Venice, 1989–99) 2: 67–68, 387–88; the bishop of Bergamo was involved

FIGURE 26. (TOP LEFT) *Parma, Palazzo del Vescovado, eleventh-century tower in northwest corner.* (M. Miller.)

FIGURE 27. (TOP RIGHT) *Parma, Palazzo del Vescovado, entrance to eleventh-century palace on north face.* (M. Miller.)

FIGURE 28. (BOTTOM LEFT) *Parma, Palazzo del Vescovado, remains of eleventh-century bicolor bifores on north face.* (M. Miller.)

FIGURE 29. (BOTTOM RIGHT) *Parma, Palazzo del Vescovado, remains of eleventh-century crenelation on north face.* (M. Miller.)

communes established hegemony over the countryside, and many were having increased difficulties collecting rents on their rural holdings.[34] So this heavy investment in the expansion of their palaces over the late twelfth and early thirteenth centuries was

---

in a long battle with the commune in defense of his mining rights in the Val'Ardesio: *AVBergamo,* Diplomata seu Jura episcopatus Bergomensis, Racc. 2, perg. no. 36.

34. Asti is a particularly good example: Richard G. McLaughlin, *The Church and Commune in Medieval Asti* (Ann Arbor, 1973), 109–18; another good description of episcopal financial woes in this period is Dameron, *Episcopal Power,* 93–140.

not a result of new wealth or windfall profits; bishops chose to invest heavily in architecture at a time when their resources were shrinking.

Frustratingly little evidence survives on how bishops financed construction. No documentation, for example, reveals how Bishop Ugo or Cadalus paid for the new episcopal palace at Parma in the mid-eleventh century. The only hint of the resources deployed in this earlier period comes in a charter of Arezzo. In December of 1026, Bishop Teodaldus of Arezzo confirmed a series of lands and tithes to Maginardus, who is described as "a man skilled and highly learned in the architectural arts." Note here that portions of the patrimony and its resources are being alienated to pay for construction. Maginardus, who clearly had been doing work for several of Teodaldus's predecessors in the see, is credited with rebuilding both the cathedral and the episcopal palace.[35] The construction and reconstruction of palaces in several cities do coincide with campaigns to rebuild churches, and it seems likely that bishops made use of the laborers and artisans assembled for cathedral building in their domestic construction projects. The association of these endeavors temporally and in documents like the Arezzo charter suggests that funds raised for a new cathedral may also have been used to subsidize palace building.[36] Evidence for the great expansion and renovation of episcopal palaces in the late twelfth and early thirteenth centuries, however, suggests that bishops borrowed money to expand their residences. In 1182 the bishop of Pistoia borrowed money from the commune in order to complete a series of renovations.[37]

Considering these financial constraints, the doubling or tripling of the size of episcopal palaces over the late twelfth and early thirteenth centuries seems more remarkable. Bishops perceived expansion as necessary. The character and effects of this expansion, then, are important to consider: What kind of space was added? Does the character of the space added tell us anything about the perceived "needs" of the episcopal office in the wake of Gregorian reform and in the midst of local political transformations? The earliest expansions of these buildings increased the size of the bishop's great hall. Subsequent expansion not only tended to multiply the number of halls but also introduced new kinds of spaces — most notably, chapels.

35. *Arezzo-Documenti*, no. 125.

36. Bishop Tebaldus of Verona first built a new palace in the 1130s, then rebuilt the cathedral from 1139 to 1153; his successor, Omnebonus, built the cathedral's sacristy but also added a new floor to the episcopal palace. A similar alternation between work on the bishop's palace and building campaigns on the cathedral is evident at Piacenza: a new episcopal palace appears there in 1171, between the completion of the first campaign of building on the cathedral and the beginning of work on the transept arms. Miller, *Formation*, 166–67; *La cattedrale di Verona nelle sue vicende edilizie dal secolo IV al secolo XVI*, ed. Pierpaolo Brugnoli (Verona, 1987), 101; *Il duomo di Piacenza* (Piacenza, 1975), 25–28.

37. Rauty, *Palazzo*, 103. Episcopal debt is more noticeable in our documentation from the mid-twelfth century. Bishop Tebaldus of Verona, who built a new palace there, borrowed over one thousand Veronese pounds from the merchant John Monteclo; the Bishop of Fiesole by 1220 was unable to pay his debts and a later settlement of his affairs with the Florentine commune reveals he owed at least ten thousand pounds: *Biblioteca Apostolica Vaticana*, Cod. Vat. Lat. No. 1322A, fol. 284v; Dameron, *Episcopal Power*, 122.

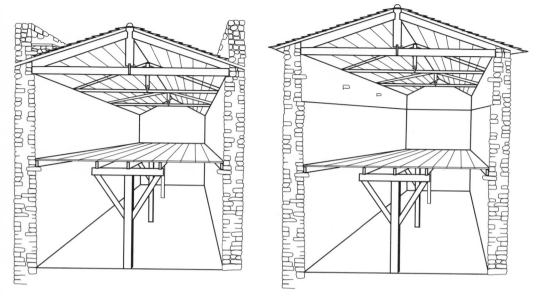

FIGURE 30. *Pistoia, Palazzo dei Vescovi, original eleventh-century support of roof and raised twelfth-century reconfiguration. (C. Ingersoll, based on Rauty,* Palazzo, *95, 98, by permission of the Cassa di Risparmio di Pistoia e Pescia.)*

The initial expansion of the bishop's great hall is well illustrated at Parma, Pistoia, and Como. In the 1170s, Bishop Bernard of Parma more than doubled the size of his palace by adding two new wings: one extended the original building farther east and the other then cut at a right angle, creating an "L"-shaped structure (see Figure 55). One would have thought this would have been expansion enough, but Bernard also had the ceiling of the original hall raised by two meters (6.5 feet).[38] At Pistoia as well, the roof of the bishop's second-story hall was raised roughly two meters (6.5 feet) in the twelfth century. The heightening here was effected not by raising the wall — as was done at Parma, a change in brick still evident to the eye along the north face of the palace (Figure 29) — but by reworking the system of support for the roof (moving it to the top of the wall rather than having it rest on stone brackets inserted into the wall) (Figure 30).[39] A similar kind of heightening could also have been effected at Como, but what we know for certain is that the bishop here expanded his hall laterally. The outer half-wall of the loggia was brought up to ceiling height, and the three bifore windows that one sees today were added. This widened the hall by roughly two meters (two yards).[40]

The bishop of Como may have wanted to accommodate more persons in his hall, but the emphasis on height rather than floor space at Parma and Pistoia suggests a desire for grandeur. What they added was the kind of wasted, nonfunctional space that befitted only God and the emperor. This extra "headroom" would have registered with

38. Pelicelli, *Vescovado*, 17–19; Banzola, "Palazzo," 31–33.
39. Rauty, *Palazzo*, 1: 96.
40. Frigerio and Baserga, "Il palazzo vescovile," 29–30.

FIGURE 31. *Verona, Palazzo Vescovile, third-floor west exterior wall of early-twelfth-century wing.* *(M. Miller.)*

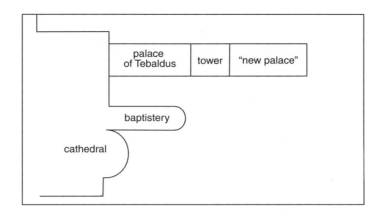

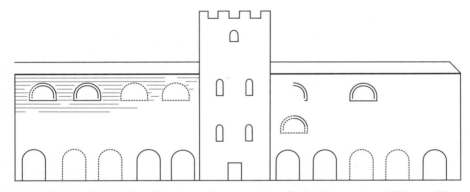

FIGURE 32. *Verona, Palazzo Vescovile, plan and reconstruction of old and new wings. (C. Ingersoll.)*

contemporaries in exactly these terms. In addition to the expansion of their halls, bishops multiplied these august spaces within their palaces. Indeed, their new additions usually duplicated the same kinds of spaces (porticos, loggias, *camere*, and halls) found in their earlier seats. Verona provides us a good example.

In 1172 a fire forced Bishop Omnebonus to restore the palace built by Bishop Tebaldus in the 1130s. The extent of the damage and of Omnebonus's rebuilding cannot be fixed precisely, but the surviving third-floor hall with wide arched windows is probably the "sala episcopi Omnisboni" where so many of the see's documents were redacted in the 1170s. The walls of this third floor — in elegant stripes of white tufa and red brick — differ noticeably from the plain brick exterior of the second floor (Figure 31).[41] A new wing was added (off the other side of the tower but in line with the original palace — Figure 32) around the time of Pope Lucius III's sojourn in the city: probably begun

41. The medieval walls of this palace closest to the cathedral are best visible on the flank facing the river. An inscription within the tower recorded that "Anno domini 1172. Omnibonus Veronen-

in the mid-1180s, charters in the 1190s mention this addition frequently as the "new palace of lord Adelard" (Bishop Adelard, 1188–1214). Several scrolls of testimony collected in disputes over the see's rights in the *contado* (the countryside surrounding the town) make clear that by the last decade of the century the palace was a more complex space. In a series of statements collected on June 30, 1183 (during Omnebonus's episcopate), Presbiterellus de Cestono prefaced his description of a conversation he overheard about the fief of Pontepossero with a clear declaration of where this conversation took place: "I was in the palace of the lord bishop Omnebonus with my lord Albert Tenca . . . " In a series of statements taken during the episcopate of Adelard, the places where actions took place were equally important to the scribe. When a witness was beginning to recount what the marquis said to him about the jurisdiction of Porto, he said that he was in the episcopal palace. The notary then asked him, "[I]n which episcopal palace did this occur?" (*in quo palatio episcopali hoc fuit*). The man responded, "[I]n that palace which is in front of the chapel which is in the bishop's tower." The same need to clarify occurred again later in the testimony: the notary "asked about the place where that contract concerning the tithes of reclaimed lands was made with lord Peccorarius," and the witness responded, "[I]n palatio novo episcopi" (in the bishop's new palace).[42] It is clear from these exchanges and the physical evidence that remains that what we would characterize as a new wing was called a "new palace" by contemporaries. Documentary descriptions suggest why: these new wings often duplicated the spaces of the initial structure so that notaries had to distinguish between old and new halls, porticos, and *camere*. The new wing at Verona had a ground-floor portico (like the original), a large hall (specified by one notary as the "sala maioris"), and a new "camera." A notary in Bergamo described an addition to that episcopal residence as "the new high room (*camera nova alta*) of the see next to the church of Santa Maria," a document from Faenza mentions the "camera nova," and notaries in Reggio in the 1190s specified a "new portico."[43] Even the Lateran was expanded with a "palatium novum" in the 1270s.[44]

The felicitous confluence of documentary and physical evidence at Parma well illustrates this duplication of "palaces." Bishop Bernard built his additions to the palace circa 1172, and from the mid-1170s notaries distinguish between the "palatio novo" and the "palatio veteri." A document of 1191 specified the place of redaction as "in the

---

sis Episcopus hoc fecit fieri opus ad honore(m) dei et sancti Zenonis et eodem anno septimo die intrante julio combusta est civitatis Verone." For Omnebonus's hall, see *ASVerona*, Clero Intrinseco, Ist. II (12) ff. 32, 127, 128; *ACVerona*, I-6-6v (AC 9 m2 n6) and Muselli, *Memorie*, at 1170 (inscription), 1174–75.

42. *ACVerona*, II-8-7r (AC 65 m5 n8), "in palacio novo dni adelardi verons epi"; I-7-2r (AC 67 m2 n15) gives Presbiterellus's testimony on Pontepossero; *ASVerona*, Mensa Vescovile, busta 1 no. 15 contains the later testimony.

43. *ACVerona*, Muselli, *Memorie*, at 1186 (f. 7, dated May 10) and 1189 (f. 2–3, dated January 7) *AVBergamo*, Diplomata seu Jura Episcopatus Bergomensis, Racc. 2, parte 1, no. 8; *BCFaenza*, Schedario Rossini, Repertorio Chronologico, July 12, 1286; *Parma XII*, nos. 687, 919.

44. The wing was probably on the southeast; Lauer, *Latran*, 209.

palace of lord Bernard, bishop of Parma by the grace of God." Additionally there is mention of "the *camera* of the new palace" (or "the new *camera* of the palace"). When Bishop Grazia expanded the palace again in the 1230s, one of the chief elements was a new great hall (twenty-five meters by fourteen meters [eighty-two feet by forty-six feet] and one and a half stories high).[45]

While much of the space added duplicated or enlarged elements that were already present in the bishop's palace, some new kinds of spaces were created. Grand staircases and emphasized foyers developed in several palaces in the thirteenth century. At Faenza, for example, numerous documents were redacted either on the stairs or on their "balcony and antechamber" (*balcone seo proaule*). The papal palace at Viterbo in this era had a magnificent projecting staircase with a broad landing, suitable for ceremonial entries and exits of the papal entourage and expansive enough to accommodate the sort of bureaucratic traffic suggested in the Faentine documents.[46] Several palaces refashioned their ground floors or devoted the ground levels of additional wings to shops that were rented out to artisans and merchants. This development is evident at the "palatio novo" at Piacenza from the 1180s. Documents, usually between private parties and not concerning episcopal business, were redacted "in a *stacione* (shop) of the episcopal palace."[47] Probably at some point in the thirteenth century there were shops in the ground floor of the episcopal palace in Florence, but leases for these properties do not survive until the early fourteenth century. These leases, interestingly, show that entrepreneurs could enter into an agreement with the bishop to build a shop on episcopal property — as two apothecaries did under the stone steps of the palace in the first decade of the fourteenth century — and receive a reduction in rent for a fixed period to encourage their commercial development of the site.[48] Ten shops were created on the ground floor of the episcopal palace in Pistoia in the fourteenth century, their entrances opening onto Piazza del Mercato (Piazza Duomo) and the streets running beside and behind the palace. Their depth, however, was shallow, leaving for episcopal use a long, narrow storage area at the center of the building (Figure 33).[49]

A more important innovation was the addition of private chapels to episcopal palaces. Although important and wealthy sees — such as Rome and Ravenna — had private chapels from Late Antiquity, there is scant evidence of such domestic sacral spaces in average episcopal residences until the eleventh and twelfth centuries. The chapel of Santa Croce at Bergamo dates from the early eleventh century, and we have reference to a chapel within the episcopal residence at Faenza in 1022. The chapel of

45. Banzola, "Palazzo," 32, 35; *Parma XII*, nos. 696, 819, app. 11, 104.

46. *BCFaenza*, Schedario Rossini, Repertorio Chronologico, August 8, 1269, June 5, 1270, Jan. 17, 1289, April 23, 1289, Feb. 25, 1289; Gary M. Radke, *Viterbo: Profile of a Thirteenth-Century Papal Palace* (Cambridge, 1996), 74–76 and Figure 1.

47. *ASPiacenza*, Archivio degli ospizi civili — Atti privati, busta 2, cartella 5, perg. 17, Nov. 23, 1183, and perg. 26, May 19, 1186; busta 3, cartella 6, perg. 29, Feb. 20, 1194.

48. Dameron, *Episcopal Power*, 154–57.

49. Rauty, *Palazzo*, 1:147–49.

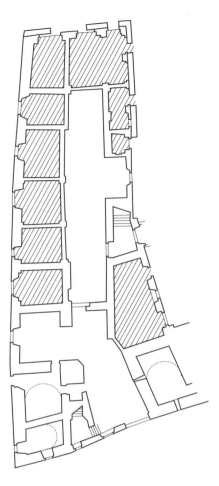

FIGURE 33. *Pistoia, Palazzo dei Vescovi, plan of ground floor of episcopal palace after the addition of shops in the fourteenth century. (C. Ingersoll, based on Rauty*, Palazzo, *149, by permission of the Cassa di Risparmio di Pistoia e Pescia.)*

San Michele, which was on the site the bishop of Como chose for his palace in the early eleventh century, probably served as an episcopal chapel, but it was not renovated and architecturally integrated into the palace until the late eleventh century. There was no chapel at the palace in Parma until Bishop Bernard's additions in the 1170s and no mention of the chapel of San Zeno within the Veronese palace until the time of Bishop Omnebonus's restorations in the 1170s. At Pistoia, the bishop's chapel was not added until about 1170.[50] In sum, by the late twelfth century a chapel within the episcopal palace was the norm. But usually this domestic sacred space was an addition to the basic palace form (tower plus two-storied rectangular building).

The significance and meaning of the addition of these chapels are discussed in a sub-

50. Bergamo: Luigi Angellini, "Scoperte e restauri di edifici medievali in Bergamo alta," *Palladio* 4 (1940): 39–41; Faenza: *AARavenna*, Fondo S. Andrea Maggiore, perg. 11394, Feb. 5, 1021 [1022]; Como: Frigerio and Baserga, "Il palazzo vescovile," 25, 31; Parma: Pelicelli, *Vescovado*, 19; Verona: *ASVerona*, Mensa Vescovile perg. 15, Clero Intrinseco, registro 12 (Ist. Ant. Reg. II), f. 198; Pistoia: Rauty, *Palazzo*, 1: 128–29.

sequent chapter, but for now let the following observations suffice. First, the dominant "old" and "new" spaces added in the expansion of episcopal palaces over the twelfth and thirteenth centuries reflect the two sides of the episcopal office that emerged from the reform era in a tense balance. The hall was the space in which the bishop exercised his secular and ecclesiastical authority; the chapel was a place of personal religious devotion cultivating an image of episcopal spirituality and charisma. Increasingly throughout the twelfth century, the worldly duties of office were represented as in conflict with the spiritual and pastoral — so much so that by the thirteenth century, bishops wishing to decline or resign the office invoked, sometimes with success, the excuse of the damage that its duties would do to their spiritual life.[51] Second, the placement of these two elements within the episcopal palace often attempted to reconcile these two sides of the office. Usually the chapel was directly adjacent to the bishop's great hall. Spatially, this juxtaposition of the worldly and otherworldly attempted to accomplish architecturally what the theologians of the reform movement tried to do intellectually: integrate the exercise of episcopal authority with the sacred foundations of the office, the precepts of scripture.

In addition to expanding spatially, episcopal palaces lost much of their fortified, castle-like appearance over the twelfth and thirteenth centuries and articulated a new architecture of lordly dominion. The heavy, unbroken expanses of wall were opened up with rows of ornamented windows, and decoration enlivened facades. Third stories were often added, bringing the palace into greater visual symmetry with the larger cathedrals constructed in the central Middle Ages. The orientation of episcopal residences shifted outward — from the cathedral and cloister to the piazza — and grand staircases invited entry. In sum, episcopal palaces in the twelfth and thirteenth centuries came to assert a dominion in the urban landscape based more on style and elegance than imposing bulk.

The only exception to this pattern is the Lateran. Its development was exactly opposite that of other sees: it became *more* fortified over the twelfth and thirteenth centuries. When Innocent II renovated the long gallery or "macrona" along the north wall in the mid-twelfth century, he added crenelated towers. Clement III at the end of the century added more fortifications, and in the 1230s Gregory IX not only raised and repaired the walls of the Lateran but also had the towers of some of his closest neighbors demolished. This did not keep the papal palace from being pillaged during the 1234 Roman revolt.[52] Indeed, the growing resistance of Roman families to papal rule made the Eternal City an increasingly dangerous place for the pope to live. As a result, in the late thirteenth century the popes had residences built in Viterbo, Anagni, Orvieto, and Rieti. In the following century they abandoned Italy altogether and took up residence at Avignon.

Note here the relation between fortification and temporal lordship. While the bishops of northern Italian cities were losing secular authority in the wake of the investiture

51. Miller, *Formation*, 174; Robert Brentano, *A New World in a Small Place: Church and Religion in the Diocese of Rieti, 1188–1378* (Berkeley and Los Angeles, 1994), 45–52.
52. Lauer, *Latran*, 174, 181–84, 195.

conflict and the rise of the communes, papal claims to direct dominion over Rome and its environs intensified. Innocent III successfully gained control over the municipal government of Rome, in addition to realizing some of the most expansive claims of earlier theories of papal plenitude. The increasingly unique character and situation of the papacy — both within the church and within European politics — were visually apparent at the Lateran. Its walls grew denser as those of episcopal residences opened up. The new episcopal architecture of dominion enunciated more indirect claims to power.

A key element in this new style was the construction of large, arched windows that broke open the heavy, fortified walls of these palaces. Usually rows of these portals of light were opened along the flanking walls of the great hall. At Como, when the half-wall of the solarium was raised in the late twelfth century, bifores were added, centered over the arches of the portico below (Figure 34).[53] The new facade added by Bishop Grazia in the 1230s to the palace at Parma had a nearly continuous row of trifores on the second floor (Figure 35). The light emitted by these windows certainly changed the character of the interiors beyond them, but the preference for bifores and trifores indicates that ornamentation was prized as much as function. The inner tympanum and the subdivided arches reduce the actual window area considerably in bifores and trifores, but this space was generative: it communicated both wealth and refinement. Each of the eleven trifore windows in Bishop Grazia's facade had two slender columns with capitals of red Veronese marble. The arches above the columns were decorated with multicolored ceramic *patera* that would catch the sun and glisten. The north wing had similarly highly decorated trifores facing in toward the courtyard: the tympanum was painted in tempera with geometric designs, and a diamond design border braces the outer arch (Figure 36).[54] Stucco painted in tempera enlivened the inner edges of windows opened into the bishop's palace at Pistoia in the thirteenth century.[55]

The walls themselves were also decorated, and this ornamentation further diminished the heavy, fortified appearance of the palace. Ceramic *patera* of different designs and colors stud the facade at Parma; besides bringing more variation in color to the wall, the glazed surfaces reflected light to give a shimmering effect that dissolved the wall further. The use of brick, instead of stone, in the twelfth- and thirteenth-century additions to episcopal palaces also offered ways to diminish the heavy character of the walls. Patterns were created by varying the lay and size of the bricks, especially around windows to emphasize their shape and open character. As we saw at Verona, stripes were created by alternating rows of brick with rows of white sandstone. The bishop of Como added a third floor to his palace, with horizontal stripes of black, white, and red stone (see Figure 34).[56]

53. Frigerio and Baserga, "Il palazzo vescovile," 33.
54. Banzola, "Palazzo," 35–37.
55. Rauty, *Palazzo*, 1: 104.
56. Banzola, "Palazzo," 35. Brick and "tufa" (white sandstone) stripes were typical of Veronese Romanesque architecture; see Wart Arslan, *L'architettura romanica veronese* (Verona, 1939). For Como, see Frigerio and Baserga, "Il palazzo vescovile," 42–43.

FIGURE 34. *Como, Palazzo Vescovile, north facade with bifores added in twelfth century and later third floor in striped stone. (M. Miller.)*

FIGURE 35. *Parma, Palazzo del Vescovado, facade. (M. Miller.)*

FIGURE 36. *Parma, Palazzo del Vescovado, decorated trifore, interior courtyard, west wing. (M. Miller.)*

The addition of third stories and the elongation of stories through heightened ceilings used the stature of the building — rather than its imposing mass — to enunciate status. The addition of upper levels seems ubiquitous: at Como, as just noted; at Verona with Bishop Omnebonus's hall; at the Lateran in 1190; at Ravenna and at Pistoia in the early fourteenth century.[57] But our bishops were not alone in this tendency to seek greater space through vertical expansion.

THE ARCHITECTURAL CONTEXT

Cities throughout northern Italy grew at a phenomenal rate over the eleventh and twelfth centuries. Demographic growth and economic expansion gave these cities the character of western "boom" towns: the revival of long-distance trade and the development of manufacturing enterprises drew people into urban centers and fueled construction. The wide-open spaces that characterized the semideserted early-medieval city disappeared, and densely populated suburbs developed along the major roads leading into the town. By the end of the twelfth century, just about every northern Italian city was expanding its walls.[58] Space within the walls became precious and this gave rise

57. Lauer, *Latran*, 181–84; Miller, "Ravenna," 154; Rauty, *Palazzo*, 1: 138–41.
58. J. K. Hyde, *Society and Politics in Medieval Italy: The Evolution of the Civil Life, 1000–1350* (London, 1973), 74–75; *EAM*, s.v. "città," 25–33.

to a new style of domestic architecture. The "casa a schiera," or row house, was a variation of the early-medieval house plan, adapting it to the spatial constraints of thriving urban centers. It was, like its early-medieval predecessor, a rectangular structure of one or more stories; two or three stories were common, with the ground floor devoted to work areas and the upper floors to living space. What was new was its orientation: the short side faced the street and its flanking walls were often shared to create a compact block of houses (Figure 37). Thus, the facade of this "casa a schiera" was a narrow strip in a continuous row of similarly slender facades (Figure 38).[59]

Here is where episcopal residences differed markedly from the other residences surrounding them: they had expansive facades, encompassing usually an entire block. Horizontal extension, more than verticality, communicated claims to lordship. Bishop Grazia's additions to the palace of Parma in the 1230s offer a particularly interesting example of the assertion of this kind of architectural dominion. While Bishop Bernard had added an east wing facing the cathedral, Grazia put a new facade on this wing, widening it by about nine meters (thirty feet) and lengthened about 4.6 meters (fifteen feet) further south (see Figure 55). On the ground floor of this new facade, a graceful vaulted portico was created. Most of the second floor (north end) was devoted to a new great hall that rose one and a half stories in height. The south end of the first floor had a lower ceiling and was used as the bishop's regular dining room, or *mensa*. Another story rose above this, and the extra half-story above the grand hall was devoted to an open-air terrace that allowed the bishop an excellent view out over the piazza.[60]

Even before it was brought to completion, Bishop Grazia's new facade offered a commanding prospect on the piazza. Salimbene de Adam recalled how Brother Benedict, one of the preachers in the spiritual movement known as the "Great Alleluia," used the rising walls as his pulpit. "Quite often," reports Salimbene, "I used to see him standing on the wall of the episcopal palace, then under construction, preaching and praising God."[61] At other points in his narrative, our Franciscan chronicler records the strong impression registered by the palace in the urban landscape. A particularly revealing anecdote is his story of the silver image of the city of Parma that some noble ladies had made and dedicated to the Blessed Virgin, beseeching her to liberate the town from the siege of Frederick II and his allies in 1247. This image, which Salimbene assures us he saw with his own eyes, included "all the major and principal buildings" of the city: the cathedral, the baptistery, the bishop's palace, and the communal palace.[62] A certain grandeur and presence in the city was clearly sought by our bishops. At Parma,

59. *EAM*, s.v. "casa," 355–56; Andrews, "Medieval Domestic Architecture," 6–12; Fabio Redi, "Centri fondati e rifondazioni di quartieri urbani nel medioevo: Dati e problemi sulle tipologie edilizie nella Toscana occidentale," *Storia della città* 52 (1989): 66–70; Laura Zanini, "L'impianto urbano e le case medievali di Priverno," *Storia della città* 52 (1989): 121–26.

60. Banzola, "Palazzo," 35; Pelicelli, *Vescovado*, 25, 27.

61. Salimbene, *Cronaca*, 100–101; trans. Baird, 48–49.

62. Salimbene, *Cronaca*, 283; trans. Baird, 187.

FIGURE 37. *Plan of "case a schiera" (C. Ingersoll.)*

FIGURE 38. *Verona, narrow facades of "case a schiere" in Via Ponte di Pietra. (M. Miller.)*

Bishop Grazia's new facade facing the piazza was the only portion of the building to have three stories.

But it was the length of this new facade that would have been most striking to the medieval viewer. It equaled in length the facade of the cathedral that stood opposite to it, creating a pleasing visual symmetry and balance across the piazza. The expanse of the facade also allowed common forms to be uncommonly deployed. Lesser examples of domestic architecture incorporated trifores and porticos, but within the narrow confines of the strip-facades offered by the "casa a schiera." The vast expanse of Bishop Grazia's facade allowed for a multiplication of these elements, creating a rhythmic series of arches, both in the ground-floor portico and in the windows of the second floor. The open space that spread before the palace was also crucial to the powerful impression of the facade: its expanse and decoration could only be appreciated with the viewer standing at a distance, and the negative space of the piazza enabled the viewer to take in the whole.

The new importance of the piazza is also evident in the orientation of the palaces and the location and emphasis of entrances to them. At Ravenna, the only see where we can trace the continuous development of the episcopal residence across the entire millennium this study traverses, there was a decisive shift in the focus of the complex from the southwest to the southeast side of the cathedral. The fourth-century core of the residence was off the end of the basilica on its southwestern side, and the impressive sixth-century additions still clustered here. In the early Middle Ages, however, two new buildings were added to the southeastern end of the church. Archbishop Felix in the eighth century added a building behind the Neonian baptistery and in the early ninth century, the Domus Valeriana was built farther southeast in line with the flank of the basilica (Figure 39). This addition had a very particular history. After the final suppression of Arian Christianity in the city, Archbishop Valerianus had the residences of his rival, the Arian bishop, dismantled; he used the stone to build this new addition to his own residence. By the thirteenth century, this Domus Valeriana had become the central part of the residence; we know this from the complaints of an archbishop who was dislodged during renovations to it in 1223. The memory of Archbishop Valerianus's triumphant pillaging of stone, however, was erased from the day-to-day invocation of the palace in the Middle Ages, and the building came to be known as the "Palatium Mercurii." This title was taken from the piazza it faced, the "platea mercurii," which was the site of the city's most important market in the Middle Ages. The entrance to the archbishop of Ravenna's palace in the Middle Ages was off this busy piazza.[63]

The main entrance to the palace at Pistoia also shifted from the small courtyard facing the cathedral and canonry to the piazza in front of the cathedral where the city's main market was held. In the late twelfth century when this occurred, the bishops added a decorous stairway that clearly marked this entrance as the main one to the

63. Miller, "Ravenna," 149–68.

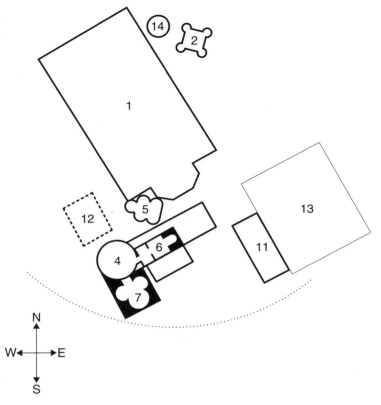

FIGURE 39. *Ravenna, archiepiscopal palace circa 1300. 1 = cathedral; 2 = baptistery; 4 = Salustra Tower; 5 = Bishop Neon's* triclinium, *the "Quinque Accubita"; 6 = chapel of Sant'Andrea; 7 = triconch hall, the "Domus Tricoli"; 11 = "Domus Valeriana" / "Palatium Mercurii"; 12 = tithe warehouse; 13 = "Platea Mercurii" / Piazza Arcivescovado; 14 = bell tower. (C. Ingersoll.)*

palace.[64] Other bishops renovated the entrances to their palaces, paying new attention to these spaces by adding staircases and covered foyers with a high degree of ornamentation. While these changes are treated at length in Chapter 4, let me point out here that the reorientation of the palace toward the piazza and the market should not be read as a decadent embrace of the world at the expense of the spirit. Remember that canons regular and the mendicant orders had claimed the piazza and the market as sites for the work of Christ. The preaching of Brother Benedict in the Great Alleluia, described by our friend Salimbene, took place in the piazza addressed by the entrance and staircase of the episcopal palace.

More important for us here is the cumulative effect of all these changes on the architectural semiotics of the bishop's palace in its urban context. Basically, it went from having the appearance of a feudal stronghold to being an example of what architectural historians call "urban civic architecture." Individual components of this new style — bifores, trifores, porticos, staircases, and other decorative elements —

64. Rauty, *Palazzo*, 1: 106.

were shared with other elite residences. "Case a schiere" incorporated these elements within the limited canvas their slender facades offered. This shared architectural vocabulary of the bishop's palace and other residential structures is important: it signifies that the bishop was a member of a broader community, a townsman among townsmen. His palace did make claims to dominion, but not through the assertion of differences in kind. Rather, it was the multiplication of these common elements across an uncommonly extensive facade that distinguished the bishop's palace. This suggests that the kind of dominion asserted was that of a supercitizen among citizens.

At least partially, this may be due to the local origins of many of the bishops renovating these palaces. While many Italian sees had imperially appointed bishops from beyond the Alps into the late eleventh century, the investiture contest did lead to the resumption of the canonical method of episcopal election by cathedral chapters. In the twelfth and early thirteenth centuries, therefore, it is common to find bishops in the sees of northern and central Italy who had been members of the cathedral chapter and who came from local families. Bishop Tebaldus of Verona, who built the new palace there in the 1130s, had been a cathedral canon and was the first Veronese to hold the see in centuries. Omnebonus, who renovated the palace in the 1170s, and Adelard, who added the "new palace" in the late 1180s, were also from families of the lesser (*capitanei*) nobility from the countryside around Verona.[65] Bishop Bernard of Parma, who first expanded the palace there, was from a local family too.[66] Even when they were not from the city of their see, bishops in this era tended to be from other towns in northern or central Italy. Bishop Grazia, who added the new facade to Parma's palace, was from Florence; Bishop Boniface, who added the chapel of San Siro to Novara's palace, came to the see from the nearby diocese of Pavia; Tedaldus, who was bishop of Piacenza when that see's "new palace" was built, was Milanese.[67] These men understood the sentiments of Italian town dwellers and the significance of local customs and styles.

The expanse of public space before the palace, the broad piazza that allows the viewer to take in this effusive rendering of familiar elements, is critical in articulating the power of the palace's resident. The only other structures in the twelfth- and thirteenth-century Italian city that similarly dominated public space were churches, imperial palaces (in the cities that had them), and communal palaces. These latter are often presented by architectural historians as the fullest expression of the new "urban civic architecture."[68] But, as we have seen, episcopal palaces preceded communal palaces and were articulating elements of this new style as these new urban governments were

65. *Chiese e monasteri a Verona*, ed. Giorgio Borelli (Verona, 1980), 70, 298; Miller, *Formation*, 144–45, 163–70. Treviso follows a similar pattern: *Storia di Treviso*, 2: 360–67, 388.

66. Pelicelli, *I vescovi della chiesa parmense*," 172.

67. Ibid., 190; *L'oratorio di San Siro in Novara: Arte, storia, agiografia tra XII e XIV secolo* (Novara, 1988), 82, 94–95; *Storia di Piacenza, II: Dal vescovo conte alla signoria (996–1313)* (Piacenza, 1984) 2: 365, 370.

68. Wolfgang Braunfels, *Mittelalterliche Stadtbaukunst in der Toskana* (Berlin, 1953), especially 214-15.

forming. The close relationship between bishops and early communal officials suggests that episcopal palaces were the dominant influence on the emergent architecture of the communes. Imperial palaces may have exerted some influence, but not every northern Italian city had an example of royal palatial architecture at hand.[69] Every city, however, had an episcopal palace, and the officials of the early communes knew these buildings intimately: in the decades before the construction of their own palaces, communal officials often conducted their business in their bishop's palace.[70] Not only did communal officials meet within their bishop's palace, but also in two notable cases they took it over. In Piacenza this happened with the agreement of the bishop. By 1171 he had built himself a new palace attached to the new north transept of the cathedral.[71] From this time until at least the second decade of the thirteenth century, the documents of the commune were redacted in the "old palace."[72] In Pavia, the commune's acquisition of the bishop's palace was pursued more aggressively. In 1197 the consuls simply commandeered a house annexed to the episcopal palace and used the site to begin building their palace (probably using some of the bishop's yard or *brolo*). In 1236 Bishop Rodobaldus II sold the main wing of his palace to the commune, and it was incorporated into the communal palace.[73]

Even when they directly appropriated episcopal structures, communal leaders and their architects did develop a dialect of "urban civic architecture" that differed in significant ways from episcopal prototypes. The different forms express different values in the exercise of lordship, and these differences were important. But they were differences of emphasis within a more broadly shared culture of civic discourse.

69. By the late twelfth century in the Po river valley there were imperial palaces at Milan, Ravenna, Pavia, Verona, Ferrara, Lodi, Imola, Parma, Reggio, Bologna, Cremona, and Mantua. Carlrichard Brühl, "Königs-, Bischofs- und Stadtpfalz in den Städten des 'Regnum Italiae' von 9. bis zum 13 Jahrhundert," in *Historische Forschungen für Walter Schlesinger*, ed. Helmut Beumann (Cologne and Vienna, 1974), 411–14; Carlrichard Brühl, *Fodrum, Gistum, Servitium Regis: Studien zu den wirtschaftlichen Grundlagen des Königstrums im Frankenreich und in den fränkischen Nachfolgestaaten Deutschland, Frankreich und Italien vom 6. bis zur Mitte des 14. Jahrhunderts*, 2 vols. (Cologne, 1968) 1: 605–15. Not enough remains of any of these buildings survive to assess their influence on communal architecture.

70. Miller, "From Episcopal to Communal Palaces," 178.

71. *ASPiacenza*, Archivio Diplomatico degli Ospizi Civili di Piacenza, Atti Privati, cartella 4, perg. 6.

72. *Il registrum magnum del comune di Piacenza*, nos. 30, 43, 44, 45, 72, 73, 95, 98, 99, 102, 103, 105, 115, 118, 121, 122, 126, 127, 129, 135, 165, 176, 178, 179, 182, 187, 187, 190, 198, 202, 205, 212, 213, 231, 232, 234, 242, 246, 251, 258, 264, 267, 268. This "old palace" where the commune was conducting its business was definitely the old episcopal palace: no. 95 was redacted "in quadam camera veteris palatii Placentini episcopi," and no. 242 (p. 503) "in veteri Placentino palatio domini episcopi."

73. This reduced the bishop's palace to one wing against the apse of the old Santo Stefano (now obliterated by the Renaissance cathedral). Gaetano Panazza, "Appunti per la storia dei palazzi comunali di Brescia e Pavia," *Archivio storico lombardo* ser. 9, 4 (1964–65): 195–97; *Nella rinascita del broletto: Il comune di Pavia* (Milan and Rome, 1928), 54–55.

The difference that would have been most striking to viewers was the shape of the great hall. An episcopal aula was rectangular, often in a rather elongated fashion. At Parma, the grand new hall in Bishop Grazia's renovated palace was twenty-five meters long, fourteen meters wide (eighty-two feet by forty-six feet). At Como, even after the widening of the hall in the twelfth century, the bishop's aula was about three times as long as it was wide (twenty meters by seven meters, or sixty-six feet by twenty-three feet). More striking still, and indicative of the values behind such elongation, are the parameters of the bishop's hall at Pistoia. Like the hall at Como, its length was over three times its greatest width (thirty-one meters by nine meters, or 102 feet by 29.5 feet). But the width of this hall was not consistent: nine meters (29.5 feet) wide at the end through which a guest would have entered, it narrowed to seven meters (twenty-three feet) at the opposite end of the hall. This narrowing architecturally focused the structure on the position of the lord seated at its culmination. The space at the focal point of the hall, like the special authority vested in the bishop, was not constructed to be shared.[74]

The halls of communal palaces, by contrast, offered greater breadth. Returning to Como, we find that the hall in the commune's palace was exactly the same length as the bishop's hall (twenty meters, or sixty-six feet); but it was over twice as wide (thirteen meters, or forty-two and a half feet as compared to seven meters, or twenty-three feet) (Figure 40). This is typical of the "broletti" of the Po valley: similar dimensions may be found in the great halls of the communal palaces of Novara, Brescia, Cremona, Piacenza, and Padua. The hall of Bergamo's palace approached a true square: it was twenty-six meters (eighty-six feet) long and 23.6 meters (seventy-eight feet) wide.[75] Functionally, such spaces were more inclusive, allowing individuals to arrange themselves in nonhierarchical groupings. Symbolically, these wider rooms communicated the more capacious interpretation of lordship pioneered by the communes. Authority, in this model, was deployed through consensus among relative equals.

The ground floors of communal palaces also communicated different values and a different relationship to public space. In the twelfth and thirteenth centuries, ground floors of episcopal palaces were more open and permeable to ordinary citizens. We have seen how they came to incorporate shops and offer covered porticos that opened to the piazza. But the communal palaces of the Po valley carried this openness to new extremes. They developed ground floors that were arcades, allowing the free flow of foot traffic right through them (Figure 41). Visually, beyond expressing a greater openness to the community, these arcades supporting the hall of the communal officials situated the exercise of governing authority above the piazza without interrupting or inhibiting the ebb and flow of life within it. This configuration of the ground floor also

74. Banzola, "Palazzo," 35; Frigerio and Baserga, "Il palazzo vescovile," tav. II; Rauty, *Palazzo*, 1: 85–86, 2: Figure 7 (for measurements).

75. Federico Frigerio, *Il duomo di Como e il broletto* (Como, 1950), 384, Figure 410B; Robert Douglass Russell, *Vox Civitatis: Aspects of Thirteenth-Century Communal Architecture in Lombardy* (Ph.D. diss., Princeton University, 1988), 36.

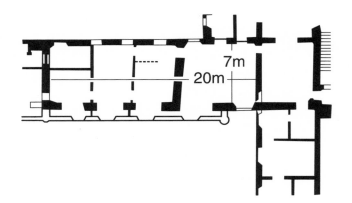

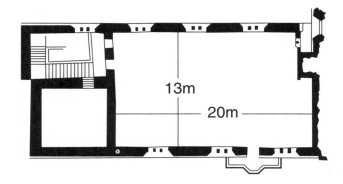

FIGURE 40. *Como, plans of episcopal and communal halls.* (*C. Ingersoll.*)

allowed the communal palace to both dominate and link more public spaces. Episcopal palaces, with their expansive facades, usually delimited one side of an open square and through this horizontality and architectural unity visually dominated the piazza. The open arcades of communal palaces, however, allowed them to jut out into a piazza without closing it off or to link two or three open spaces in the urban center.[76]

In addition to articulating a different kind of urban lordship, the building of communal palaces solidified the place of communal governments within their cities. Before their construction, the juridical gains of these emerging governments could have been erased easily. If Frederick Barbarossa had defeated the Lombard League, northern Italy might have returned to a version of the imperial rule mediated through counts and bishops that characterized the early Middle Ages. If this had happened, the modern visitor strolling around the main piazza of a northern Italian town probably would be admiring the bishop's palace and his cathedral as the city's major tourist sites. But the vic-

76. *EAM*, s.v., "Comune," 246–51; the communal palaces of Bergamo, Monza, Como, and "Il Gotico" at Piacenza are the best examples of the use of the open arcade to dominate and connect plazas.

FIGURE 41. *Bergamo, Broletto. (M. Miller.)*

tory of the communes over the forces of the emperor ensured the bishop's palace a liminal place in the modern "itinerario turistico." That victory turned the tide for the
communes. They gained juridical recognition as their city's legitimate local governments, and they solidified and celebrated that recognition by building their own
palaces.

The building of their palaces gave rise to two different patterns of development
within Italian cities. In the first, two spatially distinct centers of authority — one ecclesiastical and one communal — emerged in the urban landscape. Distinct communal
centers, for example, developed at Bologna, Mantua, Florence, Verona, Padua, Pisa,
and Treviso. The building of these new centers dramatically redefined the topography
of power in the city. In other cities, a unified center of authority developed: the communal palace was built close to the cathedral and episcopal palace — often right across
the piazza. Ravenna's earliest communal palace faced the archbishop's across the "platea

mercurii" (today Piazza Arcivescovado), and the civic palazzi of Bergamo, Brescia, Como, Cremona, Modena, Novara, Pistoia, Ferrara, Rimini, and Reggio were built on the same open space the bishop's palace already dominated.[77]

What factors produced these two very different patterns in the development of urban centers? Urban historians emphasize the free will of communal leaders: the consuls simply chose a location for their *palazzo*. Those who chose a site at some distance from the episcopal precinct, suggests Enrico Guidoni, merely sought a more central location.[78] This may have influenced the citizens of Verona and Parma, whose cathedrals were on the margins of the old city, but the cathedrals of Bologna, Treviso, Mantua, and Padua were quite centrally located.

Consideration of the preexisting topography of power in these cities provides a more reasonable explanation. The most significant factor influencing the siting of communal palaces is the power of the bishop within the city in the precommunal era and his relations with the commune as it emerged. In cities where bishops really exercised comital authority within the walls — as in Brescia, Bergamo, Cremona, Modena, and Reggio — the period of power sharing and cooperation between bishop and commune was long, and one ecclesiastical and civil center developed. In cities where the bishop's authority was limited, particularly by the presence of strong counts — as in Verona, Bologna, Mantua, Florence, and Treviso — the commune's ascendancy was established early, and an independent civic center emerged.

The bishop's lordship, then, was a force in urban development. This force was exerted on the urban landscape through the episcopal palace, where the bishop held court, heard pleas, and received distinguished visitors and the counsel of his vassals. This busy center was, in a political sense, magnetic. The palace attracted to it those who wanted a share in the bishop's power, or if their power was more organized, it kept them at a distance. The important point here is that the bishop's palace was a center of power.[79] Stronger and more determinative in the eleventh and twelfth centuries, it still

77. Jürgen Paul, *Die mittelalterlichen Kommunpaläste in Italien*, Inaugural-Dissertation zur Erlangung der Dokterwürde der Hohen Philosophischen Fakultät der Albert-Ludwigs-Universität zu Freiburg I. Br. ([Cologne], 1963), 42-44; Giancarlo Andenna, "Honor et ornamentum civitatis. Trasformazioni urbane a Novara tra XIII e XVI secolo," in *Museo novarese. Documenti studi e progetti per un a nuova immagine delle collezioni civiche*, ed. Maria Laura Gavazzoli Tomea (Novara, 1987), 52; Francesco Gurrieri, *La piazza del duomo a Pistoia* (Bergamo, 1995), 129; Grazia Gobbi and Paolo Sica, *Rimini* (Rome and Bari, 1982), 38–39.

78. " . . . quando la cattedrale appare troppo decentrata per le esigenze rappresentative e funzionali del comune, questi non esita a distaccarsi dal complesso vescovile, ristrutturando spesso l'antico foro. . . . " Enrico Guidoni, *La città dal medioevo al rinascimento* (Rome, 1981), 75–76. Lewis Mumford seems to assume town halls were always built in marketplaces, and Pierre Racine recently rearticulated this explanation for the location of communal palaces: *The City in History* (New York, 1961), 273; Racine, "Les Palais publics," 138–39. Jones repeats this desire for a central location but also recognizes one "to redirect and orientate public life from the cathedral to the civic complex": *The Italian City-State*, 445.

79. Miller, "Vescovi, palazzi e lo sviluppo dei centri civici," 27–41; for a more detailed development of this interpretation, see Maureen C. Miller, "Topographies of Power in the Urban Centers

continued to be a force to be reckoned with in the thirteenth century and beyond. When Salimbene described that silver image of his city, remember, the bishop's palace is mentioned before that of the commune. The nature of the power that the episcopal palace claimed and expressed changed, but in its more subtle and indirect expressions of authority, it pioneered structures of power that were as enduring as the elite form of representative government the communes developed.

———

of Medieval Italy: Communes, Bishops, and Public Authority," in *Beyond Florence: Rethinking Medieval and Early Modern Italy*, eds. Paula E. Findlen, Michelle M. Fontaine, and Duane J. Osheim (Stanford, 2000).

PART II
CULTURE / POWER
The Character of Space and the Meaning of Actions

The first part of this study took a panoramic view, looking at transformations in the form and character of the bishop's residence over a millennium. Architecture, from this bird's-eye view, registered broad changes in the episcopal office. This second part narrows our vista to the central Middle Ages, to interrogate more closely how space influences meaning. There are a number of reasons to focus on this era. First, our sources, although still difficult, are fuller: documentary evidence is more abundant and physical remains more legible. This allows closer analysis of specific interactions between spaces, ideas, and persons. Second, in the development of the office of the bishop and of the flock he tended, the period from the mid-eleventh to the mid-thirteenth century in Italy was a watershed. The bishop's "people" redefined themselves as a new sort of political community and created new organs of governance, the "commune." Their relationship with their bishop was crucially involved in this transformation, and as a result of these changes the bishop had to redefine his role and place within the urban community. At the same time, new sensibilities about the sacred transformed expectations of the clergy, relationships of power within the church, and the place of the church in medieval society. Closer scrutiny of the bishop's palace sheds new light on all these changes.

First, it challenges us to reconsider the role of bishops in the emergence of the communes. Scholars have acknowledged only begrudgingly the episcopal involvement in this political watershed, and the role they assign bishops tends to be negative and passive: the resistance of bishops to communal rule quickened institutional development, and public rights held by bishops devolved to communal governments. I contend here that the place of the bishop's palace within the urban community and the political uses of its space by both communes and bishops suggest that episcopal lordship was more than a politically expedient way station on the path to the autonomous commune. It was a viable political alternative with a certain appeal and impressive longevity.

Second, the bishop's palace opens a window into clerical mentalities during and after the Gregorian reform. Changes in episcopal architecture and decor reveal the emergence of a distinctive clerical culture emphasizing the power of the sacred and the priesthood's special prerogatives over it. This culture of the clergy is one of the most important results of the reform movement, one heretofore little acknowledged in scholarly discourse. Clerical culture shared themes and forms with lay culture, but its content and references were distinctively ecclesiastical. On the elite level that is our focus, episcopal culture not only distinguished the bishop's authority from that of lay persons, but also constituted both a challenge to and a critique of the power of secular elites.

Finally, aspects of this new episcopal culture attempted to maintain and redefine the bishop's authority as he lost temporal power in the city. The Gregorian imperative to separate the sacred from the profane, while maintaining the appropriate dominance of the former over the latter, resulted in bishops renewing emphasis on their spiritual powers and relying more heavily on them to achieve temporal ends. They developed a set of strategies, early technologies of power, to influence public perceptions and to order, sometimes even coerce, public compliance with ecclesiastical demands. Their attempts to maintain power in civil society, particularly their coercive use of spiritual prerogatives, contributed to the creation of a markedly more repressive church, one that emphasized submission to hierarchical authority over spiritual creativity and compassion.

These themes will be developed and pursued by focusing on particular spaces and the meanings they generated. First we will look at the space around the palace and how it changed in the central Middle Ages: what can it tell us about the place of the bishop in the city? Then we will move within the palace and consider its two most important interior spaces: the hall and the chapel. Both reveal aspects of episcopal lordship. An analysis of the character of these spaces (form, decor) and the actions they framed will reveal the distinctiveness of clerical culture and the new strategies of power bishops devised. Meaning — specifically, a particular image of the bishop and his power — was constructed through the complex interaction of individuals, images, words, music, ritual gestures, and architectural forms. The precise meaning communicated to any one individual is beyond our ken, and certainly different individuals left the bishop's palace with different impressions. As with any complex semiotic performance, the associations and experience individuals brought with them fashioned their responses, as did their reasons for entering the palace and (quite literally) where they stood within it. The Franciscan friar Salimbene de Adam, the heretic Gerard Segarello, and the consuls of Parma did not exit the bishop's palace with the exact same image of the episcopal lordship! But possibilities of meaning present in the *insieme* — in the coming together of images, actions, and spaces — can be reconstructed, and these chapters are dedicated to that pursuit, however partial the results are bound to be.

CHAPTER FOUR:
URBAN SPACE AND
SACRED AUTHORITY

Amodern reader of the life of Saint Lanfranc, bishop of Pavia, might think him a martyr to urban renewal. The saintly biography is dominated by two extended controversies with communal officials over building projects. The first was precipitated by the consuls's demand that the church pay "a huge sum of money" for rebuilding the city walls. When the bishop refused, the commune issued an edict prohibiting any citizen from selling food to him. Lanfranc suffered these trials patiently, "like a martyr for Christ," but was finally forced into exile. "Inspired to visit Rome," the good bishop obtained a papal interdict, a ban on religious services until the city yielded. This, and a few internal political shifts, finally restored peace with the church.[1] The second controversy, however, ended less favorably for the bishop and (literally) hit closer to home: when Lanfranc was taken ill, the consuls came to him demanding that he give over part of his residence — a building used as a stable — for the construction of the commune's new palace. Lanfranc, "faithful guardian and steward of the patrimony of the crucified Christ and Saint Syrus, consumed with the zeal of the Lord," and indignant at their demand that he alienate the goods of the church, "responded with an even voice that their proposal was unacceptable."[2] Despite a valiant defense, the holy bishop lost this battle. The commune took over first this one part, and then, in the thirteenth century, the entire episcopal palace.[3]

The author of this saintly biography clearly locates holiness in the defense of ecclesiastical goods, rights, and privileges. This is not a surprising theme in post-Gregorian narratives. It is significant, however, that episcopal sanctity here is defined in contests concerning urban space — in particular, the space occupied by the bishop's palace. Why was this space so charged? Why was it a focus of communal desires and a site for struggles between civic and ecclesiastical leaders? To understand how the consuls of

---

1. *AASS*, 5 Iunii: 534–35; also in Ughelli, *IS*, 1: 1094–95.
2. *AASS*, 5 Iunii: 536; Ughelli, *IS*, 1: 1095–96.
3. Gaetano Panazza, "Appunti per la storia dei palazzi comunali di Brescia e Pavia," 195–97; *Nella rinascita del broletto*, 54–55.

Pavia came to covet their bishop's palace, we need to follow a series of important shifts in the topography of Italian cities.

The first shift is in the topography of the holy: we will trace how the bishop's seat over the early Middle Ages came to be a prominent locus of the holy, particularly by fostering the cults of their episcopal forbears as the special patrons of the city. This focused civic identity in a particular way on the bishop's see. The second shift is in the physical topography of the town: we will follow how urban growth over the central Middle Ages placed the bishop's church and his residence at the very heart of the urban community. This new physical centrality is a measure of how the cathedral, its patron saint, and its bishop had become potent unifying symbols of the city. The third shift is in political topography: at the same time the bishop's see was being centered, traditional seats of public authority — comital, ducal, royal, and imperial palaces — moved to the margins. In the late eleventh and early twelfth centuries, this usually left the bishop's palace as the only palace within the city's walls. Under his lordship, in his palace, the commune emerged. This political topography is meaningful: bishops acted not just as conduits of public authority to the emergent commune but as new kinds of urban lords. The material setting of the commune's birth suggests that bishops played an active role in the reformulation of city governance. They had a vision of urban ecclesiastical lordship that was infused with the ideals of the Gregorian reform. In the wake of the wars with Frederick Barbarossa and the legitimization of communal governments with the Peace of Constance in 1183, however, our bishops found their vision of urban lordship rejected in favor of the more secular, and less hierarchical, lordship of the lay commune. In the late twelfth and early thirteenth centuries, therefore, bishops had to reconfigure their place in the urban community. They struggled to accomplish this on many levels, but the most visible was in the reconstruction of their residences. As they lost power to the lay governments and the communes began building their own palaces, bishops radically renovated and remade their palaces. The final part of this chapter will explore how bishops repositioned themselves within the urban community through these architectural changes. Hagiographic expressions of this new position also will be examined as we consider the bishop's new place in the Italian city. As the life of Bishop Lanfranc of Pavia suggests, it was sometimes an embattled one. This decentering of the bishop, in the end, had important religious and social consequences.

HOW THE EPISCOPAL CENTER BECAME HOLY

When an eighth-century poet set out to praise the city of Milan, the points of view he adopted were strikingly cinematic.[4] In the opening lines we seem to be hovering over the Po valley as the poet "once upon a times" us to his subject: "In Italy there is a

4. The wonderful observation of Gina Fasoli, "La coscienza civica nelle «Laudes civitatum»," in *La coscienza cittadina nei comuni italiani del duecento*, Convegni del Centro di studi sulla spiritualità medievale 11 (Todi, 1972), 14; see also Elisa Occhipinti, "Immagini di città. Le *Laudes civitatum* e la rappresentazione dei centri urbani nell'Italia settentrionale," *Società e storia* 14 (1991):23–52, especially 26–28.

high and spacious city, solidly built with great industry, which from ancient times is called the city of Milan."[5] As we close in on the great city, the poet praises the bounteous countryside surrounding it and then the mighty walls protecting it. Zooming in closer still we are at and then through one of the city's nine gates. Proceeding at a speed worthy of a Roman cab driver, we arrive suddenly at the old forum and after being given a split second to admire a "beautiful building" there, our poet-driver assures us that the streets are all paved and the baths still functioning. Suddenly we seem to be aloft again, looking down on the city. It is luminous: "gloriously sparkling, ornamented with holy churches."[6]

And now we have really arrived! The rest of the poem abandons visual, topographical description. As if blinded by the white light of those glistening churches, our "vision" is transformed as the poet defines the city's greatness not in terms of its physical characteristics, but through its sacred attributes. Its metropolitan status makes it "queen of cities and mother of the region," its archbishops instructing all in their synodal canons. Charity and love infuse its people, who offer their devotion and wealth at the altars of their churches. The bones and sacred presence of the saints gird and protect the city: Victor, Nabor, and Maternus, Felix and Eustorgius, Nazarius, Simplicianus, Celsus, Valeria, and the "mighty bishop" Ambrose are among its "holy defenders." Psalms and readings ring out through the "happy and blessed" city, its poor and pilgrims clothed and fed.[7]

These copious urban provisions also "maintain the princely power of the Lombards, Liutprand pious king abounding in merits, to whom Christ gave the grace of holiness." But it is Theodore, the city's great archbishop (*magnus presul*), "who embellishes the whole city, coming with bounty, born of a royal seed, whom the people raised to the see out of their love of him."[8] This contrast is telling. King Liutprand is passive: he receives bounty from the city and grace from Christ. It is the archbishop who is noble, who sustains and ornaments the city, and who is loved by its people. Milan, in this poem, is an episcopal city. Christ reigns here through his church. And the rule of bishops creates this idyllic, glimmering Christian Oz, this city of charitable souls resounding with psalms, protected by saints.

In this poem of praise, the earthly space of the city seems to disappear as soon as we encounter the holy. Walls, gates, and plazas recede from view as the poet unveils the true greatness, the true nature of the city. Yet the relationship between urban space and the holy is more complicated than this. Those saints girding about the city are, for the most part, former residents; they are the local holy, who lived and died in this place and whose bones now fortify it, fixed in this place and irradiating it with a larger power. Or they are saints who have chosen to come to this place, allowing their sacred remains to

---

5. *Versus de Verona. Versum de Mediolano civitate*, ed. Giovanni Battista Pighi, Studi pubblicati dall'Istituto di filologia classica dell'Universitá degli studi di Bologna, Facoltá di lettere e filosofia, 7 (Bologna, 1960), 145, lines 1–3.

6. Ibid., 146, line 19.

7. Ibid., 146–47, lines 23–51.

8. Ibid., 147, lines 52–57.

be translated, and whose coming has a specific history that answers local needs, celebrates local triumphs, and contributes to the providential role of *this* city. Another
early-medieval praise-poem, the *Versus de Verona*, locates a series of churches through
its catalog of holy defenders, sketching the sacred topography of the city in a much
more concrete fashion than these Milanese verses. The poet takes us to ten relic-
ladened suburban basilicas whose "most sacred sentries defend you, O happy Verona,
and conquer the iniquitous enemy."[9]

Note where our poets concentrate the holy. Although the bishop and his office are
given a high profile in these early-medieval descriptions of cities, the bishop's church is
virtually absent. The cathedral was not the resting place of confessors and martyrs:
these were in the suburban basilicas ringing the city. Their charismatic presence dominated the sacred topography of the early-medieval town. The bishop was the curator of
these sacred places and of the people entrusted to him. But his center was not a power-
house of the holy. This muted profile is one reason why scholars insisted for so long
that cathedrals originally were located on the periphery and only moved to the center
of the city later. The desire on the part of modern scholars to have holiness and the
center of episcopal ministrations coincide was strong. But bishops before the ninth
century seem relatively untroubled by this disjunction.

They did have themselves buried at the suburban tombs of martyrs and apostles:
Jean-Charles Picard's study of the burial of bishops in early-medieval Italy shows an
overwhelming preference for entombment in suburban basilicas and monasteries that
held the bodies of saints.[10] From the late sixth to the ninth century, for example, just
about all of the archbishops of Ravenna (a total of twenty-three) were buried in the
basilica of Sant'Apollinare in Classe. Many of their beautifully carved sarcophagi still
line the interior of the church. Located a few miles south of the city, Sant'Apollinare
held the body of the first bishop of Ravenna who was believed to have been a disciple of
Saint Peter.[11] In other sees, the early-medieval episcopal tombs were more dispersed. At
Brescia, for example, several seventh-century bishops — Dominator, Paul III, Anastasius, and Dominic — were buried "ad Sanctum Stephanum," a fifth-century basilica on
the hill overlooking the city, but the rest were scattered among suburban churches dedicated to John, Peter, Eusebius, Faustinus, Gervase, and other saints.[12] Bishops chose to
be buried among the holy, but in life they seemed content with the company of their
clergy and people in the cathedral.

This, however, changed in the ninth and tenth centuries. Picard's work reveals two
developments in this period. First, bishops began to have themselves buried in the
cathedral. In Milan, Angilbertus I (d. 823) was the first archbishop to be buried in the
cathedral of Santa Maria, but he was followed in this choice by seven of his successors

---

9. Ibid., 153–54, lines 55–100; and Miller, *Formation*, 17–20.
10. Picard, *Le Souvenir des évêques*, 388–91, 271–325.
11. Ibid., 116, 180–92.
12. Ibid., 228ff and Figure 44.

from Aicho (d. 915) to Gotefredus (d. 979).[13] From the end of the ninth century to the death of Anthony II (before 969), all of the bishops of Brescia were buried in the cathedral.[14] Episcopal burials within the cathedral in this period also occurred at Pavia, Grado, Como, Piacenza, Bergamo, Parma, Verona, and Padua.[15]

Moreover, having abandoned burial at the tombs of apostles and martyrs, bishops began translating relics to the cathedral. Their choices were significant: they brought the bodies of earlier bishops regarded as saints to join their own bones within their church. On April 9, 838, for example, an early bishop of Brescia, Saint Filastrius, was translated to the cathedral by Bishop Rampertus. The event gave rise to a veritable hagiographic dossier which included a copy of a sermon by Saint Gaudentius on the life and death of Filastrius, letters by Saint Augustine mentioning Filastrius's works, an account of the translation, and a song in praise of the holy bishop. Other translations by bishops of their predecessors were accompanied by these attempts to promote the cult of the cathedral's new resident. The translation of the body of the first bishop of Pavia, Saint Syrus, was remarkably successful in this regard. Bishop Donumdei (826–861) installed the saint in the cathedral of Santo Stefano (Pavia had a double-cathedral, the other basilica being Santa Maria), and ever afterwards the church was known as "San Siro."[16] Predictably, for the most prestigious sees, the translation of one saint was hardly sufficient. The decision by Archbishop Peter IV of Ravenna in about 975 to bring the body of Saint Probus to the cathedral led to the "discovery" of a veritable mother lode of episcopal relics. When the canons found the wooden casement that was the resting place of Saint Probus under the altar in the suburban basilica dedicated to him, they were amazed to discover that it also held the remains of bishops Aderitus and Calocerus. Subsequent searching turned up five more early Ravennate bishops! All were newly entombed in the cathedral, the Basilica Ursiana, amidst much rejoicing.[17]

These developments — the entombment of bishops within the cathedral, their translation of saintly predecessors to join them, and the promotion of the cults of these early bishops — combined to raise the profile of the cathedral in the local topography of the holy. This new stature of the episcopal center was related to the changes in the episcopal office and residence we saw in Part I. Bishop Teuzo of Reggio's efforts to translate the body of Saint Prosper to his cathedral will help elucidate these connections.

You will remember that after the Magyars sacked Reggio in 899, killing Bishop Azzo and burning the extramural cathedral of San Prospero, the city's new bishop rebuilt the cathedral and his residence within a section of the old Roman city that had been fortified by the Lombards. This new cathedral, dedicated to the Blessed Virgin, and the

13. Ibid., 98ff.
14. Ibid., 239–47, 359.
15. Ibid., 359–70.
16. Ibid., 211; and Bullough, "Urban Change in Early Medieval Italy," 101–2.
17. Picard, *Le Souvenir des évêques*, 205, 258, 435–36, 638, 648, 661; for other examples, see 596, 603, 646, 663.

new residence were surrounded by new walls, creating a superfortified enclave within Reggio. The political crisis engendered by continuing Magyar incursions allowed the bishops to become de facto rulers of the city. They received several royal grants of rights from beleaguered King Berengar I, and forged several more (asserting comital authority) that were validated as authentic by Otto I in 962. By the late tenth century, the bishops of Reggio were in fact, as well as in law, the temporal lords of the city.[18]

At this same time, a "life" (*vita*) of Saint Prosper was written by an anonymous cleric in Reggio. This is, indeed, the earliest known *vita* of the saint and, in fact, the earliest evidence of any cult devoted to Prosper. The "life" depicts Prosper as converting in response to Saint Paul's preaching, giving all his goods to the poor, and going to Rome. A vision tells Pope Leo I to send Prosper to be bishop of Reggio, and another tells a priest in the city that the new pastor is on his way.[19] Prosper was welcomed by his new flock with joy and he preached a sermon, which the author of this *vita* borrowed from Ennodius's *Life of Saint Epiphanius of Pavia*.[20]

In changing the setting and audience of Ennodius's words, however, our anonymous hagiographer from Reggio gave them new meaning. In the life of Epiphanius, this little sermon is given to his priests and deacons after he has been consecrated. His election to the see was depicted traditionally: although reluctant, the acclamation of people and clergy prevails and Epiphanius is taken to Milan and consecrated.[21] Prosper, however, is sent to his see by God. The Holy Spirit instructs Pope Leo to send Prosper to Reggio, and a sacred vision informs one of the priests in Reggio that Pope Leo is sending a new bishop. The people and clergy of Reggio accept the will of God and acclaim him their pastor.[22] Then, not just to the priests and deacons of the cathedral, but to all the citizens of the city, Saint Prosper begins speaking of "burdens" — his in accepting the office and theirs in living the Christian life. "Divide, oh beloved sons, my burden with me, serving one another in the love of Christ!" the saint exhorts them, "for the burden which many necks bear is easy to carry."[23] In the life of Epiphanius, these sentiments

18. See CHAPTER 2, 64–65, 78–79.

19. *Vita sancti Prosperi episcopi et confessoris* in Camillo Affarosi, *Memorie istoriche del monastero di s. Prospero di Reggio*, 3 vols. (Padua, 1733–46), 3: 16–35.

20. The insight of Golinelli, *Città e culto dei santi nel medioevo italiano*, 155.

21. Ennodius, *The Life of Saint Epiphanius*, ed. and trans. Genevieve Marie Cook (Washington, D.C., 1942), 46–51.

22. Jean-Charles Picard, "Le Modèle épiscopal dans deux vies du Xe siècle: S. Innocentius de Tortona et S. Prosper de Reggio Emilia," in *Les Fonctions des saints dans le monde occidental (IIIe–XI-IIe siècle): Actes du colloque organisé par l'École française de Rome avec le concours de l'Université de Rome «La Sapienza» Rome, 27–29 octobre 1988* (Rome, 1991), 380–81.

23. *Vita sancti Prosperi*, 37–40. Since this eighteenth-century edition is quite rare, allow me to quote the entire sermon here: "Quamvis me fratres carissimi inter primordia suscepte dignitatis judicii vestri grave pondus opresserit. memini tamen quod magna vestre debeam gratie conferre cui Deo volente maxima contulistis. Et licet vobis parendi magis quam jubendi voluntarem habuerim mutavi tamen personam per officium serviendi animum non amisi. Estote ergo caritatis amatores Deum & proximum diligentes. estote humiles estote pacifici estote misericordes estote unanimes, quatinus juxta Apostolorum acta sit vobis cor unum & anima una. quo placidum fuerit jugiter sec-

constitute expressions of solidarity and collegiality with his clergy. But in broadening the audience of these words, our tenth-century hagiographer depicts the holy bishop Prosper as making the survival of the flock a corporate concern, the burden of all the citizens of Reggio, not his task alone. The bishop has a beleaguered tone (even though, in the *vita* he has just arrived!) and seems to want to stiffen his charges for the rough road ahead. This tenth-century life, then, depicts the bishop as providentially sent by God to lead the people of Reggio. He is their "good shepherd," but he positions himself as a man of the people, in need of the help and cooperation (even correction!) of every citizen of Reggio in ensuring the survival of the flock.[24]

Thus constructed, Saint Prosper seems an interesting patron for the late-tenth-century bishops of Reggio. In fostering his cult, they rationalize their recently acquired status as lords of the city by emphasizing the figure of the bishop as divinely ordained to his see. But they soften their dominion — and surely speak to their difficult straits — by giving the community a role in its own salvation. The tone of shared struggle probably reflected the realities of urban life in the late tenth century. And the positioning of the bishop as leader of all the citizens of the town in a struggle for Christian perfection and salvation as well as communal survival set out a compelling ideal of episcopal lordship.

Joined to this text was another narrative recounting a translation of Saint Prosper in the Lombard era. In this story, the saint appears to Bishop Thomas of Reggio in a dream, demanding that the prelate build a new church for him since "barbarian invasions" had rendered his burial place uninhabitable. Note that these themes also have a

---

tantes. Onus meum dilectissimi Filii mecum dividite per caritatem Christi invicem servientes. sit enim sarcina facilis ad portandum qua multorum colla sustentant. speculanum meae conversationis interna etsi aliquid indignum cognoveritis caritate interveniente coercete. Nemo quidem Ecclesie principem ammonere timeat si probet errantem. prophetica namque auctoritate comperimus Sanctissimi Fratres ut unusquisque nostrum ex corde penitens dicat, erravi sicut ovis que periit. & quia juxta prophetam vos populus Domini & oves pascue Christi estis velocius ad observantiam mandatorum currite ut fides vestra non otiosa sed piis operibus per dilectionem pumulata reperiatur. quatinus humeris nostris supportati ad guadia superni gregis q[u]andoque pervenire valeatis."

24. My reading of this life of Saint Prosper defines a *via media* between the opposing interpretations of Paolo Golinelli and Jean-Charles Picard. Golinelli interprets this borrowed sermon from Ennodius as putting forth "the figure of the bishop as father of the city, defender and pacifier of its citizens" ("si propone la figura del vescovo padre della città, difensore e pacificatore dei cittadini"). I see some warrant in the language of the sermon for the depiction of the bishop as father of the city and as pacifier (in the general sense of Christian concord), but *none* for the bishop as defender — and this is the image Golinelli stresses in his subsequent interpretation. I agree with Picard that the text tries to identify the bishop of Reggio with Prosper of Aquitaine and thus stresses the bishop's learning, preaching, and teaching. Picard is also correct that the life does not emphasize temporal actions of the bishop and does not place the saint in the urban topography of Reggio. One should hardly leap, however, as Picard does, to reading this negative evidence as a critique of worldly bishops in the tenth century. In opposing Golinelli's reading, indeed, I think Picard has missed some of the subtleties of the hagiographer's incorporation of Ennodius and the way the text positions the bishop in relation to the "popolo" and "Urbis cunctorum civium mentes." Golinelli, *Città e culto*, 155–56; Picard, "Le Modèle épiscopal," 378–83.

distinct tenth-century feel. Indeed, both these texts — the "life" of Saint Prosper and this translation account — were clearly part of an orchestrated episcopal effort to bring the body of Saint Prosper into the new urban cathedral. The "life" defines Prosper as an ideal patron of the count-bishops of the tenth-century city, and the *Translatio* establishes a precedent for relocating the saint when barbarian invasions trouble his resting place. A new translation did occur in the late tenth century, probably the work of Bishop Teuzo (979–1030).[25]

The translation of holy predecessors into the cathedral church, then, went hand in hand with the propagation of episcopal cults. Long overshadowed as intercessors and objects of veneration by apostles and other "international" saints of early Christendom (the protomartyrs Saint Stephen and Lawrence, for example), local saintly bishops came into their own in the ninth and tenth centuries. The new popularity was not spontaneous; it was the result of the efforts of living bishops.[26] These cults served several, quite earthly, purposes. First, the fact that the promotion of these cults was tied to translation of relics shows that living bishops were not just generally interested in fostering the veneration of their predecessors. They were interested in having them venerated at the cathedral, the church that they presided over. Thus, the propagation of episcopal cults was very much about sacralizing the seat and the power of the living bishop.

Why did bishops feel a need to sacralize themselves and their centers? First, and most obviously, because few of them were reputed to be holy! This had everything to do with the changed character of the episcopal office, the alliance with power bishops entered into in order to guard their flocks. Governing and defending their cities involved bishops in royal administration, in leading armies, and in building fortifications as well as churches — and these activities did not coincide with traditional notions of sanctity (which privileged evangelization, martyrdom, and monastic virtues). Indeed, the very few ninth- and tenth-century bishops who came to be venerated as saints share the characteristics of the new model of episcopal holiness articulated in the translation narratives. Saint Ceccardus, bishop of Luni (d. 892), was "martyred" at Carrara — killed by "barbarians" — while he was procuring marble for the rebuilding of his cathedral. Saint Podius, bishop of Florence (989–1002), was also remembered as a defender of his church: he was chiefly venerated for having built many walls and castles to protect the see and its lands. He was buried in the cathedral, next to Saint Zenobius, who was appointed to the see by Saint Ambrose and considered by some Florence's "first" bishop.[27] But for the great majority of prelates of this era who were not deemed to be saints, the company of holy predecessors in their cathedrals compensated for their increasingly secular profile in the city. By surrounding themselves with holy bishops, they sought to sacralize themselves and their office. And the image of the bishop promoted in these new episcopal cults redefined holiness, locating it in the sorts of challenges

25. The translation was not uncontested; see Golinelli, *Città e culto*, 151–56.

26. Picard, *Le Souvenir des évêques*, 701–11.

27. *AASS*, 3 Iunii: 142–44; 6 Maii: 818–10.

confronting ninth- and tenth-century bishops: the defense of their cities and protection of their people.

Moreover, the burial of holy bishops within the cathedral responded to a very traditional urge: to seek protection in the bones of saints. Both of the early-medieval praise-poems of Milan and Verona describe the cities as protected by the bodies of saints buried in the suburban churches ringing the urban center. The girding of cathedrals with relics through the translation of saints had two very real structural corollaries. First, some cathedral centers — like Reggio, Modena, Piacenza, and Cremona — had been newly enclosed in walls, creating extrafortified ecclesiastical *castra* within the city. Second, as we have seen, bishops were building new highly fortified residences adjacent to their cathedrals. The presence of these newly translated saints brought divine reinforcement to the new episcopal castles just as the relics in suburban basilicas reinforced the city walls.

The translation of saintly bishops into the cathedral and the promotion of their cults correspond with and reinforce the trends in material culture and the development of the episcopal office we have seen in Part I. But what of the choice of bishops to be buried within their cathedrals? Picard relates this to the development of cathedral chapters and changing ideas about salvation. Once chapters were established, the cathedral, like monasteries, had an organized community to offer prayers for the deceased. But this also reveals, Picard argues, that in the ninth and tenth centuries prayers for the deceased were believed to be more crucial to salvation than burial in proximity to the saints.[28] It also seems, however, that bishops in the ninth and tenth centuries sought with their own bodies to reinforce their ties to the sacred space of the cathedral, a space that the canons were coming to view as their own. By having themselves buried within the church and asking the prayers of the canons for their souls, bishops created new ties, both physical and spiritual, with their cathedral. Their burials visually colonized cathedral space: mortuary inscriptions — like that of Bishop Notker of Verona (still visible in Santa Maria Matricolare) — marked their tombs around the church.[29] The burial of a succession of bishops within the cathedral (as at Milan and Brescia) seems some small revival of the visualization of spiritual genealogy that late-antique bishops pursued within their residences.

REFORM AND NEW TENSIONS

Through these episcopal efforts, the centrality of the cathedral in the sacred topography of the Italian town already had been largely secured by the late tenth century. The episcopal promotion of cults in many of these cities over the early Middle Ages had yielded a "patron" saint of the town whose veneration was focused in a particular way at the cathedral: Saint Geminianus at Modena, Saint Terence at Pesaro, Saint

28. Picard, *Le Souvenir des évêques*, 391–92.
29. Miller, *Formation*, 154–55.

Prosper at Reggio, Saint Vigilius at Trent, Saint John at Florence, Saint Donatus at Arezzo, Saint Cassianus at Imola, and Saint Syrus at Pavia.[30] Often the cult of a patron was reaffirmed through the rebuilding and reconsecration of the cathedral after the millennium. Devotion to Saint Geminianus as the patron of Modena, for example, was certainly deepened with the rebuilding of his church.[31]

The reconsecration of a newly rebuilt cathedral also offered the opportunity to add dedicatory saints, and this was another way in which the status of the cathedral as a cult site was reinforced. Many of these new cathedrals were consecrated to the Blessed Virgin. When the bishop of Como moved his see closer to the lake in the eleventh century, he abandoned his church at San Fedele and rebuilt the cathedral, consecrating it to Mary. Padua, Ferrara, and Piacenza also added Mary to their traditional patrons. Dedication to the Blessed Virgin was certainly no radical departure. Many cathedrals — those, for example, at Asti, Cremona, Ivrea, Lodi, Milan, Orvieto, Novara, Parma, Pisa, Siena, and Verona — traditionally had been consecrated to her, invoking the Mother of God as patroness of the "Mater Ecclesia" of the diocese. But for cities without a fervent identification with a particular patron saint in the eleventh and twelfth centuries, the Blessed Virgin offered a perfect devotional focus. She was especially venerated for the protection she afforded, and this was a critical function of the patron saint. And, her cult required no particular relics (although many did appear). Devotion to her flowered in the central Middle Ages, and just as many new churches in northern Europe were dedicated to "Notre Dame," many cathedrals in northern Italian towns achieved particular distinction in the topography of the holy through their dedication to "Santa Maria." Indeed, as Frederick II besieged Parma, the women of the city "besought the Holy Virgin, because her name was held in the highest reverence in the mother church of Parma."[32]

Although the centrality of cathedrals in civic devotion and identity continued to increase as these churches were rebuilt in the eleventh and twelfth centuries, episcopal relations to the holy in this period were complicated by the Gregorian reform movement. A good indicator is another shift in where bishops were buried. From the mid-eleventh century, with the intensification of the reform movement, bishops began supporting — and in many cases, founding — new monasteries outside their cities

30. Hans Conrad Payer, *Stadt und Stadtpatron im mittelalterlichen Italien* (Zürich, 1955); Alba Maria Orselli, *L'idea e il culto del santo patrono cittadino nella letteratura latina cristiana* (Bologna, 1965), reprinted in *L'immaginario religioso della città medievale* (Ravenna, 1985), 5–182; Cosimo Damiano Fonseca, "«Ecclesia matrix» e «Conventus civium»: L'ideologia della cattedrale nell'età comunale," in *La pace di Costanza 1183: Un difficile equilibrio di poteri fra società italiana ed impero*, Milano-Piacenza, 27–30 aprile 1983 (Bologna, 1984), 135–49, but especially 146–49; students may find useful Diana Webb's *Patrons and Defenders* (London, 1996).

31. Golinelli, *Città e culto*, 74 and Figure 5; on church building and episcopal cultivation of civic patriotism, see Annamaria Ambrosioni, "Gli arcivescovi di Milano e la nuova coscienza cittadina," in *L'evoluzione delle città italiane nell'XI secolo*, 193–222.

32. Salimbene, *Cronaca*, 283; trans. Baird, 187.

dedicated to a strict observance of the Benedictine rule. They also chose to have themselves buried in these reformed institutions. When Archbishop Gebhard of Ravenna died in 1044, he was buried in the choir of the monastery of Pomposa. This ancient monastery was particularly respected for the rigor of its adherence to the Benedictine rule and its ties to the reform movement; it was guided at the time of Gebhard's death by Abbot Guido of the Strambiati, venerated after his death in 1046 and later canonized. The prelates of Milan from Landulf II on preferred the reformed monasteries of San Celso and San Dionigi (both episcopal foundations, the latter restored, reconstructed, and reformed by Archbishop Aribert, 1018–45). In 1056, Bishop Rainaldus of Pavia was laid to rest in a monastery that he had founded in the suburbs dedicated to Saint Apollinare.[33]

This change in episcopal preferences for burial signals another important shift in the bishop's relation to the holy. Although the reform movement recognized the importance of the episcopal office and its pastoral work in bringing about reform, the character of the spirituality praised by the reformers was fiercely monastic.[34] It emphasized contemplation, solitude, and retreat from the world. One way, in fact, that bishops brought about reform was by raising the standards of monastic life at institutions within their dioceses and founding new monasteries dedicated to a stringent interpretation of the rule. This reaffirmation of the primacy of the monastic life and monastic virtues, however, made their own pursuit of holiness more vexed. Defending and protecting their cities and churches had deeply involved bishops in terrestrial structures of power. How could they administer the estates that supported their churches, give the emperor his due for his past and future benefactions, and cultivate monastic virtue?

The life of Saint Maurus, bishop of Cesena, shows the difficulties this posed. Written by the reformer Peter Damian, the *vita* of Maurus tries to articulate a workable model of episcopal holiness in the Gregorian age. But tensions are obvious throughout the text. Before describing Maurus's life in the see, in fact, Peter gives us explicit instructions as to how we are to interpret it: "Certainly, while neither following the leisure of contemplative life, abandoning all activity, nor running away to free himself from the fatigue of activity, withdrawing to contemplation, as I will tell you, he achieved the glorious golden mean of the celestial kingdom." This "golden mean," however, has a curiously schizophrenic quality. Maurus "governs his church vigorously" and then goes off by himself to pray. "By day he preached throughout the city, by night he pursued prayer on the mountain [Mount Spaziano]." Even glancing at the hills in the distance restored him as he bore up under the great cares and anxieties of his

33. Picard, *Le Souvenir des évêques*, 193, 107–8, 384; Mario Salmi, *L'abbazia di Pomposa*, 2nd ed. (Milan, 1966); Giovanni Tabacco, "Vescovi e monasteri," in *Il monachesimo e la riforma ecclesiastica (1049–1122)*, Atti della quarta Settimana internazionale di studio, Mendola 23–29 agosto 1968 (Milan, 1971), 105–23; Fonseca and Violante, "Cattedrale e città," 12–13.

34. Augustin Fliche, *La Réforme grégorienne*, 3 vols., Spicilegium sacrum Lovaniense, Études et documents 6, 9, 16 (Louvain and Paris, 1924–37), 1: 39–60, 75–77, 256–64; Blumenthal, *The Investiture Controversy*, 64–70; Constable, *The Reformation of the Twelfth Century*, 257–95.

office. He spends Lent in a little cell on Mount Spaziano, giving himself over to fasts and prayers: "and if he went to that little cell when he was able to steal away from ecclesiastical affairs, he was restored as if he had been at a banquet of sweet dishes." After death Bishop Maurus was buried at this retreat.[35] Peter's descriptive prose, in the end, gives us a better sense of Maurus's life as a hermit than his life as a bishop.

The model achieved greater balance in the reformed hagiography of the early and mid-twelfth century. Most of the holy bishop's monastic life in these narratives comes as the prelude to his episcopal career. Saint Bernard of the Uberti, bishop of Parma (1108–33), joined the Vallombrosian congregation at the monastery of San Salvi as a youth and rose to be abbot of the community before he answered a papal call to go to Parma.[36] John Cacciafronte entered the monastic life at age sixteen and rose to be prior of San Vittorio and then abbot of San Lorenzo (both near Cremona) before his episcopal career in Mantua and Vicenza.[37] Saint Ubaldus, bishop of Gubbio (1129–60), although educated at the city's cathedral, turned down the opportunity to enter the canonry there "because he saw that they served no religious rule and he took himself to the church of San Secundo, where he lived most virtuously for some time." Ubaldus later returns to reform the canonry. Ascetic habits and monastic interludes still crop up: Ubaldus eats and speaks sparingly, mortifies his flesh, and "frequently retreats to solitude at [the reformed monastery of] Fonte Avellana."[38] But the worldly challenges of

35. Peter Damian, *Vita sancti Mauri episcopi Caesenatis et confessoris*, cap. I in *PL*, 144: 946–48. Damian's brief life of St. Rodulphus, bishop of Gubbio, is even more unbalanced: all but two lines are given over to a description of Rodulphus's monastic life and ascetic practices. The only allusion to episcopal duties is a mention of him holding an annual synod: *Vita sancti Rodulphi episcopi Eugubini* in *PL*, 144: 1011–12. Paolo Golinelli has perceptively noted and explored this tension in Damian's hagiography between the assertion of a moderate, or "discreta," sanctity and the description of ascetic extremes: "Indiscreta Sanctitas" in *Indiscreta Sanctitas. Studi sui rapporti tra culti, poteri e società nel pieno medioevo* (Rome, 1988), 168–69. Monastic virtues also figure strongly in the lives of the great reformer Bishop Anselm II of Lucca: Edith Pásztor, "La «vita» anonima di Anselmo di Lucca. Una rilettura," in *Sant'Anselmo vescovo di Lucca (1073–1086) nel quadro delle trasformazioni sociali e della riforma ecclesiastica*, ed. Cinzio Violante (Rome, 1992), 210–14.

36. There are three lives of Bernard: I and II are published in *MGH SS*, 30/2: 1314–27; and III in *Chronica Parmensia a sec. XI. ad exitum sec. XIV*, ed. Luigi Barbieri (Parma, 1858), 491–96. All depict his monastic life as a prelude to his episcopal career: *MGH SS*, 30/2: 1316–17, 1324–25; *Chronica*, 491–92.

37. *AASS*, 2 Martii: 486.

38. François Dolbeau, "La vita di Sant'Ubaldo, vescovo di Gubbio, attribuita a Giordano di Città del Castello," *Bollettino della Deputazione di storia patria per l'Umbria* 74 (1977): 97–98 (7.1–8.3), 102 (16.1), 104 (19). This life by Giordanus, prior of the cathedral of Città del Castello and a contemporary of Ubaldus, is considered the earliest; Ubaldus's successor in the see, Bishop Tebaldus, wrote a somewhat fuller life, incorporating most of Giordanus's text. Tebaldus's life is in *AASS*, 3 Maii: 628, 630. The monastic life as preparation for the episcopal office is one of the characteristics Pierre Toubert notes in the hagiographic ideal of the Gregorian bishop in Latium: *Les Structures du Latium médiéval; Le Latium méridional et la Sabine du IXe siècle à la fin du XIIe siècle*, 2 vols. (Rome, 1973), 2: 812–14; see also Anna Benvenuti Papi, *Pastori di popolo: Storie e leggende di vescovi e di città nell'Italia medievale* (Florence, 1988), 188–90. The hagiography of imperial bishops in the same period did not share this monastic emphasis: Paolo Golinelli, "Negotiosus in causa ec-

the episcopal ministry are more prominently and realistically portrayed in these twelfth-century lives.

These holy bishops actually had to travel farther and farther out of their cities to find monastic solitude. The reformed houses they founded and the burial sites they chose tended to be miles beyond the suburban basilicas that were the powerhouses of the holy in Late Antiquity and the early Middle Ages. Archbishop Aribert of Milan's reformed monastery of San Dionigi was only brought within the city walls in the Renaissance; Sant'Ambrogio was within the walls at the end of the twelfth century.[39] This is because the eleventh and twelfth centuries saw more than reform. The era saw prodigious urban growth in northern Italy, which brings us back to topography and the bishop's see.

HOW THE EPISCOPAL CENTER BECAME CENTERED

To the see's centrality in the topography of devotion, urban growth during the eleventh and twelfth centuries added a visible, physical centrality in the city's layout. Some cathedrals had originated in the centers of the old Roman towns, and they remained centrally located as the city expanded in the eleventh and twelfth centuries. Milan, Pavia, Padua, Faenza, and Bergamo are good examples of this continuity. More commonly, as we have seen (see Chapter 1), the cathedral arose on the margins of the Roman city. Subsequent development, however, over the early and central Middle Ages, tended to centralize the bishop's church. A dramatic example is Modena. The site of the Roman city flooded and became swampy in the fifth and sixth centuries. The population shifted and reconstituted the "city" around their bishop and cathedral, which had been located just outside Roman Mutina on the Via Emilia.[40] Usually, however, it was the growth of the eleventh and twelfth centuries that centered the cathedral. On the Roman grid of Brescia, the cathedral complex was in the southwest quadrant, close to the western wall. Just outside of this wall, along the road leading to Milan, was where the city expanded in the eleventh and twelfth centuries. The communal walls built in the late twelfth century, in fact, follow the line of the old Roman walls on the east and south; the new area they enclosed was the western suburb outside the Porta Mediolanensis. After this expansion, the cathedral was just slightly west of the exact center of the area enclosed by urban walls (Figure 42).[41] The more rapid expansion of Cremona in this period to the north and

---

clesiae: Santi e santità nello scontro tra impero e papato da Gregorio VII ad Urbano II," in *Les Fonctions des saints dans le monde occidental (IIIe–XIIIe siècle)*, Actes du colloque organisé par l'École française de Rome avec le concours de l'Université de Rome «La Sapienza», Rome, 27–29 octobre 1988 (Rome, 1991), 278–79.

39. On bishops and reformed monastic houses, see Tabacco, "Vescovi e monasteri," 105–23.

40. Golinelli, *Città e culto*, 28–33; *Modena: Vicende e protagonisti*, ed. Giordano Bertuzzi, 3 vols. (Bologna, 1971), 1: 62 (maps).

41. *Storia di Brescia*, ed. Giovanni Treccani degli Alfieri, 5 vols. (Brescia, 1963–64), 1: map between 1104 and 1105.

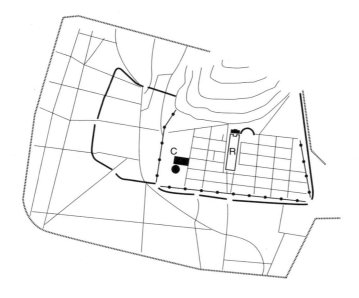

C cathedral group
R Roman forum
Roman walls
12th-century walls
mid-13th-century walls

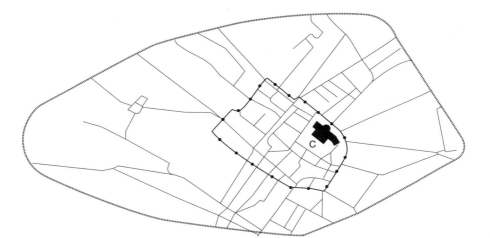

C cathedral group
early medieval walls
12th-century walls

FIGURE 42. (TOP) *Brescia, urban expansion and centering of the cathedral. (C. Ingersoll.)*
FIGURE 43. (BOTTOM) *Cremona, urban expansion and centering of the cathedral. (C. Ingersoll.)*

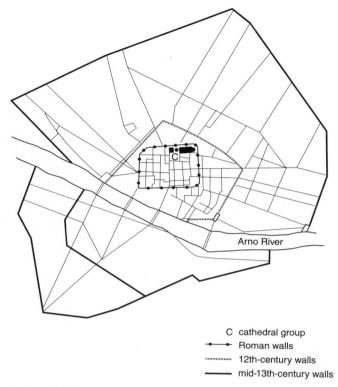

C cathedral group
Roman walls
12th-century walls
mid-13th-century walls

FIGURE 44. *Florence, urban expansion and centering of the cathedral. (C. Ingersoll.)*

west also worked to centralize the cathedral group (Figure 43).[42] Probably the most familiar example of this process, however, is Florence. The cathedral of Santa Reparata was located right against the north wall of the Roman city. Although the first communal expansion of the walls in 1172 extended only slightly farther north, the second expansion in the late thirteenth century placed the cathedral at the exact center of the city (Figure 44).[43]

42. Agostino Cavalcabò, "Le vicende dei nomi delle contrade di Cremona," *Bollettino storico cremonese* 3 (1933): map between 140 and 141.

43. *Il bel San Giovanni e Santa Maria del Fiore: Il centro religioso di Firenze dal tardo antico al rinascimento*, ed. Domenico Cardini (Florence, 1996), especially 31; Frank Sznura, *L'espansione urbana di Firenze del dugento* (Florence, 1975), 91, 95–96; an excellent map of the expansion of thirteenth-century Florence may be found in Carol Lansing, *The Florentine Magnates*, 6–7. There are exceptions to this trend: in Pisa, Turin, Verona, Rimini, and Asti the cathedral remained eccentrically located. Neither Asti, Turin, nor Rimini experienced the sort of suburban expansion characteristic of the cities of the Val Padana and Tuscany. At Pisa and Verona, rivers influenced the direction of urban expansion and, as a result, their cathedrals remained decidedly off-center.

The episcopal residence shared this central location at the heart of the medieval city. This conjunction of spiritual, temporal, and physical centrality was quite potent. It crystallized the several roles that bishops had claimed for themselves in most cities by the early eleventh century: charismatic leader, temporal lord, symbol of unity, and guardian of both civic and spiritual destinies. So successful were bishops in establishing their seats as the spiritual and physical centers of their cities, that other competing seats of power moved to the margins. As Carlrichard Brühl's exhaustive research has demonstrated, "by around the year 1020, at Rome, Milan, Ravenna, Verona and Lucca — that is, in cities very important and often visited by sovereigns — the imperial palace was located outside the city walls."[44] The Carolingian preference for *Klosterpfalzen*, palaces within a monastery or convent, certainly contributed to the movement to the suburbs. But such transferences continued throughout the eleventh century, and these cases indicate a popular animosity toward imperial seats within the walls. When the citizens of Pavia heard of the death of Emperor Henry II in July of 1024, "they destroyed the entire palace down to the very foundation stone, lest any future king decide to put a palace within that city."[45] The Pavians withstood an imperial army's attempts to enter the city to rebuild the palace; they held firm even as the emperor's forces devastated the surrounding countryside and blocked navigation on the Po.[46] The imperial palace at Bologna also was destroyed by its citizens, an act only revealed in the document recording the city's "reconciliation" with Henry V. The reconciliation did not involve the rebuilding of the palace.[47] Imperial documents also record more peaceful accords concerning the relocation of royal seats. In a diploma of 1081, Henry IV reaffirmed to the citizens of Lucca that no royal palace would be built within the city walls, and Henry V in a 1114 privilege to the Cremonese conceded "that we have hereafter our palace and reception outside the walls of their city."[48] A diploma two years later to the citizens of Mantua gave them "power of destroying the palace and all its fortifications and removing it outside the city to the suburb of Saint John the Evangelist."[49]

Ducal and comital residences also were beyond the walls. Lucca's was outside the

44. Carlrichard Brühl, " 'Palatium' e 'Civitas' in Italia dall'epoca tardo-antica fino all'epoca degli Svevi," in *I problemi della civiltà comunale, Atti del Congresso storico internazionale per l'VIIIo centenario della prima Lega Lombarda (Bergamo, 4–8 settembre 1967)*, ed. Cosimo Damiano Fonseca (Milan, 1971), 161; Carlrichard Brühl, *Fodrum, Gistum, Servitium Regis: Studien zu den wirtschaftlichen Grundlagen des Königtums im Frankenreich un in den fränkischen Nachfolgestaaten Deutschland, Frankreich und Italien vom 6. Bis zur Mitte des 14. Jahrhunderts*, 2 vols. (Cologne, 1968), 1: 485–90.

45. Wippo, *Vita Chuonradi* c. 7, in *MGH SS*, 11, 263; Arrigo Solmi, *L'amministrazione finanziaria del regno italico nell'alto medio evo* (Pavia, 1932), 187.

46. Solmi *L'amministrazione finanziaria*, 189.

47. Brühl, *Fodrum, Gistum*, 1: 493–94; Alfred Hessel, *Storia della città di Bologna dal 1116 al 1280*, ed. Gina Fasoli (Bologna, 1975), 29–30.

48. *MGH DD*, 6 no. 334; *Carte Cremonesi*, no. 262; Brühl, *Fodrum, Gistum*, 1: 493–94; Brühl, " 'Palatium' e 'Civitas,' " 161–62.

49. *Reg. Mantua*, no. 170.

Porta Donati, Turin's just beyond the Porta Doranea.[50] Although the seat of the counts of Pisa was probably at the center of the early-medieval city at "Cortevecchia," by the early eleventh century the judicial hearings of the March of Tuscany were being held just outside the western walls on the Arno.[51] Similarly, Verona's counts had abandoned their urban residence at Cortalta by the late tenth century. During Bishop Ratherius's last sojourn in the city, they had taken up residence across the Adige in the *castrum* and the San Bonifacio in the eleventh century preferred their castles in the countryside. While a *placitum* of 913 was held " in the city of Verona, at the house that was the well-remembered Count Vualfredus's," those of the eleventh century were held either at the bishop's *domus*, at the imperial residence outside the walls at San Zeno, or as in 1073 when Count Boniface himself presided, in the count's *curtis* in the village of Illasi.[52] In Asti by the early tenth century, the counts heard pleas "in a suburb of the city of Asti, not far from the church of San Secundo . . . in the place where once there was a ducal court." This was the site of the old Lombard ducal residence, southeast of the city. Meanwhile, the bishop held the *castrum vetus* within the city: this was the fortified comital residence built by the Carolingians.[53]

Historians usually attribute this relocation beyond the walls of residences representing imperial power to the emergence of the commune. Indeed, it is undoubtedly evidence of popular stirrings toward self-governance within northern Italian towns. And, certainly, the political regimes we call "communes" were the ultimate development of these sentiments. But I suggest that we abandon the usual teleological view for a moment. Imperial, ducal, and comital palaces were out of the urban center in the second half of the eleventh century. Communal palaces were not built until the closing decades of the twelfth century or the early thirteenth. For about a century then, and in some towns even longer, the only "palace" in the city was the bishop's. If the transference of imperial palaces outside the walls is read by historians as a politically significant movement (as it is), and if the building of the "broletti" is also celebrated as the coming of

50. Isa Belli Barsali, "La topografia di Lucca nei secoli VIII–XI," in *Atti del 5o Congresso internazionale di studi sull'alto medioevo*, Lucca 3–5 ottobre 1971 (Spoleto, 1973), 509–10; Vito Tirelli, "Il «palatium» a Lucca fino al sec. XIII," in *Il palazzo pubblico di Lucca: Architetture opere d'arte destinazioni*, Atti del Convegno, Lucca 27–28 ottobre 1979, ed. Isa Belli Barsali (Lucca, 1980), 10; Stefano A. Benedetto and Maria Teresa Bonardi, in "Lo sviluppo urbano di Torino medievale," *Paesaggi urbani dell'Italia padana nei secoli VIII–XIV* (Bologna, 1988), 134.

51. Gabriella Garzella, *Pisa com'era: Topografia e insediamento dall'impianto tardoantico alla città murata del secolo XII* (Naples, 1990), 59–60, 84–86.

52. Manaresi, *Placiti*, nos. 125 (*civitate Verona, ad casa qui fuit bone memorie Vualfredi comiti*), 128 (urban church of Santa Maria Antiqua), 170 (at the suburban monastery of Santa Maria in Organo), 218, 240, 267, 299, 320 (at the episcopal residence), 277, 326, 355, 440, 441, 442, 449, 460 (suburban imperial palace at monastery of San Zeno), 335 (at house within city of the Archdeacon Azeli — Count Tado presiding), and 423 (*in comitatu Veronensi in vico Illas in curte propria in vescopado*).

53. Manaresi, *Placiti*, no. 137; Renato Bordone, *Città e territorio nell'alto medioevo. La società astigiana dal dominio dei franchi all'affermazione comunale*, Deputazione subalpina di storia patria, Biblioteca storica subalpina 200 (Turin, 1980), 14–15, 31, 168–69.

age of the communes (as it is), then shouldn't we read the centrality of the bishop's palace in the late-eleventh- and twelfth-century city as *politically* meaningful? Obviously, we should.

I do not intend any radical reinterpretation of the emergence of the communes here, just a shift in perspective. For decades now, historians have acknowledged the prominent role that bishops played in the early development of communal governments. Lay leaders, however, are still always the central actors in these historical narratives. Bishops, at best, are depicted as assisting or reluctantly cooperating with them. "Already in 1105," writes Augusto Vasina, the commune of Ferrara "was functioning along side the new bishop Landolf." A consul named Ubertus represented the commune "together with the bishop" when Pope Pascal II issued a privilege in that year. In fact, the pope directed the document to Bishop Landolf, first, and then to Ubertus and two of his colleagues.[54] The reforming bishop of Brescia, Arimmanus, is described as being in solidarity with the commune, but the author reminds us, "it was a solidarity imposed by political circumstances, inspired by convenience. . . ."[55] This kind of language is the heritage both of modern Italian antipathies toward the church and of a more general tradition of history written from the point of view of the winners. The lay communes did, indeed, win. But the centrality of episcopal palaces in the topography of these cities, and the great energy and force with which these very same bishops pursued political programs — papal or imperial — during the late eleventh and early twelfth centuries, suggest that they were hardly passive companions on the road to communal independence.

The very invocation of the word *palatium* to designate their residences is evidence of an episcopal bid for a new kind of lordship. This "speech act" was not lost on the citizens of Parma. Their bishop was the very first to invoke this imperial word; but then he rebuilt his residence — and the cathedral — outside the Roman walls. Given the violent insistence of the citizens of other cities that imperial palaces move outside the walls, and given the bishop of Parma's close ties with imperial authority, it seems likely that public opinion had much to do with the bishop's relocation. But Parma was the only see in which the episcopal palace was beyond the walls (and even in Parma, the relocation of the cathedral and urban growth soon centralized the bishop's abode). As the century progressed and other bishops began invoking the term, episcopal claims to

54. " . . . risulta attestata e operante accanto al nuovo vescovo *Landolfo* . . . la magistratura collegiale dei consoli: dapprima rappresentata nella persona di un *Ubertus consul*, destinatario assieme al vescovo cittadino e ad altri notabili di un privilegio di papa Pasquale II . . . " Augusto Vasina, "Comune, vescovi e signoria estense dal XII al XIV secolo," *Storia di Ferrara*, 5 vols. (Ferrara, 1987), 5: 76; "Paschalis episcopus, servus servorum Dei, venerabili fratri Landulfo Ferrariensi episcopo, Guillelmo filio Bulgari, Petro filio Arimundi, Uberto consuli, et per eos tam Ecclesiae quam civitati Ferrariae, in perpetuum." *PL*, 163: 159 (no. 152).

55. "É una solidarietà, s'intende, imposta dalle circostanze politiche, ispirata dal convenienza . . . ," Alfredo Bosisio, "Il comune," *Storia di Brescia*, 1: 587. Philip Jones goes somewhat further and sees the commune intentionally using a "condominium" with the bishop as "a mask for revolution, an expedient or subterfuge"; Jones, *The Italian City-State*, 141. Later (335) in the same work, however, Jones acknowledges the longevity of these condominia, some traces lasting into the thirteenth century.

lordship probably looked markedly less threatening to urban autonomy than other possibilities — and it may even have seemed a compelling model of public order.

By this, I mean that we should not discount the religious sensibilities of urban dwellers. These were the same people who boycotted the services of concubinous clerics and, in some cities, violently cast out simoniacal bishops. They generously supported, through alms and donations, new reformed religious institutions and the rebuilding of their cathedrals. The insistence of reformers that the sacred took precedence over the temporal surely had some resonance among common people. And it was this basic idea that fueled Gregorian politics. The emperor may rule in this world, but if he wanted eternal life even he had to follow the precepts of prelates. This view of the order of things translated easily to urban governance. The administration of worldly matters was appropriate to laymen, but their bishop had care of their souls. His involvement in public life was necessary, and the primacy of his concerns (eternal life) over the temporal sphere of the consuls was probably accepted with little debate. Reform ideals also facilitated lay acquisition of governing faculties as the separation of the sacred from the profane was a powerful theme within the movement. Bishops, remember, had entrusted many of the temporal rights they held to a special official: the *vicedominus*. At first a high-ranking cleric from within the bishop's household or the cathedral canonry, over the eleventh century this office was entrusted to a layman. Often it became hereditary, creating a powerful family tied to the see and its patrimony. Such arrangements were what allowed Saint Maurus to run off to his little cell on the mountain!

The kind of lordship bishops offered their cities at this juncture was unifying on many levels. The sacred could suffuse all things; Christian values were meant to inform all acts. Regular preaching reinforced this view. The cathedral, the city's "mater ecclesia," brought together the entire Christian community, seen as coterminous with the civic community. Thus was the urban baptistery increasingly a focus of civic sentiment and new architectural extravagance in the communal age: all urban dwellers — from beggars to artisans to wealthy merchants — entered the Christian community at this font. They came under the bishop's purview as they were claimed for Christ through baptism.[56] The unifying force of the bishop's lordship, however, went well beyond the sacraments — and the urban walls. Over the early Middle Ages, particularly through royal and imperial donations, bishops had amassed substantial rural patrimonies. These estates were granted as "benefices" (*beneficium*) — fiefs, really — to armed retainers, and a whole class of lower nobles emerged around the bishop. They formed the bishop's court — sometimes called the *curia vassallorum* or the *curia parium* — and this community of feudal notables met in the bishop's palace. Moreover, in the eleventh and twelfth centuries it integrated urban and rural interests. New families who had made money in trade and who aspired to social distinction matching their wealth became episcopal vassals, receiving lands and interests in the countryside. The rural nobility, through attendance on their lord the bishop, were also brought

56. *EAM*, s.v. "battistero," 3: 233–38.

into the orbit of urban commerce and values. Some of them acquired houses in the city.[57]

It was, then, really not so odd to see "consuls" appear in these gatherings in the bishop's great hall. The first appearance of consuls — these earliest officials of communal government — was often in the bishop's palace, in his curia. Let us visualize this scene well. The bishop was not "alongside" or "acting with" the consuls; he was presiding over a diverse assembly of local elites. Remember the geometry of the bishop of Pistoia's hall: it was long and it narrowed at the end where the bishop sat. Although historians are fond of characterizing the bishop's relationship with the early commune as a "condominio," a sort of shared agreement among legal equals, the spatial semiotics of this relationship are quite different. The bishop was the one with the palace. He presided in his hall as he presided in his cathedral. No contemporary would have confused him as an "equal." This is not to denigrate the power of the oath-bound alliances of lay elites that were the "communes." Economically, administratively, and, as time went on, juridically, they were very powerful. But power also resides in beliefs, images, and physical relationships. Material culture reminds us of this power in the unsaid and the unwritten: literally, of where one stands in relation to another.

The buildings they were standing in were also powerful. During the formative age of the early commune, when the bishop was a key constituent and often representative of its claims to independence, the palace was a heavily fortified castle-like structure. Its name had changed, but the structure was the traditional tower and two-story rectangular building that emerged in the early Middle Ages. Its architecture was that of force, of readiness for battle and siege. This is, indeed, at least one reason why lay elites would not have mistaken their involvement with the bishop for chummy collegiality. The bishop's place was unmistakable: his was the armed fortress at the heart of the urban center. This architectural profile did change. But the chronology of these changes is worth pondering.

Parma offers a particularly clear and well-documented example. Its bishops held, in addition to a large patrimony, *districtus* over the city from 879. This grant of public authority was widened under the Ottonians to include a significant swath beyond the walls, the *territorium civitatis*. In 1020, the bishop's residence is first called a "palace." In 1029, Emperor Conrad II gave another privilege to the see, bringing the entire county under the bishop's lordship. Sometime before 1055, the bishop built his new palace and began work on the new cathedral. Over the second half of the eleventh century, the cit-

57. Ovidio Capitani, "Città e comuni," in *Storia d'Italia*, ed. Giuseppe Galasso, vol. 4: *Comuni e signorie: Istituzioni, società e lotte per l'egemonia* (Turin, 1981), 14–15, 18–21; Tabacco, *Struggle for Power*, 326–30; Jones, *The Italian City-States*, 81–82, 104–7, 147–50, 298–305; Cinzio Violante, *La società milanese nell'età precomunale* (Rome and Bari, 1981), 170ff; Hagen Keller, *Adelsherrschaft und städtische Gesellschaft in Oberitalien 9. Bis 12. Jahrhundert* (Tübingen, 1979), 251–302; Pierre Racine, "Évêque et cité dans le royaume d'Italie," *Cahiers de civilisation médiévale* 27 (1984): 129–39; Pierre Racine, "Città e contado in Emilia e Lombardia nel secolo XI," in *L'evoluzione delle città italiane nell'XI secolo*, eds. Renato Bordone and Jörg Jarnut, Annali dell'Istituto storico italo-germanico, Quaderno 25 (Bologna, 1988), 99–136; and in the same volume (241–53), Romeo Pavoni, "L'evoluzione cittadina in Liguria nel secolo XI," especially 244, 247–50.

izens began asserting rights, particularly through the old institution of the "good men" (*boni homines*) who participated in judicial cases as authorities on local customs. With the election of Bernard of the Uberti as bishop in 1104, the city passed to the reform party. "Citizens of Parma" (*cives Parmenses*) participated in a judicial hearing presided over by Emperor Henry V in 1116; consuls appear in 1149 making a treaty concluding Parma's war with Piacenza. The balance of juridical power in practice was already with the commune, but the bishop continued to preside and his palace was frequently the site of communal business. With Frederick Barbarossa's descent into Italy, Bishop Aicardus in 1167 briefly led the city as *podestà* (governor or chief executive), but after the Peace of Constance (1183) episcopal leadership seems largely eclipsed. Aicardus's successor, Bishop Bernard expanded his palace in this period, raising the ceiling in his great hall and adding a new wing that included a chapel. In 1221, the commune of Parma had its own palace. From 1232 to 1234, Bishop Grazia added the new wing to the episcopal palace that faces the piazza.[58]

This chronology is significant. The real changes in episcopal architecture occurred not when the bishop was seeking a new autonomy for the city in alliance with the lay leaders of the commune, but when he was losing his leadership role. The "new look" is an architecture of defeat, contemporaneous with lay rejection of the potent Gregorian version of episcopal lordship. As the communes were solidifying their power and institutions in the closing decades of the twelfth century — after the great contest with Barbarossa — bishops had to refigure their place and role in the city. And this was the great age of expansion in episcopal palaces. This was when Bishop Omnebonus in Verona added his new third-floor "sala" and his successor Adelard doubled the size of the palace with a whole new wing.[59] There was a "palatio novo" at Piacenza by 1171 and at Como by 1195.[60] The bishop of Pistoia added his chapel and covered over his courtyard in the late twelfth century. Expansion continued in the early thirteenth century: a new palace was built in Bergamo by 1222 with a "new high hall." And the successors of Bishop Lanfranc of Pavia, with the commune already having appropriated part of their abode, built a new palace across from the cathedral and ceded the rest of their old palace to the commune in 1236.[61]

EPISCOPAL REDEFINITION: ARCHITECTURE

These new buildings and wings transformed the entire character of the bishop's palace. Chiefly, they brought it into a new relationship with the piazza. Two kinds of changes accomplished this. First, the residence lost its castle-like demeanor and culti-

58. Schumann, *Authority*, 225–53; *Parma XII*, no. 357; Juergen Schulz, "The Communal Buildings of Parma," *Mitteilungen des kunsthistorischen Istitutes in Florenz* 26 (1982): 282; on the episcopal palace, see Chapter 3, 103, 108.

59. *ACVerona*, II-8–7r (AC 65 m5 n8) and Chapter 3, 101–103.

60. *ASPiacenza*, Archivio Diplomatico degli Ospizi Civili di Piacenza-Atti Privati, busta 2 cartella 4, perg. no. 6; Frigerio and Baserga, "Il palazzo vescovile," 81.

61. For Pistoia, see this chapter, 147–52; *AVBergamo*, Diplomata seu Jura Episcopatus Bergomensis, raccolta 2, parte 1, perg. no. 8; Gaetano Panazza, "Appunti per la storia dei palazzi comunali di Brescia e Pavia," 195–97; *Nella rinascita del broletto*, 54–55.

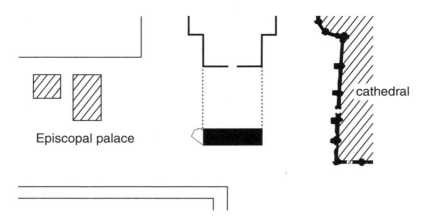

Episcopal palace

cathedral

FIGURE 45. *Como, eleventh-century episcopal complex showing separation of palace and cathedral. The dotted lines indicate the nave of Santo Stefano before it was truncated in the fourteenth century. (C. Ingersoll.)*

vated the more open, ornamented style of what we have come to call urban "civil architecture" (*architettura civile, Profanenbauten*).[62] The heavy walls of the palace were opened up with porticos on the ground floor, with rows of wide, arched windows on the upper floor, and through decorative elements (see Chapter 3). The new emphasis on windows put those within the palace in visual communication with the plaza below, and ground-floor porticos actually allowed the piazza and those in it some entry into the palace. The decorated expanse of the facade also required the piazza: it could only be fully appreciated visually through the spatial void spreading out before it. Second, palaces themselves were repositioned or their entrances reworked so that the buildings communicated with public space.

Repositioning of palaces happened most often as a result of rebuilding cathedrals. In some cases — notably those in which both the cathedral and the palace were reconstructed on a brand new site — the bishop's new house had no physical connection to the church. Indeed, the examples of both Como and Parma reveal not only detachment, but also a significant spatial separation. As we have already seen (see Chapter 2), in the opening decades of the eleventh century the bishop of Como built himself a new residence at the north end of the city near the lake. At this time he also began the construction of a new cathedral on a site south of his new *domus*. Figure 45 shows the locations of these two buildings. Not only is the palace physically detached from the cathedral, but also a long plaza separates the two. A similar set of choices is evident at Parma. In the middle of the eleventh century, the bishop built a new palace just outside the old Roman walls. At the end of the century a new cathedral was raised on a site east of the palace; it was consecrated to the Virgin by Pope Pascal II in 1106. Again, a broad piazza (about forty-five meters, or fifty yards) separated the church and palace (see Figure 57).

62. Braunfels, *Mittelalterliche Stadtbaukunst in der Toskana*, 174–215.

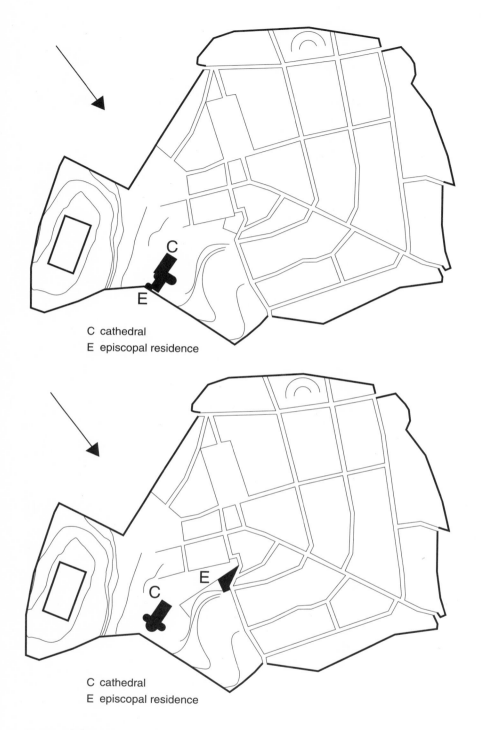

C cathedral
E episcopal residence

C cathedral
E episcopal residence

FIGURE 46. (TOP) *Spoleto, cathedral group after eleventh-century expansion of the church; episcopal residence still attached to rear. (C. Ingersoll.)*

FIGURE 47. (BOTTOM) *Spoleto, cathedral group after late-twelfth-century enlargement of the church; episcopal palace now opposite cathedral at top of piazza separating the two. (C. Ingersoll.)*

In other cases, the reconfiguration of cathedral and palace was less radical, but the result was still a new relationship with open space. Often if the cathedral was being rebuilt on its traditional site, the desire to enlarge the church necessitated the relocation of the bishop's residence. Spoleto offers an excellent example of this process. Bishop Andrew had rebuilt the cathedral in the eleventh century, more or less retaining its earlier dimensions. The bishop's residence remained in its early medieval location, attached to the cathedral apse and incorporating parts of the old city wall (Figure 46). In the 1170s, however, the cathedral was again rebuilt and, this time, enlarged. The extension of the nave in the new structure prompted the relocation and rebuilding of the bishop's palace at a site west of the facade of the church, where there had been a monastery dedicated to Sant'Eufemia.[63] A long plaza now separated the cathedral and palace (Figure 47). At Piacenza too, a new episcopal palace was built in conjunction with the new Romanesque church. The first notice of the new palace comes in 1171, a few years before the final campaign on the duomo began. This late-twelfth-century phase of construction completed the transept arms, and this suggests that the episcopal residence was restructured in preparation for this lateral extension of the church. The remains of a doorway on the north transept, in fact, indicate where the new palace was connected to the cathedral (Figure 48).[64]

As the example of Piacenza demonstrates, some restructured episcopal palaces retained a direct connection to the cathedral. But even in these cases, a new relationship with the piazza developed through restructuring of entrances. The well-excavated remains at Pistoia give the most clear and chronologically precise evidence of this development. When the new palace was built in the eleventh century, it had two entrances. An entrance off the piazza in front of the cathedral gave access only to the ground-floor service and storage areas. The bishop's hall was not accessible from this entrance. To get to the bishop's hall, one had to enter through the *curtis episcopi*, an enclosed fortified courtyard between the main building of the palace, the tower, and the facade of the cathedral. At least one entrance to this area definitely opened on the east wall, facing the canonry and cloister (a narrow lane separated the episcopal courtyard and canonry).[65] The way into the bishop's hall was a stone stairway rising along the north face of the tower (Figure 49).[66]

Several aspects of this arrangement deserve notice. First, this main entryway is not very open. The lane it faces is no more than an alley and it was not a public thorough-

63. Bruno Toscano, "Cattedrale e città: Studio di un esempio," in *Topografia urbana e vita cittadina nell'alto medioevo in occidente*, 2 vols. (Spoleto, 1974), 2: 711–47.

64. *ASPiacenza*, Archivio Diplomatico degli Ospizzi Civili di Piacenza, Atti Privati, cartella 4, perg. 6; *Il duomo di Piacenza (1122–1972)*, 22 (plan), 45.

65. This wall was entirely rebuilt in the late twelfth century and so it is impossible to tell exactly where the eleventh-century entrance was. I thank dott. Rauty for clarifying this point on the site. The original entrance may have been in the same location as the portal in the twelfth-century wall, or it could have been closer to the cathedral.

66. Rauty, *Palazzo*, 1:88–93.

FIGURE 48.
*Piacenza,
cathedral, blind
doorway still
remaining on
north flank facing
episcopal palace.
(M. Miller.)*

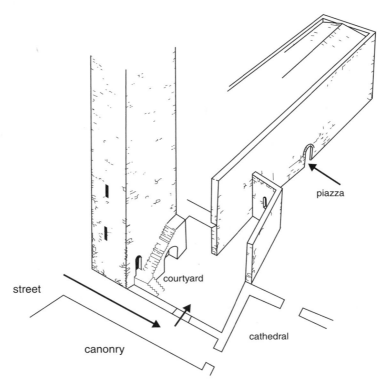

piazza

street

courtyard

canonry

cathedral

FIGURE 49. *Pistoia, Palazzo dei Vescovi, entrances to palace in eleventh and early twelfth centuries. (C. Ingersoll, based on Rauty,* Palazzo, *89, by permission of the Cassa di Risparmio di Pistoia e Pescia.)*

fare (*via publica*). The walls of the cathedral, the canonry, and the courtyard rise on every side. Nothing about the entryway invites the public in, and in fact, the entire arrangement seems designed defensively. The narrow lane could be blocked off easily, and the portal into the courtyard similarly closed and defended. The fortified, bunker-like, character of access continues within the courtyard. Although it may have been simpler merely to support the staircase against a wall than to build a freestanding stairway, the result is that one ascends to the bishop's hall very much under the shadow of his tower. One was quite aware of the bishop's military might when entering his hall.

Second, in orientation the entrance addressed the church and canonry — ecclesiastical, sacred space. Although the evidence is quite limited and fragmentary, this Pistoian arrangement shares similarities with some late-antique configurations. We know certainly that the entrances to the *episcopia* at Aquileia (late-fourth- and mid-fifth-century configurations) and Parenzo were off the atrium of the cathedral basilica. This arrangement was even prescribed by one early set of church canons, the *Testamentum Domini* (see Chapter 1). The only known entrance to the *episcopium* at Grado was from the nave of the cathedral; this entrance, similarly, led to a courtyard and then into the bishop's hall. As I argued earlier, this derived from the spatial unity of the church and

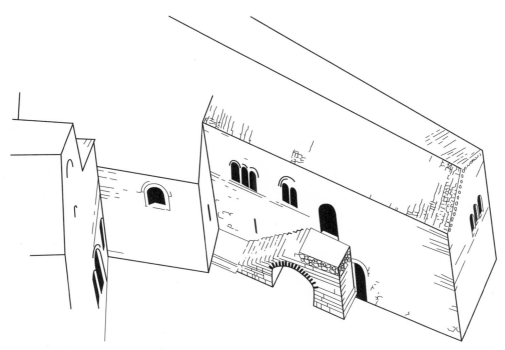

FIGURE 50. *Pistoia, Palazzo dei Vescovi, new piazza entrance to great hall added in late twelfth century. (C. Ingersoll, based on Rauty,* Palazzo, *108, by permission of the Cassa di Risparmio di Pistoia e Pescia.)*

residence in Late Antiquity. The entry arrangements at Pistoia suggest that some of this unity survived through the early Middle Ages: the bishop's residence communicated primarily with sacred rather than public space.

This changed, however, in the second half of the twelfth century. The courtyard was enclosed at this time, and a new entrance to the palace opened. This new entrance opened onto the piazza. A second-floor doorway was cut into the middle of the north wall of the palace facing the square, and a marble staircase leading to it was constructed (Figure 50). This was a decisive shift: the entrance to the bishop's hall was now from the piazza. Further, this entrance was emphasized decoratively: the staircase rested on an arch with bicolor flashing against a background of black and white stripes of marble. Successive renovations added more ornamentation. When the entire facade of the palace was extended in the early fourteenth century, the staircase was covered and four high gothic arches created along its edge. This series of graceful arches was continued down the facade at the end of the century.[67]

This shift toward the piazza is significant in many ways. The palace now chiefly addressed public, not ecclesiastical, space. And the piazza in front of the cathedral and palace was very public space indeed. The city's market was (and still is) held here; it was the city's central public gathering space. This strongly affected movement in and out of the palace. First, it meant that those going into the palace were very much on display.

67. Ibid., 1:96–97, 106–9, 129, 139–41.

Everyone would know who was being received in the bishop's hall. And, before the extension of the facade of the palace in the early fourteenth century — which opened a foyer or corridor running next to the hall — those waiting to see the bishop would have to wait on the staircase or around its base. Second, this highly emphasized staircase onto the piazza offered new possibilities for episcopal movement. The bishop retained a direct entryway into the front of the cathedral, so he could pass from his palace directly into the church. But he could also choose to make a more visible exit from his palace, down the staircase into the piazza. This made the bishop, in some significant ways, more visible.

At Pistoia, these shifts are intimately bound up in the bishop's relationship with the commune and the commune's relationship with the holy. From the eleventh century, the cathedrals were spaces central to lay conceptions of the urban community and were increasingly a focus of civic identity and pride. The involvement of lay people in the rebuilding of their cathedrals in this period, and the sentiments clustered about the cults of the patron saints of these towns, made the bishop's church a space of ever greater importance to citizens. Before communes built their own palaces, one of the places they met to solemnize acts was in or in front of the cathedral, and the symbols of communal identity — particularly the *carroccio* — came to be lodged in the church. The new lay governments of northern Italian cities increasingly laid claim to cathedral space as their own. Thus, when the bishop of Pistoia acquired a relic of Saint James and had it translated to the cathedral in July of 1144, the citizens responded with enthusiasm, devotion, and claims to space. The bishop installed the relic in the sanctuary, but the commune insisted on building a special chapel for the saint in the vestibule of the church. The consuls then created a special organization, the Opera San Iacopo, to ensure officiation in the chapel, and they built a hospice to house pilgrims to the shrine.[68]

The position of this new communally sponsored chapel for the saint is significant and it initiated a whole series of architectural changes that resulted in the new piazza entrance to the bishop's palace. The chapel was built in the entryway to the church, at its west end. The only appropriate space for a sacristy to service the chapel was just within the bishop's courtyard, and indeed, this was the solution chosen. But the building of the sacristy significantly reduced the area of the courtyard. Other changes then followed: the bishop built himself a chapel (San Niccolò) on top of the sacristy, the entrance onto the piazza with its staircase was created, and the entire courtyard began to be enclosed.[69] In response to the commune's claims on San Iacopo and the space of the cathedral, the bishop responded architecturally by creating his own special sacred place and, moreover, by connecting and opening his palace to the piazza. This new architectural relationship between the bishop's palace and the public space of the piazza was articulated in response to the commune's new public authority and attempts to associate it with the sacred.

This new episcopal relationship with the piazza is also evident in other cities. From the ninth century, with the building of the "Domus Valeriana," the focus of the episcopal residence at Ravenna was shifting from the southwest end of the cathedral to the

68. Ibid., 1:111–13.
69. Ibid., 1:113–17, 124–29, 134–35.

southeast. This "Domus Valeriana" became the main building of the complex by the thirteenth century. Then, as today, it faced onto a broad piazza. In the Middle Ages, however, this piazza was not the quiet, tree-shaded refuge it is now. The city's main market was held here, and the thriving commerce of the piazza gave the bishop's palace its medieval nickname, the "palatium mercurii" (Mercury being the deity of commerce).[70] The contemporaneous rebuilding of Spoleto's cathedral and episcopal palace in the late twelfth century also resulted in the creation of a massive piazza between them. Formerly located at the rear of the cathedral, the palace was moved to the monastery of Sant'Eufemia, in front of and above the cathedral on the main road leading to the church. This road was widened out, so that it formed the narrower end of one long, sweeping, funnel-shaped piazza culminating in the cathedral.[71] Later, the commune's palace joined the bishop's on this end of the piazza, and the space became the locus of public life and festivities.

The sort of ornamented staircase we saw in the late twelfth century at Pistoia — descending from the episcopal hall into the piazza — was also found at other palaces. A charter redacted April 12, 1180, reveals a stairway at the episcopal palace in Novara: it recorded the settlement of a dispute between the cathedral canons and a priest of San Salvatore "in the bishop's court, next to the stairs of the new palace."[72] Most of our evidence for these exterior staircases, however, comes from the thirteenth and fourteenth centuries. At Parma, Bishop Grazia's grand new hall facing the piazza (added in the 1230s) was entered from a stairway at the north end of the facade. Two carved lions that probably flanked the entrance survive.[73] The most revealing notices of an episcopal stairway come from the thirteenth-century charters of Faenza. When the palace's entrance was first mentioned in 1269 and 1270, it was simply called a "stone staircase" (*scala lapidea*). Several documents redacted in 1289, however, suggest that at least the landing had been broadened or enclosed: charters dated January 17, February 25, and April 23 were redacted "on the stairs or balcony" (*super schalis seu balchone*). This "balcony," also called an antechamber (*proaula*), was a site where a good deal of business was transacted: at least twenty-five charters from 1289 to 1291 were drawn up there.[74]

---

70. Miller, "Ravenna," 164–65.

71. Toscano, "Cattedrale e città," 713–15, 745–46. Toscano frames his inquiry around the anomalous character of the Via dell'Arringo, the street which is widened to form the base of the "nuovo, vasto invaso imbutiforme" which is "lo spazio ove defluiranno nel medioevo tardo le grandi occasioni pubbliche, le feste, le processioni, le assemblee popolari indette dal Comune . . ." (746).

72. *Le carte dello archivio capitolare di Santa Maria di Novara*, ed. F. Gabotto, et al., 3 vols. (Pinerolo and Turin, 1913–24), 3: no. 512.

73. Pelicelli, *Vescovado*, 24; for other examples from Padua and Florence see R. Zanocco, "Il palazzo vescovile," 175, and Dameron, *Episcopal Power*, 157.

74. BCFaenza, Schedario Rossini, Repertorio Chronologico, Aug. 8, 1269; June 5, 1270 (*scala lapidea*); Jan. 17, Feb. 25, April 23, 1289 (*super schalis seu balchone*); Feb. 22, 1289 (*proaule seu balchone*); Jan. 25, Feb. 2, 4, 5, April 4, 14, 1289; May 27, Oct. 27, 1290; Feb. 27, March 24, Nov. 18, 1291 (*balcone*); March 26, June 21, July 21, 26, 29, Aug. 1, 20, 1289; Jan. 26, Feb. 7, 28, April 11, 14, Oct. 11, 1291 (*proaule*); June 19, 1290 (*scale del palatio novo*).

These descriptions may refer to the kind of covered hallway created at the top of the staircase at Pistoia in the fourteenth century.

Most exterior staircases, like the one at Pistoia, ran parallel to the facades supporting them. Smaller examples, called *profferli* in Italian urban domestic architecture, and even grand examples from royal palaces in northern Europe, were arranged in this fashion. Some papal palaces, however, demonstrate an alternative arrangement. The papal palace at Viterbo had a projecting staircase, jutting out into the piazza perpendicular to the facade. Built in the late 1260s or early 1270s, the broad staircase rose steeply to "a generous landing, supported on a depressed barrel vault"; two columns ornamented the corners of the landing at the top step (Figure 51).[75] The papal palaces at Orvieto and Rieti also had projecting staircases of this sort, and the Lateran had the monumental "Scala Santa."[76]

It seems important to note here that papal palaces followed the example of the Scala Santa at the Lateran and included a projecting staircase that extended the palace entrance out into the piazza. From the few examples we have, it seems that bishop's palaces in northern Italy did not follow this papal model. While they did address the piazza with new ornamented staircases, the expressive forms they chose conformed more with those of urban domestic architecture. The bishop of Pistoia's new staircase in the late twelfth century, for example, used a Romanesque arch to support the landing, just like the *profferli* of urban row houses throughout central Italy (Figure 52). Good examples are extant in Viterbo, Orvieto, Tuscanio, and Vitorchiano.[77] As most of our bishops seem to have been adding such staircases from the late twelfth century on, their reliance on models from local domestic architecture must be read as choice rather than ignorance of papal styles.

This choice seems to me significant in understanding the place bishops defined for themselves in Italian cities. Documentary sources and the Guelph-Ghibelline political history of the thirteenth and fourteenth centuries tend to define bishops as the local

75. Radke, *Viterbo*, 74–76, 223–24.

76. Ibid., 75–76. The exact date of this grand entrance to the Lateran palace is impossible to discern. There were stairs and a main entrance to the palace at this point in the north facade from at least the ninth century and probably earlier. The sixteenth-century antiquarian Panvinius related that the "stairs which are now called holy were from the earliest times part of the patriarchium"; by his time, through a corruption of "scalae palatii" to "scalae Pilati," the stairs were believed to be those of Pilate's praetorium, which Jesus ascended to be sentenced to death. In the sixteenth century, the Scala Santa was actually three parallel projecting sets of stairs, with the bronze doors of the palace at the top of the central set and a covered portico at the base. Lauer, *Latran*, 100, 173, 185, 482 (Panvinius).

77. Andrews, "Medieval Domestic Architecture," 46–52 (prominent among these examples is the staircase on the Palazzo del Vescovo at Vitorchiano); Laura Contus, "Edilizia medievale a Viterbo: Una casa con 'profferlo' nel quartiere San Pellegrino," *Storia della città* 52 (1990): 109–14. Rauty, in his discussion of the staircase at Pistoia, contends that it is one of the earliest examples of the "profferlo" form in Italy and argues for French influence. Other contemporaneous examples, however, have since been noted, and Contus points out (109) that the term was in use from at least the eleventh century. Rauty, *Palazzo*, 1:107.

FIGURE 51. *Viterbo, Palazzo dei Papi, projecting staircase on southern facade from southeast. (G. Radke.)*

agents of papal monarchy. It is true that bishops came to have much greater contact with Rome from the time of the investiture conflict: papal correspondence with Italian sees increased, Roman synods were more frequent, and the development of the papal judicial system fueled contact with the curia. Also, once bishops had lost much of their power to the communes, they more frequently resorted to the papacy for support in their difficulties and disputes: Lanfranc of Pavia, when exiled from his see as a result of his conflict with the city's consuls, went to Rome. Finally, with the decretal *Licet ecclesiarum* of 1265, the papacy asserted the right to dispose of all benefices, and increasingly bishops were appointed to their sees by the pope. As papal provision became the "normal" route to a see, very strong links were established between Rome and the bishops of these northern Italian cities.[78] Indeed, if one pursued the history of episcopal palaces into the Renaissance, it would be interesting to see if local bishops began mimicking papal architecture as they remodeled their residences (and all of these palaces

78. Good overviews in English of the growth of papal power are Gerd Tellenbach, *The Church in Western Europe from the Tenth to the Early Twelfth Century*, trans. Timothy Reuter (Cambridge, 1993), especially 205–18, 304–34; and Colin Morris, *The Papal Monarchy: The Western Church from 1050 to 1250* (Oxford, 1989), especially 212–26, 528–29; see also Wilfried Hartmann, "Verso il centralismo papale," in *Il secolo XI: Una svolta?*, Annali dell'Istituto storico italo-germanico, Quaderno 35 (Bologna, 1993), 99–130; and on the history of papal provisions, Geoffrey Barraclough, *Papal Provisions: Aspects of Church History Constitutional, Legal and Administrative in the Later Middle Ages* (Oxford, 1935).

FIGURE 52. *Tuscanio, Palazzo Spagnoli, facade with portico,* profferlo *staircase, and bifore window. (C. Ingersoll, after a drawing by Sheila Gibson in David Andrews, "Medieval Domestic Architecture in Northern Lazio,"* Medieval Lazio *[Oxford: BAR, 1982], 51, by permission of author.)*

underwent massive renovations in this period). But in the Middle Ages, regardless of stronger ties to the curia, bishops cultivated a decidedly local image. In remaking their palaces, they drew on the common elements of urban domestic architecture: trifores and bifores, ground-floor porticos, *profferlo*-style staircases. Their decorative schemas also usually drew upon and reinforced local conventions: the black and white marble stripes on the bishop of Pistoia's staircase match the striped marble work on the facade of the cathedral, and the brick and tufa stripes of Bishop Omnebonus's hall in Verona can be found in ecclesiastical and secular architecture throughout the city.

The architectural image that bishops constructed as they lost power seems not to have been a retreat from engaged membership in a local community. In fact, by using the architectural vocabulary of urban domestic architecture and indigenous decorative details, bishops seem to have been reasserting their status as members in that community, residents of the city. But the bishop's house was no ordinary house. It was bigger than even a wealthy citizen's house, and it got bigger still. Episcopal palaces often doubled (in the case of Parma, tripled) in size over the late twelfth and early thirteenth centuries. It displayed prodigious wealth: these remodeled palaces had multiple expensive decorative elements (marble columns, colorful ceramic tiles, stucco moldings, painted tympana) across their expansive facades. And finally, it asserted an intense connection to the public space of the piazza and the life of the urban community that animated it. But what exactly was the relationship to public life that these bishops were articulating? In order to understand this reconfiguration of the bishop's place, we must return to the narrative accounts of this process.

EPISCOPAL REDEFINITION: HOLINESS AND PUBLIC LIFE

Most revealing are a cluster of lives of holy bishops that survive from this decisive period. Lives of Bishop Ubaldus of Gubbio (1129–60) and Lanfranc of Pavia (1180–98) were written by their immediate successors in their sees. The canonization process for John Cacciafronte, bishop of Vicenza (1179–84), held in 1223–24, yielded a life of the bishop and sworn testimony from Vicentine citizens about his life, death, and miracles. Finally, although the hagiographical sources for Galdinus della Sala, archbishop of Milan (1166–76), date from a later era, much can be known about his life from contemporary documents and chronicles. Several persistent themes emerge from these lives.

First, these bishops are "martyrs." In the case of John Cacciafronte, this was literally the case: he was assassinated by a disgruntled vassal in 1184. Saint Adalpretus, bishop of Trent (1156–77) was also murdered — "run through with a spear" (*hasta transfixum*) — by one of the lords of Castrobarco, but accounts of this incident and the bishop's life are quite late.[79] Even those not murdered in the line of duty, however, are portrayed as suffering for their people. Lanfranc of Pavia, already ill when the consuls of the city visit him demanding part of his palace, and "seeing iniquity and opposition in the city" (*videns iniquitatem et contradictionem in Civitate*), withdraws to a monastery and dies shortly thereafter. The author of the *vita* gives Lanfranc a dramatic end: as the moment of death approaches, the bishop dons the robes symbolizing his office (*indumenta pontificalia*), takes the crucifix offered to him, and "with tears kisses the feet of the Savior's image, saying: 'Into your hands, Oh Lord, I commend my spirit.' "[80] The juxtaposition of images — the bishop in his episcopal robes, the Savior on the cross — with the words

79. The information collected by the Bollandists in *AASS*, 3 Martii: 704–5 is from sixteenth- and seventeenth-century sources; see also *Dizionario biografico degli Italiani* 1: 227–28 (s.v. "Adalpreto"). André Vauchez noted this new twelfth-century emphasis on martyr-bishops, focusing primarily on Thomas Becket but also mentioning John Cacciafronte: *La Sainteté en occident aux derniers siècles du moyen âge d'après les procès de canonisation et les documents hagiographiques* (Rome, 1981), 197–203.

80. "Demum Crucem sibi afferri praecipiens imaginis Salvatoris pedes instanter cum lachrymis deosculabatur, dicens, In manus tuas Domine commendo Spiritum meum." *AASS*, 5 Iunii: 536; Ughelli, *IS*, 1: 1097.

of Jesus as he sacrificed himself for our redemption, makes a Christ figure of the belea-guered bishop. And as Lanfranc is assimilated to Christ in the narrative, then the con-suls and "leading men of the people" (*Popoli maiores*) are left in the roles of the Romans and Jews of the passion story.

A different relationship with citizens is articulated in the life of Saint Ubaldus of Gubbio, but a martyr theme is still prominent. This *vita*, like Lanfranc's, highlights contention over urban space. The first vignette in the recounting of Ubaldus's career as bishop is a dispute occasioned by the building of a new city wall. The workers making cement for the construction of the wall were trampling and damaging an episcopal vineyard. The bishop ordered them "humiliter" (humbly) to stop injuring his vines, but the foreman stubbornly refused and "striking him with insolence, threw him into the liquid cement being prepared there."[81] Continuing the "humiliter" theme, the bishop picked himself up and with great patience, "as if nothing had happened," returned home. When the citizens were outraged on his behalf — demanding that the scoundrel foreman be dispossessed, have his house leveled, and be expelled from the city — the saintly bishop refused to endorse the punishment and instead, kissed the man and for-gave his sins. This story is immediately followed in the life by an even more dramatic depiction of the bishop suffering from the willful wrongheadedness of his people. One day, a great insurrection arose in the city plaza, with fierce fighting among the citizens and many casualties. The bishop ran to the scene, and unable to calm the fighting through reasoned words, he rushed into the fray to try to impede the vicious blows. Nearly immediately, he fell to the ground "as if mortally wounded" (*quasi mortaliter vul-neratus*), and the shocked citizens threw down their arms, began tearing their hair, and raising a great clamor of grief. But the bishop rose slowly and indicated that he felt no pain from the wound. "And so it was," concludes the author, "that while the bishop gave himself over to death for the people, the people lived, and the bishop did not perish."[82]

This, you'll notice, is a more upbeat account of episcopal suffering: Ubaldus's hu-miliation instructs his people in Christian forgiveness, and his selfless concern for them is vindicated when the citizens throw down their arms. The bishop's suffering is efficacious — it brings about concord — and the bishop lives on. The final vignette in the life reminds us of its chronology. When Frederick Barbarossa lays siege to Gubbio to punish it for its subversion, Ubaldus goes to the emperor, and through God's grace,

81. ". . . qui operi praeerat, pertinaciter recusavit: et eum cum injuria impellens, in liquidum caementum, quod paratum erat, dejecit." *AASS*, 3 Mai: 630. This story is also in the life by Gior-danus: Dolbeau, "La vita di Sant'Ubaldo," 99–100 (11.1–4). I've used the life by Tebaldus as the ba-sis for analysis here because, having been compiled and written by another bishop of the see, it in-cludes more descriptions of Ubaldus's episcopal career. The Giordanus life circulated, it seems, through communities of regular canons: the manuscript Dolbeau uses for his edition was copied by the canons regular of San Giovanni in Monte in Bologna.

82. "Atque ita factum est, ut dum Episcopus se tradit morti pro populo, et populus viveret, et Episcopus non periret." *AASS*, 3 Mai: 630. The Giordanus life includes this story, but its conclu-sion does not emphasize the bishop's sacrifice of himself for his people: "Agunt cuncti gratias Deo quod et populus a periculo pugne est liberatus et episcopus ut putabatur non fuit peremptus." Dol-beau, "La vita di Sant'Ubaldo," 100 (13.1–4).

the stern ruler is able to recognize the bishop's holiness and is peacefully reconciled with the city. In many ways, this life sketches out a fantastic version of the kind of episcopal lordship that prelates sought in the late eleventh and early twelfth centuries, and that was undeniably rejected in favor of lay communal governance in the wake of the struggle with Barbarossa. No consuls appear in Ubaldus's Gubbio. The bishop seems to be the only authority in town. When fighting breaks out, Ubaldus quells it. When the city is attacked by a coalition of eleven other cities and the forces of Gubbio are outnumbered forty to one, the "man of God" leads a procession around the city, fervently beseeching God "for the safety of his people" (*pro salute populi*), exhorts his people to put their hopes for victory in heaven, and blesses the armed citizens as they march out to battle. The bishop, however, does not lead them (no crusading prelate here) but climbs up on the rooftop of the cloister so that he can see "*populum suum,*" his people. The Gubbians win, but the miraculous victory instills in them a sober fear of the Lord (*timor Domini*), and instead of rejoicing riotously, they return to their homes trembling.[83]

To this image of episcopal lordship, the life of Lanfranc offers a significant contrast. In Lanfranc's Pavia, there are definitely consuls; they are repeatedly depicted as harrying the bishop and trampling on ecclesiastical rights. The bishop tries valiantly to protect the rights of his church, but he appears rather powerless. He is starved into exile and has to seek help in Rome. The papal interdict seems to have little effect, however, and it is the rise of a new lay rector in the city that brings about a resolution to the dispute. What that resolution is, however, remains unclear; the author does not trumpet any details of a great victory of church over state.[84] And Lanfranc's second confrontation with the consuls results in retreat, defeat, and death. The author casts the bishop's demise as Christ like, but if the bishop's death was salvific, its redemptive results are unclear in the text.

Martyrdom is always used in these narratives to underscore specific episcopal roles and virtues. In Ubaldus's life, it is the bishop's role as peacemaker, restoring unity and concord among citizens of the town, "his people." Obviously, in Lanfranc's life it is linked to the bishop's defense of the rights and property of his church from the predations of the laity (specifically in this case, the commune). This theme, as we have seen, also appears in Ubaldus's life and is dramatically represented in John Cacciafronte's

83. *AASS,* 3 Mai: 631; in the Giordanus life, the defense of the city and the bishop's legation to the emperor are similarly portrayed, but a "consul et rector" appears at the end. As the saint is dying, this figure (*vir magnificus nomine Bambo qui erat ei carissimus et eodem anno illis civitatis consul et rector*) articulates the people's love for their bishop. Dolbeau, "La vita di Sant'Ubaldo," 105 (20.3). In the life of Bruno Bishop of Segni (written c. 1178–82), there seems to be no other public authority in the city save the bishop. The counts of Segni, who kidnap Bruno, have their seat outside the city at "Castrum Viculi." *AASS,* 4 Iulii: 481.

84. *AASS,* 5 Iunii: 535; Ughelli, *IS,* 1:1094–96. The author of the *vita* simply says of the conclusion of the first battle with the commune, "Surrexit interea in praedicta civitate Rector novus, Dei amicus, impietatis inimicus; cives ad poenitentiam commonefecti, et pro ipsis et cum ipsis satisfaciens, sanctum Dei famulum revocavit: sicque per Dei gratiam reddita pace Ecclesiae, vir Deo dilectus Clerum et populum pastorali diligentia gubernavit."

martyrdom. Bishop John was involved in a protracted dispute with several powerful local lords over their usurpation of episcopal lands on the estate of Malo. A cleric named Henry testified in the canonization process that the bishop had died "for the liberty of the church, for the maintenance and rights of the see," and that episcopal property at Malo "was being destroyed by rich men, nobles, and magnates."[85] One of these murdered the bishop in the piazza in front of his palace and the cathedral.

The location of his martyrdom — in the piazza — seems to me quite significant. What he was doing in the piazza when he was killed is also striking. The cleric Henry quoted earlier was with the bishop moments before he was slain. He recounted that coming out of the episcopal palace, he and Bishop John encountered a pauper before the door. The man needed clothing, and the bishop sent Henry to fetch some. While doing so, Henry heard noise, and when he returned he found the bishop already dead; the killers drove Henry off and would not allow him to approach the body. That the bishop was murdered while ministering to the needs of the poor is repeated several times in Henry's testimony, and other witnesses at the canonization proceeding reiterated the care he showed to "paupers": the bishop showed "the greatest charity" (*maxime caritatis*), he fed the poor from the wealth of the see in times of famine, and he honored the poor by washing their feet.[86] This image of the bishop as friend of the poor also appears in other lives. Lanfranc of Pavia is described as caring for the lesser people and having compassion for the poor (*cura subditorum, compassio pauperum*): everyday he dined with twelve paupers and gave bread to many more.[87] Galdinus of Milan was also venerated for his sustenance of the poor. As archdeacon of the Milanese church, he helped found a hospital for "the poor and infirm" of the city, and he was remembered in popular songs and sayings (*detti*) as giving bread to prisoners. This "pane di San Galdino" was recalled in a special procession on his feast day that was held into the seventeenth century.[88]

While the poor are the prime objects of care, ministrations, and concern in the lives of bishops John, Lanfranc, and Galdinus, the early life of Bishop Ubaldus of Gubbio reveals a broader canvas of episcopal solicitude. Ubaldus's concern is always for "his

85. Giorgio Cracco, "Ancora sulla «Sainteté en occident» di André Vauchez (con un appendice sul processo Cacciafronte del 1223–1224)," *Studi medievali* ser. 3, 26 (1985): 905: "Et dixit [Henricus clericus] quod fuit mortuus pro libertate Ecclesie manutenenda et iuribus episcopatus, quia pro manutenendis pauperibus de Villa Maladi, qui destruebantur per divites et nobiles et magnates qui ocupabant bona ipsorum et episcopatus. . . . "

86. Aldigerius of Quinto said of the bishop "caritativus erat multum"; Sigonfredus of Lançade characterized him as "maxime caritatis"; and the priest Americus of Saint Peter affirmed that John "erat homo maxime caritatis." Henry, who tells the narrative of the bishop's death, related, "Et semper in omni die iovis sancte faciebat me Henricum caniparium emere vestes et dare et dividere inter multos pauperes; et faciebat congregare pauperum quantitatem quandoque duodecim et quandoque viginti et plus aut minus, secundum quod esse poterant, quibus abluebat pedes." Ibid., 904–5. See also *AASS*, 2 Martii: 487–88.

87. *AASS*, 5 Iunii: 534; Ughelli, *IS*, 1: 1093.

88. Enrico Cattaneo, "Galdino della Sala Cardinale Arcivescovo di Milano," in *Contributi dell'Istituto di storia medioevale: Raccolta di studi in memoria di Sergio Mochi Onory*, vol. 2, Pubblicazioni dell'Universitá cattolica del sacro cuore, Contributi ser. 3, scienze storiche 15 (Milan, 1972), 373–74.

people," *populum suum*, the citizens of Gubbio. (*Cives* is used alternately with *populus* in this broad sense.) After being convinced to accept his election as bishop, Ubaldus "returns to the see of Gubbio with its citizens rejoicing and leaping for joy." He is constituted pastor "super populum suum." The "citizens" are outraged at his treatment by the surly foreman, and it was the "citizens" who were fighting in the piazza. But when he intervenes to stop the fighting, the author says he offers himself "pro populo."[89] This undifferentiated civic body is the object of the bishop's ministrations, solicitude, and care. The later episcopal *vitae* position the bishop differently: he is portrayed in conflict with communal leaders and the nobility, and as the champion of the "poor." We must recall here the meaning of the social category of "the poor" in the Middle Ages. Included in this designation are the sorts of people we consider "poor": beggars in the street, those without adequate food and clothing. But it also included all those perceived as powerless.[90] Thus, just after Lanfranc is praised for feeding twelve paupers every day, the author of the *vita* lauds his care of widows and orphans — persons considered vulnerable and in need of special protection even if they came from wealthy families. The bishop's *cura subditorum* — literally, care of "those having been put under," "underlings" — is also praised.[91] These were, indeed, traditional episcopal virtues but they are given particular emphasis in these lives. It should perhaps not surprise us that as they were losing their own power, these bishops identified themselves with the powerless. They are certainly associating themselves with the same spirituality that gave rise to the Franciscans and the Humiliati, but they are also positioning themselves politically as the champions of the "opposition," of all those not in power.

More interesting still is the way in which being a champion of the "poor" is linked in these lives with fighting heresy. Several of the witnesses at John Cacciafronte's canonization process juxtapose these roles. Just after describing how charitable the bishop was, the priest Aldigerius of Quinto said, "[H]e loved good, orthodox men and hated bad, heretical ones." The priest Sigonfredus of Lanzade similarly mentioned the "great charity" of Bishop John and how he "loved those loving the church and hated those hating the church, and this was widely known." It was known because the bishop had founded a special school of theology in Vicenza to combat heresy, and as the cleric Henry described, the bishop was on his way to the school when he was murdered.[92]

89. *AASS*, 3 Mai: 629–31.

90. Michel Mollat, *The Poor in the Middle Ages*, trans. Arthur Goldhammer (New Haven and London, 1986), 2–5; and more recently Otto Gerhard Oexle, "*Potens* und *Pauper* im Frühmittelalter," in *Bildhafte Rede in Mittelalter und früher Neuzeit: Probleme ihrer Legitimation und ihrer Funktion*, eds. Wolfgang Harms and Klaus Speckenbach (Tübingen, 1992), 131–49, but especially 148 on its continuing use in the central Middle Ages. Gilles Couvreur's study of how theologians and canonists evaluated the culpability of the poor for their actions reveals a profound shift in attitudes in the thirteenth century that worked to redress the radical imbalance of power in property relations: *Les Pauvres ont-ils des droits? Recherches sur le vol en cas d'extrême nécessité depuis la Concordia de Gratien (1140) jusq'à Guillaume d'Auxerre (d.1231)*, Analecta Gregoriana 111 (Rome and Paris, 1961).

91. *AASS*, 5 Iunii: 534; Ughelli, *IS*, 1: 1093–94.

92. Aldigerius of Quinto: " . . . et diligebat bonos homines et catolicos et malos et hereticos odebat."; Sigonfredus of Lançade: " . . . et diligebat diligentes Ecclesiam et odebat odientes Ecclesiam;

This connection between loving the poor and fighting heresy is also made in the other lives. The author of Lanfranc of Pavia's *vita* devotes twenty-six lines to his care of the poor, concluding that the bishop "used to say of himself that he was not lord, but custodian, not possessor, but dispenser of the goods of the church." Then, he continues,

> He was also a skilled champion of Catholicism, a defender of the faith, a very strong conqueror of heretics, who mark themselves out by their impious pride, not to mention their cruelty. Indeed, this one [Lanfranc] because he considered Christ such great gain, went about untroubled among both the infamous and the well regarded. In fact, his preaching was to Catholics the scent of life in life and to heretics of death in death. As a result of his efforts, the Catholic faith was strengthened day after day and the chattering of pseudo-preachers diminished. He persecuted the detractors of the faith with perfect hatred, expelling them from his diocese, prohibiting their conventicals, destroying their houses, and vice versa, he most patiently endured the unjust persecutions of these heretics and the many disparagements of their supporters, knowing that Abel was unable to be any other than the one whom Cain's malice followed.[93]

Yet more striking is the case of Galdinus of Milan. Venerated for his charity, he was also famed for his preaching against the Cathars. He was believed to have met his end in this pursuit. On the second Sunday after Easter, although ailing, Galdinus was "enflamed with the zeal of God against the heretics." Too weak to say mass, the cathedral provost said the rites. The archbishop, however,

> having recited the creed with his brothers, and before reading the Gospel to the people, ascended the pulpit and gave a splendid oration against the aforementioned Cathars and their accomplices, manifestly confuting their errors with many arguments and explanations as well as proving the Catholic faith with many stories of the

et de hoc publica fama erat." Cracco, "Ancora . . . ," 904–5; and Francesca Lomastro Tognato, *L'eresia a Vicenza nel duecento: Dati, problemi e fonti* (Vicenza, 1988), 12–14; Giorgio Cracco, "Religione, chiesa, pietà," in *Storia di Vicenza II: L'età medievale* (Vicenza, 1988), 393–97; *AASS*, 2 Martii: 487–88. For the theological connections between the Gregorian notion of "caritas" and the tendency to conflate disobedience with heresy, see Giuseppe Fornasari, "S. Anselmo e il problema della «caritas»," in *Medioevo riformato del secolo XI. Pier Damiani e Gregorio VII* (Naples, 1996), 477–90.

93. *AASS*, 5 Iunii: 534; Ughelli, *IS*, 1: 1094: " . . . dicebat enim se rerum ecclasiasticarum non dominum, sed custodem; non possessorem, sed dispensatorem. Erat et fidei Catholicae prudens assertor, fidelis defensor et haereticorum fortissimus expugnator: qua de causa plerique sibi superbiae, nonnulli crudelitatis et impietatis notam imponebant. Ipse vero, propter Christum talia reputans tamquam lucra, securus ambulabat inter infamiam et bonam famam: sua etenim praedicatio, Catholicis erat odor vitae in vitam, mortis in mortem haereticis. Unde per ipsum fides Catholica de die in diem roborabatur, et pseudo-praedicatorum garrulitas minorabatur. Perfecto odio detractores fidei persequebatur, eos de suis finibus expellendo, ipsorum conventicula prohibendo, et ipsorum domos destruendo. Et versa vice ab ipsis haereticis injustas persecutiones, et ab eorum fautoribus detractiones plurimas patientissime sustinebat; sciens quod Abel esse nequit [*IS*-renuit], quem Cain malitia non exercet."

Holy Fathers and Gospel passages. After he stopped speaking, his brothers gently helped him lie down. The gospel having been read, the solemn mass said, as he lay in that very pulpit [Galdinus] gave up his spirit to God.[94]

The way in which these lives link the episcopal "virtues" of being a champion of the powerless and a persecutor of heretics prompts us to reconsider Giaocchino Volpe's emphasis on the politicized character of denunciations for heresy in Italian cities. "Religious rebellion and heresy," he wrote, "were able to flourish in the same places where political rebellion and heresy flowered."[95] Volpe noted that this connection was particularly strong in exactly the period we are considering — the late twelfth and early thirteenth centuries — and he located its origins in friction between bishops and communes. More recent work on heresy has abandoned this line of inquiry and focused, instead, on explicating the beliefs of heretical sects and showing their ties to popular religion. In this endeavor the persecution of heretics is cast mainly as repression of the lower classes and of alternative belief systems.[96] Politically motivated accusations and denunciations of elites tend to be portrayed as infrequent, unimportant, and evidence merely of the corruption of the church hierarchy. E. Dupré Theseider criticized Volpe, for example, for not distinguishing between real heresy and political heresy (implying that political heresy was not "real") and characterized politically motivated accusations against Ghibellines as "of no more than secondary and incidental importance."[97]

94. "Ipse vero, confessione cum fratribus facta, priusquam Evangelii lectio populo recitaretur, pulpitum ascendens, contra praememoratos Catharos eorumque complices praeclarissimam habuit orationem, eorum errores multis argumentis et rationibus apertissime et quantum oportebat confutans, fidemque catholicam multis sanctorum Patrum exemplis et Evangelicis comprobans scripturis. Posteaquam vero finem dicendi fecit . . . fratres . . . eum ibidem levi motu deposuerunt. Perlecto autem Evangelio et peractis Missarum solemniis, cum ipse in eodem pulpito jacens . . . spiritum Deo reddidit . . . " Cattaneo, "Galdino della Sala," 374 (note 76).

95. Giaocchino Volpe, *Movimenti religiosi e sette ereticali nella società medievale italiana (secoli XI–XIV)* (Florence, 1926), 98.

96. Herbert Grundmann, *Religiöse Bewegungen im Mittelalter*, 2nd ed. (Darmstadt, 1961), trans. as *Religious Movements in the Middle Ages: The Historical Links between Heresy, the Mendicant Orders, and the Women's Religious Movement in the Twelfth and Thirteenth Century, with the Historical Foundations of German Mysticism*, by Steven Rowan (Notre Dame, 1995); *Heresy and Literacy, 1000–1350*, eds. Peter Biller and Anne Hudson (Cambridge, 1994); Malcolm Lambert, *Medieval Heresy*, 2nd ed. (Oxford, 1992); Raniero Orioli, "Le correnti spirituali nel regno d'Italia," *Bullettino dell'Istituto italiano per il medio evo e Archivio muratoriano* 96 (1990): 283–302; Grado Giovanni Merlo, *Eretici ed eresie medievali* (Bologna, 1989); Manselli, *Il secolo XII*; R. I. Moore, *The Origins of European Dissent* (London, 1977). Particularly important in solidifying this approach to heresy have been Emmanuel Le Roy Ladurie's *Montaillou, village occitan de 1294 à 1324* (Paris, 1975), trans. Barbara Bray as *Montaillou, the Promised Land of Error* (New York, 1979); and Carlo Ginzburg's *Formaggio e i vermi* (Turin, 1976), trans. by John and Anne Tedeschi as *The Cheese and the Worms* (Baltimore, 1980).

97. " . . . ma d'importanza non più che secondaria e accidentale," E. Dupré Theseider, "Gli eretici nel mondo comunale italiano," in *Mondo cittadino e movimenti ereticali nel medio evo* (Bologna, 1978), 234.

Such distinctions, it seems to me, are not very useful. Clearly, heterodox belief systems did exist. This does not, however, necessarily mean that everyone accused of heresy was actually being denounced because of defects in belief. In fact, there is clearly a tendency from the time of the investiture conflict to expand the notion of heresy to include not only heterodox belief but also rejection of ecclesiastical authority in matters of discipline. Nicolaitism (clerics being married or having concubines), for example, was clearly a problem of clerical discipline, of the refusal of clerics to obey ecclesiastical dictates. So too simony (the buying or selling of church offices) was a nonconformist practice more than a heterodox belief, yet the radical wing of the reform movement (Humbert of Silva Candida and his followers) held that the simonist was a "heretic." Thus, when the church began seriously attempting to combat heterodox belief, the sternest punishments were accorded the obdurate, those who refused correction and obedience to constituted authority. One of the reasons why the efforts at correcting heretical belief through preaching and instruction were fast deemed inadequate was that heretics rejected the authority of the orthodox hierarchy. Rejection of the authority of the church, disobedience to its dictates, was perceived to be at the heart of the problem. Thus does the author of Lanfranc's life underscore the "impious pride" of the heretics, their sinful reliance on their own faculties rather than humble obedience to ordained authority. It is a short step from this to the definition of any resistance or opposition to ecclesiastical authority as heresy. In 1139, the Second Lateran Council ordered all rulers to force heretics to obey ecclesiastical precepts. When the potentates themselves resisted the authority of the church, they too joined the ranks of "heretics." Lucius III in 1184 decreed that rulers must take an oath before their bishop, pledging their full cooperation in enforcing laws against heretics. Failure to do so would result in excommunication. This decree (known as *Ad abolendam*), in fact, was issued from the new episcopal palace that Bishop Adelard of Verona had built.[98]

Ad abolendam was the foundational document of episcopal inquisitorial powers. It enjoined bishops to announce on all feast days the ecclesiastical and temporal penalties that awaited heretics and their supporters: excommunication, confiscation of goods, loss of office, and abandonment to the secular arm for execution. The bishop, or his trusted delegate, was to visit any parish rumored to harbor heretics and require people to swear oaths binding them to denounce heretics. And, as mentioned earlier, public officials also were required to promise under oath to cooperate with the bishop in persecuting heretics. The decree is careful to stipulate that even those not usually under episcopal jurisdiction were bound to follow his dictates in the pursuit of the purity of the faith.[99] This constituted a powerful reassertion of episcopal authority just as the communes received imperial legitimation. It was issued the year after the Peace of

---

98. Edward Peters, *Inquisition* (New York, 1988), 44–52; Henry Charles Lea, *A History of the Inquisition of the Middle Ages*, 2 vols. (New York, 1922), 1: 224–25.

99. Jaffé, *Regesta*, 2: no. 15109; text in Mansi 22:476 or *PL*, 201: 1297–300; Mariano D'Alatri, "Il vescovo e il «negotium fidei» nei secoli XII–XIII," in *Eretici e inquisitori*, 2 vols. (Rome, 1986), 1: 114–15.

Constance recognized the communes; this, rather than any sudden upsurge of heresy, more likely explains the timing of this decree. It used a spiritual prerogative of the church (the defense of orthodox belief) to place the leaders of the commune in a relationship of subservience and enforced obedience to the bishop. The insistence on an oath, indeed, had ritual significance. It placed the leaders of the commune back in the early-twelfth-century position of acting as vassals of the bishop: they had to take an oath to him, promising to do his will, to obey his commands. True, it was a more circumscribed oath. It subjected them in regard to a specific area, heresy. But this is why the expansion of the notion of what constituted "heresy" becomes so important. In 1253 a crusade was preached against the Ghibelline lord Ezzelino da Romano, and the papacy invited Charles of Anjou in 1266 to lead a Guelph crusade in Italy to quell Ghibelline opposition to papal rule.[100] In sum, political opposition to the church was being assimilated to heresy.

There was, actually, good reason for conflating these categories. As Carol Lansing's study of Cathar heresy in Orvieto demonstrates, "Catharism became an alternative understanding of the relations between public authority and the sacred, an understanding that by disengaging the sacred could sustain the creation of independent corporate institutions. . . . "[101] Her meticulous reconstruction of the social world of Orvietan Cathars reveals them to have been at the forefront of the popular commune, a concerted movement to build strong, independent, corporate institutions of governance within the Italian city. The bishops of Orvieto, weakened and impoverished at the end of the twelfth century, understood the threat this posed to ecclesiastical power. Lansing shows how a key text in the history of heresy in Orvieto — the "Legend of Peter Parenzo," a passion narrative of the martyrdom of a papally appointed rector at the hands of "heretics" — was "concerned to exonerate the bishop, rebuild episcopal fortunes, and, to that end, get Parenzo canonized."[102] The text blames the flourishing of heresy within the town on the pope's detention of Bishop Richard in Rome for several months; the earlier chapters of the *Leggenda* characterize this bishop as an impassioned opponent of the heretics, condemning many to death or loss of citizenship. The rector, Peter Parenzo, is depicted as an episcopal ally: he lives in the episcopal palace and together they fight heresy. After he is murdered, he is still the bishop's best friend: dead, he is a martyr and the bishop vigorously promotes his cult.

Politics and belief were intertwined, and Lansing's study demonstrates that their interconnection was hardly straightforward but nonetheless extremely important: there was a significant "association between ecclesiastical statebuilding, the early Cathars, and attempts to repress them as heretics."[103] Alternate beliefs did exist and did consti-

100. Lea, *History of the Inquisition*, 2: 226–33; Volpe, *Movimenti*, 126–35, 153–59.
101. Carol Lansing, *Power and Purity: Cathar Heresy in Medieval Italy* (Oxford, 1998), 11.
102. Ibid., 25.
103. Ibid., 23.

tute a serious challenge to ecclesiastical authority. And politics were related to the repression of divergent beliefs: it was a political shift consolidating Guelph rule in Orvieto and weakening popular institutions that resulted in the "successful" inquisition of the 1260s in that city.[104]

Not every ecclesiastical censure for heresy, then, was aimed entirely at combating unorthodox belief. Denunciation for heresy too easily became an ecclesiastical tool in friction between the lay leaders of the commune and the bishop. In 1190 the consuls of Piacenza demanded a sum of six hundred pounds from the church to help the commune meet Emperor Henry VI's demand for "contributions" toward his coronation. The bishop refused. The commune responded by carrying off the doors of the churches and refusing to return them. The bishop, with the support of Pope Clement III, threatened the consuls with excommunication and interdict. The archbishop of Milan on March 28, 1191, published these sentences throughout Lombardy. What happened at this point is unclear. But a new round of discord is noted by local chroniclers in 1203. The commune was again demanding a sum from the church (at first two thousand pounds, later raised to sixteen thousand) to help pay off its debts. The bishop again refused. This time the commune countered by prohibiting all its subjects from paying tithes to the church. In protest, the bishop and his clergy left the city, going first to Cremona, but then establishing themselves at Castel'Arquato, twenty-six kilometers (sixteen miles) south of the city. Pope Innocent III on December 15, 1204, wrote to the archbishop of Milan, asking him to make it known throughout the province that the citizens of Piacenza had been excommunicated by their bishop and that their goods were to be sequestered until the conflict was resolved. This economic threat quickly brought the commune to heel, but it took years of negotiations to resolve all the grievances between the church and the city government.[105] Whereas early in the struggle the commune was accused of "iniquitas" — which can be translated as "unfair demands," "injustice," or "sin" — as the wrangling dragged on and the bishop remained in exile, the language of papal condemnation stiffened. On October 7, 1206, Innocent III addressed the *podestà*, consuls, and people of Piacenza about the oppression of its mother church. Accusing the city of trying "to enslave" the church, "reducing it to a piece of

---

104. Lansing's study significantly complicates an older, more straightforwardly political interpretation of accusations of heresy expressing Guelph-Ghibelline factional struggles. These interpretations tend to minimize the significance of real religious differences, highlighting instead the political usefulness of accusations: see Volpe, *Movimenti*, 106–9; Daniel Waley, *Mediaeval Orvieto: The Political History of an Italian City-State 1157–1334* (Cambridge, 1952), 13–15, 49–50; and Lansing's discussion of this literature, *Power and Purity*, 7–8. The nuanced reading of Catharism Lansing articulates, however, reveals the real political threat in divergent belief, particularly in the social networks underpinning both it and the popular commune; the result is a narrative of ecclesiastical repression that is about religion, but also very really about politics.

105. Pierre Racine, *Plaisance du Xème a la fin du XIIIème siècle: Essai d'histoire urbaine*, 3 vols., Thèse présentée devant l'Université de Paris I, le 5 mars 1977 (Paris, 1979), 850–52; Lea, *History of the Inquisition*, 2: 196–97.

property to be taxed," the pontiff contended that the city acted "with contempt for all our warnings and mandates, seduced by the fallacies of heretics."[106]

The bishop of Brescia's persecution of heretics in 1224–25 illustrates how politically enmeshed such campaigns could be. During the opening decades of the thirteenth century, Brescia was ravaged by a veritable civil war between two factions. Its bishops, who before 1183 had ruled the city with full comital authority, took the opportunity to try to recover some of their power. At a certain point in the struggle, the bishop and his allies tried to bring in a *podestà* (governor) from Parma, Matthew of Correggio. On December 27, 1219, when Matthew arrived in the city under the protection of the bishop, the ceremony to invest him as *podestà* was quickly organized. But it was interrupted by a group of leading Brescian citizens who refused to swear in Matthew. The ceremony dissolved in rock throwing and other violence, the would-be-*podestà* barely escaping the city without injury. He and the commune of Parma soon began a suit demanding payment from Brescia of the salary Matthew was to have received, plus damages. Meanwhile, in Brescia, those who had disrupted the ceremony elected their own *podestà*, Obertus Gambara. Those opposing the bishop had won.

Three years later, this faction was still in power and late in 1223, hostilities reopened. According to a papal letter, "heretics and their supporters burst forth in such madness that, having armed their towers against the Catholics, they not only destroyed several churches with fire and ruin, but even threw burning torches from these, ranting with the mouth of blasphemy that they excommunicated the Roman church and those following its doctrine." The pope, Honorius III, urged the bishop to destroy the towers of these "heretics and their supporters," and named the Gambara, Ugoni, Oriani, and the sons of Botatius. Six months later the conflict was still going strong. Another papal letter names the vicar of the *podestà*, Gerard of Modena, and the consuls, along with certain nobles and others of the city, as being in open opposition to the Holy See. Gerard is described as "having cut himself off from ecclesiastical unity, showing himself to be a supporter of heretics." The pontiff, indeed, had received a delegation of nobles asking him "to excuse their fault and that of those absent, asserting that the city of Brescia had been divided into factions for a long time, as everyone knows, whence if some of one party by chance are suspected of the aforesaid depravity, they are keen to defend them not so much as heretics but as members of their party." The bishop's actions were definitely interpreted as an assault on his opposition, and, indeed, families and individuals named as heretics or supporters of heretics — most notably the Gambara — had defeated the bishop's attempt three years earlier to bring Matthew of Correggio in as *podestà*. It would be naive to think that politics had nothing to do with the sanctions for heresy against the Gambara and their faction. Indeed, Matthew's suit against the commune of Brescia was only settled in 1225, as the Gambara and their allies had their

---

106. *PL*, 215: 487–78 (Dec. 18, 1204, no. 175), 998–1000 (Oct. 7, 1206, no. 167). A similar sort of dispute occurred at Fano from 1218 to 1222: see Waley, *The Italian City-Republics*, 3rd ed. (New York, 1988), 57–58.

towers destroyed and were being forced to seek reconciliation with their bishop and the Holy See.[107]

Taking seriously the political context and capital of heresy allegations makes this period in the history of the commune — the late twelfth and early thirteenth centuries — much more intelligible. The vantage point of the bishop's palace is key. It suggests that we take seriously the idea that bishops had their own vision of the independent commune, an ideal of a Christian city presided over by its lord bishop, guarded by its patron saint, and supported and administered by its faithful lay sons and daughters. The ideal had deep roots. We can see elements of it in those early-medieval *laudes civitatis*: recall the image of Milan, girded about by saints and presided over by its *magnus praesul*, its great archbishop. The ideas of the eleventh-century reform movement intensified some elements of this image — the primacy of the sacred and of the power of church leaders — but also opened up new room for lay initiative. By advocating the clearer separation of the sacred and profane, the clergy and the laity, reform sentiments paved the way for ceding many aspects of worldly activity, the *negotium mundi*, to the ambitious burghers of northern Italian towns. The *negotium fidei*, matters of faith, remained the bishop's. Of course, in the eyes of reformers the concerns of the faith touched all things, so in reserving this to the bishop they probably thought they had secured his primacy. As we know, this was not to be; communal leaders came to have a different vision of the city's independence. This was being forcefully articulated in the period after the Peace of Constance: the lay commune's institutions of governance take on greater definition, and its rule was visually solidified in the building of the *broletti*.

This contemporary term for the communal palace is, itself, revealing. From the Latin *brolo* — a lord's hayfield, or more generally an open field — the word well expressed the way the architecture of the communal palace sought to dominate the open, public space at the heart of the city. This was why the consuls of Pavia wanted Bishop Lanfranc's stable; they wanted their palace to have a place on the piazza. And this had been the terrain of the bishop's palace. Bishops countered the new self-confident stance of the commune with a sort of architectural compensation. They expanded the size of their palaces. They articulated in these new palaces a whole new style: one that was decidedly urban and local, drawing on the vocabulary of the city's domestic architecture and decorative traditions, and one that sought a new relationship with the piazza, with public space. The openness of the new look, with its broad windows and porticos, and its engagement with the piazza through staircases and entries, constituted a recasting of the bishop's place in the urban center. It seems a bid to be a sort of lordly first citizen, someone whose place of primacy in the city is based not on feudal power (the image of the palace from at least the tenth century), but on wealth and refinement. If we read this architectural image against the hagiographical one being articulated at the same time, a quite particular view of this

<hr />

107. *Storia di Brescia*, 1: 1063–64, 655–59; *MGH Epist.*, 1: 189–90 (no. 264, Jan. 9, 1225), 197–98 (no. 275, July 15, 1225); Volpe, *Movimenti*, 101–2; Lea, *History of the Inquisition*, 2: 198–99.

lordly first citizen emerges. His wealth is evident in his new palace, but the *vitae* insist that the bishop uses his wealth to sustain the poor: remember Bishop Lanfranc's assertion that he was "not lord, but custodian, not possessor, but dispenser of the goods of the church." By positioning themselves as champions of the poor, the advocates of those without power, bishops claimed for themselves a voice as a sort of moral opposition within the political community. They may have lost real dominance and power to the lay leaders of the commune, but they were not leaving town. They rearticulated their membership in the urban community and claimed the role of ombudsman for those not in power.

This role had moral force because of the bishop's religious position, and bishops focused more intensely on the spiritual powers that remained to them, the *negotium fidei*. As the lives of holy bishops suggest, persecution of heretics was quickly defined as their leading concern in this area and, in fact, the phrase *negotium fidei* comes to mean, par excellence, the defense of the purity of the faith. I believe it became their leading concern not only because heterodoxy was a real threat to the church, but also because it gave bishops some power over the lay leaders of the commune. As bishops were coming to grips with the loss of real power within the city over the late twelfth and early thirteenth centuries, they repositioned themselves as defenders of the downtrodden and moved to solidify and institutionalize the one sure hold they had over lay rulers: their primacy in matters of faith. Sadly, this attempt to hold on to some power within their cities laid the groundwork for the inquisition.

This episcopal repositioning in the late twelfth and early thirteenth centuries seems to me particularly significant. Paradoxically, the bishop became both champion of the oppressed and oppressor. By using the defense of the faith as their most powerful coercive tool to move lay authorities, bishops helped usher in a significantly more repressive phase in the history of the Catholic church. And the move backfired on them. By the mid-thirteenth century, bishops were deemed too inefficient and preoccupied by other concerns to shoulder the primary responsibility of persecuting heretics. Specialists were needed. Increasingly, the papacy appointed members of the new mendicant orders to dedicate themselves to discovering heretics, and bishops saw their powers markedly diminished. The obvious intermingling of politics in accusations for heresy, moreover, compromised the bishop's other roles. The powerless whom he tried to champion were more wary, and contempt for the political involvement of the see often yielded alienation from both the church and the faith.

CHAPTER FIVE:
WHAT KIND OF LORD?
The Bishop in His Hall

In the summer of 1284, Bishop Obizzo of Parma invited some guests to dinner. One was our Franciscan chronicler, Salimbene de Adam, who left an account of this particular evening in the bishop's hall. As we shall see, Salimbene was a frequent guest in episcopal palaces, and his chronicle reveals a great deal about their inner spaces and the activities taking place within them. What prompted the good friar to record this dinner was the bishop's invitation of a certain Benevenutus Asdente. Salimbene identifies Asdente as "a certain poor man" (*quidam pauper homo*), an artisan who made sandals and who lived on the outskirts of the city next to the sewer. He describes him as being

> pure and "simple and God-fearing" [Job 2.3] and courtly (*curialis*), that is having wit and [although] uneducated he had great enlightened understanding, in that he understood the writings of those who predicted the future, namely the abbot Joachim [of Fiore], Merlin, Methodius and the Sibyls, Isaiah, Jeremiah, Hosea, Daniel and the Apocalypse, and even Michael the Scot, Frederick II's astrologer.[1]

Bishop Obizzo had invited Asdente to dinner to question him closely (*diligenter quaesivit*) about the future, and before a large number of people gathered in the hall, this local prophet foretold the death of Pope Martin IV and hard times for Reggio and Parma. The bishop was probably curious about the future, but his invitation to Asdente certainly also was motivated by a desire to observe and question directly this man within his diocese who was developing a reputation as a prophet. Unlike other local aspiring holy men, whom we will encounter later, Asdente allayed any concerns the bishop may have had about his orthodoxy. Salimbene reports that he was humble, without pomp and vanity in his bearing, and that "he never said anything with assurance, but said 'it seems to me' and 'this is how I understand this writing.'"[2]

1. Salimbene, *Cronica*, 749.20–27; trans. Baird, 522.
2. Salimbene, *Cronica*, 776.24–777.26; trans. Baird, 541.

Certain things stand out about this gathering in the bishop's hall. The topics of discussion were probably broad; we know that Asdente's prophecies concerned both general events (bad times coming) and specifically ecclesiastical concerns (the demise of the pope). But the main focus of the evening was religious: the words of a prophet and the bishop's questioning of him. The latter was part of the duties of the conscientious prelate: as bishop he was responsible for the orthodoxy of belief and practice within his diocese, the spiritual well-being of his flock. It is also significant that the man was "poor" and that our account of it comes from a man who had renounced wealth and status to become "poor" as a follower of Saint Francis. These, as we shall see, were important guests at the bishop's table. Obizzo was lord of this hall, but his lordship had a distinctly ecclesiastical flavor.

The hall — a large, open room built to accommodate significant gatherings — is a particularly important place in medieval culture. In elite residences, it was where nobles held court and exercised power. Monarchs were counseled by their vassals in their halls; counts issued judgments and collected dues in theirs. In addition to being a stage for the exercise of power, the hall was also the center of social life. Here great feasts and everyday meals were held. Guests slept here at night, and during the day, genteel conversation and the arts of poetry and song were cultivated.

As we have seen, bishops always had halls. In Late Antiquity, these episcopal *aule* could take several forms. Some *episcopia* had triconch halls (the "Domus Tricoli" in Ravenna, for example), others had basilica-style single-apsed halls (Parenzo), and still others had rectangular halls either on the ground floor (Aquileia, Grado) or on upper floors (the hall next to the chapel of Sant'Andrea at Ravenna). Grand residences — the Lateran, and the archiepiscopal residence at Ravenna — had more than one hall. This diversity in number, style, and siting, however, ended with Late Antiquity. The episcopal *domus* of the early Middle Ages was a much simpler structure; it had only one hall. Both the location and the character of the hall assumed a new uniformity. It was on the second story, sometimes occupying it entirely and in other cases sharing it with one or two smaller rooms. It was rectangular, in length usually three to four times its width. If it had windows, they were few and small. In the central Middle Ages, the bishop's hall became more commodious. Large windows brought light, air, and gracious decor to the hall; ceilings were raised. The number of halls within the episcopal residence often multiplied as new wings were added in the late twelfth and thirteenth centuries, but in location and basic form they continued early-medieval traditions.

The location of our medieval Italian episcopal halls on the second, not ground, floor was typical of aristocratic halls in continental Europe. In Britain, an entirely different tradition of hall building developed. The elite hall there was a free-standing, ground-floor structure, its interior spacious and open to the rafters. In a peculiarly Anglo-centric fashion, architectural historians seem to see the second-story hall dominant throughout the continent — rather than the uniquely insular ground-floor hall in Britain — as the development requiring a causal explanation. Michael Thompson, in fact, recently argued that on the continent halls moved to the second floor during the disturbances of the Viking invasions in the post-Carolingian era.[3] Why, one wonders, did not a similar development occur in England during its century and a half of severe Viking onslaughts? Other architectural historians trace the origins of the second-story hall to Charlemagne's revival of Roman architectural forms.[4]

The documentary and archeological evidence on the emergence of episcopal *domus* in early-medieval Italy presented in Chapter 2 suggests the need to reconsider and perhaps reframe this debate. Basing their developmental model on only physical remains, architectural historians heretofore have thought that the second-story hall originated "at the very top of the social tree" (e.g., Carolingian sovereigns) and then spread downward. The documentary evidence of the *Codice Bavaro* — that collection of early-medieval leases from the archdiocese of Ravenna containing extraordinarily detailed descriptions of houses — indicates that at least in Italy, second-story halls were a common feature of urban domestic architecture and not reserved only for rulers. The residences of the powerful were distinguished by towers, but otherwise their dwellings were simply variants of a two-story rectangular structure, with service areas on the ground floor and living areas above, common in urban centers. This suggests, indeed, that the aristocratic second-story hall developed out of common forms of early-medieval domestic architecture rather than being an innovation of ruling elites. Moreover, remember that archeological evidence from Italy now suggests that these forms of domestic architecture in early-medieval towns were urbanized versions of late Roman rural architecture. This suggests that before positing a Carolingian importation of Italian styles, scholars may want to explore late Roman domestic architecture in Gaul as a source for the elite halls that develop in France and Germany. And, clearly, the early-medieval documentary evidence must be brought into play and used in conjunction with archeological evidence of early-medieval domestic architecture.

Although one can point to general similarities between our Italian episcopal halls and other continental aristocratic halls, such as its second-story location, scholars have overemphasized broad similarities in the elite architectural forms of the twelfth and thirteenth centuries. Generally, they treat examples of ecclesiastical and lay residences interchangeably as evidence of one homogeneous elite palatial architecture. Moreover, the cultural practices taking place within palace halls are also homogenized, with lay and clerical elites depicted as sharing one, pan-European "courtly" culture.[5] Some "na-

3. Michael Thompson, *The Medieval Hall: The Basis of Secular Domestic Life, 600–1600 AD* (Aldershot, England, and Brookfield, Vt., 1995), 45–48.

4. Jacques Gardelles does begin his genealogy of the typical second-story palace hall at Aachen, but he does not place his comments in the context of any debate over a change in the location of halls from the ground to the second floor (as Thompson states, *Medieval Hall*, 41, "Jacques Gardelles [1976], in a penetrating article, thought this change had taken place in the reign of Charlemagne [768–814]"). Jacques Gardelles, "Les Palais l'Europe occidentale chrétienne du Xe au XIIe siècle," *Cahiers de civilisation médiévale Xe–XIIe siècles* 19 (1976): 119.

5. Authors describing courtly culture tend to use examples from secular and clerical elites interchangeably: Thompson does this throughout his work on halls and so too does Joachim Bumke, *Courtly Culture: Literature and Society in the High Middle Ages*, trans. Thomas Dunlap (Berkeley and Los Angeles, 1991), good examples being 54, 56–57, 104–5, 109, 458–88. C. Stephen Jaeger goes

tional" or geographical variation is acknowledged, but there is no distinction between prelates and the secular nobility. The scholarly drive to define and describe one broadly shared elite culture in medieval Europe, I submit, has ended up obliterating important distinctions between secular and ecclesiastical residences, between lay and clerical culture. What follows, I hope, will constitute one step toward reinscribing these significant distinctions.

RELIGIOUS MEANING IN HALL ARCHITECTURE

Let us start with our buildings. We have already noted (in Chapter 3) the elongated proportions of some episcopal halls. The eleventh-century hall in Como is an extreme example: it was five times as long as it was wide. The contemporary Pistoian episcopal *aula* was roughly four times longer than it was wide and Parma's roughly three times longer. As there are no excavated Italian comital or ducal residences from this period, it is impossible to compare the narrow character of these eleventh-century episcopal halls with their direct secular equivalents. The late-twelfth- and early-thirteenth-century halls built by the new communal governments of these cities, however, were proportioned quite differently: they were nearly as wide as they were long or they were square. These differently configured halls certainly enunciated different styles of lordship and statements about power: in the way these spaces structured human interaction, the wider dimensions of the communal hall bespoke collective lordship and a more broadly shared access to power, while the narrower confines of the bishop's hall suited personal lordship and a more hierarchical conception of power.

In France, where more remains of episcopal and comital palaces survive, a comparison of the proportions of clerical and lay halls does show some preference for elongation among ecclesiastics.[6] Our Italian prelates, however, were more likely influenced by

---

further in his book *The Origins of Courtliness: Civilizing Trends and the Formation of Courtly Ideals, 932–1200* (Philadelphia, 1985), arguing that courtly culture originated with the clergy.

6. The twelfth-century episcopal hall at Angers was two and a half times longer than it was wide (26 meters by 10 meters, or 86 feet by 33 feet); the episcopal hall at Meaux in the same era had the same proportions (25 meters by 10 meters, or 82.5 feet by 33 feet). The thirteenth-century hall of the bishop of Laon was smaller, 13 meters by 5 meters (43 feet by 16.5 feet), but similarly proportioned (2.6 times long as wide). Bishop Maurice de Sully's residence in Paris, dating from the late twelfth century, was also over twice as long as it was wide. The halls of secular elites tended to be wider. The comital hall at Le Mans measured 30 meters by 19 meters, or 99 feet by 63 feet (1.57 times long as wide); at Estampe, 11 meters by 7 meters, or 36 feet by 23 feet (1.57); at Mans, 31 meters by 23 meters, or 102 feet by 76 feet (1.3). The halls of great princes, such as the dukes of Aquitaine at Poitiers, were more elongated like the ecclesiastical *aule*: Poitiers measured 50 meters by 16 meters, or 165 feet by 53 feet (3.12), the ducal hall at Caen 30 meters by 11 meters, or 99 feet by 36 feet (2.7), and that at Troyes 30 meters by 12 meters, or 99 feet by 39.5 feet (2.5). Was prodigious length, a certain narrowness of space, an assertion of status? Points of comparison are few, but episcopal halls tend to approximate the proportions of those of greater, rather than lesser, lords. The bishop of Winchester's hall measured 30 meters by 9 meters, or 99 by 29.5 feet (proportion: 3.33); the royal hall at Westminster was much larger (70 meters by 21 meters, or 231 feet by 69 feet), but in proportion (3.33) the same. Pierre Héliot, "Nouvelles remarques sur les palais

the imperial German tradition. In the tenth and eleventh centuries, many of the bishops in Italian sees were from north of the Alps and came to Italy with the imperial entourage. From the Ottonian era, German bishops were prodigious builders, and Wolfgang Giese has eloquently demonstrated that improvement of the material fabric of both their sees and their cities was a prominent element in the reigning ideal of the good bishop. Building churches, palaces, and even city walls was not just a practical good; these activities were conceived as spiritual contributions, improvements of the religious life of their sees.[7] The close relations between sovereigns and bishops in the empire certainly may have influenced episcopal building programs: were episcopal and imperial halls similarly proportioned?

The well-documented remains of Paderborn offer an interesting example (Figure 53). This had been a royal site from Carolingian times and a favored residence of the Ottonian emperors. The city burned, however, in the year 1000, leading to a massive rebuilding program under Bishop Meinwerk of Paderborn (1009–36). Meinwerk rebuilt the cathedral, built himself a residence (*domus episcopalis*) south of the church, raised a royal chapel north of the cathedral dedicated to Saint Bartholomew (in a Byzantine style, using Greek artisans: *per operarios graecos*), and probably oversaw the reconstruction of the imperial palace (his *vita* does not mention his involvement, but the remains date to this era). The proportions of all these structures reveal interesting relationships. The hall of the imperial palace was larger and wider than the hall in the bishop's residence: it measured forty meters by fifteen meters (130 feet by 49 feet), roughly two and half times long as it was wide. Meinwerk's own hall was more elongated, three and a half times longer than it was wide (thirty-five meters by ten meters, or 114 feet by 32.5 feet). What is interesting is that the proportions of the cathedral built by Bishop Meinwerk match those of his hall: the church measured eighty-eight meters by twenty-four meters, 3.66 times long as it was wide.[8]

A similar relationship may be found at Parma. The construction history of the cathedral of Santa Maria is complex, but intimately related to the building and rebuilding of the episcopal residence. You may remember that the bishop of Parma moved his see to a site just beyond the old Roman walls in the mid-eleventh century. Either

épiscopaux et princiers de l'époque romane en France," *Francia* 4 (1976): 197–99, 203, 209; Gardelles, "Les Palais," 121; E. Viollet-Le-Duc, *Dictionnaire raisonné de l'architecture française du XIe au XVIe siècle*, 10 vols. (Paris, 1858–68), 7: 15–18.

7. Wolfgang Giese, "Die Bautatigkeit von Bischofen und Abten des 10. Bis 12. Jahrhundert," *Deutsches Archiv für Erforschung des Mittelalters* 38 (1982): 344–438. There was criticism of overly luxurious building. Bernard of Clairvaux, Hugh of Fouilloi, and Peter the Chanter all decried lavish episcopal architecture: Victor Mortet, "Hugue de Fouilloi, Pierre le Chantre, Alexandre Neckam et les critiques dirigées au douzième siècle contre le luxe des constructions," in *Mélanges d'histoire offerts a M. Charles Bémont* (Paris, 1913), 105–37.

8. Wilhelm Winkelmann, "Die Königspfalz und die Bischofspfalz des 11. und 12. Jahrhunderts in Paderborn," *Frühmittelalterliche Studien* 4 (1970): 398–415; Friedrich Oswald, *Vorromanische Kirchenbauten: Katalog der Denkmäler bis zum Ausgang der Ottonen*, rev. ed., 2 vols. (Munich, 1990–91), 2: 323–24, plan between 328 and 329.

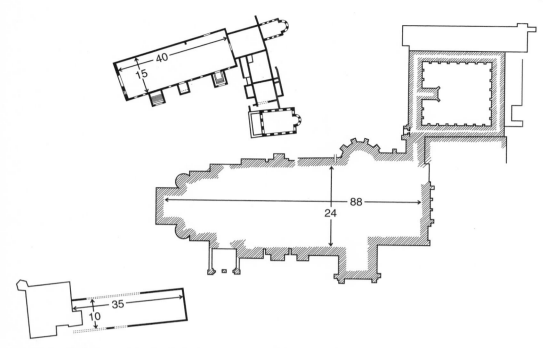

FIGURE 53. *Paderborn, plan of cathedral, royal (top) and episcopal (bottom left) halls. (C. Ingersoll.)*

Bishop Ugo (1027–44) or Bishop Cadalus (1045–71) first built a new residence, calling it a *palatium*. Then a new cathedral was begun on a site across from the new palace; it was consecrated by Pope Paschal II in 1106. Damage to the structure from an earthquake in 1117, however, necessitated a new building campaign; the church and its extraordinary sculptural program were not completed until about 1160.[9] The plan (Figure 54) of the church reveals the cultural connections of its eleventh-century imperial bishops: It was clearly influenced by the eleventh-century cathedrals of Goslar, Metz, and Speyer.[10] It combines a basilical (nave) and a central (transept) plan, the two merged in its seventh bay. In the 1170s, after the cathedral was completed, Bishop Bernard expanded the episcopal palace, adding at least one other hall. After the commune built its palace (1221–23), Bishop Grazia (1224–36) renovated and expanded his, adding both a gracious facade and a new hall (Figure 55).

The proportions of all these episcopal halls are related to the proportions of the cathedral. Moreover, they emphasize different liturgical positions of the bishop in his church. Both the original mid-eleventh-century hall, and one added by Bernard in the 1170s, measured fifteen by seven meters, or 49.5 feet by 23 feet, (2.1 times longer than it is wide). The distance from the high altar to the entrance of the cathedral was fifty-five meters, or 181.5 feet, and the width of the nave 25.5 meters, or eighty-four feet

9. Arturo Carlo Quintavalle, *La cattedrale di Parma* (Parma, 1974), 31–89.
10. Ibid., 83.

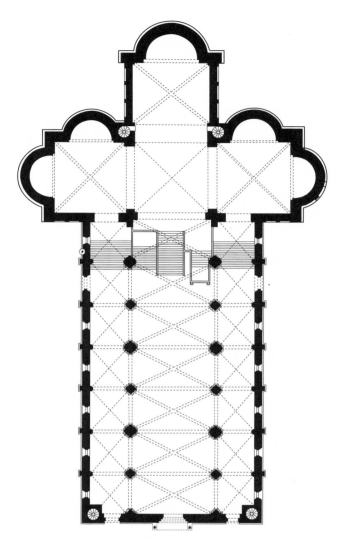

FIGURE 54. *Parma, plan of cathedral. (C. Ingersoll.)*

(2.1 times longer than it is wide) (Figure 56).[11] This geometry assimilated the role of bishop as celebrant of the Eucharist to his role as lord holding court from one end of his hall. His sense of space, whether gazing out over his flock assembled in the church or over those gathered before him in his hall, would have been similar. Conversely, those coming into the bishop's hall were placed in a spatial relationship to him that approximated their relationship to him in the cathedral. The siting of these halls on an

11. See Figure 57 based on Quintavalle, *Cattedrale di Parma*, Plate XXXVIII, and Banzola, "Vescovado," 41. I thank don Bianchi at the Curia of Parma for giving me access to the east wing of the palace while restoration of the great hall was underway (1998) and plans of this floor (Banzola only publishes plans of the ground floor). The renaissance renovations to this floor broke the area of Grazia's great hall into a smaller hall, a chapel, and three anterooms, and this is the configuration preserved today.

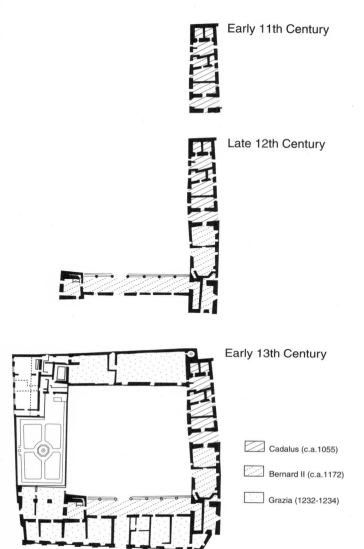

Early 11th Century

FIGURE 55. *Parma, Palazzo del Vescovado, expansion over the Middle Ages. (C. Ingersoll.)*

Late 12th Century

Early 13th Century

Cadalus (c.a.1055)

Bernard II (c.a.1172)

Grazia (1232-1234)

east-west axis, like the cathedral, intensified this association. The spatial relationship created by these shared proportions was one of dependence. The salvation of the believer standing in the nave of the cathedral depended on the mystical sacrifice of the Eucharist offered by the bishop at the altar. The bishop assumed the same place, spatially, in his hall, constructing a similar position of dependence for the petitioners and guests who encountered him there. Their salvation there also depended on him.

The proportions, axial alignment, and spatial relations of Bishop Grazia's new hall were different, but also related to the cathedral (Figure 57). The new hall measured twenty-five by fourteen meters, or 82.5 feet by forty-six feet (1.8 times longer than wide) and was oriented north-south; its seven beautiful trifore windows looked out over the piazza and across to the facade of the cathedral. If the proportions of the earlier

The Bishop in His Hall (177)

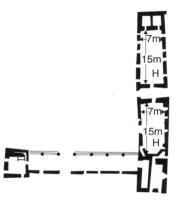

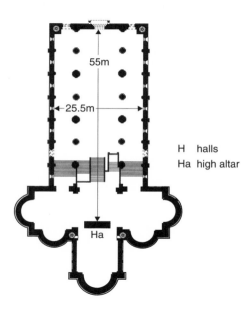

H   halls
Ha high altar

episcopal halls placed the bishop at the altar, where did the proportions of Grazia's hall position the bishop in his church? Significantly, they placed him at the dividing line of lay and clerical space in the cathedral. Like many Romanesque churches, the cathedral in Parma had a raised choir. At the seventh bay of the nave (note the correspondence here with the seven windows establishing a rhythm down Grazia's hall), a series of staircases led down into the crypt and up into the sanctuary. This demarcation between the space reserved to the clergy for the celebration of the sacred mysteries of the mass and the space of the laity in the nave of the church was quite pronounced: the sanctuary was raised above the nave and the staircases visually marked the point of division. The di-

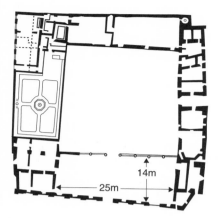

FIGURE 57. *Parma, Palazzo del Vescovado, Bishop Grazia's thirteenth-century hall in relation to the cathedral. (C. Ingersoll.)*

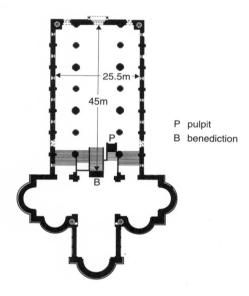

P pulpit
B benediction

mensions of the nave from the top of the stairs were forty-five by 25.5 meters, or 148.5 feet by eighty-two feet (length-width ratio, 1.8). These proportions assimilate the space of the bishop's hall to the place of the people in the church; if the bishop sits at the end of this hall, he occupies the same place that in the cathedral demarcates the transition from lay to clerical space. This point of transition was emphasized liturgically through pontifical benediction: it was exactly at this point, at the top of the stairs leading into the presbytery, where processions into the church paused and the bishop turned to the people to give them his blessing.[12]

In choosing this place for himself, the bishop both underscored the separateness of

12. Quintavalle, *Cattedrale di Parma*, 346.

the more worldly concerns of the people in the hall from his function as high priest, and claimed a liminal status for himself as a figure negotiating the boundary of the lay and clerical, secular and spiritual worlds. Note what has been abandoned in the changed configuration of the episcopal hall. In its proportional relationship to the cathedral, previous halls had joined the bishop's spiritual role as priest to his secular roles (as lord to his vassals, landlord to his tenants) exercised in the hall. This was an optimistic view of a seamless lordship of the bishop in his city. It echoed that "golden mean" that Peter Damian attributed to Saint Maurus of Cesena, the Gregorian vision of balancing the worldly with the spiritual duties of the episcopal office. Bishop Grazia's early-thirteenth-century hall abandons this optimistic vision of a lordship that encompassed both the spiritual and the worldly and acknowledged the changed position of the bishop in the Italian city. He was no longer both spiritual and secular lord of the town. Now he was a negotiator of boundaries, standing at the edge of the sanctuary defending the rights of his church against the predations of the laity. Bishop Grazia's hall reflects the position of the saintly bishops whose lives we visited in the last chapter: Bishop Lanfranc of Pavia defending the rights of his church against the consuls of the commune; Bishop John Cacciafronte defending the poor and the lands of the see against "rich men, nobles, and magnates."

It also echoes the position of Saint Galdinus, who died in his pulpit preaching against heretics. The approximation of the bishop's place in his hall to the point of division between lay and clerical space in his cathedral assimilates his holding court to his preaching in church. The bishop's pulpit stood at that point of demarcation in the seventh bay at the edge of the sanctuary. Ornately decorated with the sculptured reliefs of Benedetto Antelami and jutting out into the nave, the pulpit visually associated the bishop with a sovereign and majestic image of Christ.[13] This was the site from which both the Word of God was proclaimed and the sermons of the bishop preached. This association of the bishop's pulpit with his position in the hall is highly meaningful. First, it assimilates his words in the hall to both the Word of God and his pastoral teaching. Second, it emphasizes how his power in the city was now based on moral suasion rather than juridical rights; his weapons in disputes with the commune, for example, were verbal exhortation and denial of access to the sacraments of the priestly sanctuary (also symbolized in this liminal position). Third, it reflects a new emphasis on preaching in the thirteenth century. This trend is most evident in the immense popularity of the new mendicant orders (the Order of Friars Minor, or Franciscans, and the Order of Preachers, or Dominicans). With these new voices emerging, the bishop underscored his preaching authority by assuming this place in his hall. Moreover, the bishop's new hall allowed him to compete with these other preachers in their own domains. Both the Franciscans and Dominicans were famed for attracting mass audiences to sermons preached in the open piazza. This is at least one reason for the reorientation of Bishop Grazia's hall: its windows looked out onto the piazza, and sermons were preached from the windows of the palace: Bruno Bishop of Segni preached his final ser-

13. For the reconstruction of both the decoration of the pulpit and its placement in the church, see Quintavalle, *Cattedrale di Parma*, 345–50.

mon to his flock from the window of his palace, and Salimbene de Adam recalled Pope Innocent IV preaching from the window of the episcopal palace in Ferrara. Even before Grazia's new hall was finished, preachers found it a perfect vantage point for addressing the throngs in the piazza: during the Great Halleluia of 1233, Salimbene reports that he saw Brother Benedict "standing on the wall of the episcopal palace, then under construction, preaching and praising God."[14]

RELIGIOUS DECOR

Not only the dimensions of the episcopal hall had religious meaning. The decor of the hall also articulated ecclesiastical themes. The Lateran offers abundant evidence of these preferences. The theme for the paintings decorating Leo III's great eleven-apsed *triclinium*, later called the Hall of Councils (*Aula Concilii*), was the Apostles preaching to the gentiles: each of the ten side apses was decorated with an apostle and the main apse depicted Christ and the Blessed Virgin with saints Peter and Paul. In another of Leo's halls, a central image of Christ and the Apostles was flanked by images announcing the transfer of empire from East to West and a very particular view of the relationship between sacred and secular authority. To His right, Christ gives the keys to Pope Sylvester and an oriflamme to Emperor Constantine; to His left, Saint Peter gives the pallium to Pope Leo III and an oriflamme to Charlemagne. The emperor receives his authority from Christ, but through Saint Peter and his successors.[15] Decorative messages were updated with later popes, but sacred themes always predominate. In the twelfth century, the area just outside the Sancta Sanctorum was painted with full-length images of saints and prophets, and a varied array of scenes from sacred history: the Crucifixion, the martyrdom of Saint Sebastian, a blessing Christ, episodes from Genesis. No theory of an iconographic program has yet been advanced for these images.[16] But some additions to Lateran decor were more pointed (and more polemical). Calixtus II (1119–24) celebrated his triumph over Emperor Henry V and his supporters in the Concordat of Worms by having a very particular set of frescos painted in an anteroom just off the great *Aula Concilii*. The paintings depict reforming popes — Alexander II, Gregory VII, Victor III, Urban II, Paschal II, and Calixtus himself — victorious over the imperial antipopes set up against them. The victorious pontiffs are enthroned in full pontificalia; the antipopes (Cadalus / Honorius II, Guibert of Ravenna /

14. *AASS*, 4 Iulii: 484; Salimbene, *Cronica*, 101, 242, 647; trans. Baird, 48, 157, 454.

15. Lauer, *Latran*, 103–13, especially Figure 44; Cäcilia Davis-Weyer, "Die Mosaiken Leos III. und die Anfänge der karolingischen Renaissance in Rom," *Zeitschrift für Kunstgeschichte* 29 (1966): 111–32; Hans Belting, "Die beiden Palastaulen Leos III. im Lateran und die Entstehung einer päpstlichen Programmkunst," *Frühmittelalterliche Studien* 12 (1978): 55–83; Di Berardo, "Le aule di rappresentanza," in *Il palazzo apostolico lateranense*, ed. Carlo Pietrangeli (Florence, 1991) 39–42; Gerhard Ladner, "I mosaici e gli affreschi ecclesiastico-politici nell'antico palazzo lateranense," *Rivista di archeologia cristiana* 12 (1935): 267–69; Christopher Walter, "Papal Political Imagery in the Medieval Lateran Palace," *Cahiers archéologiques* 20 (1970): 157–60, 170–76.

16. Radke, *Viterbo*, 91.

Clement III, Theodoric, Albert, Maginulf / Sylvester IV, and Maurice Burdinus / Gregory VIII) crouch under their feet, serving as footstools (*scabella*).[17]

Many of these fresco cycles within the Lateran treated themes of sacred genealogy. The emphasis in Calixtus's frescos is on visually depicting the true genealogy of Peter — the legitimate popes of the reform era — while execrating pretenders to the lineage. Other images, such as Pope Sylvester receiving the keys from Peter, associated specific popes with the Apostles. We know that this motif of sacred genealogy was used in the decoration of bishop's halls in Late Antiquity. Agnellus recorded how Archbishop Maximian of Ravenna in the sixth century had images of all the bishops of the see painted in the hall of the Domus Tricoli, with inscriptions giving the name of each prelate. Thirteen epigrams of Ennodius on individual archbishops of Milan also clearly were meant to accompany and identify painted images of them.[18] This decorative scheme — a depiction of the series of bishops of the see — was definitely the norm for the episcopal *aula* when palaces were renovated in the Renaissance. Many of these cycles still survive and some are still being continued with the addition of portraits of present-day bishops! The bishop's hall in Verona, for example, is decorated with a cycle painted by a local artist, Domenic Riccio Brusasorzi (1494–1567), and then continued in an anteroom down to the present by other artists (Figure 58). At Padua we know that several artists over the fifteenth century painted the series decorating the great hall of that see's episcopal residence. A register of expenses recorded in 1456 that Bishop Fantino Dandolo commissioned Peter Calzetta to paint "in the great hall, 39 bishops at 3 lira a piece." As R. Zanocco has suggested, these thirty-nine bishops probably represented the number necessary to bring the series up to Bishop Dandolo; another artist most likely painted the early bishops of the see (up to Rorio in the late ninth century), and we know that a "Maestro Lunardo da fiorenza depintore" added ten more bishops in the late fifteenth century.[19]

Unfortunately, these Renaissance renovations of episcopal palaces and their audience halls often obliterated earlier decorative programs, so we have only one fragment of a possible medieval example of this sacred lineage motif. This one fragment survives in the remains of the bishop's palace at Novara. In a ground-floor room adjacent to the cathedral (and now used as the sacristy) are frescos dating from the late twelfth century depicting figures of bishops, each posed in the arch of a loggia, crowned by a bal-

17. Mary Stroll, *Symbols as Power: The Papacy following the Investiture Contest* (Leiden, 1991), 16–35, Plates 8–10; Ladner, "I mosaici," 269–80; Walter, "Papal Political Imagery," 162–66, and its continuation in *Cahiers archéologiques* 21 (1971): 109–23.

18. Picard, *Le Souvenir des évêques*, 505–6.

19. A cycle of bishops was painted in the *aula* of the oldest part of the Castello di Buon Consiglio in Trent under Count-Bishop Johannes Hinderbach (1465–86) and then renovated by the Venetian artist Marcello Fogolino in the sixteenth century. Hans Schmölzer, *Die Fresken des Castello del Buon Consiglio in Trient und ihre Meister* (Innsbruck, 1901), 48–53; Renzo Chiarelli, *Verona — Guida Artistica* (Florence, 1963), 70–71; Bartolomeo Dal Pozzo, *Le vite de'pittori, de gli scultori et architetti veronesi*, 2 vols. (Verona, 1718; reprinted, Verona, 1967), 2:17; R. Zanocco, "Il palazzo vescovile," 180–81.

FIGURE 58. *Verona, Palazzo Vescovile, hall with series of paintings of bishops by Domenic Riccio Brusasorzi, 1494–1567. (M. Miller.)*

dacchino (Figure 59).[20] The best preserved, however, is identified with an inscription as "S. SYRUS," who was the first bishop of Pavia, not Novara. The chapel adjacent to this hall, its entrance just next to this image, was dedicated to Saint Syrus and, as you will read later (see Chapter 6), there were political reasons why the bishops of Novara were invoking Syrus in the late twelfth century — mainly their desire to escape the authority of the archbishops of Milan. Were the bishops of Novara reconfiguring their own genealogy in their selection of holy bishops depicted in the hall? The remains of these wall paintings are too fragmentary to say.[21]

20. Costanza Segre Montal, "La pittura medievale in Piemonte e Valle d'Aosta" in *La pittura in Italia. L'altomedioevo*, ed. Carlo Bertelli (Milan, 1994), 40–41.
21. But Maria Laura Gavazzoli Tomea has noted a compositional parallel between the Novarese series of arches framing saintly figures topped with a baldacchino and both reliquaries (where the figures are usually apostles and prophets) and ivory diptychs. The latter form is attested in Novara recording the episcopal lineage: a fifth-century Ravennate diptych was reused in the thirteenth century to record the bishops of the see from 1125 to 1240. Maria Laura Gavazzoli Tomea, "Considerazioni sulle pitture medievali della curia episcopi di Novara," *Arte medievale* ser. II, 9 (1995):

FIGURE 59. *Novara, cathedral sacristy, fragments of frescos of bishops formerly within the episcopal palace. (Giacomo Perolini.)*

The only complete surviving set of frescos we have for a medieval bishop's palace does not illustrate sacred genealogy, but it is intensely religious in character. These frescos date from the early thirteenth century and are found today in the Curia of Bergamo. The siting of the hall in which they are found is highly significant. In the early twelfth century, the area between the episcopal residence (just north of this hall, along the west end of the old forum) and the cathedral of San Vincenzo was much less crowded. This was the site of the forum of Roman Bergamo, and before the twelfth century it retained this character of open, public space.[22] There was, somewhere in this zone, another "church" (*ecclesia*) dedicated to Mary; some scholars have suggested that it formed, with San Vincenzo, a double-cathedral complex (Figure 60). Over the twelfth century, this relatively open space between the bishop's residence and his liturgical complex became much more densely populated. Two new buildings that separated

---

69–83, 76–77 for the compositional parallels. On the Novarese diptych, *The Age of Spirituality: Late Antique and Early Christian Art, Third to Seventh Century*, Catalogue of the exhibition at the Metropolitan Museum of Art, November 19, 1977, through February 12, 1978, ed. Kurt Weitzmann (New York, 1979), 56–58 (no. 54); Eduard Hlawitschka, "Die Diptychen von Novara und die Chronologie der Bischöfe dieser Stadt vom 9.-11. Jahrhundert," *Quellen und Forschungen aus italienischen Archiven und Bibliotheken* 52 (1972): 767–80.

22. Bruno Cassinelli, Luigi Pagnoni, and Graziella Colmuto Zanella, *Il duomo di Bergamo* (Bergamo, 1991), 6–8, 16–17.

the bishop from his cathedral were raised (Figure 61). First, was the church of Santa Maria Maggiore. Local scholars, following the great eighteenth-century historian Mario Lupo, see the origins of this structure in a rebuilding of the Santa Maria believed to be the "twin" church of San Vincenzo in the proposed double-cathedral complex.[23] But much is ambiguous about the building of this new church: the very date of its construction is still debated, and although the canons of San Vincenzo were involved in its officiation, it had a distinct patrimony. A late-twelfth-century account identifies Santa Maria as a baptistery and reports that "the church of Santa Maria and San Vincenzo is one church and the mother [cathedral] church."[24] What is clear, however, is that by the thirteenth century, Santa Maria had the character of a communal chapel. It became known as the "Chapel of the City," and the commune not only supported it, but also intervened in its administration. Communal business was conducted within the church, and the weights and measures ordained for the city's commerce were inscribed on its north wall facing the piazza.[25] Many visitors to the city today mistake it for the cathedral, and this visual impression no doubt served the commune's purposes: built on a grand scale and after an innovative design, it both dwarfed and marginalized the old basilica of San Vincenzo. Next to it, at the end of the twelfth century, the commune had built its palace. The "broletto" is parallel to Santa Maria and occupies a portion of that public space of the old Roman forum.[26] By the thirteenth century, then, when one entered the center of old Bergamo, this communal palace, with the church of Santa Maria rising behind it, dominated the vista. Both the bishop's palace and his church were occluded (Figure 62).

But the bishop of Bergamo did not gracefully cede the entire central public space of the town to the new commune. He built a new hall abutting the church of Santa Maria (Figure 63). Local observers have long noted, and detested, the curious siting of this hall. It sits exactly where the facade of the church should be. Earlier in this century, Luigi Angelini affirmed in his restoration of the hall that it had not destroyed or covered over a decorated facade; Santa Maria Maggiore had never had one. Since medieval churches were usually built from east to west, from the apse to the facade, this would have been the last section to be completed. Recently, several local scholars have suggested that the episcopal *aula* was added after the 1222 earthquake and that it was posi-

23. Giuseppina Zizzo, "S. Maria Maggiore di Bergamo «Cappella della Città»: La basilica bergamasca nei secoli XII e XIII," *Archivio storico bergamasco* 2 (1982): 216–19.

24. On its dating, see Porter, *Lombard Architecture* 2: 106–118; Zizzo, "S. Maria Maggiore," 213, 215–20. In testimony taken in 1187 regarding the ongoing feud between the canonries of San Vincenzo and Sant'Alessandro, the witness Lanfranc Mazoco reported that on Holy Saturday the bishop celebrated the divine office in San Vincenzo, "et cum processione inde vadit ad ecclesiam Sancte Marie ad benedicendum fontem et celebrandum baptismum. . . . Item dixit quod ecclesia Sancte Marie et Sancti Vincentii est una ecclesia et mater ecclesia." Zizzo, "S. Maria Maggiore," 219.

25. Zizzo, "S. Maria Maggiore," 213–14, 225–29, and generally on this theme, Mauro Ronzani, "La 'Chiesa del Comune' nelle città dell'Italia centro-settentrionale (secoli XII–XIV)," *Società e storia* 6 (1983): 499–534.

26. Russell, *Vox Civitatis*; Paul, *Die mittelalterlichen Kommunalpaläste*, 123–26.

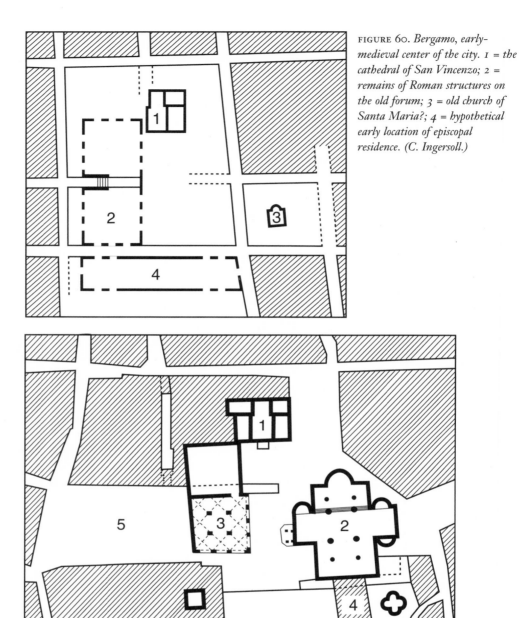

FIGURE 60. *Bergamo, early-medieval center of the city. 1 = the cathedral of San Vincenzo; 2 = remains of Roman structures on the old forum; 3 = old church of Santa Maria?; 4 = hypothetical early location of episcopal residence. (C. Ingersoll.)*

FIGURE 61. *Bergamo, center of the city in the thirteenth century. 1 = cathedral of San Vincenzo; 2 = new "chapel of the city" dedicated to Santa Maria; 3 = the communal palace; 4 = the bishop's new decorated hall; 5 = Piazza Vecchia. (C. Ingersoll.)*

FIGURE 62. *Bergamo, view of civic center from base of Piazza Vecchia, the communal palace at center and the church of Santa Maria Maggiore rising behind it. (M. Miller.)*

tioned in order to stabilize the church.[27] This would be one explanation for the large diaphragm arch running through the center of the hall, perpendicular to the west wall

27. First suggested by Angelini, "Scoperte e restauri di edifici medievali in Bergamo alta," 38; and repeated by Miklós Boskovits, his introducton to *I pittori bergamaschi dal XIII al XIX secolo, vol. I: Le origini* (Bergamo, 1992), 70, note 9, and Laura Polo D'Ambrosio and Anna Tagliabue, "Un ciclo bergamasco di primo duecento: Gli affreschi dell'aula della curia," *Arte cristiana* ns. 77 (1989): 269.

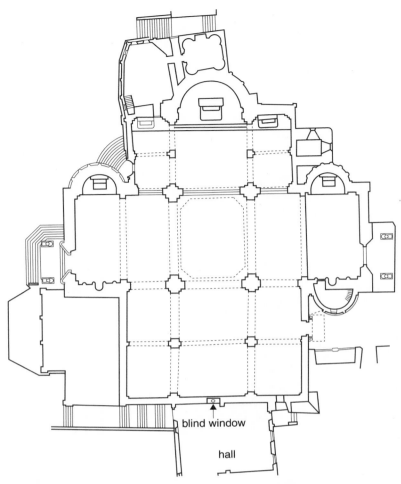

blind window

hall

FIGURE 63. *Bergamo, plan of Santa Maria and new episcopal hall. (C. Ingersoll.)*

of Santa Maria. But this arch, in fact, neither lines up with any of the piers nor is positioned centrally to counter the thrust of the building. There is also no other evidence of stabilizing repairs on other sides of the building (would only this side be unstable?).[28]

The siting of the bishop's new hall, I think, has more to do with destabilizing the triumphalist building program of the commune than with shoring up one of its central elements. The new hall enlarged the episcopal palace and impeded further expansion of the "Chapel of the City." Were the consuls planning a nave? Since they hadn't put a facade on the west end of Santa Maria, one has to wonder. If such a development of the church's plan was under discussion, the bishop's extension of his residence decisively closed off this possibility. Moreover, it positioned the bishop's new hall as a "nave" to the commune's church. In light of the proportional relationship between Bishop Grazia

28. Both don Bruno Caccia and arch. Pino Calzana concur that the arch does not serve as a buttress.

of Parma's new hall and the nave of his cathedral, the siting of the bishop of Bergamo's new hall is striking. More interesting still is a fake "window" at the east end of the hall — which, if Santa Maria had a nave, would have been that point of demarcation between lay and priestly space — that is perfectly centered with the main aisle of the church and contains images of two early bishops of the see giving the pontifical benediction (Figure 64). In the deployment of these images and the placement of his new hall, the bishop of Bergamo seems to be reasserting a particular relationship with his people that the commune, in adopting Santa Maria Maggiore as its own church, had been subverting.

That relationship is one of receiving, and needing, the bishop's blessing. The interior decoration of the hall amplifies this theme. It was a hall of judgment, but not one, as has been suggested, belonging to *"miles iustitie,* that is, the officials of the commune who oversaw fairs and markets."[29] It was the bishop's hall. Several indicators tell us this. First, this land has always been associated with the see: the hall is still part of the Curia of Bergamo, and just next to it is the bishop's chapel, Santa Croce, dating from the eleventh century.[30] Moreover, an episcopal document dated 1225 was redacted "in the new high room of the see, next to the church of Santa Maria" (*in camera nova alta episcopatus iuxta ecclesiam sancte marie*).[31] In this document, it was the bishop who presided over a dispute settlement concerning lands belonging to the see. No contemporaneous communal documentation mentions a hall of justice next to Santa Maria.

The fresco cycle, on stylistic considerations, has been dated to the second or third decade of the thirteenth century. It consists in several registers of decoration. Just below the ceiling was a band of animal figures, much like the top border of the Bayeaux Tapestry. A band with vine and leaf interlacing set this off from the main register, which contains scenes from the life of Christ. Below this narrative register was another of equal width divided into squares containing geometric designs and some small figures (Figure 65). Finally, the lower part of the wall was frescoed with drapery; only a small fragment of this survives on the north wall, but it indicates that the hall was originally much taller. The current flooring was inserted during the Renaissance, probably owing to problems of water infiltration (Figure 66). This means that during the Middle Ages this space would have been more grandiose and that the narrative scenes that concern us here were probably about three meters (roughly ten feet) higher off the floor.

29. "L'Aula poteva essere uno degli spazi usati per trattare questioni del genere. In particolare si può ipotizzare fosse la sede dei *miles* [sic] *iustitie:* cioè degli ufficiali del comune che svolgevano funzione di sorveglianza su fiere e mercati . . . " Laura Polo D'Ambrosio, following Giuseppina Zizzo, in Boskovits, *I pittori bergamaschi,* 79.

30. Both don Bruno and arch. Calzana believe that a passageway originally connected the two structures on what was then the ground level. The present flooring, both in the chapel and in the hall, was inserted in the early modern era, probably due to water infiltration.

31. On the long association of the property with the see, Angelo Mazzi, "I «confines domi et palatii» in Bergamo," *Archivio storico lombardo* 19 (1903): 27, and 20 (1903): 332, 342–46, 354–61 with the "Schizzo topografico"; the original north doorway is evident in the hall and in the map of the site there by Luigi Angellini; for the 1225 document, see *AVBergamo,* Diplomata seu Jura Episcopatus Bergomensis, Raccolta 2, parte 1, perg. 8.

FIGURE 64. Bergamo, *Aula della Curia, blind window on east wall with early bishops Narnus and Viator.* (*Fototeca della Diocesi di Bergamo / Archivio Edizioni Bolis.*)

animal
figures
and
flora

vine and leaf
interlacing

pictorial
narrative

geometric
designs

drapery

Renaissance
flooring

FIGURE 65. *Bergamo, Aula della Curia, divisions of wall décor. (C. Ingersoll.)*

With these conditions in mind, let us consider the narrative portion of the fresco cycle as it would have greeted the eyes of a viewer entering from the piazza on the north side of Santa Maria Maggiore (Figure 67). The large arch dividing the room would first command the viewer's attention. Closest to you, on the east end of the arch, a dynamic angel points across its expanse, its wings emphasizing the urgent gesture of its hands

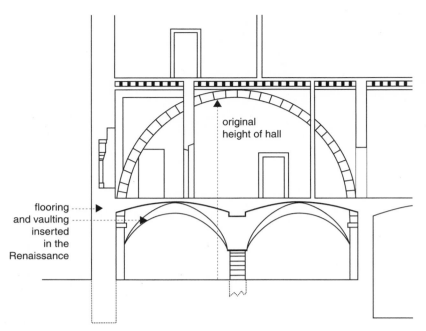

FIGURE 66. *Bergamo, Aula della Curia, section showing original height of hall. (C. Ingersoll.)*

(Figure 68). The eye follows this cue and finds on the other end of the arch a placid *An-nunziata*, an image of the Blessed Virgin receiving the news that she is to bear a son (Figure 69). Her hands reach out toward the angel, indicating her acceptance. Behind her, along the northwest corner, cascade scenes from the infancy of Christ: him as a newborn, resting in the manger; his birth announced to the shepherds; his first bath; his adoration by the Magi; him carried into Egypt as Herod has the innocents slain (Figure 70). Below the Virgin, facing in toward the center of the room, a bishop kneels in full pontifical vestments addressing a petition to Mary, his hands clasped and raised in a gesture of supplication. On your left begins another narrative. The Last Supper is above your shoulder (Figure 71). As you look up, you share the view of the one child-like-looking apostle on your side of the table who is being fed by the hand of Christ. A sleepy Saint John has put his head down, and Judas gestures toward Jesus; his other hand rests on the outstretched arm of the Savior. You walk forward and see Christ kneeling to wash the feet of an apostle (Figure 72). Below the seated apostle is the blind window: across its tympanum, Saint Alexander rides, armored as a knight, his cape fly-ing out behind him, his bannered lance emblazoned with *fleur-de-lis* (Figure 73). The leaping posture of his horse pulls you farther along the wall. Below him, in the arched portals of the bifore, the two earliest bishops of Bergamo — saints Narnus and Viator — offer you their blessing: their faces are solemn, one hand raised in benediction, the other holding the crosier (see Figure 64). You pass under the arch and the Passion cy-cle continues on your left: Christ prays in the Garden of Gethsemane as you stand with the huddled sleeping apostles, their rounded forms like bundled infants. In the center of the wall, a mob of soldiers seizes Christ, and Peter strikes the servant of the High

FIGURE 67. (TOP) *Bergamo, Aula della Curia, interior. (Fototeca della Diocesi di Bergamo / Archivio Edizioni Bolis.)*

FIGURE 68. (BOTTOM LEFT) *Bergamo, Aula della Curia, north face of central arch, east end: Angel of the Annunciation. (Fototeca della Diocesi di Bergamo / Archivio Edizioni Bolis.)*

FIGURE 69. (BOTTOM RIGHT) *Bergamo, Aula della Curia, north face of central arch, west end: Blessed Virgin Mary receiving the Annunciation. (Fototeca della Diocesi di Bergamo / Archivio Edizioni Bolis.)*

FIGURE 70. Bergamo, *Aula della Curia, west end of central arch, wall facing north: scenes from the infancy of Christ. (Fototeca della Diocesi di Bergamo / Archivio Edizioni Bolis.)*

FIGURE 71. *Bergamo, Aula della Curia, east wall: Last Supper. (Fototeca della Diocesi di Bergamo / Archivio Edizioni Bolis.)*

FIGURE 72. *Bergamo, Aula della Curia, east wall: Christ washing the feet of a disciple. (Fototeca della Diocesi di Bergamo / Archivio Edizioni Bolis.)*

FIGURE 73. *Bergamo, Aula della Curia, tympanum of blind window on east wall: Saint Alexander.* *(Fototeca della Diocesi di Bergamo / Archivio Edizioni Bolis.)*
FIGURE 74. *Bergamo, Aula della Curia, east wall: agony in the garden, the soldiers seize Christ, Jesus before Pilate. (Fototeca della Diocesi di Bergamo / Archivio Edizioni Bolis.)*

Priest. In the corner scene, Christ stands before Pilate while Peter denies him three times in the courtyard (Figure 74). The story continues on the wall facing you. Only fragments remain, but the raised-fist postures of the figures in profile and the placid autocephalous figure at the center suggest the Derision of Christ by the soldiers. Nothing remains of the final scene on this south wall, but it must have been the crucifixion: just on the other side of this wall was the bishop's chapel, Santa Croce, dedicated to the cross on which Jesus suffered.

The bishop, coming out of his chapel, could enter his hall through a door on the south wall, diagonally across from the piazza entrance. He would have sat just within the door at the west end of the hall. As he looked out into the room, he faced the images of Christ praying in the garden, betrayed to the soldiers by Judas's kiss, and arraigned before Pilate — images of a flawed and corrupt "judicial" process necessary for our salvation. Christ the innocent — betrayed, abandoned, and denied by his followers — was the backdrop against which those brought before the bishop's judgment stood (probably not altogether reassuring to the petitioner with the Crucifixion in his peripheral vision). Other images appropriate to a judicial setting were within the bishop's view along the arch dividing the room. Just above where we entered, was a wheel of fortune (Figure 75). Lady Fortune sits at the center. Above her, with the inscription "I reign" (*REGNO*), is a seated figure raising a branch in his right hand. Toppling head first off the right curve of the wheel is a figure inscribed "I ruled" (*REGNAVI*). Prostrate under the wheel is a barefoot figure murmuring, "I am without kingdom" (*SVM SINE REGNO*) and rising on the left, one looking expectantly upward with the inscription "I will rule" (*REGNABO*). Flanking the center of the arch are images of King David and the prophet Jeremiah: both would have been looking at the image of the crucifixion I hypothesize on the south wall, for both were related in medieval exegesis to suffering and redemption. Jeremiah was the somber prophet of mourning and of the suffering of God's people; King David was cast as a messianic forerunner of Christ (his early shepherd's life pointing to Christ the Good Shepherd, the five stones he used to fell Goliath symbolizing the five wounds of the Savior, his betrayal by his counselor Ahithophel and passage to Cedron recalling the Passion). And closest to the bishop, at the west end of the arch, is the Archangel Michael weighing souls in a balance.

The backdrop to the bishop is equally unambiguous (Figure 76). Above his left shoulder, presiding over the Last Judgment, is the apocalyptic Christ with the two-edged sword issuing from his mouth, the sword that destroys unrepentant sinners (Rev. 1:16, 2:16, 19:15). Damned souls writhe in a tomb on Christ's (and the bishop's) left and on his (and the bishop's) right are the happy souls of the saved. Over the bishop's right shoulder is an image of Christ in glory adored by the blessed; he holds a scroll proclaiming, "Let he who wishes to come to me, deny his very self. . . . " The wording of the scroll stops there, but most in the room would have known that this passage from the Gospel of Matthew (16:24) continues: " . . . take up his cross and follow me." Farther to the bishop's right, of course, was the cross: the image of the crucifixion on the south wall and behind it the cross-shaped little chapel dedicated to the "holy cross." As if all this visual association of the bishop with both Christ the eternal judge and Christ our Savior wasn't sufficient to reinforce the prelate's authority, slightly above and behind him in the patterned squares of the geometric register are little images of legal experts, some pointing at books, others reading scrolls, all looking sage and gesturing didactically.

In a rather simple way, aspects of this decorative program tried to reinforce the bishop's judicial authority by associating it with Christ's authority to pass eternal judg-

FIGURE 75. *Bergamo, Aula della Curia, central arch, south face, east end: wheel of fortune. (Fototeca della Diocesi di Bergamo / Archivio Edizioni Bolis.)*

FIGURE 76. *Bergamo, Aula della Curia, west wall: Christ in Glory and apocalyptic Christ. (Fototeca della Diocesi di Bergamo / Archivio Edizioni Bolis.)*

ment on all men and women. This powerful linkage between the bishop's justice and God's has to be set in the context of jurisdictional change within the city of Bergamo. The bishop here had been count of the city since the early tenth century: this means that he by right administered all justice, criminal and civil, within the walls.[32] Although a commune emerged in the city at the very end of the eleventh century, judicial authority seems to have remained in the bishop's hands. Indeed, Bergamo was one of the few cities where some titular role for episcopal power survived the wars with Barbarossa. In 1156 the emperor had even extended the bishop's *districtus* (control of all public functions) to the countryside, which no previous monarch had ceded. These rights were confirmed in 1183, and even in the provisions of the Peace of Constance, the bishop of Bergamo was accorded the right to nominate the city's officials (in other

32. Jörg Jarnut, *Bergamo 568–1098: Verfassungs-, Sozial- und Wirtschaftsgeschichte in einer lombardischen Stadt im Mittelalter*, Vierteljahrschrift für Sozial- und Wirtschaftsgeschichte, Beiheft Nr. 67 (Wiesbaden, 1979), 112–32, and his "Lo sviluppo del potere secolare dei vescovi bergamaschi fino alla lotta per le investiture," in *Bergamo e il suo territorio nei documenti altomedievali: Atti del convegno Bergamo 7–8 aprile 1989*, ed. Mariarosa Cortesi (Bergamo, 1991), 69–79.

cities the consuls derived their authority directly from the emperor).[33] Regardless of these imperial affirmations, however, in the opening decades of the thirteenth century the commune was exercising judicial authority in the city and challenging the bishop's lordship in the *contado* as well. In 1219 a "consul of justice" appears in a charter, and some of the laws incorporated into the earliest communal statutes (the *Statutum vetus*, redacted sometime before 1248) date from 1211, 1220, and 1221.[34] Claudia Storchi, recognizing that the bishop still technically held public authority in the city, has suggested that the character of the justice offered by the commune was rooted in neighborhood organizations (the *vicinie*) and drew on traditions of private arbitration and dispute settlement.[35] A particularly intense bout of factional violence within the city in these opening decades of the thirteenth century probably fostered the commune's more aggressive involvement in maintaining public order: the earliest laws in the *Statutum vetus* bring homicide and "injuries" under the purview of the *podestà* We know from a lengthy dispute between the bishop and the commune, extending from about 1215 to the early 1230s, that the consuls were also trying to legislate for the *contado*, specifically in the Valle Ardesio where the bishop held lucrative mining rights. The commune responded to the bishop's denunciations by recognizing that the church held *honor et districtus* (public authority) there, but claiming that the commune was still "lord over the men of this valley" (*dominus super hominibus illius Vallis*).[36]

It is within the context of these competing notions of law that we must read both the building of the bishop's new hall and the semiotics of its fresco cycle. The bishop, by virtue of relatively recent imperial *diplomata* and constitutions, held title to rights of justice in both the city and its surrounding countryside. In the face of the city's long tradition of episcopal rule and these imperial affirmations, the commune fostered and began to systematize traditional private methods of arbitration and dispute settlement, integrating them with their emergent institutions. It basically developed a new parallel and competing system of law and justice, rather than trying to take over the bishop's. The building of the bishop's new hall of justice was a clear reply to the commune's legislation, and its fresco cycle answers the consuls' use of "tradition" by invoking a more ancient, powerful, and eternal tradition: God's just ordering of the world and his plan for our salvation. The bishop was shifting the grounds of his authority, appealing not to the imperial documents he had received, but to his consecrated authority and his liturgical role as Christ's representative in Bergamo. In the arrangement of his new hall, the bishop associated himself with the apocalyptic Christ separating the damned from the blessed. The other frescos spelled out a particular reading of salvation history, but the historical character of these scenes is important: it served to concretize the salvific char-

33. Claudia Storti Storchi, *Diritto e istituzioni a Bergamo dal comune alla signoria* (Milan, 1984), 71–72, 82, 87.

34. Ibid., 161, 228–33. On the date and character of the *Statutum vetus*, 153–76.

35. Ibid., 181–233, but especially 197, note 45; on the general outline of her view of the neighborhood associations, 49–55.

36. Ibid., 255–61; *AVBergamo*, Diplomata seu Jura Episcopatus Bergomensis, Racc. 2, perg. 36, 37.

acter of the bishop's justice and to set it in a worldly context. The bishop's new hall was an artful rejoinder in an ongoing public discourse within the city about the source of justice.

But the fresco cycle is even more semiotically complex; it is not just a reassertion of episcopal authority. It acknowledges the fallibility of the judicial process while offering both a deeply Christian exhortation to submission of the will and the reward of holiness to those who do. What immediately confronts the petitioner entering the room is the Annunciation depicted across the central arch facing north: Mary placidly, willingly, accepts what God had decreed for her. The inscription across the center of the arch underscores the Virgin's submission. This is not the surprised Mary, so favored by Renaissance artists, wondering, "[H]ow can this be when I do not know man?" (Luke 1:34). The Annunziata of Bergamo responds, "[B]ehold the handmaid of the Lord; let it be done to me according to your word" (Luke 1:38). Accepting God's will is part of the divine plan for our salvation. That this message is depicted through Mary has another level of meaning: the commune of Bergamo had taken Mary as its patron and had patronized the church next door dedicated to her. The bishop, in emphasizing Mary's submission to the divine will, prescribed a certain attitude of submission for the commune. The submission the bishops sought, however, from their lay "subjects" was not an abject one. The route of the petitioner into the bishop's presence was also the route of Christ to Calvary: the placement of the Passion frescos in the room associates the petitioner with Jesus. Significantly, the submission and humility of Jesus are emphasized in the frescos. The first scene depicts not the moment of the institution of the Eucharist, but Jesus receiving Judas's denial of his betrayal. In the second, he kneels to wash the apostle's feet. After the agonizing prayer in the garden to be spared his ordained suffering and sacrifice, he accepts his Father's will in words that resonate with the Virgin's: " . . . but let your will, not mine, be done" (Matt. 26:42; Mark 14:36; Luke 22:42). In the next scene Jesus allows himself to be arrested (and tries to keep Peter from defending him). He stands bound before Pilate in the following scene, refusing to deny the charges against him and give Pilate some out. In the "Derision" he accepts the scornful blows of the soldiers. Humble acceptance and submission are visually emphasized every step of the way into the bishop's presence, but the redemptive purpose of this submission is also embraced. Thus, not only the bishop sitting in judgment is associated with Christ. So too is the petitioner. That all the roles in these encounters are patterned on Christ is no accident. The spirituality of the late twelfth and early thirteenth centuries placed the life of Christ — and our imitation of it — at the center of Christian devotion.

The religious character of these decorative wall frescos in the bishop's hall is clear. Fragments from other sites suggest, not surprisingly, that bishops surrounded themselves with religious imagery. At Parma, no medieval decor from Grazia's great hall survives, but in the large room on the third floor (at the south end of the building) there are remains of a thirteenth-century fresco. The image is of Christ offering his blessing, flanked by the Blessed Virgin and Saint John the Evangelist.[37] At Como, photographs

37. Banzola, "Vescovado," 36.

survive of some medieval frescos from the west wing of the palace (destroyed early in the century). One fragment shows the bishop of Como giving a blessing; in addition to his vestments and mitre, he wears a comital crown indicating his dominion over Chiavenna. Other fragments show mythical beasts — their bottom halves animal, their tops human — fighting, playing musical instruments, gesturing.[38] Such creatures usually were understood metaphorically to represent the constant human struggle with our lower selves, our bestial natures. A frescoed wall in a ground-floor hall within the episcopal palace in Spoleto depicts the Blessed Virgin enthroned (Figure 77). The baby Jesus, sitting on her lap, raises one hand in blessing while holding a tiny book in his other hand. The Madonna's throne is flanked on the left by Archangel Michael and on the right by Saint Lawrence. A tiny figure of the donor (probably the bishop's chancellor) kneels at the Virgin's feet. This fresco, dating from the early fourteenth century, was the work of an Umbrian artist known as the "Maestro della Fossa," whose refined Gothic-inflected style is considered one of the finest of the Trecento.[39] Finally, although the fresco itself does not survive, an episcopal chronicle from Orvieto mentions a painting within the palace depicting a pious donation to the see by Count Pepo and his son Farolfus the Bald.[40]

Only one fragment from an episcopal decorative program seems to belie my point. When the bishop of Pistoia raised the ceiling in his hall in the late twelfth century, he also added a set of frescos on the newly created space running along the top of the long walls. A fragment has survived on the south wall: the images are of battle scenes (Figure 78). Confronting ranks of war-horses clash as a lance unseats a mailed knight; he and his eagle-crested shield tumble toward the ground. Under the galloping hooves, two decapitated warrior corpses lie. With the closed eyes of death one head looks toward his *fleur-de-lis*–crested shield; the other head, wearing a ruler's crown, looks away from its eagle-emblazoned shield. The frescos seem to depict an imperial defeat. This, of course, would be a perfect post-Gregorian ecclesiastical topic! Natale Rauty considered this possibility and rejected it in his discussion of these fragments, because Pistoia had returned to the imperial camp after the investiture conflict. In fact, Frederick Barbarossa not only had given gifts to the see, but also was guest of Bishop Rinaldus, whom he invested with an imperial fief, in 1181. Further, no twelfth-century emperor died in battle. Barbarossa, it is true, died on the third crusade, but he drowned in the river Saleph; the bishop would have been creatively rewriting his end if this were a crusade tableau. The general style and disposition of the fragments recall the Bayeux Tapestry, but a compositional parallel closer to home suggests that the theme of the decorative

38. Frigerio and Baserga, "Il palazzo vescovile," 45, and Figures 21–28.

39. Elvio Lunghi, "Umbria," in *Pittura murale in Italia dal tardo duecento ai primi del quattrocento*, ed. Mina Gregori (Bergamo, 1995), 163, 166; Giampiero Ceccarelli, *Il museo diocesano di Spoleto* (Spoleto, 1993), 18. I thank dott. Giuliana Nagni for showing me this fresco while the building was undergoing earthquake repairs.

40. David Foote, *The Bishopric of Orvieto: The Formation of Political and Religious Culture in a Medieval Italian Commune*, Ph.D. diss., University of California Davis, 37. I thank the author for allowing me to read his dissertation and for his permission to cite it.

FIGURE 77. *Spoleto, episcopal palace, Blessed Virgin and saints by "Maestro della Fossa." (Arcidiocesi di Spoleto-Norcia.)*

program may not have been secular. As Rauty has pointed out, a manuscript of Augustine's *City of God* in the Laurentian Library (Florence) includes a battle scene with a figure falling from a horse in its depiction of the "earthly city," suggesting this as a possible theme for these frescos on the south wall of the bishop's hall. Might the frescos on the north side of the bishop's hall have depicted the "heavenly city"?[41] The remains of the decorative cycle are too partial to assay its meaning. But the manuscript illustration Rauty calls to our attention serves as a salutary caution to interpreting every knightly figure as evidence of profane decoration.

Moreover, several Italian fresco cycles depicting secular subjects that were once credited to episcopal patronage have been attributed more convincingly to lay lords. A good example is the fresco cycle in the "Hall of Justice" within the fortress of Angera on Lago Maggiore. The fortress did belong to the see of Milan before 1314, and the

41. Rauty, *Palazzo*, 1:99–103.

FIGURE 78. *Pistoia, Palazzo dei Vescovi, fragments of frescos from hall, south wall. (Natale Rauty and the Cassa di Risparmio di Pistoia e Pescia.)*

frescos within the hall depict the victory in 1277 of Archbishop Ottone Visconte over Napo Della Torre for control of Milan. The construction of the hall was contemporary with the battles the frescos depict, but the frescos themselves are obviously later. The question is, how much later? Some scholars, basing their arguments on archaic stylistic characteristics of the cycle, have attributed the frescos to the last years (1290–95) of the victorious archbishop himself, Ottone Visconti. But since two bishops hostile to the Visconti (one a Della Torre) followed him in the see, it is difficult to imagine these celebratory frescos surviving their episcopates. Most scholars, in fact, have come to date the frescos — on stylistic as well as historical grounds — to the period just after 1314.[42] In that year, Matthew Visconti permanently wrested the fortress from the Della Torre and from the see. The decoration of the hall with scenes of his ancestor's victory at the site served to commemorate its acquisition by Matthew for the Visconti family. It also celebrated the Visconti lordship over Milan, for which Archbishop Ottone laid the foundation: the victory at Desio depicted in the frescos was the foundation of the Visconti signoria. The fact that this family established its rule over Milan through the

42. The best overview of the scholarship on the Rocca di Angera is in *EAM*, s.v. "Angera" (1:641–44); the key interventions in the debate over the date, and therefore the sponsorship, of the frescos are Pietro Toesca, *La pittura e la miniatura in Lombardia* (Milan, 1912), 156–70; and Fernando Bologna, *La pittura italiana dalle origini* (Rome, 1962), 91. The famous Iwein frescos in the castle of Rodengo were also once attributed to episcopal patronage, but are now recognized to have been commissioned by a ministerial elite: Nicolò Rasmo, *Pitture murali in Alto Adige* (Bolzano, 1973), 7–13; Volker Schupp, "Kritisch Anmerkungen zur Rezeption des deutschen Artusromans anhand von Hartmanns 'Iwein.' Theorie — Text — Bildmaterial," *Frühmittelalterliche Studien* 9 (1975): 424–34 on Rodengo and especially 431–33 on the reattribution.

archbishopric shows the political significance of episcopal lordship even after the rise of the commune.

The Visconti at Angera were, in fact, following a well-established theme for the decoration of secular halls. The decorative cycles adorning the halls in communal palaces in the thirteenth century often depicted significant military victories. At Mantua, a twelfth-century cycle in the great hall depicts an unidentifiable battle involving ships, knights, and foot soldiers. In the thirteenth century, this was replaced with a cycle depicting the victory of the Mantuan commune in 1251 over a group of Ghibelline "traitors" who had taken over the castle of Marcaria.[43] Fragmentary frescos at Brescia in the hall of the commune's *palatium maius* depict prisoners chained together; the names inscribed below identify them as "traitors" to the commune. Sometimes, however, more peaceful events were commemorated. The communal hall in San Gimignano was frescoed with scenes from a ceremonial tournament and hunting party the city put on for Charles of Anjou after he was victorious over Ghibelline forces at Poggibonsi in 1274.[44] Fragments recently discovered at the *broletto* in Milan appear to be the depiction of constituent groups within the commune: groups of men, some armed and some not, are drawn in full length, with inscriptions below the clusters identifying them as representatives of different quarters of the city (Porta Vercellina, Porta Comasina, Portanuova) or various communities in the *contado* (Galliano, Corneno).[45]

My point here is simple. Evidence for the character and meaning of decoration within communal, princely, and episcopal halls in the twelfth and thirteenth centuries is quite fragmentary. But several patterns seem clear. Secular topics dominate secular halls: communes and noble families alike tended to commemorate important military victories on their walls or to depict the jousts and hunting parties that entertained courtly society. The evidence for episcopal halls is different: religious imagery predominates. Bishops surrounded themselves with scriptural narratives, theocratic allusions, and icons of holiness. There were, I submit, both secular and clerical dialects within the aristocratic, or "courtly," culture of medieval Italy. Some themes and types of imagery were shared in common. Both prelates and lay nobles, for example, liked to visualize their genealogies.[46] And communal decorative cycles often did include some religious

---

43. *Matilde, Mantova e il palazzi del borgo. I ritrovati affreschi del palazzo della ragione e del palazzo dell'abate*, ed. Aldo Cicinelli, et al. (Mantua, 1995), especially 117–90.

44. Gaetano Panazza, "La pittura del secolo XI all'inizio del secolo XIV," in *Storia di Brescia*, 1: 793–812; *Pittura murale in Italia*, ed. Mina Gregori (Bergamo, 1995), 62–64; and now C. Jean Campbell, *The Game of Courting and the Art of the Commune of San Gimignano, 1290–1320* (Princeton, 1997), 44–106.

45. Maria Laura Gavazzoli Tomea, "Le pitture duecentesche ritrovate nel broletto di Milano, documento di un nuovo volgare pittorico nell'Italia padana," *Arte medievale* ser. 2, 4 (1990): 55–70.

46. A popular decorative schema in imperial halls was the "family of kings." Gottfried of Viterbo described such a cycle of depictions of rulers in Frederick I's palace at Hagenau. Family genealogies also graced the walls of the palaces of lesser nobles. Bumke, *Courtly Culture*, 118–19; Andrew Martindale, "Heroes, Ancestors, Relatives and the Birth of the Portrait," in *Painting the Palace: Studies in the History of Medieval Secular Painting* (London, 1995), 75–111; Andrew Martindale, "Painting for Pleasure — Some Lost Fifteenth Century Secular Decorations of Northern

imagery: a fresco of the Virgin and Child, for example, or of a patron saint. Metaphorical images of virtues and vices (beasts and partially bestial figures) seem to have been popular with both lay and ecclesiastical lords; floral and geometric decoration can be found in all halls. But the differences between clerical and lay elites in their decorative choices are more important than the similarities. Scholars are quick to acknowledge that secular elites articulated their social status and their power in their halls. We also need to acknowledge that prelates did too and that both their status in medieval society and the character of their authority were distinctive.

Did the character of visual decor within halls matter to what went on within them? I think so. We know that the visual cues in a library and a sports arena suggest different "appropriate" behaviors. Wouldn't a hall decorated with religious imagery establish different expectations than one decorated with images of hunting and dancing? Decorative narratives in medieval buildings seem designed to frame the actions that occurred within them. When one stood in the hall of Rocca di Angera, one was surrounded by images that proclaimed the divinely ordained foundation of the Visconti lordship over Milan. If one came into this hall to dispute possession of a piece of land the Visconti claimed, for example, the frescos unambiguously communicated a particular balance of power. The paintings in Adele of Blois's room that linked the deeds of her immediate ancestors to Biblical history likewise framed her, and those who approached her, in a context of dynastic power and destiny.[47] Likewise, a series of solemn portraits of all the bishops of the see, reaching back to the age of the apostles, lent a weight of sacred tradition to even the most minor administrative acts of a reigning prelate.

CLERICAL COURTLY CULTURE

Just as the decor of secular and clerical halls embraced some common motifs and significant elements of difference, so the activities that took place in these spaces varied. Bishops, like their lay counterparts, had estates and other economic resources that required regular management. Notarial charters reveal the bishop in his hall investing vassals with fiefs, leasing properties, and exchanging, buying, and selling lands.[48] Lay elites did the same sorts of things in their halls. But bishops, by virtue of their ecclesiastical office, also performed a wide array of religious acts, many of them of economic

Italy," in *The Vanishing Past. Studies of Medieval Art, Liturgy and Metrology Presented to Christopher Hohler*, ed. Alan Borg and Andrew Martindale ([Oxford], 1981), 109–31.

47. Bumke, *Courtly Culture*, 117–19; the text of this poem may be found in Philippe Lauer, "Le poeme de Baudri de Bourgueil adressé a Adèle fille de Guillaume le Conquérant et la date de la tapisserie de Bayeux," in *Mélanges d'histoire offerts a M. Charles Bémont* (Paris, 1913), 43–58.

48. *CDP*, no. 714, Bishop John, "in urbe Padua in episcopali aula," invests Peter of Naticherio with a fief; two other investitures of fiefs, both by the bishop of Vicenza "in aula episcopali," are registered in Tommaso Riccardi, *Storia dei vescovi vicentini* (Vicenza, 1786), 66–67; Raynerius, bishop-elect of Volterra, "in curia episcopi," leased some lands of the see in 1255, *Reg. Volterra*, no. 660; *Codice diplomatico laudense*, ed. Cesare Vignati, 2 vols. (Milan, 1879–83), 1: no. 127, and 2: no. 58 are leases of episcopal property enacted "in aula"; Rauty, *Palazzo*, 1:284, app. no. 13, a sale of episcopal lands in 1114.

significance. They received pious donations to their own see and renunciation of claims involving churches and their property; they witnessed and ritualized benefactions made to individual churches or monasteries within their diocese and presented gifts to religious institutions.[49] Bishops were the traditional protectors of widows and orphans, and so frequently the legal guardians of such vulnerable individuals came into the bishop's presence to transact business on their behalf. The bishop could withhold sanction of actions that harmed the interests of those commended to his care.[50] All manner of ecclesiastical appointments could also take place here: in 1285, for example, the bishop of Rimini "in aula maiori palatii episcopalis" designated two canons as collectors of a special tithe to support papal campaigns in Sicily.[51] Disputes between individual clerics and between ecclesiastical institutions also came into the bishop's hall.[52] He settled these "lis et querimonia," and in his presence the right order of things was restored and visualized through the exchange of "fustes" (staffs denoting power) and kisses of peace. The acting out of the proper arrangement of things was a frequent activity in the hall: offerings that symbolized institutional and spiritual ties were often made here. In 1180, for example, a priest of San Pietro in Carnario in Verona brought the half-pound of wax that acknowledged his church's dependence on the cathedral canons to the bishop's court and presented it there to the archpriest of the chapter.[53]

49. *Arezzo-Documenti*, no. 718, the bishop of Arezzo, "in sala maioris palatii episcopali," approved the foundation of a monastery in the see's castle at Civitella (no. 714 records a similar transaction); *AARavenna*, perg. 2190, doc. 2 (Sept. 8, 1122), in which Archbishop Gaulterius receives Guido Traversaria's renunciation of all claim to the churches he had been detaining; *Reg. Mantua*, no. 210, the bishop of Padua, "in aula," donates tithes to the church of San Benedict of the monastery of Santa Croce; *ACTreviso*, perg. no. 215 (Dec. 24, 1196), Bishop Conrad, for the good of his soul and remission of his sins, gave houses to the cathedral canons, asking that they commemorate the anniversary of his death (also published in *Antichi documenti della diocesi di Treviso, 905–1199*, ed. Antonio Sartoretto, (Treviso, 1979), 192, no. 25); Bishop Aribert of Vicenza donated tithes to his canons in 1172 "in aula episcopi," Riccardi, *Vescovi vicentini*, 56.

50. *ASPiacenza*, Archivio storico degli ospizi civili — Atti privati, busta 2 cartella 5 perg. no. 43 (Jan. 23, 1189) in which Bishop Tebaldus makes public the will of Anselm Marthanus and its provisions concerning his three daughters (Athelasia, Lombarda, and Bellahonor) and his wife Donella, and perg. no. 45, doc. 2 (June 25, 1189) in which Obertus Scorpionus, acting as tutor and "curator" for the daughters, came before the bishop concerning a sale of lands involving Marthanus's estate.

51. *BCRimini*, SC-MS. 200 "Schede Garampi 439–1145, scheda 467; the appointment of priests to churches might also be done here: *Codice diplomatico laudense*, 2: no. 43, "in aula suprascipti domni episcopi."

52. *BCFerrara*, mss. G. A. Scalabrini, cl. I #445 "Uomini e donne illustri per santità" vol. 2, f. 292 (Nov. 7, 1149), "in curia mansionis episcopii Ferrariensis," Bishop Grifo heard a dispute between the abbot of the monastery of San Bartolomeo and a canon of Santa Maria in Reno over lands near the monastery; the bishop of Pistoia settled disputes in 1176 between the nuns of San Mercuriale and a certain Ubertellus over unpaid rent and in 1190 between the parish of Montecuccoli and the abbot of the monastery of San Salvatore over a church in Periano, Rauty, *Palazzo*, 1:287–89, app. nos. 23, 28.

53. *ACVerona*, III-8-7v (AC 10-m5 n15), "in sala domini Omniboni episcopi"; in 1170 the same bishop in his hall had interrogated Paris of Lazisio, archpriest of the church of San Michele in Cal-

This conjuring of correct order also went on in secular halls: this is why palaces were such charged places and why communes and bishops competed for space and prominence in the urban center. Different visions of the right ordering of the world, however, were enunciated. The consuls of our communes also settled disputes and received tokens of submission in the halls of their new palaces, but the meanings generated by these exchanges differed from those in episcopal halls. Context here was key. The squared shape of the communal hall framed these meetings as gatherings of relative equals. Those making decisions were several (not singular), and the power they wielded was depicted as the fruit of consensus and valor in defense of the community. The frescos surrounding them placed their actions in the context of civic unity — the ranks representing different neighborhoods and outlying communities depicted on the walls of the Milanese *broletto* — or military victories in defense of civic freedom (the battles that adorn the walls of communal palaces in Mantua, Novara, and Brescia). The religious imagery of the bishop's hall framed his right ordering of human and institutional relations in the context of God's plan of salvation.

This is even true of the "courtly" culture practiced in these places. Much has been made of the image of the courtly prelate: it is usually presented in the course of depicting the medieval church as corrupt and hypocritical. There were, it is quite true, ecclesiastics who lived in an ostentatiously secular fashion. They offended the sensibilities of contemporaries, both clerical and lay, whose censorious reports of their behavior are our chief sources for these images. The offensive cultivation of some secular courtly customs by prelates, however, does not mean that all courtly behavior was considered inappropriate for clerics. What I want to establish here is that there was a religious strain of courtly culture, articulated by prelates and regarded as appropriate to their status, that differed from the culture of secular courts. The chronicle of Salimbene de Adam provides us a rich view of clerical courtly culture and contemporary attitudes toward it.

First of all, Salimbene uses the terms "courtly" (*curialis, curialiter*) and "courtliness" (*curialitas*) throughout his chronicle in a strongly positive sense to mean courtesy, kindness, benevolence. He even attributes these qualities to God: to those who humbly seek understanding, "the Lord bestows it *curialiter et abundanter* (benevolently and lavishly)."[54] Many clerics are praised for their "courtliness." His fellow Franciscans, Brother Jacobinus of Reggio, Brother Gerard of Modena, and Brother Matthew of Cremona, are commended in this fashion, as are Tancred, the abbot of San Giovanni in Parma, and Pope Innocent IV.[55] Bishops too are praised for their *curialitas*. An excellent example for our concerns is Salimbene's initial description of Bishop Nicholas of Reggio:

> On the first of June, 1211 Lord Nicholas was enthroned as bishop of Reggio. He was nominated bishop and was something of a military man. He had the grace of both

---

masino, about whether he held his parish from the cathedral canons and whether he owed them tribute (*censum*): mss. Muselli, VI, DCCCXXXVI at 1170, f. 3.

54. Salimbene, *Cronica*, 209.16. Baird suppresses *curialiter* in his translation, 132.

55. Salimbene, *Cronica*, 102.28, 106.14, 149.27, 459.20, 140.15, 75.20, 331.13.

Emperor Frederick II and the Roman curia. He was a Paduan, born of the noble Maltraversa family, a handsome man, generous, courtly, and liberal. He had a great episcopal palace built at Reggio.[56]

Note the association here of palace building with courtliness and liberality. Salimbene returns to Bishop Nicholas later in his chronicle and expands on this description.

He was a cleric among clerics, a religious with religious, a layman with laymen, a knight among knights, a lord among lords, a great barterer, a great manager, generous, liberal, and courtly. At first, he took many lands and possessions of the see and gave them to shady men. For this Ghibert de Gente accused him before Pope Urban as being an embezzler, destroyer, and squanderer of episcopal property. But, as time went on, he recovered the lands he had given and accomplished many good things in the see. He was a learned man, highly skilled in canon law and ecclesiastical service; and he knew the game of chess. He kept the secular clergy firmly under control (sub baculo), and he gave parishes and churches to those who comported themselves well. He loved the religious, especially the Friars Minor.[57]

Nicholas was clearly the kind of person we might call a real "operator." He got along famously with all sorts of people; he loved making deals and brought a certain gamesmanship to his administration of the see. But Salimbene clearly regarded him as a good bishop, and among the "good" qualities he brought to the office was his *curialitas*, his courtliness.

Indeed, the patterns of praise and blame in Salimbene's appraisal of contemporary prelates give us a good sense of the expectations contemporaries had of bishops. Some of these expectations upset our own. Many contemporary Christians don't think their church leaders should live in big new residences, have large entourages of servants, and entertain lavishly. But these are exactly the sorts of things praised repeatedly by our thirteenth-century Franciscan. Salimbene noted about Bishop Grazia of Parma, for example, that

. . . in 1233 the part of the episcopal palace facing the cathedral was built; at that time, Grazia of Florence governed the see of Parma and caused palaces to be built in

56. Ibid., 38.16–21: "Anno Domini MCCXI dominus Nicholaus Reginus episcopus positus fuit in cathedra die prima Iunii. Hic fuit nominatus episcopus et quasi vir militaris. Gratiam habuit imperatoris Friderici et Romane curie. Paduanus fuit, nobili genere ortus de Maltraversis, pulcher homo, largus, curialis et liberalis. Maius palatium episopii Regini fieri fecit."

57. Ibid., 87.4–16: "Fuit enim cum clericis clericus, cum religiosis religiosus, cum laycis laicus, cum militibus miles, cum baronibus baro, magnus baratator, magnus dispensator, largus, liberalis et curialis. Multas terras et possessiones episcopatus baratavit in principio et quibusdam trufatoribus dedit; quapropter accusatus fuit Urbano pape a Ghiberto de Gente quod baratator et dissipator et alienator erat episcopalium rerum; sed, procedente tempore, recuperavit terras quas dederat et multa bona fecit in episcopio. Hic fuit litteratus homo, maxime in iure canonico et in ecclesiastico offitio valde expertus; et de ludo scaccorum noverat; et clericos seculares multum tenebat sub baculo. Et plebes et Ecclesias dabat illis qui bene sibi facerent. Religiosos dilexit et specialiter fratres Minores."

many places in the diocese. And, therefore, he was considered a good bishop by the Parmese, because he did not disperse, but rather increased and conserved episcopal goods.[58]

The large entourages of bishops seemed unremarkable to Salimbene. He tells of a newly elected bishop who had come to the papal court only to succumb to a sickness there along with twenty-five members of his household (this obviously not the entire retinue). He condemns bishops who treated their servants badly, particularly the abusive Philip, archbishop of Ravenna, who had forty armed retainers. One he had dragged through a marsh for forgetting to bring the salt, and another he had burned on a spit for some misdeed. Throughout the "Book of the Prelate" that constitutes a large section of the chronicle, Salimbene censures those in power who mistreat subordinates: those who act like tyrants, remain angry with their servants, or demand obsequiousness from them. He records a popular preacher's criticism of the bishop of Rieti for having his servants genuflect before him as they served him at table.[59]

Humility was often praised as a personal quality in bishops, but their households were not expected to look humble: a certain level of decorum was expected. Salimbene's exegesis of the story from the book of Kings of Naaman — who brought ten sets of clothes when he sought out the prophet Elisha — seems a defense of aristocratic clerics: "he can be excused for a number of reasons. First, because he was a prince. For many more things are conceded to the noble, both in food and clothing, than to private citizens, because of their high positions."[60] Most revealing is Salimbene's critique of the "excessive mode of living" of the head of his own order, Brother Elias. The friar castigates Elias, head of a religious order dedicated to poverty, for behaving "like a bishop." He kept well-fed and strong palfreys and rode everywhere on horseback (in violation of the rule). "Also, he had, just as bishops do, secular boys as servants, dressed in multicolored clothing, who assisted and ministered to him in all things." Elias also had his own personal cook.[61] While Salimbene considered such behavior outrageous in the successor of Saint Francis, he accepted it as normal in bishops.

Salimbene repeatedly praised bishops for entertaining lavishly, but key to his positive appraisal of episcopal feasting is the attitude shown to the poor. When he criticized bishops for sumptuous living, it is because their liberality did not encompass the needy. Of Bishop William de Fogliani of Reggio he wrote, "He held great feasts frequently for rich men and his relatives, but for the poor he shut off the means of mercy."[62] Indeed, both Salimbene's chronicle and saints' lives reveal that good bishops fed the poor in their halls. There had been a long and deep tradition of episcopal responsibility for the

58. Ibid., 97.16–21; trans. Baird, 46.
59. Salimbene, *Cronica*, 861.32–862.1, 576.1–10, 472.9–11; trans. Baird, 598, 400–401, 324.
60. Salimbene, *Cronica*, 409.23–25; trans. Baird, 279.
61. Salimbene, *Cronica*, 231.11–25; trans. Baird, 149.
62. Salimbene, *Cronica*, 758.3–5: "Magna convivia faciebat frequenter divitibus et propinquis, pauperibus vero clausit viscera pietatis." See also 161.17–20 and 628.11–14, praising liberality toward the poor at the bishop's table.

poor and poor relief. The property of the church from very early on was conceived of as the patrimony of the poor and the bishop as their special protector.[63] As we saw in Late Antiquity, the poor would come to the bishop's residence to ask for alms; Gregory the Great's *Dialogues* frequently depict this custom. But the practice idealized in these twelfth- and thirteenth-century texts is of the bishop actually dining with the poor or personally giving them food. This ideal, moreover, seems to be newly emphasized in the same period in which bishops were expanding their palaces and changing their appearance, in the closing decades of the twelfth century. In episcopal hagiography of the eleventh and early twelfth centuries, mention of any relationship with the poor is rare. In his *vita* of Saint Rodulphus of Gubbio, Peter Damian did add that the bishop "distributed generously to the poor whatever he managed to steal away from the household stores." But the narrative focus of these lives is the bishop's monastic formation and his continuation of the ascetic and contemplative life after being raised to the see.[64] In the life of Bruno of Segni, written about 1178–82, however, a renewed emphasis on episcopal poor relief is evident. The author asserts that Bishop Bruno "was attentive to works of charity and alms-giving, so much so that he seemed to think of nothing else. He clothed the naked, fed the hungry, gave lodging to pilgrims, and cared to relieve all the indigent equally."[65] John Cacciafronte, bishop of Vicenza (1179–84), was remembered as someone who established new customs in poor relief: he bought up clothing and distributed it "with his own hands" (*suis manibus*) to the poor on Good Friday, he washed their feet, and he brought "food prepared with his own hands" (*suis manibus praeparatum cibum*) for the sick and women in labor. The author of the life of Lanfranc of Pavia also portrays his bishop as an innovator in these matters. He notes first that Lanfranc's predecessors were accustomed everyday to feed twelve paupers and to give out pieces of bread to others. Bishop Lanfranc, however, not only maintained this number but also "instituted the giving of an entire sextarius [a large measure of grain] every day to other paupers, which by the grace of God to this very day is served in his house."[66]

Salimbene's chronicle reveals much about episcopal tables, mainly because Franciscans were numbered among the "poor" deserving the bishop's charity. He wrote of the

63. Mollat, *The Poor*, 20–23, 38–42; Evelyn Patlagean, *Pauvreté économique et pauvreté social à Byzance 4e–7e siècles* (Paris, 1977).

64. None of the three vitae of the great reforming bishop Bernard of the Uberti of Parma depicts him as showing concern for the poor, and Peter Damian's *Life of Saint Maurus of Cesena* makes no mention at all of episcopal poor relief; for his *Vita sancti Rodulphi episcopi eugubini*, see *PL*, 144, 1011–12.

65. *AASS*, 4 Iulii: 480: "Circa vero opera charitatis, et eleemosynarum ita erat attentus, ut nihil aliud cogitare videretur. Vestiebat nudos, esurientes alebat, peregrinos hospitio recipiebat, et omnibus pariter indigentibus subvenire curabat."

66. *AASS*, 2 Martii: 487; *AASS* 5 Iunii: 534; Ughelli, *IS*, 1: 1093: "In honestate vitae antecessores secutus, eos in eleemosyna superavit. Cum enim antecessores ejus duodecim pauperes quotidie reficerent, & aliis minam panis erogarent, hic eundem numerum reficiendorum servans, aliis pauperibus integrum sextarium instituit quotidie dari, quod per Dei gratiam adhuc hodie in eadem domo servatur."

archbishop of Embrun that he "wanted every day to provide dinner for two Friars Minor and he always had all sorts of dishes served to them at his table. And if Friars came, they had [these dishes]; if not, he had them given to other paupers (*aliis pauperibus*)."[67] Salimbene recalled eating frequently with the papal legate Cardinal Ottavianus: "And he always placed me at the head of his table, so that between me and him there was no other except my companion friar, and he himself took the third place at the head of the table . . . the entire hall (*sala*) of the palace was full. Truly, we ate abundantly and well."[68] Another vignette he offers us is of Bishop Obizzo of Parma at table with the "pseudo-holyman" Gerard Segarello. Salimbene had low regard for this enthusiast for the apostolic life; he describes him as "lowly born, an illiterate layman, ignorant and foolish." Bishop Obizzo had him chained up and put in prison for practicing syneisaktism, an ancient ascetic practice of testing one's chastity by sleeping among women.[69] After a period of imprisonment, however, the bishop

> released him and kept him in his palace. And when the bishop ate, this one also ate in the hall of the palace (*sala palatii*) at the lower table, where others were eating with the bishop, and he enjoyed drinking exquisite wines and eating delicate foods. When the bishop began drinking wine, that one called out to all hearing that he too wanted that wine, and immediately the bishop sent it to him.[70]

It appears on the whole from Salimbene's stories that most of the "poor" at the bishop's table were clerics and religious. The bishop's interest in them, it is also true, was not entirely charitable: Salimbene tells of declining an invitation to the archbishop of Embrun's table because he did not wish to be delayed and he knew the archbishop "would detain us and impede our journey inquiring news of us because we were coming from the curia."[71] Certainly Bishop Obizzo's interest in having Gerard Segarello in his palace was as much for surveillance as charity, but the impulse seems to have been pastoral nonetheless. Even if the most abject of the poor were not physically at the bishop's table, mindfulness of them seems to have been ritually cultivated. Salimbene narrated how Brother Rigaud, a Franciscan who was archbishop of Rouen, "had before him at table two large silver serving bowls in which were placed food for the poor." Two dishes of every sort of food would be served the archbishop and he "would retain one for himself, from which he would eat, and the other he would put into the serving bowls for the poor."[72]

67. Salimbene, *Cronica*, 469.17–21; trans. Baird, 322.

68. Salimbene, *Cronica*, 556.4–8; trans. Baird, 386.

69. Although it had been roundly condemned in the patristic era, several adherents of the new apostolic life cultivated this practice, among them the wandering preacher and founder of Fontevraud, Robert of Arbrissel. See Dyan Elliott, *Spiritual Marriage: Sexual Abstinence in Medieval Wedlock* (Princeton, 1993); Bruce L. Venarde, *Women's Monasticism and Medieval Society* (Ithaca, 1997), 59; Constable, *The Reformation of the Twelfth Century*, 68.

70. Salimbene, *Cronica*, 369.21 (description), 383.23–384.2; trans. Baird, 260.

71. Salimbene, *Cronica*, 469.28–29: "Ipse vero detineret nos et impediret iter nostrum inquirendo rumores, cum audiret quod venimus a curia." Also Baird, 322.

72. Salimbene, *Cronica*, 628.22–29; trans. Baird, 440–41.

Lay elites were not unsympathetic to the plight of the poor, but they did not invite them to table. Lay nobles made charitable bequests: they founded and supported monasteries, the institutions that were the main sources of poor relief in our period, and they gave alms. Their almsgiving generally took place in public and at ritualized moments: the distribution of alms was expected, for example, at funerals and on feast days on the way to, just outside, and within the church. Feasts were not viewed as the appropriate forum for almsgiving. On the contrary, for lay elites feasts were primarily a means of visualizing the social distance between themselves and non-nobles. They consumed "noble" foods (white bread, meat, fish, wine) in abundance, reveling in the variety and presentation of dishes. Seating arrangements were by rank, and those eating were waited on by a troop of servants. Greeting of guests and distribution of gifts also called attention to differences of rank. The feasting of secular elites reinscribed hierarchies and celebrated the patrons' position at the top.[73]

Although feasting was an important part of courtly life for both clerical and secular elites, clearly the manner in which they feasted and the social meanings generated differed in significant ways. This is also true of how both groups cultivated courtly entertainment. Salimbene mentions minstrels and jongleurs in several descriptions of encounters with prelates; they were clearly commonly encountered in episcopal halls. We know this as well from episcopal account books. The earliest and most notable is that of Bishop Wolfgang von Erla of Passau. A fragment of his record of expenditures from 1203 to 1204 reveals sums paid to jongleurs in Germany and in Italy and, most famously, to the courtly love poet Walther von der Vogelweide.[74] No doubt bishops enjoyed some of the same sorts of entertainment that secular elites did: the "jongleurs with knives" Bishop Wolfgang paid in Verona, for example, surely also performed for lay patrons, and the viol player Salimbene describes as entertaining the archbishop of Embrun would have deployed the same repertoire in secular and clerical courts. Salimbene does criticize clerics who spend too much on minstrels and jongleurs but he also praises prelates for taking time out from their duties to enjoy courtly entertainment. Moreover, in his description of interactions between prelates and jongleurs, he seems to value most the display of a sort of benevolent wit. After praising, for example, Pope Innocent III as "a man who took time out from his duties now and then for light courtly entertainment," he recounts an exchange between the pope and a jongleur from the

73. Bumke, *Courtly Culture*, 178–230; on 229 he notes, "In the descriptions of feast we hardly ever hear of gifts to the truly poor. Only in works that were more legendary in nature is this motif sometimes found. And then we discover that alms for the poor were reckoned in pennies, whereas the gifts for the wealthy were measured in pounds."

74. The text is published in Hedwig Heger, *Das Lebenszeugnis Walthers von der Vogelweide: Dei Reiserechnungen des Passauer Bischofs Wolfger von Erla* (Vienna, 1970), 80.35, 12 denarii to "a certain jongleur" (*Joculatori cuidam. Xij. den*); 90.188, 30 denarii to "the bishop's jongleur" (*Ioc[u]latori episcopi .xxx. den*); 91.199 to "three jongleurs" (*Tribus ioculatoribus . Xxiiij. den*); 93.20, at Ferrara "to a certain little old jongleur in a red tunic, 5 Paduan solidi"; 93.26 to "Flordamor the jongleur"; 93.30, "[a]t Siena, to a certain singer and two jongleurs, 7 solidi and 6 denarii Sienese," etc.; for Walther von der Vogelweide, 81.98, 86.55.

Marches of Ancona. The jongleur recited a brief poem for the pope, praising him as "doctor of all people" and enunciating a desire to have him as his lord. The poem rhymed, but its Latin was flawed. Salimbene praises the pope for answering the jongleur "in kind" with a doggerel Latin so as not to point out the poverty of the jongleur's skill. In another vignette, Salimbene admires Cardinal Ottavianus's cleverness in dealing with a jongleur who was heckling him during a procession; the cardinal, knowing that "all things obey money," had one of his servants give the man a coin, and the jongleur changed his tune. Salimbene praises similar qualities in secular lords. He notes with special admiration how Emperor Frederick II suffered the derision of jongleurs with good humor. The powerful, whether clerical or lay, should not take themselves too seriously, and the ability to enjoy courtly entertainment seems to be taken as showing a healthy lighter side to themselves.

What is clear from Salimbene's chronicle is that the clergy enjoyed poetry and song. We should consider carefully, however, what kind of poetry and song they enjoyed. First, our chronicler never depicts bishops listening to courtly love lyrics or romances. The secular verse he mentions and repeats is on common pleasures and annoyances of everyday life: the joys of wine, the aggravation of fleas. Second, when he does depict clerics enjoying poetry and song, the material is religious. Salimbene praised Brother Vita of Lucca, a fellow Franciscan, as being "the best singer of his time anywhere, in both styles, plainsong and harmony." He credits Brother Vita with composing a harmonic accompaniment to the hymn "Having Been Born and Having Suffered, the Lord is Risen Today" (*Natus, passus Dominus resurrexit hodie*) and the words and music of the sequence beginning "Hail Mary, hope of the world" (*Ave, mundi spes, Maria*). "He sang" says Salimbene, "for bishops, archbishops, cardinals, and popes, and they gladly heard him."[75] Another "courtly" friar Salimbene mentions is Brother Henry of Pisa. The chronicler praises his ability to converse with all sorts of people, to preach well, to illuminate manuscripts, and to compose and perform music. "He was a man of high morals," wrote Salimbene, "devoted not only to God and the Blessed Virgin, but also to Mary Magdalene." Brother Henry wrote many hymns to the Magdalene, and Salimbene gives the titles of nine of his compositions, all on sacred themes.[76] Prelates supported these talented clerical musicians in their households just as lay elites supported troubadours.[77]

75. Salimbene, *Cronica*, 264.18–65.15; trans. Baird, 174, seriously mistranslates part of this passage. His translation reads in part, "[h]e [Brother Vita] wrote many worldly songs with harmonious melodies, which greatly delighted secular clerks." The Latin text is the following: "Hic fecit multas cantilenas de cantu melodiato sive fracto, in quibus clerici seculares maxime delectantur," better translated as "[h]e wrote many songs in both melodious and harmonized style, which secular clerics greatly enjoyed." Salimbene uses the word "cantilena" at other points in his chronicle, but there is nothing in his usage which suggests that he means "worldly" or "profane" songs when he employs this word. Indeed, Baird does not translate it in this fashion elsewhere.

76. Salimbene, *Cronica*, 262.15–64.16; trans. Baird, 172–73.

77. Brother Henry was in the household of the patriarch of Antioch and Brother Vita was taken into the entourage of the archbishop of Ravenna: Salimbene, *Cronica*, 262.15, 265.27–28.

Salimbene also praised bishops who both sang and composed poetry and music. The archbishop of Embrun was "a good singer, a good cleric, who loved so much the Alleluia canticle of blessed Francis, namely 'Oh patriarch of the poor,' that he composed a hymn in honor of the glorious Virgin using the same melody. The verse went like this:

> Oh Mary, comforter of the poor,
> By your prayers, increase the number of your [people] in the love of Christ!
> Those whom you, oh mother,
> Snatch from the clutches of death
> Through your humble son.[78]

Salimbene depicts the archbishop of Ravenna strolling through his palace singing antiphons in honor of the Blessed Virgin, and he relates how Pope Gregory X composed a prophetic poem about his own ascent to the see of Peter.[79]

Our evidence here is limited, but I think it sufficient to suggest that the courts of bishops differed in significant ways from those of secular elites. The proportions of their halls evoked those of their cathedrals; their decorations established a religious context for the actions transpiring within their walls. Although some of those actions, particularly administrative dealings and the exercise of lordship, were shared with secular elites, others were distinctly ecclesiastical. Bishops brought the poor and religious to their tables, feasting them in their halls. The songs performed were in praise of the Blessed Virgin and the saints; the poems recited celebrated sacred themes. This clerical strain of courtly culture distinguished the higher clergy — and the power they wielded — from their secular counterparts. It is to the character and sources of this power that we now must turn.

---

78. Ibid., 630.34–631.9; trans. Baird, 442.

79. Salimbene, *Cronica*, 621.24–28, 717.20–719.15; trans. Baird, 435, 502–3. Cinzio Violante interpreted this same evidence differently, emphasizing the worldliness of Salimbene's outlook: "Motivi e carattere della *Cronica* di Salimbene," in *La «cortesia» chiericale e borghese del duecento* (Florence, 1995), 13–80.

CHAPTER SIX:
SPIRITUAL SPACE, INTERIORITY,
AND CHARISMATIC AUTHORITY
The Bishop's Chapel

In the late eleventh century, the people of Anagni were at odds with their bishop. Although he had entered the see with great energy — restoring its patrimony and beginning the rebuilding of the cathedral — the papal conflict with Henry IV over investiture seemed to curtail Bishop Peter's local restoration of the church. Work on the cathedral had stopped and when the bishop spent money on the care of the poor, local citizens were outraged at a perceived misuse of funds. The bishop's critics maintained that "if he were of sound mind he would have, at least, better illuminated the old churches and would have more usefully distributed what remained among their servants." They indicted Bishop Peter for "theft of property" (*furto pecuniarum*). The good bishop responded by fleeing his diocese, setting off for the Holy Land in the company of Bohemund of Taranto (on what would become known to history as the First Crusade). After two years of pilgrimage, however, a vision of one of the see's early bishops, Saint Magnus, warned Peter to return to his see. As soon as he got back, not surprisingly, he turned his attention to building:

> The fabric of the unfinished church was well brought to completion with all the workshops [contributing]; it was endowed with many houses and possessions, all of which Blessed Peter supported through many great gifts. In honor, therefore, of the Savior and Blessed Benedict, he built a chapel behind the palace, and with his own hand consecrated it, placing a room for himself, between that chapel and the hall, where after ceaseless vigils of prayer and exacting religious observances he might recline on a very hard couch and apply himself to the study of [sacred] readings. He ordained the lower floor as a reception area for taking in pilgrims and guests so that he might more vigilantly visit guests and paupers through an added stairway.[1]

1. *AASS*, 1 Aug.: 238: "Ecclesiae praetaxatae fabrica perbene cum omnibus officinis perficitur, in amplitudine domorum et possessionum augmentatur, [quae omnia B. Petrus] per plures largitiones suscepit. In honore praeterea Salvatoris et beati Benedicti post palatium capellam construxit, et manu propria consecravit, constituens sibi cameram inter ipsam capellam et aulam, ubi post orationum indefessas vigilias, et religionis exactam observantiam accubitu durissimo quiescebat, et [se] exercebat studio lectionum; in cujus partem cubiculi infimam in susceptionem peregrinorum et hospitum, receptaculum ordinavit, quo vigilantius hospites et pauperes per descensus aditum visitabat."

This story of how Bishop Peter of Anagni built a chapel in his palace is, in many ways, paradigmatic. A self-confident and vocal citizenry challenged the bishop: they had fixed ideas about how their church should be administered and they did not hesitate to criticize him. The bishop responded by avoiding conflict, in this case by leaving the diocese altogether, and by reaffirming his spirituality: he went on pilgrimage. His holiness and relationship with his see are affirmed in the narrative by the apparition of Saint Magnus to the bishop. Returning to the diocese, he gives the town folk the church they want, but he also builds a church for himself. This new chapel in his palace is the site of his virtue, his "ceaseless vigil of prayer," his study of the scripture.

In the eleventh and twelfth centuries, bishops throughout northern Italy, like Peter, added chapels to their palaces. The addition of these devotional spaces to episcopal residences reveals an important element in the redefinition of the bishop's power in the postreform era. That element is the reemphasis of the bishop's spiritual power and a much more marked tendency to use religious authority to achieve temporal ends. The latter is critical in understanding the increasingly oppressive character of the church as an institution from the thirteenth century. In exploring this development, we will look first at the chronology of the addition of chapels to bishops' residences and why they were added. Then we will consider the forms these chapels took and the models they were based on. Finally, we will explore the character of the spirituality they defined for the bishop through their dedication to saints, their decoration, their uses, and their spatial semiotics.

THE ADDITION OF CHAPELS

There was no pressing functional reason for episcopal residences to have chapels. Unlike imperial palaces or noble residences, episcopal residences usually were physically attached to a sizable church: the cathedral. The bishop was not wanting for a place to pray and to celebrate mass. Before the millennium, in fact, evidence for bishops having chapels within their residences is quite limited. Only the most wealthy and powerful sees had chapels and even these were additions and not elements of the original residence. The Lateran, for example, had several oratories but our earliest evidence of them in the *Liber Pontificalis* is from the mid-seventh century and later. The most famous papal chapel, San Lorenzo, also known as the *Sancta Sanctorum* (an allusion to the temple in Jerusalem and to the chapel's many relics), is not mentioned until the late eighth century.[2] A chapel was only added to the archiepiscopal residence at Ravenna in the early sixth century.[3]

2. The chapel of San Sebastiano was built by Pope Theodore (642–649), and the chapel of San Silvestro is mentioned in the life of Pope Sergius (687–701); Pope Gregory II (715–731) built a chapel dedicated to Saint Peter within the Lateran *episcopium*, and San Lorenzo is mentioned in the life of Pope Stephen III (768–772). Duchesne, *LP*, 1: 333, 371, 402, 469; trans. Davis, 1989, 68, 83; 1992, 9 (91.9), 89 (96.4). The Sancta Sanctorum is believed, however, to be much older than this first reference; see Marina Righetti Tosti-Croce, "Il Sancta Sanctorum: Architettura," in *Il palazzo apostolico lateranense*, ed. Carlo Pietrangeli (Florence, 1991), 51–57, and *Sancta Sanctorum* (Milan, 1995).

3. See discussion Chap. 6, pp. 219–22.

But evidence of average sees adding chapels comes much later and seems to coincide with the eleventh-century reform movement and its aftermath. Both physical remains and documentary evidence reveal that most bishops added chapels to their residences in the eleventh and twelfth centuries, particularly in the late-twelfth-century renovations that so changed the character of the bishop's palace. The beautiful little cruciform chapel of Santa Croce at Bergamo dates from the first half of the eleventh century, and a similar style chapel at Como probably to the same era.[4] This early chapel of San Michele at Como was rebuilt and joined to the palace with a new wing in the early twelfth century. A chapel was added to the Pistoian palace and to the bishop's palace at Parma during the 1170s.[5] Documentary notices of chapels begin in the early twelfth century, but are most frequent in the late twelfth and early thirteenth centuries. A document of 1101, for example, was redacted in the episcopal chapel at Padua; one in 1128, within the archbishop of Lucca's chapel; and one in 1156, in the bishop's chapel at Lodi.[6] By the mid-twelfth century too, we know that the bishop of Ferrara had a chapel dedicated to the apostle Thomas at his residence.[7] Episcopal chapels are mentioned at Vicenza in 1172, Treviso in 1187, Modena in 1189, Verona in the 1190s, Bolzano and Cremona in 1199, Ivrea in 1213, and Faenza in 1222.[8] Bishop Matthew of Orvieto (1202–11), amidst other renovations, added a chapel to his palace and consecrated it to San Silvestro.[9] Chaplains within the episcopal household are mentioned at Piacenza in 1169, in Forlimpopoli in 1214, and in Fano in 1217.[10] All of this documentary evidence of chapels clearly postdates the actual addition of a chapel, but it is impossible to esti-

4. For Santa Croce in Bergamo, see Angelini, "Scoperte e restauri di edifici medievali in Bergamo alta," 40–41; for San Michele at Como, see Frigerio and Baserga, "Il palazzo vescovile," 21–26, 77, and tav. II. Mariaclotilde Magni more recently dated the lower level of San Michele to the early eleventh century: *Architettura romanica comasca* (Milan, 1960), 116–17.

5. Rauty, *Palazzo*, 1:129; Banzola, "Palazzo," 32 and plan on 41.

6. *CDP*, 2: no. 1, in which Bishop-elect Peter made a donation to the monastery of Santa Giustina "in capella episcopi"; *Regesto del capitolo di Lucca*, ed. Pietro Guidi and Ovidio Parenti, 3 vols. (Rome, 1933), no. 860; and Tirelli, "Il «palatium» a Lucca," 17; *Codice diplomatico laudense*, 1: no. 157, Dec. 31, 1156.

7. In the mid-twelfth century, the bishops of Ferrara moved their cathedral and residence from a site outside the city walls to one within. On May 5, 1141, Bishop Grifo donated the old residence to found a regular canonry, beginning "in primis palatium nostrum domnicatum cum ecclesia sancti apostoli Dei Thome, capella meam in eo sita, . . ." BCFerrara, Mss. Scalabrini, "Documenti trascritti," c. I #445, vol. 1, f. 270.

8. *CDP*, 2: no. 1079; ACTreviso, perg. 120, March 5, 1187; Pistoni, *Il palazzo arcivescovile di Modena*, 24–25; ASVerona, Mensa Vescovile, busta 1, perg. 15; Franz Huter, *Tiroler Urkundenbuch: I. Abteilung: Die Urkunden zur Geschichte des deutschen Etschlandes un des Vintschgaus. I. Band: Bis zum Jahre 1200.* (Innsbruck, 1937), no. 568, June 16, 1199; *Parma XII*, no. 883, March 21, 1199, "Act. Cremone in capella inferiori memorati d. episcopi"; *Le carte dello archivio vescovile d'Ivrea fino al 1313*, no. 72, May 17, 1213; BCFaenza, Schedario Rossini, March 24, 1222.

9. Foote, *The Bishopric of Orvieto*, 316.

10. ACPiacenza, "Investiture," perg. 12, March 6, 1169 (although indiction, 13, corresponds with 1165); Ughelli, *IS*, 2: 604; Pietro Maria Amiani, *Memorie istoriche della città di Fano* (Fano, 1751), 1: XXVII–XXIX — I thank dott. Roberto Bernacchi for this reference.

mate the era of construction using some assumed chronological lag. In the several cases where we have both physical and documentary evidence, the time between the addition of the chapel and its mention in episcopal documents varies considerably. At Bergamo, we know from physical evidence that the chapel dates from the early eleventh century, but it is not mentioned in a document until 1177. At Parma, however, where we know that the chapel was added in Bishop Bernard's additions to the palace in the 1170s, it begins appearing in documents within two decades (from 1195).[11]

The important point here is that chapels were not part of the original episcopal residence; they were added after initial construction. And most of these chapels were added in the eleventh and twelfth centuries. Both of these patterns require explanation. What prompted bishops to add chapels to their residences? Why did most add them in the eleventh and twelfth centuries? In answer to the first question, as Bishop Peter of Anagni's story and several other cases reveal, bishops added chapels to their residences when their authority in spiritual matters was contested. As to the second, my evidence suggests a connection between the addition of chapels and the ideals of the eleventh-century reform movement. It also suggests that residential chapels only became ubiquitous when the bishop's relationship with his primary sacral space — the cathedral — was contested. The story in Anagni of the citizens' discontent with their bishop's progress on rebuilding the cathedral is concluded with his construction of the palace chapel.

Two particularly well-documented cases, Ravenna and Pistoia, show how bishops added chapels to their residences when their authority over the holy was challenged. Consider first the beautiful chapel of Sant'Andrea that Archbishop Peter II of Ravenna added to his residence in the early sixth century (see Figures 4–6). At this time, the Ostrogothic emperor Theodoric — an Arian Christian — ruled the city, and this certainly left the Catholic archbishop somewhat marginalized if not embattled. Theodoric was sponsoring plenty of buildings for the Arian church: a cathedral, baptistery, and (in particular) two residences for the Arian bishop, one of which included a chapel.[12] We know that the Catholic archbishops were keenly aware of these buildings and their significance: a later archbishop had the Arian *episcopia* demolished and used the stone to build an addition to the Catholic residence. This physical appropriation of the Arian episcopal residences is an apt symbol of the triumph of orthodoxy and, in particular, of the Catholic archbishop.

It seems likely, therefore, that Archbishop Peter's construction of a substantial building and a sumptuously decorated chapel within it sprung from a desire to keep up with his Arian rivals. Several motifs in the chapel's decoration — the depiction of Christ the Victor in the narthex, for example, and the prominence of the evangelists in its central mosaic (Figures 79, 80) — reaffirm orthodox doctrines reputed by the Arians.[13] Arch-

11. *AVBergamo*, "Diplomata seu Jura Episcopatus Bergomensis," vol. I, perg. 27, Jan. 1177; *Parma XII*, app. no. 147, June 14, 1195.

12. For these Arian *episcopia*, see Agnellus, *LP*, Chaps. 70, 86.

13. See Deichmann, *Ravenna*, 1: 203: the text in the book held open by the Christ figure, "EGO SUM VIA VERITAS VITA," is one quoted by Athanasius and his followers repeatedly against the Arian Christology.

FIGURE 79. *Ravenna, Palazzo Arcivescovile, Sant'Andrea, mosaic of Christ the Victor.* *(Alinari / Art Resource, N.Y.)*

bishop Peter's chapel not only contested the Arians' control over church building in this period, but also identified the orthodox Catholic archbishops with the martyrs of the early church and with the Roman see. The faces of the Apostles and a series of male and female martyrs stare down from the chapel's four arches, and the energetic angels along the vaulting mimic a decorative scheme in the chapel of Santa Croce built at the

FIGURE 80. *Ravenna, Palazzo Arcivescovile, Sant'Andrea, vault mosaics. (Alinari / Art Resource, N.Y.)*

Lateran baptistery in the 460s by Pope Hilary.[14] The pope converted a second- or third-century structure into this shrine for a piece of the true cross, changing four caryatids holding aloft a laurel of victory into four angels supporting a wreath enclosing a cross.[15] At Ravenna the four angels hold aloft a chrismon, a symbol of Christ. Through this allusion to Rome and through the iconographic alignment of the Catholic archbishop with both persecuted predecessors and theological orthodoxy, Archbishop Peter was making his resistance to Arian domination of Ravenna quite apparent in his chapel. The Arian challenge to his power over the holy in the city seems the essential context in understanding the archbishop's addition of a chapel to his residence.

A less dramatic, but also perhaps more common scenario, is evident at Pistoia. In the late eleventh century, Bishop Ildibrandus of Pistoia had rebuilt his residence; by 1112 it was being called a palace. As we have seen, this palace consisted of a tower and a two-story rectangular building with a large hall on the second floor. A chapel was added in the 1170s; its construction is linked to the foundation of a chapel consecrated to the city's patron, Saint James, within the entry of the cathedral.[16]

This cathedral chapel celebrated the acquisition in July 1144 of a relic of Saint James (San Iacopo). The relic was placed in the cathedral by the bishop, but the commune — wanting to cultivate the saint as its patron — insisted on constructing a special chapel at the entry of the duomo. The commune then created a special organization, the Opera di San Iacopo, to ensure officiation in the chapel, and built a hospice to house pilgrims to the shrine. While the bishop is mentioned in the earliest documentation of the Opera, by 1163 this organization was clearly independent and subsidized by the commune.[17]

Around this time, the Opera arranged to build a sacristy to service the chapel, the only space appropriate being along the south wall, essentially in the bishop's courtyard (Figure 81). The rectangular building opened into the rear of the chapel and was completed between 1163 and 1170. The bishop's chapel of San Niccolò was built over the sacristy.[18] It seems then that the chapel has its origins in the competition between the bishop and the commune over control of the relic and cult of the city's patron, Saint James. The construction of the bishop's chapel on top of the sacristy of San Iacopo seems even more significant considering that the sacristy served as the commune's treasury and archive.[19] At least spatially, if not juridically, the bishop came out on top in this contest.

But notice here who ended up in the cathedral. One of the reasons why chapels became common elements in episcopal residences during the eleventh and twelfth cen-

14. Gerola, "Il repristino," 112 and note 1.

15. The chapel was destroyed in 1588 but is known from Renaissance drawings. Duchesne, *LP*, Chap. 1.242; Lauer, *Latran*, 57–62; Richard Krautheimer, *Rome: Profile of a City, 312–1308* (Princeton, 1980), 50–51.

16. Rauty, *Palazzo*, 1:113–19, 124–29.

17. Ibid., 111–13; see also Sabatino Ferrali, *L'apostolo S. Jacopo il Maggiore e il suo culto a Pistoia* (Pistoia, 1979), especially 11–34.

18. Rauty, *Palazzo*, 1:111–20, 124–26.

19. Rauty, *Palazzo*, 1:119–20.

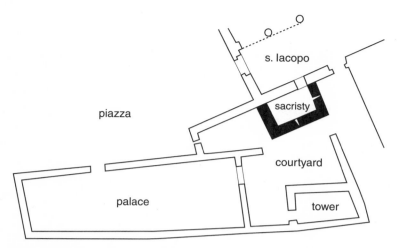

FIGURE 81. *Pistoia, Palazzo dei Vescovi, plan of chapel of San Iacopo and sacristy. (C. Ingersoll, based on Rauty,* Palazzo, *115, by permission of the Cassa di Risparmio di Pistoia e Pescia.)*

turies is that bishops lost their undisputed sovereignty over the sacred space of the cathedral in this period. This loss was the fruit of two complex and not unrelated developments: the rise of cathedral chapters and of communal governments. Although the cathedral clergy in Italy were generally organized into chapters by the late ninth century, few were wealthy or powerful enough to be a serious challenge to their bishops until the postreform era. As we have seen (see Chapter 2), chapters had slowly developed a significant claim to the cathedral space by their maintenance of its day-to-day liturgical life and by virtue of the often-extended absences of their bishops. That many bishops of Italian sees in the tenth and eleventh centuries were foreigners (from imperial territories north of the Alps) meant that cathedral chapters increasingly became the representatives of local ecclesiastical tradition and culture. This, and the fact that their members were usually drawn from the same social groups that constituted the early commune, meant that the cathedral became an intense focus for civic identity in the eleventh and twelfth centuries. Before they had their own buildings, the communes frequently met in the cathedral, and communal governments involved themselves in the wave of rebuilding and beautification of cathedrals that has left us so many wonderful examples of the Romanesque in northern Italian cities. By the late twelfth century, then, the cathedral had become not only the bishop's space but also the commune's space, so bishops created sacred spaces undisputedly and exclusively their own in reaction to these changes.

The creation of these devotional spaces within episcopal palaces, moreover, was usually part of a whole series of architectural changes in the late twelfth and early thirteenth centuries that radically refashioned the bishop's visual presence in the Italian city. Consider again Pistoia. The commune's new chapel to Saint James asserted an association with the holy and a claim to cathedral space. The bishop not only responded by creating his own private sacred space, but also countered with claims to public space.

Previously the bishop's great hall — the physical space in which he exercised lordship — had only been accessible from the fortified courtyard at the base of the tower; its entrance addressed ecclesiastical space (the cathedral and the canonry). In the late twelfth century, just after building the chapel, the bishop created a new entrance to his hall that opened out onto the piazza (see Figure 50). This entrance was emphasized through a decorated *profferlo* staircase — its marble facing matching the black and white marbling of the cathedral. Thus, in response to the commune's claims to the sacred and sacred space, the bishop not only created new sorts of sacred space entirely his own, but also asserted a new relationship to the public space of the piazza. This new relationship of discourse with the city's central plaza, site of its chief market, was also accomplished by opening larger windows onto the piazza and by adding decorative elements (stucco moldings, brick facing) to the facade. This two-pronged response — the addition of private chapels and the assertion of a new relationship with public space — occurred at episcopal palaces throughout northern Italy in the late twelfth and early thirteenth centuries. Later we will return to the significance of this linkage, but now let us consider the kinds of sacred structures bishops built when they wanted to reaffirm their authority over and connection to the holy.

MODELS AND INFLUENCES

The forms of episcopal chapels are quite diverse, but they are all based on ecclesiastical models. This needs to be articulated because art and architectural historians tend to treat episcopal chapels merely as examples of seigneurial chapels and they emphasize secular models — chapels built by monarchs, like Charlemagne's palatine chapel at Aachen and Louis IX's Sainte-Chapelle, in particular.[20] Northern Italian bishops, however, were clearly looking to ecclesiastical models and, in the twelfth century, increasingly to papal and other episcopal chapels.

20. Viollet-le-Duc's entry for "chapelle" in his *Dictionnaire raisonné de l'architecture* (2: 423–80) is a classic example: it begins with the Parisian Sainte-Chapelle and then traces the relations of other chapels to this prototype. The section on "chapelles de chateaux, d'évêchés" begins with several twelfth-century episcopal chapels but leads inevitably to Sainte-Chapelle and its influence. The entry in the much more recent *Enciclopedia dell'arte medievale* (s.v. "cappella") recognizes greater diversity, but still emphasizes the influence of the palatine chapel at Aachen and Sainte-Chapelle and uses genealogical language (". . . da Aquisgrana discendono . . .") to describe the place of these royal chapels in the development of the architectural type. See also Inge Hacker-Sück, "La Sainte-Chapelle de Paris et les chapelles palatines du moyen âge en France," *Cahiers archeologiques* 13 (1972): 215–57; and Gardelles's discussion of chapels in "Les Palais," 124–28. So dominant is this framework that a recent treatment of the papal chapel of San Lorenzo in the Lateran tried to link the results of Pope Nicholas III's late-thirteenth-century renovations to the model of Sainte-Chapelle despite "evidenti differenzi formali": Julian Gardner, "L'architettura del Sancta Sanctorum" in *Sancta Sanctorum*, 32–33. Han J. Böker has persuasively challenged the idea of the bishop's chapel at Hereford as a "copy" of Aachen, but he still prefers imperial to ecclesiastical models in his reinterpretation: "The Bishop's Chapel of Hereford Cathedral and the Question of Architectural Copies in the Middle Ages," *Gesta* 37 / 1 (1998): 44–54.

FIGURE 82. *Bergamo, Santa Croce.* (*M. Miller.*)

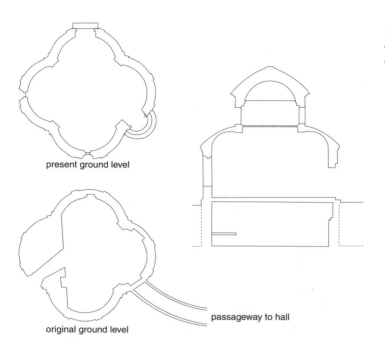

present ground level

original ground level

passageway to hall

FIGURE 83. *Bergamo, Santa Croce, plan and elevation. (C. Ingersoll.)*

Two early episcopal chapels — Santa Croce in Bergamo and San Michele in Como — both built in the opening decades of the eleventh century, demonstrate the primacy of ecclesiastical models. Santa Croce in Bergamo is a centrally planned chapel: a quadrilobed structure with an octagonal second story finishing in a dome (Figures 82, 83).[21] The original chapel of San Michele in Como was probably quite similar. A groin vaulted base still remains, and its restorers conjecture that it had an upper domed section (Figure 84).[22] The architectural models for Santa Croce, and this early San Michele were Lombard baptisteries. The baptisteries of Biella (circa 1040), Mariano Comense (circa 1025), and Galliano di Cantù (circa 1015) are roughly contemporary (Figures 85, 86).[23] Their ground plans and elevations are similar.

It should not surprise us that these bishops used the form of the baptistery for their residential chapels. In the eleventh century, baptism was one of the most important sacral powers of the bishop. Within the city and its immediate suburbs, only the bishop

21. Angelini, "Scoperte e restauri," 39–43. The chapel was originally taller than it is today: by the sixteenth century a new floor was inserted and entrances reworked, probably because water had invaded the original level. There is still a crawl space beneath the present flooring. It was probably Angelini who filled in around the structure to create the present ground level that gives the chapel its squat look. I thank don Bruno Caccia of the Ufficio dei Beni Culturali Ecclesiastici della Curia di Bergamo for sharing these observations on the chapel and for giving me access to it.

22. Frigerio and Baserga, "Il palazzo vescovile," 24–25, tav. V.

23. Angelini, "Scoperti e restauri," 41; Porter, *Lombard Architecture*, 2: 121, 517, 439; Ferdinando Reggiori, *Dieci battisteri lombardi, minori, dal secolo V al secolo XII* (Rome, 1935), 3 and tavole XXI, XXII.

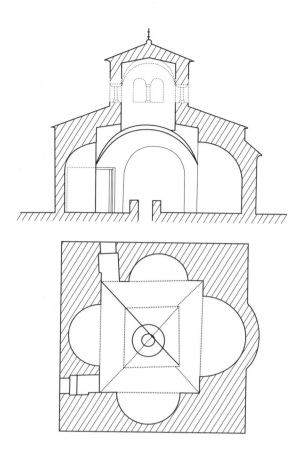

FIGURE 84. *Como, Palazzo Vescovile, reconstruction of San Michele I. (C. Ingersoll.)*

performed baptism. Later these rights would devolve to parish churches, but in the eleventh century it was the bishop who made Christians, removing original sin with sacred water and chrism at the most holy juncture of the liturgical year, the Easter vigil.[24] It seems then that these bishops underscored this particular sacramental power in their chapels. This reminder of sacramental power, however, also had political connotations. It is exactly at this time that urban dwellers began reemphasizing and distinguishing their status as "citizens" (*cives*), and historians have correctly seen in this new self-consciousness the first stirring of urban autonomy, the earliest signs of the communal identity that would be the foundation for the new lay governments that emerged in the late

24. The classic study of this devolution is Paolo Sambin, *L'ordinamento parrochiale di Padova nel medioevo*, Pubblicazioni della Facoltà di lettere e filosofia 20 (Padua, 1941); in English, see Catherine E. Boyd, *Tithes and Parishes in Medieval Italy* (Ithaca, 1952), 52–53. Although the Eucharist was beginning to receive greater emphasis among theologians in the eleventh and twelfth centuries, "baptism continued to be seen as fundamental, sometimes even as 'chief among the sacraments that Christ instituted in the church,' because it alone was necessary for salvation": Jaroslav Pelikan, *The Christian Tradition: A History of the Development of Doctrine*, vol. 3: *The Growth of Medieval Theology (600–1300)* (Chicago, 1978), 205.

FIGURE 85. *Mariano Comense, baptistery, elevation. (C. Ingersoll.)*

FIGURE 86. *Mariano Comense, baptistery, plan. (C. Ingersoll.)*

eleven and early twelfth centuries. Baptism at the bishop's font, at the urban baptistery, to a large degree defined membership in the urban community. This is why baptisteries (and one need only think of the Florentine example) became such important foci of communal patronage: all citizens of Florence were reborn in the spirit at the font of San Giovanni. By choosing the form of the baptistery for their chapels, these early-eleventh-century bishops were reaffirming a powerful role for themselves as creators or "fathers" of the urban community, who fashioned "citizens" as they effected their spiritual rebirth in baptism.

In the twelfth century, bishops looked increasingly to other bishops in designing their chapels. In rearticulating their charismatic authority, they increasingly identified themselves with the distinctive clerical culture emerging out of the reform movement. At Como in the early twelfth century, two stories were added atop the base of San Michele, and a new chapel was created on the second of these added levels. This new

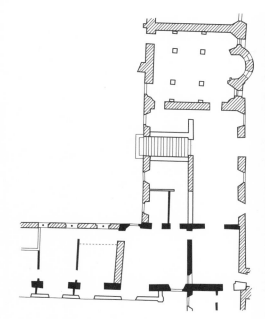

FIGURE 87. *Como, Palazzo Vescovile, San Michele II, plan. (C. Ingersoll.)*

FIGURE 88. *Como, Palazzo Vescovile, apse of San Michele II. (M. Miller.)*

chapel had an orientation quite different from the first incarnation of San Michele. It was square, with nine vaulted compartments sustained by four columns and an apse with a monofore (narrow, undivided) window on the east (Figures 87, 88).[25] San Niccolò in Pistoia, an example from the second half of the twelfth century, is a rectangular room covered by a barrel vault with a pensile apse (one protruding only from the second story) on the east pierced by a monofore (Figure 89).[26]

Both these structures generally conform to the "Doppelkapellen" or double-chapel model that architectural historians identify as the classic seigneurial chapel. The pri-

25. Frigerio and Baserga, "Il palazzo vescovile," 24–36, 75–81, and plates; Magni, *Architettura romanica comasca*, 116–17.

26. Rauty, *Palazzo*, 1:111–35.

FIGURE 89. *Pistoia, Palazzo dei Vescovi, interior of San Niccolò. (Natale Rauty and the Cassa di Risparmio di Pistoia e Pescia.)*

mary chapel is on the second floor so that it communicates with the princely living quarters on the "piano nobile." There are two types of double-chapels. The first type, generally preferred by the lay nobility,[27] has two chapels, one on top of the other but communicating through a large opening, often in the center of the floor / ceiling. Architectural historians see the palatine chapel at Aachen — with its two altars, one on

27. The classic examples of this type are the palatine chapels of Ottmarsheim, Nuremburg, Saint Ulrich at Goslar, and Saint Klemens at Schwarzrheindorf. Only two episcopal chapels — Saint Gothard at Mainz and the palace chapel at Hereford in England — follow this type. On the latter see Richard Gem, "The Bishop's Chapel at Hereford: The Roles of Patron and Craftsman," in *Art and Patronage in the English Romanesque*, eds. Sarah Macready and F. H. Thompson, Occasional Papers (New Series) 8 (London, 1986), 87–96.

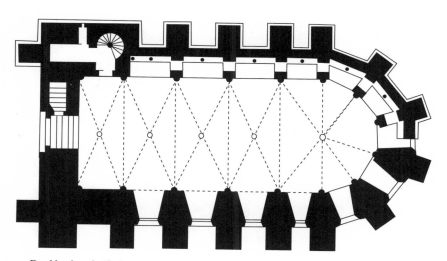

FIGURE 90. *Double-chapel. (C. Ingersoll.)*

the ground floor and another in the gallery — as the prototype for this design. The opening allowed mass said in the lower chapel to be heard in the upper (and vice versa). In an elite household, the design also visualized the social order: servants and dependents were consigned to the lower chapel and their noble masters received the sacrament above them. The second type of double-chapel lacked the central aperture: the only communication between the two levels was, in some but not all cases, a stairway. This is the form, for the most part, used by bishops (Figure 90). The lower level was often a chapel, as at the French episcopal residences of Beauvais, Laon, Noyon, Reims, and Meaux, and within Italy at San Lorenzo in Laterano, at the bishop's palace in Cremona, and probably also at Faenza.[28] But often the lower level was devoted to other uses. As we saw at Anagni, Bishop Peter used the level below his chapel as a place to receive the poor and sick. At Piacenza, the space below the chapel seems to have been used as just another "camera": several administrative documents in the late thirteenth century were drawn up "sub capella palacii episcopalis."[29] The episcopal chapel at Pistoia and the Lateran chapel of San Niccolò had sacristies (*vestiaria*) on their lower levels.

The models our bishops of Como and Pistoia were looking to in the twelfth century were ecclesiastical. San Michele most closely resembles the roughly contemporary Saint Gothard chapel in Mainz built by Archbishop Adelbert (died 1137).[30] The floor plan and vaulting are quite similar, although it lacked the aperture of the Mainz double-chapel (Figure 91). San Niccolò in Pistoia is a simpler and smaller structure, its most notable feature being its pensile or hanging apse (Figure 92). As Natale Rauty has argued, the Pistoian chapel most closely resembles several French episcopal chapels — notably that of Laon (also featuring a pensile apse) and Bishop Maurice de Sully's two-story chapel in Paris. Although the pensile apse was much developed in the French Gothic, there are very few examples of it in Italy, making the bishop of Pistoia's use of it even more striking.[31]

28. On the French episcopal chapels, see Thierry Crépin-Leblond, "Une Demeure épiscopale du XIIe siècle: l'exemple de Beauvais," *Bulletin archéologique* ns 20–21 (1984–85): 19, 46–49; and Hacker-Sück, "La Sainte-Chapelle," 224, 232–35. The lower level of San Lorenzo is presently filled with rubble, but Lauer's excavations revealed a well for relics and fragments of fresco, indicating that it had been used as a chapel, Righetti Tosti-Croce, "Il Sancta Sanctorum," 52; a document of March 21, 1199, was drawn up in Cremona "in capella inferiori memorati d. episcopi," *Parma XII*, no. 883; thirteenth-century Faentine documents regarding the episcopal palace mention both a chapel of Sant'Ordinazione and one dedicated to Santi Giovanni e Paolo, suggesting a true double-chapel arrangement: *BCFaenza*, Schedario Rossini, June 8, 1286, April 13, 1289, May 27, 1290, July 16, 1290, Jan. 1292 in Sant'Ordinazione and July 15, 1291, Nov. 25, 1298, March 3, 1299 in Santi Giovanni e Paolo.

29. *ASPiacenza*, microfilm of holdings of Archivio Capitolare di S. Antonino, bobina 7, *Liber Parvus*, aa. 997–1338, f. 10v, 26v, 34v.

30. G. Dehio and G. von Bezold, *Die kirchliche Baukunst des Abendlandes*, 2 vols. + plates (Stuttgart, 1884–1901) 1: 459–60, taf. 170, Figures 14–16.

31. The only contemporary use of it in Italy is in the abbatial chapel of Santi Severo e Martirio, a benedictine monastery near Orvieto. Rauty, *Palazzo*, 1:129–34.

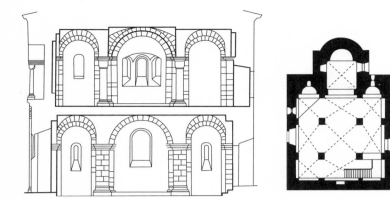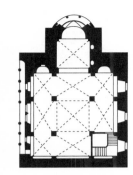

FIGURE 91. *Mainz, Saint Gothard chapel, plan. (C. Ingersoll.)*

The dedication of this Pistoian chapel to Saint Nicholas, however, suggests other influences. Earlier in the century, Pope Calixtus II had built a chapel dedicated to Saint Nicholas in the Lateran to celebrate the victory of the papacy over the empire in the Concordat of Worms (1122).[32] The bishop of Pistoia's chapel does share some general characteristics with this earlier Lateran chapel. Like the Lateran San Niccolò, the Pistoian chapel was on the second floor of a structure that housed a *vestiarium* — a treasury for liturgical objects and vestments — on the ground floor. The Lateran chapel was also a simple rectangular structure with an apse (see Figure 18), although their roofing solutions differed.[33]

The architecture of San Michele II and, particularly, San Niccolò in Pistoia suggests that in the twelfth century, bishops looked chiefly to other prelates when seeking models for their own devotional spaces. This accords well with the impact of the reform movement, which stressed the distinctive character of ecclesiastical authority and the pivotal role of the bishop as leader of the Christian flock. Consideration of the saints to whom these chapels were dedicated, their decoration, their liturgical uses, and the placement of the chapels within episcopal palaces strengthen this connection.

Two patterns appear in the saintly affiliations bishops chose in consecrating their chapels. The first is a strong devotion to the Apostles. The archbishop of Ravenna's chapel was dedicated to the apostle Andrew, the brother of Peter. Archbishop Maximian, roughly three decades after the chapel was built, supposedly acquired a bit of Andrew's beard on a visit to Constantinople. The iconography of the chapel — with its medallion images of all twelve Apostles — underscores the importance of Christ's disciples in episcopal devotion. The twelfth-century episcopal chapel of Bishop Grifo of Ferrara was dedicated to "the Holy apostle of God Thomas" and the bishop of Faenza's chapel commemorated the saints John and Paul. French episcopal chapels built in the twelfth century also show this predilection for Apostles: both of the chapels at the episcopal palace in Beauvais were dedicated to Saint John the Evangelist, one of the chapels

32. Lauer, *Latran*, 162–71; Stroll, *Symbols as Power*, 16–19, 132–49. Stroll attributes the ornamentation within the chapel to Anaclet rather than Calixtus.

33. Stroll, *Symbols as Power*, 17 n. 5, 17–18, 132.

FIGURE 92. *Pistoia, Palazzo dei Vescovi, pensile apse of San Niccolò. (M. Miller.)*

at Laon was devoted to Saint James, and the lower chapels at the episcopal palaces of Noyon and Reims were dedicated to Saint Peter.[34]

The upper chapels at Noyon, Reims, Meaux, and Laon were all dedicated to Saint Nicholas, and the devotion to this saint is the second pattern evident in the naming of episcopal chapels. It also brings us back to the papal influence already noted in the chapel of San Niccolò at Pistoia. All of these chapels dedicated to Saint Nicholas were built in the late twelfth century, after Pope Calixtus II had built his chapel of San Niccolò in the Lateran explicitly intended to celebrate the triumph of the reform movement. Nicholas was an apt patron for the reform movement, but particularly for prelates. He was bishop of Myra (in Asia Minor) in the fourth century, and many legends associated with him depict Nicholas as the exemplary bishop, guarding his flock zealously.[35] Moreover, one of the earliest tales associated with him is one in which he berates Emperor Constantine — the saint threatening to "stir up an uncontrollable revolt against you, and hand over your carcass and your entrails to the wild beasts for food!"[36] This righteous tongue lashing of an emperor, obviously, made Nicholas the perfect patron of the reforming popes. For Italian bishops slowly losing power to communal governments in the twelfth century, the image of Nicholas standing up to secular authority surely also had a special resonance. The saint was venerated as the patron of clerics and seemed to have been of special personal significance to the reformers Peter Damian and Pope Urban II.[37] Thus, the dedication of episcopal chapels to Saint Nicholas suggests a connection between the reform movement and the addition of these devotional spaces to bishops' residences.

Both the devotion to the Apostles and the cult of Saint Nicholas were joined in the early-fourteenth-century decoration of the bishop of Pistoia's chapel of San Niccolò. Two fresco cycles, both likely the work of the "Maestro di Città di Castello," decorate the walls of this chapel, running like comic strips in bands around the interior. The top register depicts the martyrdom of the Apostles, beginning at the front to the left of the apse with Saint Peter's crucifixion and finishing (hypothetically, since the series is damaged) at its right with the death of Paul. The surviving scenes show the heroic ends of Andrew, James (the Elder), Thomas, James (the Younger), Matthew, Philip, Judas Thadaeus, and Bartholomew. The latter apostle is given special prominence, the narrative of his being flayed alive after converting the king of India filling the entire rear wall. Ada Labriola convincingly links the prominence of this particular martyrdom with the bishop who likely commissioned the frescos, Bartholomew of Guittoncino Sinibuldi (1303–7).[38] Below these gruesome apostolic ends is a series of frescos depicting the life of Saint Nicholas and some of his postmortem miracles.[39]

34. See note 26 above.

35. Charles W. Jones, *Saint Nicholas of Myra, Bari and Manhattan: Biography of a Legend* (Chicago and London, 1978), 28, 58–66.

36. Ibid., 29–36 (quote 34).

37. Ibid., 127–35, 140–42, 159–60, 209–17.

38. Ada Labriola, "Gli affreschi della cappella di San Niccolò nell'antico palazzo dei vescovi a Pistoia," *Arte cristiana* ns 76 (1988): 247–66; on the prominence of Bartholomew, 248–50.

39. Ibid., 248.

These decorative choices suggest certain themes appropriate to the episcopal office. First, note that this artist and his episcopal patron chose to depict not the preaching of the Apostles and their leadership of the early Christian community, but their martyrdom. This emphasis underscores a self-representation noted earlier (see Chapter 4) of bishops as martyrs. Hagiographical texts in the late twelfth and thirteenth centuries (Bishop John Cacciafronte of Vicenza, Bishop Lanfranc of Pavia, Bishop Ubaldus of Gubbio) depicted prelates as real or metaphorical martyrs, suffering for their people at the hands of rebellious nobles and iniquitous communal officials. The martyrdom of ecclesiastical leaders is definitely underscored in these depictions of the Apostles. Other themes are evident in the choice of episodes depicted from the extremely rich hagiographical dossier of Saint Nicholas. The saint's miraculous selection as bishop and his consecration were obvious choices for an episcopal chapel. The scenes depicting Nicholas's wonderworking in this life represent his most popular miracles and even follow the order of stories given in the popular *Golden Legend*.[40] Less obvious choices, however, appear on the opposite wall: there are two panels devoted to the "Miracle of Adeodatus" and one to the depiction of the "Cup of Gold" miracle. Both stories tell of men praying to Nicholas for a son. The saint answers their prayers, but tragedies befall the sons. Nicholas intervenes and returns the boys safe and sound to their fathers. Both stories, then, depict the saint as miraculously intervening to preserve the lineage: is this a metaphorical reassertion of the traditional episcopal concern with sacred lineages?

An earlier pictorial cycle in the episcopal chapel of Novara, San Siro, also reveals interests in apostolicity and in the bishop's relationship both to Rome and to his flock. Like other chapels, San Siro was added in the late twelfth century to the episcopal palace in Novara: the chapel was built and decorated under Bishop Boniface (1172–94). Formerly provost of the canons regular of Santa Croce di Mortara in the diocese of Pavia, Boniface was certainly influenced in his decision to dedicate the new chapel to Pavia's first bishop and patron Syrus by his long association with the diocese and its devotions. But the choice of Saint Syrus was much more ladened. First, it associated Novara with a tradition of Christian evangelization that totally obscured the traditional dominance that the archbishops of Milan claimed over the see. Novara's patron and earliest bishop, Saint Gaudentius, was probably passed over by the bishop because the traditions surrounding the saint emphasized the see's relationship with Milan. Gaudentius also lacked an apostolic lineage: he was sent to evangelize Novara by Eusebius of Vercelli. Saint Syrus, on the other hand, could be proffered as another possible early source for Novara's Christianization. Syrus was famed for bringing Christianity "to all the villages, villas, and cities" around Pavia, and his *vita* depicts him performing mira-

40. After the difficult-to-identify infancy scene, the panels depict his dowering of the three neighbor girls, his selection as bishop and consecration, and his rescue of the ship at sea. Then there is a destroyed panel followed by the phial of oil miracle. These scenes follow the order in the *Legenda Aurea*, suggesting that the missing scene was the saintly bishop's relief of a famine in his diocese. Jacobus a Voragine, *Legenda Aurea*, ed. Th. Graesse (Wratislav, 1890) 1: 22–25; *The Golden Legend*, trans. William Granger Ryan, 2 vols. (Princeton, 1993), 21–25.

cles much farther afield (in Verona, Brescia, and Lodi) than nearby Novara. More importantly, Syrus's see, Pavia, remained independent of Milan even though it was only forty kilometers (twenty-five miles) away from the great metropolis. This seems to have been an important element in Bishop Boniface's devotion to Syrus. Novara in the second half of the twelfth century was constantly at odds with Milan politically. The city supported Emperor Frederick Barbarossa in his war against Milan and the other Lombard cities. At the Peace of Venice in 1177, Bishop Boniface had represented the sees adhering to the emperor while the archbishop of Milan had represented the Lombard communes. Thus, Boniface's decision to dedicate his new chapel to the patron of Pavia, a city that had remained independent of the Milanese see even though it was quite near it, seems to reinforce Novara's anti-Milanese posture.[41] Second, the choice of Saint Syrus also associated Novara with a more venerable apostolic lineage and with Rome. Syrus was sent to Pavia by Hermachore, bishop of Aquileia, who was a disciple of Saint Mark, who in turn was the disciple of Saint Peter. The cultivation of Saint Syrus associated Novara with the apostolic lineage of the "Prince of the Apostles." Moreover, part of Pavia's independence from Milan was its direct dependence on Rome: its bishops were consecrated in Rome, and this right was upheld against attempts by the archbishops of Milan to claim dominion.[42]

The decoration of Bishop Boniface's chapel narrated the life of Saint Syrus. The cycle is arranged in two registers (an upper and lower, running clockwise and beginning on the south wall) and begins in Aquileia with Saint Hermachore consecrating Syrus and sending him to evangelize Pavia (Figure 93). The scenes following recount the saint's journey to the city, emphasizing especially his miraculous raising from the dead of the son of a Veronese woman. We see the woman entreating Syrus outside the gates of Verona, then the boy being brought back to life, then the woman and her family accepting baptism from the holy bishop. Centrally located over the main entrance to the chapel is a depiction of Saint Syrus being received joyfully by the people of Pavia, who are gathered outside the city gate in a huge crowd (Figure 94). Syrus's preaching and miracle working in other towns are also depicted: the saint casts a demon out of a boy in Brescia and cures a blind man at Lodi. Most striking in the artistic composition of these scenes is the prominence and beauty of the cities: Verona, Pavia, Brescia, and Lodi are all depicted, their encircling walls crowded with houses and towers (Figure 95). As Giancarlo Andenna has noted, "one could say that the city, represented four times in all its grandeur and splendor, is co-protagonist with Saint Syrus in the cycle."[43] The holy bishop is portrayed in relation to the city, and that relationship is one of heal-

41. Giancarlo Andenna, "Un palazzo, una cappella, un affresco," in *L'oratorio di San Siro in Novara*, 80–82.

42. Mario Perotti, "La leggenda di San Siro," in *L'oratorio di San Siro*, 62.

43. "Si potrebbe dire che la città, rappresentata per ben quattro volte in tutta la sua grandezza e in tutto il suo splendore, sia coprotagonista con Siro della vicenda." Andenna, "Un palazzo," 83. I thank Giancarlo Andenna for showing me these paintings and others within the episcopal palace of Novara and for sharing with me the results of his research on them.

FIGURE 93. *Novara, San Siro, Saint Hermachore consecrating Saint Syrus. (Giacomo Perolini.)*

ing and ministering to its people. The crowd of citizens pouring out of Pavia to receive their bishop's benediction posits a unity between bishop and people that Bishop Boniface seems eager to reinforce. Indeed, as this cycle was being painted, relations between bishop and commune were deteriorating in the wake of the Peace of Constance.

These decorative cycles within episcopal chapels emphasized the figures of holy bishops (Saint Nicholas, Saint Syrus), the bishop's relationship to the city and its people, and the bishop's genealogical and spiritual relationship to the Apostles. Ties to Rome — through the dedication to Saint Nicholas at Pistoia and through the association with Pavia and the lineage of Saint Syrus at Novara — are evident in both cases. All of these associations, and the very act of adding sacred spaces within their residences, suggest that bishops in the wake of the reform were cultivating their own devotional practices focused on their office and its spiritual powers. This certainly reinforces the conclusions of recent work on Biblical exegesis revealing that bishops in the eleventh and twelfth centuries brought the ecclesiological issues of their time and their own immediate pastoral concerns to their reading of sacred scripture.[44] More specifically, the creation of a special place within the palace for episcopal piety and asceticism

44. Giampaolo Ropa, "Studio e utilizzazione ideologica della Bibbia nell'ambiente matildico (sec. XI–XII)," in *Studi Matildici: Atti e memorie del III Convegno di studi matildici*, Reggio Emilia, 7–9 ottobre 1977 (Modena, 1978), 395–425; William L. North, *Exegesis and the Formation of a Clerical Elite, 1049–1123*, Ph.D. diss., University of California, Berkeley, 1998.

FIGURE 94. *Novara, San Siro, the citizens of Pavia greeting Saint Syrus. (Giacomo Perolini.)*

marks the successful integration of the spiritual demands of the reform movement into the day-to-day reality of the bishop's office.

THE NEW EPISCOPAL IMAGE

The early attempts at reformed episcopal hagiography, as we have seen, could not imagine monastic spirituality and the dutiful performance of office in the same place. Peter Damian's *vitae* of Saint Rodulphus, bishop of Gubbio, and Saint Maurus, bishop of Cesena, depict these prelates cultivating a life of contemplation and prayer, but they do so in "little cells." Maurus's was well outside the city on Mount Spaziano. We have already noted the schizophrenic effects this bifurcation of office and spirituality had on this *vita* (see Chapter 4). The location of Rodulphus's *cellula* is unclear, but it is also described in opposition to his see and its duties: " . . . what he [Rodulphus] learned in the desert, he did not abandon in his church. . . . While he considered the church his guest house, he ordained his little desert cell his home."[45] When these early *vitae* extol the

45. For Maurus, see *PL*, 144: 947–48; for Rodulphus, 1010 in the same volume: " . . . quod in eremo didicit in Ecclesia non omisit. . . . Ecclesiam porro deputabat hospitium, solitudinis autem cellulam habitaculum decernebat." On the dating of this life, see Giovanni Lucchesi, "La «vita S. Rodulphi et S. Dominici Loricati» di S. Pier Damiano," *RSCI* 20 (1965): 166–77; on Maurus, Pietro Burchi, "Il vescovo di Cesena s. Mauro e il monastero della Madonna del Monte," *RSCI* 11 (1957): 95–106.

FIGURE 95. *Novara,
San Siro, detail of city
of Pavia. (Giacomo
Perolini.)*

"monastic rigor" a bishop maintained after being promoted to his see or praise him for "having joined monastic religion and the pastoral office," it is the solitude and contemplation of monastic life that they emphasize.[46]

Asceticism is more prominent when an integration of monastic virtues and the episcopal office emerges in the anonymous prose life of Saint Anselm, bishop of Lucca. Anselm turns the demands of his office into ascetic practices: "All the allurements of the world and delights of the body, which men rejoice in, this one [Anselm], by detesting each, turned into tortures." When he must hold court and entertain guests, the saintly bishop takes mouthfuls of food but does not chew so as to avoid tasting its sweet flavors. He drinks nothing at table (especially not wine!), but takes a sip of water at vespers. Instead of enjoying the companionable sociality of a public figure, he remains solitary and devoted to the study of scripture: "whether he was with the battle host in the field or at home in his residence, he gathered around his bed only a modest circle and there alone either read or wrote."[47]

The breakthrough of this anonymous hagiographer is that he asserts the possibility

46. Damian asserts of Rodolphus that "nihil de rigore monastico deponit in episcopatu" and the life of Peter of Anagni praises how he "se gerebat sanctitas juncta religioni monasticae simul et officio pastorali." *PL*, 144: 1010; *AASS*, 1 Aug.: 236.

47. *MGH SS*, 12: 21–22; Pásztor, "La «vita» anonima di Anselmo di Lucca," 210–11; Paolo Golinelli, "Una agiografia di lotta: Le «vitae» di Sant'Anselmo di Lucca," in *Indiscreta Sanctitas*, 117–55.

that the bishop can be practicing a quasi-monastic life while dutifully performing all the outward appearances of his office. He has feasts in his hall (but denies himself the taste of the fine foods); he rides out to battle with his vassals (but sequesters himself reading the scriptures); he lives in a palace (but cultivates a hermit's life within it). The addition of the bishop's chapel literally builds on this juxtaposition of exterior appearances and interior spiritual states. It architecturally integrates the monastic cell with the palace. Behind the increasingly splendid and ornate facades of episcopal palaces, the bishop's real home was the "little cell" of his chapel, where (as Peter of Anagni's *vita* shows us) he undertook "endless prayer vigils and exacting religious observance."[48] Peter had been a monk before becoming bishop, but most of the bishops adding chapels were not: Bishop Boniface of Novara had been a regular canon, Bishop Matthew of Orvieto had been a cathedral canon, and all the bishops during the period in which Verona's chapel was added were secular clerics who had come to the see through the chapter.[49] These additions then reveal the wide diffusion of reform values among the clergy. By adding chapels to their residences, bishops were fostering a reputation for a more personal piety, the interiority of these chapels and their relative inaccessibility working to lend the bishop an aura of sorts, the knowledge of this architecturally interior sacred space imputing a sacred interiority to the prelate. Here the insights of Christian Metz and other film theorists can help us appreciate the power of the unseen in relation to the seen. What is offscreen exerts a powerful influence on how we see, interpret, and react to what is onscreen. As we all know from watching film, what is offscreen is left to our imaginations.

Here we need to stop and consider who would have had access to these episcopal chapels. Certainly the bishop and the other clerics in his household would. We have frequent references to episcopal "chaplains" from the late twelfth century, and these priests would have had charge of the chapel and its maintenance. Other individuals, from time to time, were brought into the chapel; the documents recording these occasions sometimes provide our only evidence of the chapel's existence. These gatherings were not different in legal intent than others enacted in the great hall: lands were bought, exchanged, surrendered, and leased. Fiefs were invested and renounced; disputes were settled. But one senses that a certain need to mobilize the sacred determined the choice of locale. Sometimes this mobilization of the sacred seems pastoral. In 1189 Bishop Ardicio of Modena chose his chapel as the site to hear the confession of wrongdoing and offer of repentance of one of his priests who, in his own words, had "done wrong . . . and did not then obey all the mandates of the lord bishop."[50] Sometimes it seems more strategically political: investitures and renunciations of fiefs are particularly

48. *AASS*, 1 Aug.: 238.

49. Foote, *Bishopric of Orvieto*, 188; *L'oratorio di San Siro*, 94–95; for Verona, see Chap. 3, note 65.

50. *Reg. Modena*, no. 816: "Albertus de eccl. S. Andree fuit confessus quod male fecerat, quia non steterat cum eis, qui erant capellani ecclesiarum civ. Mutine, olim de procurationibus cardinalium et archiep., et quod non obediverat olim omnia mandata d. Ardicionis Mutin. Ep., sic dicens: ego male feci, quod non steti ita vobiscum in predictis procurationibus et in cunctis vestris factionibus, ut debebam; et quod non obedivi omnia mandata d. Ardicionis, unde vos multum exhoro, et mihi

common among the notarized acts performed in the chapel. Were these especially difficult vassals whose oaths the bishop wished to undergird by deploying all the sacred trappings at his disposal? Were more relics placed under the oath taker's hands when such rituals were enacted in the bishop's chapel? Several such enactments in the bishop of Padua's chapel suggest that particularly powerful lords were brought there: an investiture of 1149 made in the chapel was to one of the Carrara, and a renunciation in 1152 was from the hands of one of the Pallavicino, both of these extremely powerful families with castles in the countryside.[51] Some lay people, therefore, did know the bishop's chapel. But clearly more people knew of it by word of mouth than by direct experience. This perfectly suited the orchestration of the bishop's reputation. Although few people in any city were invited into the bishop's chapel, knowledge of its existence could shape how he was seen. In terms of bolstering his reputation for sanctity, the location "offscreen" of the bishop's devotional space removed his actual piety from public surveillance and allowed it to be fashioned by public imagination and artful clerical propaganda.

And what sort of religious observances might be imagined in this space? The life of Peter of Anagni mentions "ceaseless vigils of prayer and exacting religious observances." Some form of the cathedral or "secular," as opposed to monastic, divine office was the major constituent element in this devotional regimen. From the time at least of Saint Augustine, secular clerics were supposed to perform a version of this series of psalms, prayers, and readings spread at intervals ("hours") across the day and night. This requirement was reiterated and enlarged by the Carolingian reformers (Chrodegang of Metz's rule for canons including extra services such as psalms for the dead and penitential psalms). Although the number of psalms and readings in the secular office was slightly reduced from the monastic cycle, the number of hours was the same: matins (or nocturns, performed at about 2:00 A.M.), lauds at daybreak, then prime, terce, sext, none, vespers, and at bedtime, compline. By the eleventh century, perhaps not surprisingly, the secular clergy were having difficulty maintaining this regimen. The renewed emphasis among reformers on restoring the communal life of the clergy derived at least in part from the requirements of performing the office, but the persistence of small communities of clerics and the isolated circumstances of rural priests made its recital (especially the antiphonal chanting of the psalms) difficult. Reformers responded to these difficulties by designing a new liturgical book — the breviary — that compiled in one place all the material (psalms, prayers, antiphons, readings) necessary for the performance of the divine office. This at least would have made its performance markedly less complicated, as previously material from several different books had to be organized and prepared prior to each office.

---

de hoc, quod erga nos feci, parcatis, et ut predictum d. ep. Deprecemini up ipse mihi parcat. . . . Act. In capella ep. Mutin."

51. *CDP*, 2: nos. 521, 566.

Bishop Sicard of Cremona (1185–1215) devoted an entire book of his liturgical commentary, the *Mitrale*, to the divine office, and since this work was clearly written for the use and edification of his clergy, it demonstrates the expectation that even the average priest engaged in this devotional regimen. Moreover, Bishop Sicard emphasizes the office in the overall structure of the work. After first discussing the physical setting and requirements of the church (its parts, its consecration, its decoration), Sicard describes the orders of clergy and how they should deport themselves. Then he turns to the liturgical duties or work of the clergy: first he comments extensively on the mass and then he turns to the divine office. After these disquisitions, he goes through the liturgical year commenting on the weekly Sunday liturgy and the great feast days. He then goes through the year again, commenting on saints' feast days. The mass and the divine office are the central topics in the work and the essential spiritual exercises of the clergy. The voice Bishop Sicard employs throughout these expositions is collegial, invoking his own devotion while extending the gift of his learning to his clergy. After, for example, linking each of the daytime hours (prime, terce, sext, etc.) to an act of Christ in the Gospels that took place at that time of day, he offers these associations as meditations during the office. "At sext on the day of his Ascension," Sicard set forth,

> He reclined at table with his disciples. At nones, before their eyes, he ascended into heaven (Matt. 16:14–19). In vespers [through the foundation of the church, Acts 1] he came to save the world; at the end, let him come to restore [it], He who even at vespers before his passion dined with his disciples, washed their feet, and gave to them his own body.

The bishop then continued, priest to priest:

> At vespers, let us reflect upon the evening sacrifice of the king [the sacrifice of Aaron in Exodus 29 instituting the priesthood] that prefigured the new sacrifice instituted in vespers. Let us be buried together with Christ and institute our heirs by the testament of our humility in the washing of the feet and by the bond of charity forging this new mandate; and having been inspired by the fire of love let us be incited to the care of the poor and be illumined in the understanding of Scripture.[52]

The voice Sicard adopts and the hagiographer's allusion to "vespers" when describing Bishop Anselm's ascetic fluid intake certainly suggest that bishops performed the

52. Sicard of Cremona, *Mitrale, sive de officiis ecclesiasticis summa*, in *PL*, 213: 161–62. On Sicard generally and his work, see Leonard E. Boyle's entry in the *New Catholic Encyclopedia* (s.v. "Sicardus of Cremona") and Roger E. Reynold's contextualization of his liturgical work in *DMA*, s.v. "Liturgy, treatise on," 632. Book I of the *Mitrale* is treated extensively by Joseph Sauer in his *Symbolik des Kirchengebäudes und seiner Ausstattung in der Auffassung des Mittelalters* (Münster, 1964) and Book III on the mass by Mary M. Schaefer in *Twelfth Century Latin Commentaries on the Mass: Christological and Ecclesiological Dimensions*, Ph.D. diss., University of Notre Dame, 1983. I thank William L. North for the latter reference and for sharing with me his observations on the language of liturgical commentaries.

divine office. Indeed, when one of the witnesses testifying in the canonization process for Bishop John Cacciafronte of Vicenza wanted to describe the bishop's piety, he said simply that Cacciafronte "most willingly celebrated the divine office with great devotion."[53] The postmortem inventory of the palace of a later prelate, Archbishop Rinaldus Concorezzo of Ravenna (1303–21), offers confirmation of this impression: in the archbishop's room the auditor found "about 20 volumes of books, of which he believed more related to the divine office than to other services."[54] In the early Middle Ages, bishops would have joined their canons in the cathedral for these rites (and they still did from time to time even after the construction of their chapels).[55] The demands on the bishop that took him out of his diocese — particularly in the ninth and tenth centuries when royal service was added to pastoral travels — fostered the development of an episcopal household distinct from the chapter. These clerics, like the "chaplains" that traveled with the monarch to serve his religious needs, would have been the bishop's spiritual companions as well as his close counselors. The addition of chapels to episcopal palaces solidified the development of this community around the bishop.

Here, certainly, the influence of the papacy was a factor. From at least the time of Pope Sylvester II (999–1003), a few especially trusted clerics in the pope's circle were called "chaplains." Little is known about this group and the organization of the papal chapel even in the high Middle Ages. Most of the papal chaplains then seem to have been subdeacons and to have served in the chancery in addition to their liturgical duties in the Lateran.[56] What is clear is that these papal chaplains not only maintained the divine office in the Lateran chapel of San Lorenzo but also played a significant role in the elaborate liturgies of the great feasts of the Christian year. Indeed, liturgical documents

53. Cracco, "Ancora . . . ," 905.

54. ". . . in camera domini XX volumina librorum vel circha quos credit pocius ad divinum officium spectare quam ad aliud ministerium." Renzo Caravita, *Rinaldo da Concorezzo Arcivescovo di Ravenna (1303–1321) al tempo di Dante* (Florence, 1964), 251. A late-eleventh-century inventory of John, cardinal bishop of Porto, gave the contents of "the chapel of our palace," listing a collection of liturgical books (a missal, a "nocturnal" with psalter and hymns, a passionary, an antiphonry, the gospels) and vestments: Georg Swarzenski, "Ein unbekanntes Bücher- und Schatzverzeichnis des Cardinalbistums Porto aus dem XI. Jahrhundert," *Römische Quartalschrift für christliche Alterthumskunde und für Kirchengeschichte* 20 (1900): 128–31 (Latin text of chapel inventory on 131); Hubert Mordek, "Bemerkungen zum mittelalterlichen Schatzverzeichnis . . . ," *Studia Gratiana* 20 (1976): 233–40. I thank Bill North for bringing this to my attention. A similar inventory survives for Bishop Capitaneus of Orvieto, made by his successor Ranerius in 1228. Three liturgical books (an evangeliary, epistolary, and ordinal) were found in the bishop's room, and in the chapel were vestments, "a silver chalice, a vase of wine and water for mass," other altar furnishings, and the bishop's staff and mitre. Foote, *The Bishopric of Orvieto*, 311.

55. A twelfth-century liturgical manual from Milan, Beroldus's *Ordo et caeremoniae ecclesiae Ambrosianae Mediolanensis*, only gives directions for matins and vespers, but in the directions for each, changes are indicated "si archiepiscopus adfuerit" (if the archbishop was present) and "si archiepiscopus defuerit" (if the archbishop was missing). *Beroldus, sive ecclesiae Ambrosianae Mediolanensis kalendarium et ordines saec. XII*, ed. Marcus Magistretti (Milan, 1894), 37, 53.

56. Schimmelpfennig, *The Papacy*, 115, 161.

of the reform era suggest that this set of papal customs was overtly being offered to bishops as correct, "Roman" practice in the twelfth century.

Driving the reform movement were varied concerns about the correct performance of ecclesiastical rites and factors affecting their efficacy. The debates over clerical celibacy and simony, for example, evinced grave concerns about the efficacy of the sacraments performed by clerics guilty of these practices. Were the ordinations of a simoniacal bishop valid? Was the bread and wine consecrated by a priest sullied by sexual activity actually the body and blood of Christ and therefore a purveyor of grace to communicants? The importance of rites to the reform movement is easily understood in its most dramatic political contest: at the heart of the investiture conflict was a disagreement over who should invest bishops with the symbols of their office. Not surprisingly, then, the reformers were quite concerned with liturgy and from the mid-eleventh century, numerous commentaries and compilations were undertaken. One of their main goals, under the guise of ridding the liturgy of "abuses," was to eliminate practices imposed by the Ottonian and Salian emperors when the papacy was in disarray in the tenth and early eleventh centuries. Thus, the new liturgical manuals compiled by the reformers overtly aimed at a Romanization of the liturgy. One of their first efforts in this direction was a revision of the liturgical manual (called a "pontifical") for bishops. This book included all the prayers and ritual directions needed for the rites that were the special prerogatives of bishops: consecration of churches, the ordination of clerics, the profession of monks and nuns, the chief cathedral liturgies of the Christian year, and a wide variety of benedictions. The new Roman pontifical of the twelfth century was distributed as part of a self-conscious attempt to impose papally sanctioned practices throughout the church.[57]

Largely, this was achieved in the work by simply replacing most of the old Germano-Roman pontifical of the ninth century with new material based on Roman practice. The authors, indeed, make constant asides underscoring the Roman origin of these rites, inserting phrases like "according to the true custom of the Roman church" and "according to the ancient usage of the Romans."[58] More importantly, in the descriptions of the ritual actions that will necessarily differ for the bishop using the manual because he is not in Rome, the authors still describe what the Roman practice is. After generally setting out, for example, the order of the procession that opens the Palm

---

57. Roger Reynolds, "Liturgical Scholarship at the Time of the Investiture Controversy: Past Research and Future Opportunities," in idem, *Law and Liturgy in the Latin Church, 5th–12th Centuries* (Aldershot, 1994), 112; Michel Andrieu, *Le Pontifical romain au moyen-âge*, vol. 1: *Le Pontifical romain du XIIe siècle*, Studi e testi 86 (Vatican City, 1938), 5–19. On this genre of liturgical books, see Aimé-Georges Martimort, *Les "Ordines," les ordinaires et les cérémoniaux*, Typologie des sources du moyen âge occidental fasc. 56 (Brepols, 1991), 107–9; Eric Palazzo, *Histoire des livres liturgiques: Le moyen âge des origines au XIIIe siècle* (Paris, 1993), 204–20; Joaquim Nabuco, "La Liturgie papale et les origines du cérémonial des évêques," in *Miscellanea liturgica in honorem L. Cuniberti Mohlberg* (Rome, 1948), 1: 283–300.

58. Andrieu, *Pontifical . . . XIIe siècle*, 137, 221, 230.

Sunday celebration, the authors add: "One should also know that since the Roman pontiff arises in his palace at Rome, he gives palms there to the cardinals, dressed in vestments as they would be when at Mass with him, and to the clergy and people."[59] A description of the procession at the Lateran follows. While this might be for the general education and edification of the prelate, it is more likely meant as a guide so that the bishop can reproduce Roman custom as closely as possible in his own diocese. Significantly, then, in the description of the rite for solemn celebration of the Lord's Last Supper on Holy Thursday, the authors omit any directions for orchestrating the reenactment of Christ's washing of the feet of his disciples (a ceremony called the *mandatum*), which is a dramatic part of the liturgy. They list the psalms and antiphons to be sung and then continue:

> In the true Roman church, the aforementioned communion antiphon "Lord Jesus" having been sung, the Roman pontiff solemnly completes the mass. And after having been vested, he goes up with the cardinals to his chapel, where, while he washes the feet of twelve subdeacons, his chaplains sing the aforementioned psalms and antiphons until vespers.[60]

This model, however, seems not to have been followed in local churches. The later pontifical of William Durand, bishop of Mende (1285–96), shows that a different siting of this liturgical sequence was propagated: Durand's pontifical had a wide diffusion not only in his native France but also throughout Europe. This work was so popular that ultimately it was used as the basis for the first printed edition of the Roman pontifical in 1485.[61] For this ceremony of the washing of feet, Durand directs:

> . . . in this day, the feet are washed. Indeed, at the hour of vespers, the *tabula* having been struck or sounded, the pontiff entering the chapter with the canons and clergy

59. Ibid., 214: "Sciendum quoque est quoniam Romae pontifex romanus sursum in palatio suo dat palmas cardinalbus, indutis quidem sicut debent esse in missa cum eo, et clero et populo."

60. Ibid., 233: "in ecclesia vero romana, cantata communione praenotata *Dominus Iesus*, romanus pontifex solemniter perficit missam. Et postea indutus cum cardinalibus ascendit ad capellam suam, ubi dum ipse lavat pedes duodecim subdiaconorum, capellani sui cantant praedictos psalmos et antiphonas ad vesperam."

61. Roger Reynolds deems Durand's liturgical writings, particularly the *Rationale divinorum officiorum*, as "the most important and influential of all thirteenth-century treatises on the liturgy." See *DMA* s.v. "Liturgy," 632 and s.v. "Pontifical." On the manuscript diffusion of the *Pontificale romanum*, see Michel Andrieu, *Le Pontifical romain au moyen-âge*, vol. 3: *Le Pontifical de Guillaume Durand*, Studi e testi 88 (Vatican City, 1940), ix–xiii, 17–19, 23 et seq. Two of the late-medieval Italian pontificals assessed by Marc Dykmans tended to reproduce large sections of the pontifical of the twelfth century or the curial pontifical of Innocent III, but that of John Barozzi, bishop of Bergamo (1449–65) and then patriarch of his native Venice (1465–66), follows Durand, and Augustine Patrizi-Piccolomini did as well for the revision of the pontifical commissioned by Innocent VIII (and ultimately printed as the standard version). Barozzi reproduces Durand's chapter on the washing of the feet, prefacing it with the phrase "as some are accustomed to do," but Piccolomini acknowledged the diversity and primacy of local customs by simply abandoning attempts to describe a norm. Marc Dykmans S.J., *Le Pontifical romain révisé au Xve siècle*, Studi e testi 311 (Vatican City, 1985), 21, 35, 67, 78, 120.

begins to wash the feet of the canons in order chiefly by their rank. That having been done, let the chief person of the chapter wash the feet of the bishop. Meanwhile, the *schola* chants the antiphon "I give you a new mandate" and others customary [for this rite].[62]

The differences with the Lateran rite set forth in the twelfth-century pontifical are significant. The Lateran ceremony casts the pope in the role of Christ and his chaplains as the Apostles. In Durand's late-thirteenth-century pontifical, the bishop is in the Christ role, and the cathedral canons — not the bishop's household clergy — are in the position of the Apostles. The Lateran basilica, it should be noted, did not lack canons but their status had always been subordinate to that of clergy within the papal retinue. In episcopal practice, I think it significant that this rite was regularized in late-medieval pontificals as one performed with the cathedral canons. It is a powerful ritual: the bishop humbles himself before his canons by washing their feet, and their leader humbles himself before the bishop by washing his. Given the propensity in the later Middle Ages for chapters and bishops to be at odds, usually over rights and lands, this ceremony offered an annual opportunity for reconciliation before the celebration of the Easter vigil. This was a highly functional liturgical choice: concord between bishop and chapter was good for the local church. The fact that Durand's pontifical locates the rite on the canons' turf — in their chapter hall — and instructs that the bishop wash their feet in order by rank — visualizing and acknowledging the power structure within the chapter — suggests the aim of cultivating respect for the chapter in its role as representative of the local church and community (since canons tended to come from the leading families in the city).[63]

62. Ibid., 581 (Liber Tertius, II, 98): "Quarto loco in hac die pedes lavantur. Hora enim vespertina, tabula percutitur, vel cornatur, et pontifex, cum canonicis et clericis capitulum intrans, incipit lavare pedes canonicis, precipue in dignitatibus constitutis. Quo facto, maior persona ipsius capituli lavat pedes episcopi. Et interim scola cantat antiphonam *Mandatum novum do vobis*, et alias solitas." The *tabula* was a wooden board that was struck; it was used instead of bells at particularly solemn rites.

63. These local ecclesiopolitical factors are probably the primary reason episcopal chapels were not incorporated into diocesan liturgies following the Roman model. Physical characteristics did not preclude the replication of Lateran customs. The surviving examples we have of medieval episcopal chapels indicate that they were small, but not significantly smaller than their papal counterparts. The chapel of San Niccolò at Pistoia was roughly 8 meters by 5 meters, or 26 feet by 16.5 feet; Santa Croce at Bergamo has a diameter across the longest section of the quadrilobe of 8 meters, or 27.5 feet; the twelfth-century chapel of San Michele at Como measured 7.5 meters by 7 meters, or 26 feet by 23 feet; San Siro in Novara is roughly 6 meters by 4 meters, or 20 feet by 13 feet. San Lorenzo, the most important Lateran chapel, indeed, was slightly smaller (measuring roughly 7 meters by 7 meters, or 23 feet by 23 feet). Calixtus II's later chapel of San Niccolò was more spacious (15 meters by 7.5 meters, or 49 feet by 26 feet) but its larger interior did not lead to any relocation of ceremonies formerly conducted in the Sancta Sanctorum or San Silvestro. The sacred associations of the space seem to have been more important than the amount of performance area provided for the rite. Rauty, *Palazzo*, 1:114; Angelini, "Scoperte e restauri," 42 (confirmed in the recent plans of the structure drawn up by architect Pino Calzana, whom I thank for sharing his drawings with me); Frigerio and Baserga, "Palazzo vescovile," tav. 3; *L'oratorio di San*

A thirteenth-century *Ordo* (or liturgical manual) drawn up for the cathedral chapter of Pistoia confirms that the bishop's chapel was not incorporated into the Holy Week liturgies of the diocese and reveals, indeed, a different role for the chapel. The *mandatum*, or washing of the feet on Holy Thursday, took place in the choir of the cathedral of San Zeno, with the bishop and his canons participating (as in Durand).[64] But the chapel was visited by the cathedral canons on the feast of Saint Nicholas. The *Ordo* instructs that vespers on the day preceding the feast were to be celebrated in the chapel, and on the day of the feast "we canons go in a procession to the chapel of blessed Nicholas singing prime." The office and a mass were celebrated there in honor of the saint.[65] A similar custom is attested at Novara. An *Ordo* composed for the Novarese church between 1332 and 1358 instructed the canons to process to the chapel of San Siro on the vigil of the saint's feast day (December 9) to sing vespers. After vespers the bishop was to provide them a good meal ("with excellent wine"). They returned the next day on the feast to sing vespers and to recite the *Commemoratio* (excerpts from the life) of the saint.[66]

The fact that episcopal chapels were not integrated into the Holy Week liturgies certainly reveals another example of episcopal independence in relation to the papacy.[67]

Siro, 21; Righetti Tosti-Croce, "Il Sancta Sanctorum," 52; Lauer, *Latran*, 162 and plan; the thirteenth-century pontifical of the curia still locates the washing of the feet on Holy Thursday in San Lorenzo (the only option added being the use of the chapel of San Martino in the Vatican if the rites were performed at Saint Peter's): Michel Andrieu, *Le Pontifical romain au moyen-âge*, vol. 2: *Le Pontifical de la curie romaine au XIIIe siècle*, Studi e testi 87 (Vatican City, 1940), 463.

64. *ACPistoia*, Cod. 102, *Ordo divinorum officiorum Ecclesiae Pistoriensis*, fol. 22v-23r. Other churches and chapels were included in the Holy Week liturgies. The procession on Palm Sunday, for example, went to the churches of Sant'Andrea and San Pietro Maggiore. The chapel of San Iacopo at the entrance to the cathedral was where the chrism was prepared on Holy Thursday and where the Easter fire was kindled and the candle lit for the Easter vigil: fol. 21r-21v, 22v, 26r.

65. Ibid., fol. 35r.

66. Cod. LII in the Biblioteca Capitolare di Santa Maria: Andenna, "Un palazzo," 74.

67. As Pierre-Marie Gy has noted, the liturgy of the papal chapel came to replace the liturgy of the Lateran basilica as the paradigm of "Roman," and therefore universal, practice. Two thirteenth-century *Ordinals*, one compiled under Pope Innocent III (circa 1213–16) and the other under Gregory X (circa 1274), show that the integration of the Lateran chapels with the celebration of the great feasts of the year and the complex Roman liturgical duties of the pope intensified. These manuals reveal that not only were the chapels the sites where the pontiff heard daily mass in the morning and performed the nine divine offices, but also particular saints' feasts were celebrated there with special masses (notably that of Saint Nicholas). More parts of the major liturgies of the Christian year were enacted in the Lateran chapels. The blessing of the palms for Palm Sunday and the beginning of the procession that reenacts Christ's entry into Jerusalem before his passion took place in the oldest chapel in the Lateran, San Silvestro. The washing of the feet on Holy Thursday, as we have seen, took place in the chapel of San Lorenzo. Both of these rituals place the celebrant quite dramatically in the role of Christ. That these rituals were chosen to take place in the Lateran chapels also sheds interesting light on some of the more seemly mundane activities described as occurring in the chapels: that is, dressing and undressing the pope in the complex vestments that were the markers of the pontiff's liturgical and ecclesiological roles. This also makes sense of the way in which several chapels — San Niccolò in Pistoia and Calixtus's chapel of Saint Nicholas in

While some papal influence is evident in bishops' adding chapels to their palaces, they did not use their chapels in exactly the same way the popes used theirs. Instead of becoming a ritual site in the great liturgies of the year, the chapel became incorporated into the calendar of saints' feasts. Just as the canons of Pistoia went to the church of San Paolo to celebrate the feast of Saint Paul, and to the church of San Pietro Maggiore to commemorate the feast of Saints Peter and Paul, and to the altar in the cathedral dedicated to Saint Michael on his feast, so they processed to the bishop's chapel of San Niccolò on the feast of Saint Nicholas.[68] The canons' celebration of the saint's feast in the episcopal chapel honored the bishop as well as the saint, just as the bishop (at least in Durand's pontifical) honored the canons by performing the *mandatum* in the chapter hall. But the extant liturgical sources suggest that episcopal chapels remained a distinct sacral space, for the most part the bishop's own. They seem to have been used for the personal devotional life of the bishop, attended by the clergy of his household. As such, episcopal chapels helped construct a religious persona for the bishop that responded to the heightened spiritual expectations for the secular clergy coming out of the reform movement.

The precise location of chapels within episcopal palaces, moreover, suggests that they were designed to sanctify not only the person of the prelate, but also the temporal aspects of his office that were most undermined by the reform movement. To appreciate the significance of the location of episcopal chapels, we must first briefly consider chapels in lay residences. Lay chapels are usually located adjacent to the lord's private chambers — this is thought to be the originating functional principle of the double-chapel (the second-story chapel could then communicate directly with the princely apartments). The imperial palaces at Paderborn and Goslar, for example, follow this arrangement (see Figure 53).[69] The sacral space is associated with the persons of the lord and his family, quite literally with the lord's bedroom and its products; the chapel sanctifies the fruit of the lord's loins, his lineage. Some of these chapels became mini-reliquaries of the lineage through the burial of members (or parts thereof) within it.

Episcopal chapels, however, communicated with the bishop's audience hall.[70] Sant'-Andrea in Ravenna was directly adjacent to the archbishop's hall, the apse and its relics

---

the Lateran — were located above vestries. The chapels seem to be associated, then, with the prelate's assumption of his role through the ritual doffing of the symbols of his office, a role that is ritually linked to that of Christ Himself. *The Ordinal of the Papal Court from Innocent III to Boniface VIII and Related Documents*, ed. Stephen J. P. Van Dijk and completed by Joan Hazelden Walker, Spicilegium Friburgense 22 (Fribourg, 1975), 90, 152, 356, 453, 589, 214–17, 240–41; Pierre-Marie Gy, "La Papauté et le droit liturgique aux XIIe et XIIIe siècles," in *The Religious Roles of the Papacy: Ideals and Realities 1150–1300*, ed. Christopher Ryan (Toronto, 1989), 229–245. When the papacy was at Avignon, ceremonial became much more restricted to the papal residence: Bernhard Schimmelpfennig, *Die Zeremonienbücher der römischen Kirche im Mittelalter* (Tübingen, 1973).

68. *ACPistoia*, Cod. 102, fol. 48r, 54r, 59r, 63v.

69. Gardelles, "Les Palais," planches II (Paderborn), VI (Goslar).

70. In addition to the Italian examples cited, the episcopal chapel of Hereford in England is aligned with the great hall: John Blair, "The 12th-Century Bishop's Palace at Hereford," *Medieval Archaeology* 31 (1987): 68–69; a staircase linked the great hall of the bishop of Beauvais to the

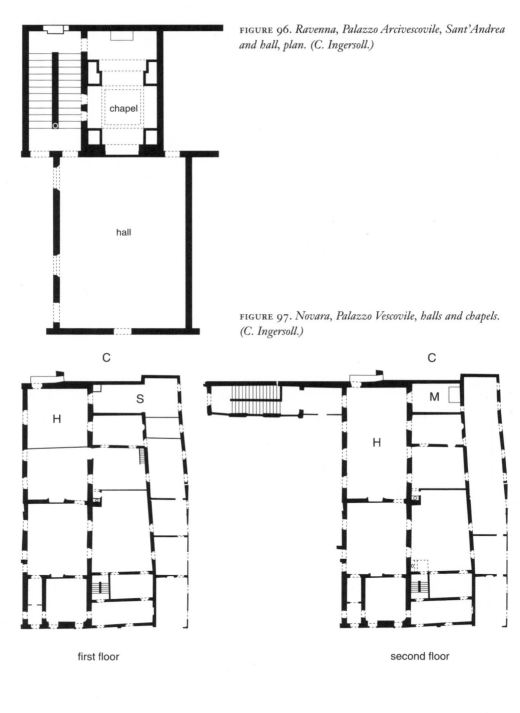

FIGURE 96. *Ravenna, Palazzo Arcivescovile, Sant'Andrea and hall, plan. (C. Ingersoll.)*

chapel

hall

FIGURE 97. *Novara, Palazzo Vescovile, halls and chapels. (C. Ingersoll.)*

C

S

H

C

M

H

first floor

second floor

M S. Maria Maddalena
S S. Siro
H hall
C cathedral

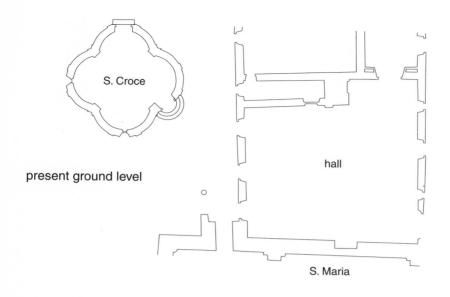

present ground level

hall

S. Maria

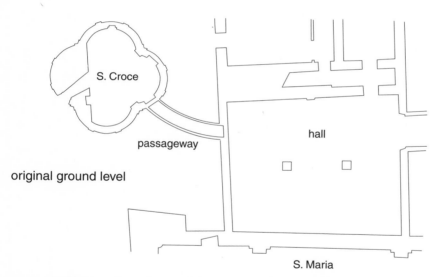

original ground level

passageway

hall

S. Maria

FIGURE 98. *Bergamo, Santa Croce and the Aula della Curia, plan. (C. Ingersoll.)*

chapel, Thierry Crépin-Leblond, "Une Demeure épiscopale du XIIe siècle," 34; the chapel in the palace built by Bishop Maurice Sully of Paris (1160–96) extended directly off the great hall, as did the chapels in the palaces of the bishops of Anger and Le Mans: Gardelles, "Les Palais," planches I, III; and Inge Hacker-Sück, "La Sainte-Chapelle," 229–31; Annie Renoux, "Palais èpiscopaux des diocèse de Normandie, du Mans et d'Angers (Xie-XIIIe siècles)." In *Les évêques normands du XIe siècle,* ed. Pierre Bouet and François Neveux (Caen, 1995), Figures 1, 5, 182, 190–91.

pointing toward it (Figure 96). In Novara, the twelfth-century chapel of San Siro was off the ground-floor hall next to the cathedral used for the bishop's judicial activities, and another chapel added later above San Siro (dedicated to Mary Magdalene) was just off the great audience hall (Figure 97). At Bergamo, the entrance to Santa Croce faced an entrance to the bishop's *aula* (Figure 98): just within were two fresco images of Christ, one blessing the souls in paradise and the other sitting in judgment on the souls consigned to eternal hellfire. It was here that the bishop of Bergamo sat in judgment on his vassals, his serfs, and his clergy. And if the bishop were sitting just below these frescoes, facing those assembled before him in the *aula*, on his left would be the image of Christ judging the damned and on his right the image of Christ blessing the saved. Also on his right, the side of the saved, is his chapel, which (you will remember in Bergamo) is in the form of a baptistery, associating it with the bishop's removal of original sin through baptism, offering the Christian the possibility of eternal life. This chapel in Bergamo was also dedicated to the holy cross through which Christ achieved salvation for believers, ransoming the faithful from sin and death. This powerful constellation of iconographic and theological meaning at Bergamo, and the general placement of chapels in relation to these spaces where the bishop exercised his extraliturgical and secular powers, seem to me to be attempts to sacralize the bishop's power in this world by associating it with the bishop's spiritual role in his church and with Christ's salvific role in Christian history.

CONCLUSION

The cultural expression of claims to power has been the central focus of this book. Ideas about power, relations of power, competition for power — all are evident in the bishop's palace. Architecture both articulated and provided a theater for these expressions. The forms taken by the episcopal residence from Late Antiquity through the thirteenth century reveal ideas about the apostolic origins of episcopal power and realities entailed by the actual exercise of public authority. The most elegant forms bishops created were the products of competition with, and ultimately loss of power to, the communes. These two powers, bishops and communes, were closely related: they inhabited the same urban terrain, and they shared some values and goals (the independence of the city, the salvation of its people). But ultimately their visions of urban lordship and their cultural expressions of claims to rule were quite different. The differences involve relations between the holy and public life, but these relations were hardly resolved: they remained contested and often paradoxical.

The spiritual power of the bishop was used not only to buttress his authority. As bishops in northern Italian cities lost secular powers to the communes, they increasingly attempted to use sacred prerogatives to accomplish temporal ends. We have already seen one example of this: in the late twelfth and early thirteenth centuries bishops increasingly used accusations of heresy to retain influence over the communal government or to resolve financial disputes with the commune. Another example is the more frequent deployment of interdict and excommunication. An interdict was a ban on the performance of essential religious services (communion, absolution of sins, Christian burial) usually within a certain geographical area. It penalized an entire community, or specific groups within it, through deprivation of the sacraments, but it did not entirely cut individuals off from the church. Excommunication, a more extreme measure, was usually directed at individuals and it did place the person outside the church and its saving grace. Moreover, other Christians were prohibited from having anything to do with an excommunicate: social as well as spiritual shunning were entailed. Both these weapons derived from the bishop's religious authority, his control over the administration of the sacraments within his diocese and his judgments in the care of souls.

Significantly, it was only in the reform era that these two types of ecclesiastical censure were being distinguished and defined in church law. Both were characterized by the formula "anathema sit" (let him be anathema) and were frequently deployed together. Changes in the usage of each contributed to their definition. The interdict from at least the sixth century had been used as a coercive measure, usually against a city or diocese in order to prompt penitence or reparation for grievous acts of violence. Not surprisingly, the interdict came to be used much more frequently in the early eleventh century when the plague of internecine warfare in western Europe moved bishops to invoke the "Peace and Truce of God" in an attempt to protect innocents and limit violence. The Council of Limoges in 1031, for example, imposed an interdict on the entire diocese for a breach of the Peace of God, but its bishops also defined some mitigating clauses to ease its burden on the innocent.[1] Such uses of the interdict to force lay compliance to ecclesiastical orders escalated across the twelfth and thirteenth centuries.

Excommunication underwent a more interesting development. Before the eleventh century, it was used in the administration of penance, chiefly to constrain public sinners to seek reconciliation with the church. Under Gregory VII, however, excommunication came to be used much like interdict as a penalty to coerce Christians to obey ecclesiastical decrees. During the investiture contest, Gregory excommunicated not only the emperor Henry IV (several times) and his advisors, but all the bishops who remained loyal to the imperial party. This meant that most of the bishops of Lombardy — and their clergy and people if they continued to consort with the excommunicate — were placed outside the church's grace for much of the conflict. As Elisabeth Vodola has noted, although many of Gregory's legal innovations were not widely disseminated and influential, his changes in the use and character of excommunication were nearly immediately incorporated into canonistic collections that did enjoy a broad popularity.[2]

But, judging by documentary notices, Italian bishops did not begin to deploy this power frequently until after their loss of temporal authority to the communes. In the well-documented see of Arezzo, for example, there are no notices of the bishops using the penalty of excommunication until the thirteenth century. Then, however, its use was frequent. The bishop's deployment of this weapon in relation to Cortona is particularly revealing. This smaller city just south of Arezzo was within the Aretine diocese. The bishop of Arezzo claimed to have received temporal jurisdiction over the city in a diploma from Emperor Charlemagne, but by the early thirteenth century a communal government was ruling Cortona. In an attempt to compensate for urban jurisdictions

1. Mansi, 19: 541–44.
2. Elisabeth Vodola, "Sovereignty and Tabu: Evolution of the Sanction against Communication with Excommunicates. Part 1: Gregory VII," in *The Church and Sovereignty c. 590–1918: Essays in Honor of Michael Wilks*, ed. Diana Wood (Oxford, 1991), 35–55; on the development, generally, of these censures, see *DMA*, s.v. "excommunication" and "interdict"; *DDC*, s.v. "interdit" and "excommunication"; Cyrille Vogel, "Buße und Exkommunikation in der Alten Kirche und im Mittelalter: Ein historischer überblick," *Concilium* 107 (1975): 446–52; Elisabeth Vodola, *Excommunication in the Middle Ages* (Berkeley and Los Angeles, 1986), 1–43. An excellent case study of the increasing episcopal resort to ecclesiastical censures and their mixed results is Brian A. Pavlac's "Excommunication and Territorial Politics in High Medieval Trier," *Church History* 60 (1991): 20–36.

lost to the commune, the bishops of Arezzo shifted their focus toward exercising lordship in their outlying and rural holdings. In the early thirteenth century, then, the Aretine bishops became much more interested in exercising dominion over Cortona. Guelph-Ghibelline politics made this interest avid: Arezzo was strongly allied with the papal or Guelph party and other leading Guelph cities (such as Florence), but Cortona's commune had adopted a pro-imperial, or Ghibelline, stance. With the aid of Perugia, the Cortonese were able to defend themselves against an attack by the forces of Arezzo in 1230, and their defeat of the Aretine army is the background for the series of ecclesiastical censures that followed: by 1234 the citizens of Cortona were excommunicated for their "rebellion and insolence" in ignoring the interdict already laid on them. Tensions continued. In 1252 Pope Innocent IV confirmed the decree of excommunication that a papal legate had issued against the city, again for its resistance to the bishop of Arezzo. On February 1, 1258, finally, the bishop, assisted by the communal forces of Arezzo and Guelph exiles from Cortona, took the city by force and burned it. The bishop thereafter appointed the city's *podestà* and levied taxes. But resistance to these taxes and contact with imperial legates again brought an interdict on the city, and in 1277 all of Cortona's public officials had again been excommunicated by the bishop. The ends sought through the use of these penalties were clearly temporal: the political subordination of Cortona.[3]

Other political results were cultivated through this ecclesiastical censure. An important one was maintaining the Guelph (papal) allegiance of the city. In 1248–49 Bishop Guglielminus had excommunicated the provost of the cathedral chapter, the abbot of the monastery of San Fiora, a certain canon named Bernardinus, and twenty other unnamed men and women of the city of Arezzo, for supporting Emperor Frederick II and the imperial (Ghibelline) party.[4]

Examples can be multiplied. The bishops of Florence used excommunication repeatedly against rural communities that resisted the consolidation of episcopal properties and exercise of episcopal lordship in the countryside. When the men of Sesto rebelled against episcopal jurisdiction, they were excommunicated because they "injured and molested the bishop and the episcopal office by damaging his properties and rights." Bishop John of Velletri excommunicated the notaries of the syndic of San Lorenzo di Borgo in 1207 for opposing his authority and in 1232 excommunicated the leaders of this rural commune for refusing to accept the bishop's *podestà*. Bishop Anthony excommunicated all the residents of Rabbiacanina for their resistance to paying a traditional due, the *census*.[5]

The deployment of these weapons was not always effective, and worse, this constant resort to spiritual censures to achieve temporal ends yielded cynicism and contempt for the church's authority. By the mid-thirteenth century there was a movement among

3. Girolamo Mancini, *Cortona nel medio evo* (Florence, 1897; reprinted Rome, 1969), 12–63; *Arezzo-Documenti*, nos. 516, 578, 622, 650.

4. *Arezzo-Documenti*, nos. 556, 557, 563.

5. Dameron, *Episcopal Power*, 96, 99, 100, 139, 165.

canonists, for example, to restrict the use of interdict because of grave qualms about punishing the innocent along with the guilty. In the decretal *Romana ecclesia: Ceterum* (1246), Pope Innocent IV even limited excommunication to individuals, arguing that to excommunicate entire communities punished the innocent and the guilty. "[L]ong after its fundamental injustice had been acknowledged at the highest levels of the church," notes Elisabeth Vodola, interdict was still exploited because it "was needed as a political and diplomatic weapon."[6]

The use of spiritual penalties to achieve temporal ends brings us back to the linkage already noted between the addition of chapels to episcopal residences and the reorientation of these palaces toward the public space of the piazza. The spiritual power the bishop cultivated in his chapel was, indeed, mobilized to influence and attempt to control the increasingly laicized public sphere. Michel Foucault, in his famous reading of the architecture of Bentham's *Panopticon*, located power in seeing and being seen.[7] Elements of this architectural semiotics of power are present in our bishops' palaces: from their new large windows they gaze on the life in the piazza they seek to control and they heighten their visibility in the piazza (as they process through it from their new entrances, and force their clients to stand waiting in it at the foot of their staircases). But their real power is unseen. It is concentrated in the chapel within the palace, a place known only by rumor and hagiography to all but a few. Their real power lies in the unseen and the imagined, and it is increasingly through these precious but intangible forces that bishops tried to exercise authority.

Here we see one of the most paradoxical effects of the Gregorian reform movement. Originally, the reformers were objecting to the way in which bishops had become imperial servants, were appointed by monarchs, and involved themselves in secular affairs. They successfully "liberated" bishops from the control of rulers, but also lost their means to influence public life. In reaction, bishops begin to use religious means to achieve temporal ends: through the spiritual power cultivated in their chapels, they tried to influence life in the piazza. On the less troubling side of this development, we have bishops preaching from the windows of their palaces, exhorting their flocks, using persuasive rhetoric to accomplish moral and civic renewal. But there is obviously a more troubling side, that of bishops using accusations of heresy, decrees of excommunication, and the interdict of religious compassion in order to achieve political ends. The oppressive results of this linkage between spiritual power and public life are all too clear in the fate of the bishop of Pistoia's chapel of San Niccolò: in the fourteenth century it was converted into an episcopal prison. Graffiti by the inmates is incised over frescoed images of the life of the exemplary bishop Saint Nicholas, one lament warning "beware the madness of this bishop which is without reason."[8]

6. *DMA*, s.v. "interdict," 496–97; *DDC*, s.v. "excommunication," 618. Richard C. Trexler's *The Spiritual Power: Republican Florence under Interdict* (Leiden, 1974) shows how effective this tool remained.

7. *Discipline and Punish: The Birth of the Prison*, trans. Alan Sheridan (New York, 1979), 195–228.

8. Rauty, *Palazzo*, 1:159–60, 303.

Lay resistance to episcopal power could be more violent: from time to time, the bishop's palace was sacked. Carlo Ginzburg and his seminar at the University of Bologna in 1987 published an analysis and interpretation of this phenomenon — the pillaging of the house and property of a pope, cardinal, or bishop upon his death. They called it "ritual sackings" ("saccheggi rituali"). Although the most extreme and well-documented examples of this custom followed the demise of cardinals and popes, its most ancient attestations concern bishops.[9] Several councils in Late Antiquity — most notably Chalcedon in 451 — condemned the looting of the deceased bishop's residence. In the mid-eleventh century, Peter Damian, writing on behalf of Pope Leo IX, warned the clergy and people of Osimo (a small diocese in the Marches) not to repeat "the perverse and detestable practice of certain people who at the death of the bishop break in like enemies and rob his house, like thieves make off with his belongings, set fire to the homes on his estate, and with fierce and savage barbarity cut down his grape vines and orchards."[10] You will not be surprised to learn that he threatened the pillagers with excommunication.

Sometimes these sackings could have the quality of a personal vendetta, the people getting even with a particular prelate whose rule was perceived as harsh or unjust. Thus contemporaries immediately understood the four days of looting that followed the death of Pope Paul IV as retribution for the sufferings he had visited on the citizens of Rome through the arrogant and avaricious administration of his nephews, through his own fanatical persecutions of heretics, and through his rekindling of the Hapsburg-Valois wars.[11] But as Ginzburg and his colleagues emphasize, the longevity of the custom and the details of specific sackings suggest that the wealth, power, and privilege of the episcopal office — more than the failings of an individual incumbent — were targeted. By ransacking the bishop's palace and violently making off with his possessions, the people at least momentarily redressed one of the gross inequalities of a vertiginously hierarchical society. In this carnivalesque exercise in "the world turned upside down," the powerless deployed a "right of spoil" and the poor seized the rich stores of the bishop's cellars and the precious objects that marked him as a "prince" of the church. Some of the irony of this inversion eluded Ginzburg and his students: how rich indeed that the bishop, "father of the poor," was so rich that his wealth could satisfy crowds of looters, who were (after all) only carrying off their own patrimony, that "patrimony of the poor" of which bishops like Lanfranc of Pavia were only stewards and

9. Seminario Bolognese coordinato da Carlo Ginzburg, "Saccheggi rituali: Premesse a una ricerca in corso," *Quaderni storici* ns 65 (1987): 615–36; Reinhard Elze, "«Sic transit gloria mundi»: La morte del papa nel Medioevo," *Annali dell'Istituto storico italo-germanico in Trento* 3 (1977): 23–41; Laurie Nussdorfer, "The Vacant See: Ritual and Protest in Early Modern Rome," *Sixteenth Century Journal* 18 (1987): 173–89.

10. *Monumenta Germaniae historica, Die Breife der deutschen Kaiserzeit* 4: *Die Briefe des Petrus Damiani*, ed. Kurt Reindel (Munich, 1983), no. 35; trans. Owen J. Blum, *Peter Damian, Letters 31–60* (Washington, D.C., 1990), 61.

11. Ginzburg, "Saccheggi," 614; Nussdorfer, "Vacant See," 179.

dispensers. Ritual sackings not only momentarily redressed great inequalities of wealth and power, but also underscored the paradox of a prelate draped in gold brocade, a bishop with a palace, figuring himself as the father of the poor.

Essential to this pillage is a trespass of space: the crowds entered the residence, roamed through its halls and rooms, scoured it from top to bottom for all that it held. For most it was probably their first visit to the bishop's palace. Even with the bishop dead, it surely communicated some of the meanings we have discerned. Did they ransack the chapel with the same gusto with which they cleared out the kitchen and cellars, or did they at least pause and steal more selectively, perhaps in silence? Did they give mock addresses out the decorous trifores of the great hall to their whooping confreres in the piazza below? Did they sit in the bishop's chair and take in his view of the frescos before hauling it off? Early modern accounts describe a great deal of mocking inversion of ecclesiastical ceremonial (like the papal grooms enthroning one of their own in Saint Peter's),[12] but in the end this play acting reinscribed the structures mocked. As Michael Taussig has observed, defacement, transgression, and sacrilege can serve to make more visible and striking the authorities against which they are perpetrated.[13]

As we have seen, the spaces created by bishops could be nuanced expressions of both the character and the claims of the power of their office. If only our sources were voluble enough to tell us whether the styles of ritual sacking changed with the development of episcopal architecture! But just as it is clear that medieval people attacked episcopal power when they sacked their bishop's house, so too it is obvious that these buildings survived. The houses of Dante's Guelph compatriots in Florence did not. They were leveled by their Ghibelline opponents and the powerful expanse of the Piazza della Signoria created in their place. Domestic architecture was commonly recognized as making claims to power but there are many responses to such claims. "Ritual sackings" were neither a renunciation nor an obliteration of the place our bishops made for themselves in the medieval Italian city. And although the commune's architectural initiatives usually decentered the bishop's palace, they did not entirely efface it.

The strategies of visuality and the ideas about power they enunciated were influential long after the bishop's authority was eclipsed. Secular elites borrowed and developed some of these practices, particularly the bishop's use of architecture to visualize claims to urban centrality and authority. In this regard, bishops contributed to the development of Italian political culture. The more coercive strategies bishops devised also contributed to this development, mainly by generating the fierce anticlericalism that is still a potent factor in Italian politics. The broader significance of these episcopal strategies of power, however, is their contribution to the development of the Catholic church. Popes maintained temporal power for much longer than did bishops, but as

12. Nussdorfer, "Vacant See," 187.
13. Michael Taussig, "By the Lake with Liz and Phil: A Story of Defacement and of Defacement of the Defacement," November 11, 1996, Stanford University, Palo Alto, Cal.

their worldly authority was challenged and diminished, they availed themselves of the practices that earlier bishops had pioneered. The artistic and architectural splendor of the Vatican, the careful construction of a charismatic spiritual image of the pontiff, and a rhetorical positioning of the church as the advocate of the poor, all had roots in earlier episcopal responses to political change.

APPENDIX

Changes in the Terms Describing Episcopal Residences

The terms used to identify and describe episcopal residences changed significantly from the fourth to the thirteenth century. But like the use of language itself, a creative process admitting much variation, these changes are neither chronologically precise nor universally consistent. The developments described here are changes in the dominant usage in northern Italian sources, that is, how bishops' residences are usually described in most cities. Important variants in usage and chronology are noted here, but the main purpose of this appendix is to lay out the evidence for the three broad phases of usage that provide the framework for the first part of this book.

I. SOURCES

I have used notarial charters, letters, conciliar acts, and various narrative sources (chronicles, histories, sermons, saints' lives) to study how episcopal residences are referred to and described. Notarial charters have been the most revealing and reliable sources for this terminology and its development. First, they are generally numerous and precisely dated, making it possible to trace changes over time in different cities. Second, their purposes — to record official acts and agreements, mostly related to property tenures and conveyances — promote the usage of careful, clear, and precise language. The formulaic character of these documents, and their provenance in official chanceries and notaries recognized by public authorities, certainly privilege formal terms of reference over popular usages. The general conservatism and formality of legal language, however, make changes in it highly significant: such changes more likely reflect developments in institutional self-representation than, for example, the linguistic choices of two preachers addressing two different audiences in different cities and centuries. For all these reasons, in constructing my three broad phases in the development of terms for episcopal residences, I have accorded greater weight to the evidence of notarial charters than to that of other sources. For the latter, I have supplemented my own reading in Italian sources with systematic searches of "Cetedoc," the computerized edition of the *Corpus Christianorum*, and Migne's *Patrologia Latina* on CD ROM.

II. *Episcopium*

The most commonly used term to describe a bishop's residence in late-antique Italy was *episcopium*. This term was well established by the sixth century and remained dominant into the eighth.

In Christianity's earliest centuries, the terminology describing its most central institutions and buildings was quite varied. A church, for example, might be called the "house of God" (*domus dei*), the "house of prayer" (*domus orationis*), or the "house of the church" (*domus ecclesiae*).[1] In the last usage, "church" denotes the congregation or Christian community; only from the fourth century did *ecclesia* become the normal term used to describe the building used for Christian worship.[2] A stable terminology to describe the bishop's residence took somewhat longer to emerge.

There are very few references to the residence in the fourth and fifth centuries, and the terms invoked are varied. The *Statuta ecclesiae antiqua*, a fifth-century set of rules for ecclesiastical discipline copied into numerous canonical collections in both Italy and Gaul, ordained "that the bishop should have his *hospitiolum* not far from the church." Meaning, literally, "little inn," this language emphasizes the bishop's duty to provide hospitality to those in need, a virtue praised repeatedly in *vitae* of holy prelates.[3] This collection of precepts also admonishes the bishops to have "a modest household and table, and also meager sustenance" and to seek "the authority of his dignity in faith and in the merits of his life."[4] Early saints' lives — such as Sulpicius Severus's *Vita sancti Martini* and Possidius's *Vita Augustini* — extol the monastic quality of life these bishops led. Thus, Saint Martin's abode is a *cellula* (little cell) or a *monasterium* (monastery).[5] Possidius relates that Augustine "instituted a monastery within the church and began to live with the servants of God according to the manner and rule established under the holy apostles."[6]

The bishop of Hippo himself, however, used the term *domus* to describe his residence. In the sermon *De moribus clericorum*, Augustine refers to his abode as "that house which is called the house of the bishop" (*in domo ea quae dicitur domus episcopi*).[7] Similarly, in his life of Saint Ambrose, Paulinus describes the bishop as living in a "house."

1. Saxer, "Domus ecclesiae—οικος Της Εκκλησιας" 167–79.
2. Franz Joseph Dölger, " 'Kirche' als Name für den christlichen Kultbau," in *Antike und Chrisentum*, Kultur- und religionsgeschichtliche Studien, 6 (Münster, 1976) 161-95.
3. "Sed et hospitalitatem semper exhibuit." Possidius, *Vita Augustini*, ed. A. A. R. Bastiaensen, *Vita di Cipriano, Vita di Ambrogio, Vita di Agostino* (Milan, 1981), cap. 22.6.
4. "I. Vt episcopus non longe ab ecclesia hospitiolum habeat"; "4. Vt episcopus uilem supellectilem et mensam ac uictum pauperem habeat, et dignitatis suae auctoritatem fide et uitae meritis quaerat." *CC*, 148, *Statuta Ecclesia Antiqua* canons 1 and 4 (pp. 166–67).
5. Sulpicius Severus, *Vita sancti Martini*, ed. Jacques Fontaine, Sources chrétienne 130 (Paris, 1967), Chaps. 19.4, 23.2; trans. F. R. Hoare, *The Western Fathers* (New York, 1954).
6. " . . . monasterium intra ecclesiam mox instituit et cum Dei servis vivere coepit secundum modum et regulam sub sanctis Apostolis constitutam." *Vita Augustini*, cap. 5.1.
7. Interestingly, however, one ninth-century manuscript renders it *domus episcopii*. Augustine of Hippo, *Sermones selecti duodeviginti*, ed. D. C. Lambot (Brussells, 1950), sermon CCCLV, 124.

In one story, demons sent to attack Ambrose were not even able to get close to his house (*domus in qua manebat Episcopus*).[8] Note that in each of these cases, as with early references to churches, additional descriptive language is used to clarify that the house discussed is that of the bishop. The clarity and verbal economy offered by the term *episcopium* were certainly among the reasons this usage became dominant.

References to the episcopal residence become much more numerous in the sixth century. These sources use *episcopium* consistently and in constructions clearly denoting the bishop's residence. Jordanes in his *Historia Romana* reports how the Augusta Agnes fled court intrigue and sought refuge with Bishop Acacius, *in episcopio*.[9] Gregory the Great uses the word when telling the story of Bishop Andrew (*Dialogues*, III, 7), who unwisely allowed a nun to stay in his *episcopium*. In several letters he invokes the term: discussing armed men breaking into *episcopia* (VI, 42; XII, 10), counseling the bishop of Corsica on the location of his *episcopium* (VIII, 1), and instructing Neapolitan electors to bring the clothes and silver of the *episcopium* for the use of their new bishop (III, 35).[10] He uses the term throughout his *Dialogues* to denote the bishop's residence.[11] Episcopal chronicles also use *episcopium* to refer to the late-antique bishop's house.[12] Finally, a copy of a very early episcopal charter, redacted in 616 for Bishop Alphanus of Benevento, was written "in episcopio."[13]

III. *Domus Sancte Ecclesie*

The emergence of a new convention in identifying the bishop's residence began in the eighth century. It was, however, gradual and largely coincides with a change in the kinds of sources surviving to illuminate episcopal residences. In Late Antiquity, our evidence was from letters and narrative sources; from the early eighth century, significant numbers of notarial charters begin to be preserved. The earliest and most numerous are from the episcopal chancery at Lucca: from 700, these documents are redacted *in domo sancte ecclesie civitatis lucensis* or, more simply, *in domo sancte ecclesie*.[14] How do we know that this *domus* is the bishop's residence? Several charters refer to the bishop's church, San Martino, and specify its location with phrases such as *ubi est domo episcopii*, *ubi est domo episcoporum*, and *domo episcopalis*.[15] In the ninth century, charters refer to the episcopal residences of Asti, Bergamo, Cremona, Florence, Milan, Novara, Pavia, Pia-

8. Paulinus, *Vita sancti Ambrosii*, Chaps. 20, 47—*PL*, XIV 34, 43.

9. Jordanes, *Historia Romana* c. 350, *MGH Auct. Ant.* V / 1, 45.

10. Gregory the Great, *Registrum epistolarum*, *CC*, CXL (Turnhout, 1982)—also IX, 195 and XI, 21.

11. Gregory the Great, *Dialogues*, I.9.11 (1:86), III.1.1 (1:256), IV.13.2 (2:52).

12. Agnellus, *LP*, cap. 23, 29, 66, 132, 157, 158; *Gesta episcoporum neapolitanorum*, *MGH SSRL*, 412, 425.

13. Ughelli, *IS*, 8: 18; also reprinted in *PL*, 80: 325.

14. *CDL*, nos. 12 (700), 85 (746), 99 (749), 114 (754), 182 (764); *Mem. e doc.* V no. 16 (770); V / 2 nos. 103 (767), 202 (785); IV nos. 34 (795), 50 (795?); Manaresi, *Placiti*, no. 7 (786).

15. *CDL*, nos. 132 (759), 140 (759), 175 (764); *Mem. e doc.*, V no. 16 (770); V / 2 no. 202 (785); IV nos. 34 (795), 50 (795?).

cenza, Siena, and Verona, as *domus*.[16] In the tenth century, there is evidence of the usage in Bologna, Padua, Parma, Pistoia, Ravenna, Reggio, and Volterra.[17]

Is this change in language the result of the change in our sources? The use of *domus sancte ecclesie* is most common in notarial charters, and *episcopium* tends to survive longer in narrative works. But use of the term *episcopium* in charters is not unknown. Although the dominant terminology in Lucca from the early eighth century was *domus*, a notary redacting a *placitum* there in 865 described the proceedings as taking place "in episscopio ipsius civitatis." Another imperial scribe located a *placitum* in Milan "in episcopio sancte mediolanensis ecclesie" in 874, but one held in 896 was described as taking place "in domum eiusdem sancte mediolanensis ecclesie."[18] Bishop Elbuncus of Parma, when he redacted his will in 913, noted carefully that he was leaving four copies of the document: "one in the royal palace in Pavia, another in the *episcopium* of Piacenza, a third in that of Reggio, a fourth in that of Modena."[19] The rental clause of a lease redacted in Parma confirms that *domus* and *episcopium* were understood as synonyms for the episcopal residence: "domum vel episcopio Parm."[20]

Some patterns are evident in late examples of the usage of *episcopium* to designate the episcopal residence. Compilation, for example, fostered the repetition of older forms. So we do find an instance of the use of *episcopium* in the early-eleventh-century *Collectio canonum in V libris* (III.249). In a chapter on "clerics who take up arms in sedition," the

16. Asti: *Le carte dello archivio capitolare di Asti (830, 948, 1111–1237)*, ed. F. Gabotto and N. Gabiani, Biblioteca della Società storica subalpina 37 (Pinerolo, 1907), no. 1 (830) and *Le più antiche carte dello archivio capitolare di Asti*, ed. Ferdinando Gabotto, Biblioteca della Società storica subalpina 28 (Pinerolo, 1904), nos. 16 (886), 24 (894), 26 (895), 27 (896), 42 (910), 45 (916), 48 (927), 56 (941), 66 (950–51), 75 (959), 87 (973), 112 (989); Bergamo: *Perg. Bergamo*, nos. 34 (897), 54 (911); Cremona: *Carte Cremonesi*, nos. 12 (851), 41 (910), 42 (910), 106 (1001), 107 (1001), 109 (1004); Florence: Manaresi, *Placiti*, no. 102 (897); Milan: Manaresi, *Placiti*, no. 101 (896); Novara: *Le carte dell archivio capitolare di Santa Maria di Novara*, nos. 13 (881), 42 (924), 44 (931), 50 (949), 103 (999); Pavia: Manaresi, *Placiti*, nos. 108 (899), 158 (967); Piacenza: *Le carte private della cattedrale di Piacenza I (784–848)*, ed. Paola Galetti (Parma, 1978), no. 13 (815) and *ACPiacenza*, cass. 5, "giudizi 830–1078" (Feb. 859); Siena: Manaresi, *Placiti*, nos. 42 (833), 92 (881); Verona: the episcopal residence was most commonly called the *domus sancti zenonis* (*CDV*, 1 nos. 71, 115, 234), but also the *domus sanctae veronensis ecclesiae* (*CDV*, 1 no. 182).

17. Bologna: "Le carte bolognesi del secolo decimo," ed. Giorgio Cencetti in *Notariato medievale bolognese* (Rome, 1977), no. 23 (997 or 1012); Padua: *CDP*, nos. 47 (964), 63 (978), 98 (1014), 144 (1045); Parma: Drei, nos. 29 (924), 41 (?), 42 (935), 74 (987); Pistoia: *Regestum chartarum pistoriensium. Alto medioevo, 493–1000* (Pistoia, 1973), nos. 80 (962), 91 (973), 93 (976), 100 (985); Manaresi, *Placiti*, no. 270 (1006); Ravenna: Fantuzzi, *Mon. rav.*, 3, no. 6 (997); Reggio: Manaresi, *Placiti*, nos. 142 (944), 143 (945), 145 (962), 146 (962); Volterra: *Reg. Volterra*, nos. 27 (947), 29 (949), 69 (985), 110 (1017), 116 (1032).

18. Manaresi, *Placiti*, nos. 69, 78, 101.

19. *Parma X*, no. 9: "Unde quatuor huius mei testamenti exemplaria scribere feci. Unum quod sit in testimonio in palatio Ticini regio, aliud in episcopio Placentino, tercium in Regiense, quartum in Motinense."

20. Ibid., no. 29.

compiler presents admonitions from the Council of Toledo, from a Roman synod, and from a capitulary of "King Wido." This was Wido, marquis of Spoleto, who was elected king of Italy in 889 by a faction headed by the archbishop of Milan. At this election, done by a gathering of bishops in the capital of Pavia, Wido promulgated a series of capitularies, mostly on ecclesiastical subjects. The wording of the law on seditious clerics, however, suggests that it was not "new law" conceived by Wido, but a canon from an earlier Lombard-era collection. It admonishes "clerics who carry arms" and who reside "at the church or at the *episcopium*" not to serve as soldiers, nor pursue worldly things, nor "live in law just as the rest of the Lombards."[21] Such genealogies are common in canonical collections and preserve earlier linguistic preferences. Choices in language and style could also be more self-conscious. Both Agnellus, who compiled his *Liber Pontificalis* in the mid-ninth century, and the anonymous compiler of the *Gesta episcoporum neapolitanorum* in the late ninth century, were copying the model of the Roman *Liber Pontificalis*. Particularly in the case of Ravenna, a see that claimed independence from Rome in the seventh century, such emulation was not without significance; Agnellus follows the format and style of his papal exemplar and, not surprisingly, uses *episcopium* to designate the archiepiscopal residence (see later section on the Roman *Liber Pontificalis*).

Another pattern in continued usage of the term is geographical. In two areas of the peninsula, *episcopium* remained a designation for the episcopal residence. One was the eastern edge of the Romagna along the Adriatic coast. In the cluster of sees around Ravenna — Cesena, Faenza, Ficocle, Ferrara, and Rimini — usage of *episcopium* to designate the building in which the bishop lived persisted into the eleventh century.[22] A likely reason is the influence of the see of Ravenna, which had extensive land holdings in this area and a rather conservative administrative tradition. Ravennate usage preferred the Greek-derived term *episcopium* into the ninth century, and other aspects of the archiepiscopal chancery were profoundly conservative: the script used by the curia into the ninth century was a slightly modified (rounded) form of the "new Roman cursive" developed in the third century A.D., and other features of Ravennate documents (the "ad latus" dating clause, the *Legimus* subscription) derived from late-antique impe-

21. "De clericis qui arma baiulant et in suis propriis resident ad ecclesiam seu ad episcopium non militant, negotia saecularia agunt, in lege uiuant, sicut et ceteri langobardi, tam ipsi quam et filii eorum." *CC Cont. Med.*, 6: 436; Wido's capitulary is in *Monumenta Germaniae historica. Legum sectio II: Capitularia regum Francorum*, ed. Alfredus Boretius, 2 vols. (Hannover, 1883-97) 2: 106; see Chris Wickham, *Early Medieval Italy: Central Power and Local Society 400–1000* (Totowa, N.J., 1981), 170 on Wido, or "Guy," and his career.

22. Fantuzzi, *Mon. rav.*, I no. 112 (1067, *in lacu Ficulensis prope Episcopio*), II no. 149.31 [p. 382] (1010, *in Episcopio Cesene*); *ASModena*, Archivio Estense, Giurisdizione Sovrana Vescovado Ferrara, busta no. 251, perg. no. 3 (1082, *in episcopio ferr.*); *Le carte ferraresi*, no. 62 (1083, *in episcopio sancti georii*); *ACRimini*, perg. ACaRn gr I n. VII [A] (1070, *iuxta prefatum episcopium*), ACaRn gr I n. XIV [A] (1086, *prope episcopium*), AcaRn gr I n. XXII [B] (1144, *ad episcopium*)—note that the transcription with n. VII incorrectly reads the abbreviation for *episcopium* as *episcopatum*; *Biblioteca Classense di Ravenna*, Archivio Storico Comunale perg. no. 12bis (1111, *in episcopio faventie*).

rial chancery forms were cultivated into the early eleventh century.[23] The other area is the region around Rome and farther south in the Duchy of Benevento. Two charters of Rieti — one from the ninth and one from the tenth century — used *episcopium*, and the ninth-century Greek scholar at Rome known as Anastasius the Librarian (a contender for the papal throne against Benedict III but then papal secretary to Nicholas, 858–867, and librarian under Hadrian II, 867–872) used the term frequently in his writings.[24] Beneventan chroniclers — such as Leo Atinensis, Leo Marsicanus, and Falco of Benevento — also continued to use *episcopium*.[25]

These geographical patterns suggest the possibility that ties with the eastern empire or lingering Greek tradition may have influenced local conventions in the language applied to the episcopal residence. The eastern Romagna was part of the Byzantine exarchate of Ravenna. There are also some examples of late usage of *episcopium* associated with Venice, another area with close ties to Byzantium.[26] The areas in the south also preserved Greek ties and traditions longer: the Beneventan rite into the eleventh and twelfth centuries contained chants in Greek as well as Latin. This evidence, although slight, associating the term *episcopium* with areas of enduring Greek influence, prompts consideration of whether the new usage of *domus* to designate the episcopal residence was fostered by Frankish influence. Gregory of Tours used the term *domus ecclesie* (or *domus ecclesiastica*) to refer to the bishop's residence, and Merovingian conciliar decrees tend to use *domus* or *episcopalis domus*.[27] Early Carolingian decrees use similar constructions, but several decrees of the Council of Tours and the "Concord of Bishops," both from 813, use the term *episcopium* to mean an episcopal residence. Canon 26 of the councils of Meaux-Paris (845–846) uses *episcopium* but then defines it: "De episcopio,

23. Jan-Olaf Tjäder, "Le origini della scrittura curiale romana," *Bullettino dell' «Archivio paleografico italiano»*, ser. 3, II–III (1963–64): 7–54, but particularly 12, 49–50; Jan-Olaf Tjäder, "*Et ad latus*. Il posto della datazione e della indicazione del luogo negli scritti della cancelleria imperiale e nelle largizioni di enfiteusi degli arcivescovi ravennati," *Studi romagnoli* 24 (1973): 91–124.

24. Manaresi, *Placiti*, no. 198: "intus ipsam civitatem [Rieti] ad ipsum episcopium et in ipsa turre" (Nov. 982). The ninth-century example is more ambiguous. In a charter dated Oct. 4, 877, the bishop of Rieti made a donation to the monastery of Farfa with the consent of the clerics and priests "aepiscopii nostri" (which could mean either his household or, more broadly, his see): *Il Regesto di Farfa compilato da Gregorio di Catino*, eds. I. Giorgi and U. Balzani, 5 vols. (Rome, 1879–1914), 3: no. 323. For Anastasius the Librarian, see *Dizionario biografico degli italiani* (Rome, 1960-) 3: 25–37 and for his use of the term, *Historia de vitis pont. Rom.*, *PL*, 128: 216, *Interpretatio Synodi VIII gen.*, 129: 145; *Epistola ad Martinum*, 129: 589.

25. Leo Atinensis episcopus, *Translatio corporis Marci pontificis*, Ughelli, *IS*, 6:541–48 (2nd ed., 426–31) and also in *PL*, 143: 1417–18, 1421; Leo Marsicanus, *Chronicon Monasterii Casinense*, 3.4, 3.21, 4.20, *MGH SS*, 7: 700, 713, 771; Falco Beneventanus, *Chronicon* in *PL*, 173: 1158, 1173, 1175, 1179, 1188, 1191, 1192, 1212, 1217, 1249, 1250, 1257.

26. Iohannis Diaconi, *Chronicon Venetum et Gradense usque ad a. 1008*, *MGH SS*, 7: 40; "Actum episcopio Cenedensi," *CDV*, 2 no. 41 (Jan. 6, 897).

27. May Viellaard-Troiekouroff, *Les Monuments religieux de la Gaule d'après les oeuvres de Grégoire de Tours* (Paris, 1976), 306–7; *Historia Francorum (MGH SRM)* II.23, IV. 36, V.48–49, VII.27, VIII.43, IX.12; *MGH Concilia* 1: 101, 125, 170.

quod domus episcopi appellatur."[28] The dates of these examples suggest that contact with Rome may have introduced the older Greek-based designation, but that common parlance in the Frankish kingdom was *domus*. Although our earliest examples in Italy (all from Lucca in the early eighth century) predate the Carolingian conquest, it is at least possible that Frankish ecclesiastical custom fostered the widespread adoption of *domus sancte ecclesie* in the Po valley and in Tuscany.

At the same time, usage of the word *episcopium* was also changing. In Late Antiquity the word was sometimes used to denote "diocese" or "see," but the word *episcopatus* was usually preferred for this sense. From the eighth century, however, *episcopium* is increasingly used to denote the see, the bishop's office, especially the territory or property of the see. We can already see this in some of the earliest *domus* examples from Lucca: *ubi est domo episcopii, ubi est domo episcoporum,* and *domo episcopalis* are all used to denote the same thing. *Episcopium* here has the sense of "episcopal" or "of the bishops."[29] Similarly, in Volterra a charter of 947 reads "in domo episcopatui nostro Voloterrensis," and one of 949 substitutes *episcopium* for *episcopatus*: "in domo episcopio nostro Voloterrensis."[30] A *placitum* from Cremona using the term twice in one sentence well illustrates the change in meaning: the judicial session took place "in caminata maiore domui episcopio ipsius civitatis per data licencia domni Odelrici episcopi ipsius episcopio." Another redacted at the same session used "domus episcopi" to indicate the bishop's residence but called Odelricus once again "episcopi ipsius episcopii."[31] Otto I in a diploma to Andrew, Bishop of Lodi, granted "iure et dominio in prefati episcopii," and Bishop John of Modena accepted a donation to his see in 994 made "ad pars predicto episcopio."[32] By the early eleventh century, the see of Reggio was identified as "episcopio sancte Regiensis ecclesie ubi nunc domnus Teuzonem episcopus hordinatum esse videtur."[33] Similar uses in notarial charters occur throughout northern Italian sees.[34]

This change in meaning and usage is also evident in other kinds of sources. Liudprand of Cremona, in his *Antapodosis* (V.29), uses *episcopium* to mean "see" when he describes how Bishop Joseph of Brescia was deprived of his by King Berengar. Ratherius of Verona also uses the word with this sense in his *Excerptum ex Dialogo Confessionali* and *Phrenesis*.[35] The author of the life of Pope Sergius II (844–847) uses the word *episcopium*

28. *MGH Concilia*, 2: 97, 213, 288–89, 297; 2: 97.
29. *CDL*, nos. 132, 140, 175; *Mem. e doc.*, V no. 16, V / 2 no. 202, IV nos. 34, 50.
30. *Reg. Volterra*, nos. 27, 29.
31. *Carte Cremonesi*, nos. 106, 107.
32. *Codice diplomatico laudense*, no. 17; *Reg. Modena*, no. 65.
33. *Carte Reggio*, no. 131.
34. Brescia: *Carte Cremonesi*, no. 89; Cremona: *Carte Cremonesi*, no. 106; Piacenza: *AAPiacenza*, no. 517; Vicenza: Manaresi, *Placiti*, no. 420. Papal confirmations of episcopal rights and properties use *episcopium* in this fashion regularly from the tenth century: *PL*, 133: 1016 (John XII); 137: 350 (Benedict VII), 905, 919, 928, 936 (Gregory V); see also Toubert, *Les Structures du Latium médiéval*, 797.
35. *Dial. Conf.*, 1.45 and *Phrenesis* 1.11 (*CC*, 46A, 97, 222).

when describing the "wicked heresy of simony": "so much did it flourish that bishoprics (*episcopia*) were sold in public, and he who paid most got the bishopric (*episcopatum*). To such avarice were they brought that a bishopric (*episcopium*) was sold for 2000 mancuses and more still if the buyers could find the funds."[36] In a more laudatory description of the relationship between a bishop and his see, Peter Damian praised Saint Maurus of Cesena for combining devotion to pastoral care with a contemplative life: "Even while in his diocese (*episcopio*) and energetically governing the church committed to him, he began to seek with an agitated searching mind that place where he might be able to leave time and the disturbances of the world and draw especially close to God alone."[37]

IV. *Palatium*

One by one, beginning in the 1020s and continuing well into the twelfth century, bishops in northern Italy started calling their residences "palaces." The two earliest examples come from Parma (1020) and Mantua (1021), followed at mid-century by Modena (1046) and Padua (1048). The most common pattern, however, is for the *domus* terminology to continue until the late-eleventh-century documentary thinning produced by the investiture conflict and its attendant changes, and for *palatium* to appear when the quantity of episcopal documentation picks up again early in the twelfth century. Piacenza is a good example. The residence is called a *domus* in 1009, 1038, and 1086.[38] In the last decade of the eleventh century and the opening decade of the twelfth, there are hardly any episcopal documents, but when we finally get an exchange by Bishop Arduin in 1121, it is enacted "in palacio episcopii civitatis placencie."[39] The use of *palatium* is stable from this point on.[40] Bergamo, Como, and Cremona follow a similar chronology. In Bergamo the residence is a *domus* in 1088 and 1091 and then after a period of thin documentation it emerges in 1129 as a "palace."[41] The residence at Como is a *domus* in 1043, 1079, and 1087; the next time we see it in a document of 1109 it is a "domo palacii eius."[42] At Cremona the bishop's residence is a *domus* until 1052 and then it reap-

36. Duchesne, *LP*, 104; trans. Davis 1995, 93.

37. *PL*, 144: 947.

38. Manaresi, *Placiti*, nos. 273, 347; *Archivio capitolare di S. Antonino—Piacenza* [microfilm, Archivio di Stato, bobina 1], "Donazioni diverse VIII-1086" no. 96.

39. *ACPiacenza*, permute cass. 12, May 14, 1121.

40. Jan. 30, 1124, "in palacium episcopi" Simona Rossi, *Arduino Vescovo di Piacenza (1121–1147)*, Tesi di Laurea, Università cattolica del sacro cuore, Milano, Facoltà di lettere e filosofia, Rel. A. Ambrosioni, 1990–91, 207–209; Oct. 20, 1133 "in palacio placentino" *Archivio capitolare di S. Antonino—Piacenza*, Atti Publici no. 27; April 8, 1134 "in palacio istius episcopus" and Feb. 13, 1135 "in palatio domni episcopi," *ASPiacenza*, Archivio storico degli ospizi civili, Atti privati cartella n. 2, perg. 15bis and 16.

41. Manaresi, *Placiti*, 467, 469, 470; Ughelli, *IS*, 5: 451–52.

42. Manaresi, *Placiti*, no. 359 "intra civitatem Cumensem data licencia Lithigeri humilis episcopi in aula domus sancte Cumensis ecclesie"; *Gli atti privati milanesi e comaschi del secolo XI*, eds. C. Manaresi, G. Vittani, and C. Santoro (Milan, 1933–69), nos. 590, 707; *Carte di San Fedele in Como*, no. 11.

pears in 1123 as the "palatio episcopali civitatis cremone."[43] Although their documentation is more problematic, Reggio and Milan also seem generally to follow this chronology. For Reggio, after a good series of tenth-century references to the residence (as *domus*) we know nothing about the building in the early eleventh century. A charter redacted on the first of June 1071, however, was redacted "in pa[l]at[ium eius]dem urbis."[44] There are no references to the residence again until the mid-twelfth century, but these do identify it as a "palace."[45] A *placitum* held in Milan in 1021 was in the "brolito domui sancti Ambrosii," and Arnulf of Milan, whose chronicle covers eleventh-century events in the city until 1077, used the word *domus* to describe the bishop's residence in his narration of its invasion by an angry mob. Unfortunately, there are few documents in the archiepiscopal archive of Milan before the mid-twelfth century. After a twelfth-century copy of a ninth-century lease, the earliest document in the collection is dated March 4, 1137, and, indeed, it is redacted "in palatio mediolanensis."[46]

Although the transition to *palatium* generally coincides with the investiture conflict, the politics of the reform movement do not explain which bishops adopt the term first. Parma, the earliest example, was the seat of an imperial antipope, and Mantua, the next to invoke the term, was a center of reform. Both imperial and papal supporters are found among the first dozen sees using *palatium*. Wealth and power are no better indicators. Some of the earliest bishops to invoke the term (those of Parma, Modena, Arezzo, Reggio, and Trent) did exercise full comital powers within their cities, but others (those of Mantua, Florence, Padua, Lucca, and Bologna) did not dominate public authority within their walls. No strong regional patterns emerge either, with cities in Emilia-Romagna, Lombardy, Tuscany, and the Veneto represented among the earliest to have a "palace." As I have argued in Chapter 3, local factors, particularly shifts in power leading to the emergence of the commune, seem most closely linked to the invocation of *palatium* to describe the episcopal residence in individual cities. Listed below for each city are occurrences of the various terms used to describe the residence: "E" represents *episcopium*; "D," *domus*; and "P," *palatium* (other terms are given in brackets with the year of the document). The numbers in parentheses indicate the number of documents in that year in which the term occurs. Cities are listed in chronological order by the year in which *palatium* is first used and I have appended comments on patterns in the data.

43. *Carte Cremonesi*, nos. 106, 107, 109, 191, 284. In the 1060s and 1070s there are episcopal documents, but they are redacted largely at castles in the countryside; the bishop is absent from Cremonese documentation from 1086 to 1120.

44. *ASReggio*, Monastero dei SS. Pietro e Prospero, June 19, 1071: The document records a sale enacted "coram predictum domum Gandulfum presulem in ipsius pa[l]a[tium eius]dem urbis feliciter."

45. *ACCReggio*, ser. A no. 219, Oct. 19, 1162 "Actum in palatia regini"; no. 243, April 1171 "in palatio domni regini episcopi Albrizonis"; no. 273, April 21, 1179 "in palacio regini episcopi"; nos. 278–80, Feb. 11, 1180 "in palatio regini episcopi Alberizonis."

46. Manaresi, *Placiti*, no. 308; *MGH SS*, 8: 25, Arnulf of Milan, *Gesta archiepiscoporum mediolanensium* III.25; *Regesto delle Pergamene dell'archivio arcivescovile di Milano*, ed. Ambrogio Palestra (Milan, 1961), 15, and *Archivio storico diocesano*, sez. 15, Pergamene.

Parma[47] — D: 924, 935, 982, 987, 1015, 1046, 1055, 1060, 1061, 1069, 1081; P: 1020, 1074, 1081, 1153, 1157, 1162, 1163, 1167, 1168, 1170, 1171, 1175, 1179, 1186, 1191, 1192, 1194, 1195; both D and P from 1020 to 1081, then only P.

Mantua[48] — D: 1088; P: 1021, 1056, 1082, 1086, 1154, 1185, 1199(2).

Florence[49] — D: 897, 967, 1038; P: 1038, 1046, 1061, 1070, 1073, 1074, 1075, 1100, 1119.

Modena[50] — D: 796; P: 1046, 1056 (2), 1068 (2), 1070 (2), 1078, 1094, 1101, 1102 (2), 1105, 1108, 1141 (2), 1143, 1147 (2), 1148, 1154, 1157 (3); P used exclusively and consistently from 1046.

Arezzo[51] — D: 961, 1084 (3), 1086; E: 1015, 1025, 1028, 1029, 1030 (2), 1031, 1041, 1043 (2), 1053, 1057 (2), 1064, 1065, 1073, 1080 [domum et episcopium], 1082 (2); P: 1046 (3), 1074, 1079 (4), 1087, 1139, 1147, 1154, 1157, 1162, 1180, 1184, 1216, 1232, 1240, 1255, 1252, 1257, 1266, 1269, 1270 (2), 1277, 1282, 1315, 1319, 1320, 1324 (4); E, early eleventh; E, D, and P 1046–86; then just P.

Padua[52] — D: 964, 978, 1014, [mansio: 1026], 1048, 1085, 1095, 1107, 1110, 1129?, 1139, 1151, 1153, 1156; P: 1048, [casa terranea: 1077], 1116, 1130 (3), 1131, 1132 (2), 1136 (2), 1138, 1140, 1145, 1147, 1148, 1149, 1152, 1153, 1154, 1156 (2), 1157, 1160 (3), 1161 (2), 1166, 1167, 1168, 1170, 1171, 1185 (2).

Ferrara[53] — E: 1082, 1083; D: 1120, 1124, 1129, 1147, 1148, 1178, 1186, [mansio:

47. *Parma X*, nos. 29, 42, 72, 74; *Parma XI*, nos. 16, 26, 80, 82, 97, 106, 109, 122, 129, 137, 138; *Parma XII*, 225, 252, 278, 279, 281, 289, 351, 355, 359, 396, 400, 460 500, 696, 819, 828, app. nos. 32, 103, 104, 140, 147.

48. *Reg. Mantua*, nos. 52, 80, 101, 106, 109, 292, 427, 637, 638.

49. Manaresi, *Placiti*, nos. 102, 157, 351, 353, 372, 413, 424, 430, 434, 480; *Le carte del monastero di S. Maria in Firenze (Badia)*, ed. Luigi Schiaparelli and Anna Maria Enriques (Rome, 1990), nos. 100, 161.

50. Most episcopal documents before 1046 were redacted "in urbe Mutina," but once the palace appeared in 1046, the use of *palatium* was consistent: *Reg. Modena*, nos. 200, 216, 217, 254, 255, 261, 263, 278, 290, 293, 294, 297, 302, 311, 408, 409, 425, 437, 438, 439, 448, 468, 469, 475, 494, 498, 501–8, 510–11, etc.

51. Manaresi, *Placiti*, nos. 373, 454; *Arezzo-Documenti*, nos. 69, 106, 116, 120, 129, 139, 141, 143, 150, 161, 163, 164, 178, 182, 183, 192, 196, 210, 213, 241, 250, 251, 255, 256, 258, 266, 271, 284, 345, 353, 359, 362, 364, 392, 399, 476, 514, 535, 584, 599, 600, 602, 634, 638, 642, 643, 650, 661, 710, 714, 718, 724, 726, 727, 729.

52. *CDP*, 1: nos. 47, 63, 98, 111, 144, 150, 151, 237, 282, 316; 2: nos. 33, 48, 79, 185, 208, 212, 213, 217, 239, 240, 287, 303, 340, 370, 383, 451, 497, 508, 524, 549, 556, 586, 600, 623, 655, 664, 666, 675, 742, 743, 745, 765, 768, 898, 902, 932, 998, 1027; *ACVerona*, III-9-3v (AC 68 p n15), III-9-3v (no other enumeration).

53. Manaresi, *Placiti*, no. 336; *ASModena*, Archivio Estense, Giurisdizione Sovrana Vescovado Ferrara, busta no. 251, nos. 2 (1062), 3 (1082), 8 (1092), 10 (1110), 11 (1113), 23 (1158), 27 (1186); *Le carte ferraresi*, nos. 44 (1063), 62 (1083), 72 (1092); *ASFerrara*, Archivio Estense-Tassoni, busta 1, nos. 8 (1083), 9 (1083), 14 (1120), 15 (1124), 16 (1129), 20 (1147), 25 (1192); *ACAFerrara*, Reparto Pergamene Sec. XII, nos. 6 (1148), 11 (1172); *BCFerrara*, Mss. G. A. Scalabrini, "Documenti

1032], 1149, 1155, 1158; P: 1062, 1063, 1083, 1092, 1110, 1113, 1127, 1192, 1193, 1197, 1204; no clear pattern until 1190s, thirteenth century.

Reggio[54] — D: 944, 945, 962; P: 1071, 1162, 1171, 1179, 1180, 1190, 1191, 1192, 1199.

Rimini[55] — D: 1070, 1087; P: 1086, 1158, 1187.

Lucca[56] — D: 700, 746, 749, 754, 759 (2), 764 (2), 767, 770, 785, 795, 803, 830, 871, 971, 1000, 1018, 1020, 1025, 1068, 1073, 1084, 1086; P: 1086, 1119, 1121, 1128, 1178, 1179, 1191, 1193, 1195, 1197.

Trent[57] — P: 1086, 1144, 1193, 1196.

Bologna[58] — D: 1012, 1062, 1105, 1121, 1126, 1139, 1142, 1143, 1170, 1172; P: 1089, 1122, 1128, 1154, 1157, 1176, 1197, 1205, 1225; both terms used from 1080s to about 1180.

Como[59] — D: 880, 1031, 1043, 1087, 1165; P: 1109, 1180, 1194, 1195 (3), 1239, 1247.

Trascritti" cl. I #445 vol. 1: f. 268 (1141), f. 292 (1149), f. 297 (1155), f. 398 (1186), vol. 2: f. 15 (1193); cl. I #459, quire 8 f. 15r (1197).

54. Manaresi, *Placiti*, nos. 142 (944), 143 (945), 145 (962); *ASReggio*, Monastero dei SS. Pietro e Prospero, June 19, 1071; *ACCReggio*, nos. 219 (1162), 243 (1171), 273 (1179), 278–280 (1180), 339 (1190), 353 (1191), 369 (1192); *Carte Cremonesi*, nos. 834, 835 (1199).

55. *ACRimini*, no. 7A (1070), 14A (1086), 16A (1086), 31A (1187); Luigi Tonini, *Rimini dal principio dell'era volgare all'anno MCC, ossia della storia civile e sacra riminese* (Rimini, 1856), 2, no. 76.

56. *CDL*, nos. 12, 85, 99, 114, 132, 140, 175, 182; *Mem. e doc.*, V / 2 no. 103, V no. 16, V / 2, 202, IV no. 34, IV no. 50, IV supp. App. 4.5, V / 2 504, IV supp. 39, IV supp. App. 57, V / 3 1427, IV supp. 89; Manaresi, *Placiti*, nos. 305, 323; Vito Tirelli, "Il «palatium» a Lucca fino al sec. XIII," *Atti del convegno Il palazzo pubblico di Lucca: Architetture opere d'arte destinazioni* Lucca 27–28 ottobre 1979, ed. Isa Belli Barsali (Lucca, 1980), 16–18 with annotation; *Regesto del capitolo di Lucca*, no. 1739; *AALucca*, Diplomatico, *D 61 (1191), A 53 (1193).

57. Odorici, *Storie bresciani*, 5: 72 (no. 7); Huter, *Tiroler Urkundenbuch*, no. 217; *ACVerona*, II-8–5r (AC 13 m2 n14); Leo Santifaller, *Urkunden und Forschungen zur Geschichte des Trientner Domkapitels im Mittelalter. I. Urkunden zur Geschichte des Trientner Domkapitels 1147–1500* (Vienna, 1948), no. 12.

58. Lodovico Vittorio Savioli, *Annali bolognesi*, 3 vols. (Bassano, 1784–1795), 1: nos. 62 (1062), 153 (1154) and 2: no. 206 (1170), 316 (1197); *San Giorgio Maggiore*, ed. Luigi Lanfranchi, 4 vols. (Venice, 1968), 2, no. 68 (1089); *ASBologna*, San Giovanni in Monte 1 / 1341, nos. 25 (1105), 42 (1121), 43 (1121); 3 / 1343, nos. 29 (1142); 5 / 1345 no. 56 (1157); 8 / 1348, nos. 1 (1172), 41 (1176); Abbazia di Santo Stefano 8 / 944, nos. 22 (1122); 9 / 945, no. 5 (1128); *Reg. Mantua*, nos. 197 (1126), 239 (1139), 253 (1142); Girolamo Tiraboschi, *Storia dell'augusta badia di S. Silvestro di Nonantola* (Modena, 1784–85), 2: 258 (1139); *Archivio Arcivescovile di Bologna*, Documenti dalla R. Mensa Arciv. di Bologna, L / 572, Lib. A nos. 17 (1205), 24 (1225).

59. Manaresi, *Placiti*, Inquisitiones et Investiture VIII and no. 359; Ughelli, *IS*, 5:285–87; *Gli atti privati milanesi*, nos. 590, 707; *Carte di San Fedele in Como*, ed. Santo Monti (Como, 1913), nos. 11, 49; Luigi Tatti, *Gli annali sacri della città di Como*, 3 vols. (Como, 1663; Milan, 1683; Milan, 1734–35), 2: 879–81, 889–90; Frigerio and Baserga, "Il palazzo vescovile," 81.

Pistoia[60] — D: 962, 973, 976, 985, 1030, 1046, 1067; P: 1112, 1114, 1131, 1142, 1176, 1182, 1190, 1220, 1223, 1226, 1245, 1246.

Piacenza[61] — D: 815, 859, 1009, 1010, 1025, 1038, 1086; P: 1121, 1124, 1133, 1134, 1135, 1143, 1144, 1147, 1169, 1171, 1178, 1183, 1182, 1193, 1194.

Cremona[62] — D: 851, 910 (2), 1001 (2), 1004, 1052; P: 1123, 1153, 1156, 1158 (2), 1159, 1161, 1162, 1163 (3), 1169, 1172 (3), 1174, 1176, 1177, 1179 (3), 1180, 1183, 1185, 1188 (2), 1189, 1192, 1194 (2), 1197 (2).

Ravenna[63] — D: 997, 1030, 1031, 1073, 1074, 1122; P: 1126, 1127, 1128, 1138, 1145, 1154, 1176, 1177, 1180, 1181, 1184, 1190, 1194, 1197, 1199.

Pavia[64] — D: 899, 967, 1115; E: 1103, 1118, 1124, 1129, 1148; P: 1127, 1150, 1153, 1157, 1188.

Bergamo[65] — D: 897, 911, 1088, 1091 (2), 1164, 1171; E: 1078; P: 1129, 1145,

60. Rauty, *Palazzo*, 1, Documenti, nos. 1–4, 7, 9–10, 12–13, 16, 23, 25, 28, 30–31, 33–35; Manaresi, *Placiti*, no. 270.

61. Manaresi, *Placiti*, nos. 273 (1009), 347 (1038); *Le carte private della cattedrale di Piacenza I (784–848)*, no. 13 (815); *Parma XI*, no. 32 (1025); *Parma XII*, no. 178 (1147); *ASPiacenza*, Archivio storico degli ospizi civili—Atti Privati, cartella 2 perg. 15bis (1134), 16 (1135); cartella 4 perg. 6 (1171), 35 (1178); cartella 5 perg. 17 (1183), 43 (1189), 45 (1189); *ACPiacenza*, Giudizi (Cass. 5, no. 14) Feb. 859; Donazioni Diversi (Cass. 4) Permute (Cass. 12 no. 74), May 14, 1121; Vendite (Cass. 16) Nov. 24, 143; Sentenze (Cass. 14) June 1, 1144, Apr. 15, 1194; Investiture (Cass. 6) nos. 12 (1169), 29 (1193).

62. *Carte Cremonesi*, nos. 12 (851–852), 41 (910), 42 (910), 106 (1001), 107 (1001), 109 (1004), 284 (1123), 358 (1153), 368 (1156), 377 (1158), 380 (1158), 382 (1159), 393 (1161), 402 (1162), 403 (1163), 407 (1163), 408 (1163), 439 (1169), 471 (1172), 482 (1172), 488 (1172), 515 (1174), 527 (1176), 545 (1177), 562 (1179), 568 (1179), 570 (1179), 577 (1180), 612 (1183), 633 (1185), 671 (1188), 672 (1188), 673 (1188), 711 (1192), 766 (1194), 777 (1194), 811 (1197), 812 (1197).

63. Fantuzzi, *Mon. rav.*, 3 no. 6 (997), 1 nos. 93 (1030), 96 (1031); 2 no. 156.4 (1079), 1 no. 139 (1176), 3 no. 33 (1181), 4 no. 72 (1184), 5 no. 51 (1194), 3 no. 37 (1197), 5 no. 3.49 (1199); *AARavenna*, nos. 1760 (1073), 2794 (1074), 2190 doc. 2 (1122), 2447 (1127), 3690 (1138); *Regesto di S. Apollinare Nuovo*, ed. Vincenzo Federici, Regesta chartarum Italiae 3 (Rome, 1907), nos. 51 (1126), 54 (1128), 118 (1180); *Regesto della chiesa di Ravenna; Le carte dell'archivio estense*, 2 vols., ed. V. Federici and G. Buzzi, Regesta chartarum Italiae 7 & 15 (Rome, 1911–1931), nos. 29 (1154), 67 (1177), 93 (1180), 110 (1184), 127 (1197); *Biblioteca Classense di Ravenna*, Archivio Storico Comunale, no. 13 (1128).

64. Manaresi, *Placiti*, nos. 108, 158; *ADPavia*, Vescovi di Pavia cartella 1 (1099–1295), fasc. 2, July 11, 1103; pergamena E4, July 21, 1115; fasc. 6, Dec. 10, 1118; pergamena E5, Oct. 6, 1124; pergamena E6, Feb. 27, 1127; Giuseppe Robolini, *Notizie appartenente alla storia della sua patria*, 7 vols. (Pavia, 1823–36), 3: 247, May 18, 1129; *Le carte del monastero di Santa Maria di Morimondo I (1010–1170)*, ed. Michele Ansani (Spoleto, 1992), nos. 98, Jan 25, 1148, and 114, Oct. 1150; *Regesto degli atti dei secoli X–XIII della biblioteca civica "Bonetta"* (Pavia, 1974), nos. 18, May 19, 1153, and July 20, 24, 1157; *Carte Cremonesi*, no. 665.

65. *Perg. Bergamo*, nos. 34, 54; Manaresi, *Placiti*, nos. 467, 469, 470; Ughelli, *IS*, 4: 451–52; *AVBergamo*, Diplomata seu Jura Episcopatus Bergomensis racc. 1 perg. nos. 3, 5, 6, 12, 13, 23, 26, 34, 40, 41, 58, 61; racc. 2 perg. nos. 26, 27, 28, 36, 52, 56, 57, 59, 73.

1153, 1179, 1180 (2), 1181, 1193, 1196, 1197, 1199, 1200, 1222, 1223; both D and P 1129–71.

Milan[66] — D: 863, 896, 1005 (2), 1021, 1125, 1136, 1154, 1173; P: 1137, 1140, 1174 (2).

Faenza[67] — D: 1021; E: 1111, 1184, 1185, 1188, 1195; P: 1141, 1144, 1146, 1163, 1166, 1181, 1185, 1186, 1194, 1195; both E and P used in second half of twelfth century.

Verona[68] — D: 806, 814, 846, 866, 926, 931, 993, 996, 998, 1001, 1018, 1023; P: 1145, 1147 (2), 1154, 1170, 1183, 1186, 1189 (2), 1190, 1193, 1194, 1196, 1207.

Novara[69] — D: 881, 924, 931, 949, 999, 1147; P: 1148, 1149, 1164, 1165, 1176, 1180, 1190.

Treviso[70] — [*casa*: 1082]; P: 1148, 1157, 1164, 1166, 1171, 1182, 1189 (2), 1196 (2), 1197, 1198 (2), 1215.

Ivrea[71] — P: 1161 (2), 1176, 1183, 1192, 1194 (2), 1195 (4).

66. *Le carte dello archivio capitolare di Santa Maria di Novara*, no. 9, but on the dating of this document to 863, see Luisa Federica Zagna, "Gli atti arcivescovili milanesi dei secoli VIII–IX," *Studi di storia medioevale e di diplomatica* 2 (1977): 28; Manaresi, *Placiti*, nos. 101, 301; *Gli atti privati milanesi*, nos. 13, 15; *Le carte dello archivio capitolare di Tortona*, ed. F. Gabotto, V. Legé, Biblioteca della Società storica subalpina 29 (Pinerolo, 1905), nos. 36, 42; *Le carte del monastero di Santa Maria di Morimondo I (1010–1170)*, nos. 58, 155; *Le pergamene del secolo XII del monastero di S. Margherita di Milano*, ed. Luisa Zagna (Milan, 1984), no. 18.

67. *AARavenna*, Fondo S. Andrea no. 11394 (1021); *Biblioteca classense di Ravenna*, Archivio Storico Comunale no. 12bis (1111); *ACFaenza*, nos. 135 (1141), 156 (1144), unnumbered charters Feb. 9, 1163, Oct. 10, 1166, Sept. 4, 1181, July 16, 1184, Feb. 9, 1185, April 20, 1185; *BCFaenza*, Schedario Rossini, Feb. 13, 1185, Nov. 29, 1186, July 24, 1188, Jan. 9, 1195, March 13, 1195, Dec. 22, 1195, Dec. 17, 1194; Mitarelli and Costadoni, *Annales Camaldulenses Ordinis Sancti Benedicti*, 3: 293, app. no. 426 (1146); *Chartularium imolense*, ed. S. Gaddoni and G. Zaccherini, 2 vols. (Imola, 1912), no. 360 (1186).

68. *CDV*, 1, nos. 71, 115, 182, 234; 2, nos. 195, 211; Manaresi, *Placiti*, nos. 218, 224, 240, 267, 299, 320; *ACVerona*, mss. Muselli DCCXXXVI at 1145 and 1189; *ACVerona*, I-6–5v (BC 44 m4 n4), II-7–4r (AC 37 m2 n1), I-6–6r (BC 27 m4 n1), III-8–5r (AC 11 m2 n3), I-7–2r (AC 67 m2 n15), II-8–2v (AC 18 m5 n8), III-9–6v (AC 10 p 15), II-8–5v (AC 18 m4 n4), II-8–6v (AC 12 m8 n10), II-8–7r (AC 65 m5 n8), II-9–6r (BC 12 m4 n11).

69. *Le carte dello archivio capitolare di Santa Maria di Novara*, nos. 13, 42, 44, 50, 103, 352, 355, 356, 425, 427, 432, 512, 577.

70. *CDP*, 1 no. 298; Sartoretto, *Antichi documenti della diocesi di Treviso 905–1199*, nos. 10, 13–15, 20, 22, 24–27; *ACTreviso*, scatola no. 1, perg. 44, 136, 215; *ACTreviso*, mss. D. Filippo Avanzini, "Series Documentorum," 1: 390 (no. 120), 400 (no. 125), 422 (no. 135), 484 (no. 157).

71. *Le carte dello archivio vescovile d'Ivrea fino al 1313*, nos. 10, 11, 13, 21, 22, 25, 26, 27, 29, 30, 31, 37, 51, 54, 55, 57, 58, 59, 60, 62, 63, 64, 65, 66, 68, 73, 76, 77, 80, 81, 82, 83, 84, 89, 91, 92, 93, 98, 99, 101, 102, 109, 110, 112, 118, 119, 121, 123, 127, 130, 131, 132, 135, 137, 148, 152, 155, 157, 162, 164, 166, 167, 168, 169, 171, 172, 174, 176, 179, 181, 182, 191.

Brescia[72] — D: 1087 (2), 1141; P: 1170, 1176, 1178, 1184, 1193, 1200.

Lodi[73] — E: 1148; D: 1169; P: 1176, 1188, 1194 (3).

Vicenza[74] — D: 983, 1050, 1066, 1146, 1166, 1177; P: 1179, 1185, 1187 (2), 1206.

Volterra[75] — D: 947, 949, 985, 990 (E), 1017, 1032; P: 1195, 1214 (2), 1216, 1218, 1239 (3).

Asti[76] — D: 830, 886, 894, 895, 896, 910, 916, 927, 941, 950–51, 989, [*mansio*: 974], [*casa*: 1043], [*castrum / castellum*: 1081, 1088, 1094, 1190, 1200]; P: 1201.

V. ROME AND THE EVIDENCE OF THE *Liber Pontificalis*

The terms used to describe the residence of the bishops of Rome at San Giovanni in Laterano differ significantly from those applied to other sees in the peninsula. This is hardly surprising: the bishops of Rome and the institution of the papacy hold a unique place in the history of western Christianity. The terminology designating the residence at the Lateran coincides with that applied to the episcopal residences at other sees only in the seventh century. Thereafter, it follows an independent pattern of development linked to the primatial claims of the See of Peter.

The *Liber Pontificalis* is our best early source for the papal residence, and references to the Lateran begin in the entry for Pope Vigilius (537–555). But in this and subsequent late-sixth-century entries, the substantive *Lateranus* is used.[77] In these references, there is no distinction made between the church of San Giovanni and the papal residence. More discriminating language occurs in the entry for Pope Severinus (640), which reports the plundering of the Lateran *episcopium* by the exarch Isaac and the *cartularius* Maurice. In the entries for Theodore (642–649), Martin (649–653), John V (685–686), Conon (686–687), and Sergius (687–701), the papal residence at the Lateran is called an *episcopium*.[78]

In the entry for Sergius (687–701), however, a new term is also introduced: *patriarchium*. When describing the schism ensuing on the death of Pope Conon, the author

---

72. Giovanni Girolamo Gradenigo, *Brixia sacra. Pontificum Brixianorum series commentario historico illustrata* (Brescia, 1755) 187, 226; *Reg. Mantua*, no. 107, 247; *Carte Cremonesi*, no. 457; Odorici, *Storie bresciane*, 6 nos. 139, 161, 7 no. 236; Gaetano Panazza, *L'arte medioevale nell territorio bresciano* (Bergamo, 1942), 190; *ACVerona*, I-8–5v (AC 13 m4 n11).

73. *Codice diplomatico laudense*, ed. Cesare Vignati, 2 vols., Biblioteca Historica Italica 2–3 (Milan, 1879–1883), 1 no. 127, 2 nos. 42, 74; *Carte Cremonesi*, nos. 665, 767, 768, 769.

74. *CDP*, 1, no. 67; Manaresi, *Placiti*, nos. 384, 420, 450; Riccardi, *Storia dei vescovi vicentini*, 53, 55, 56, 58, 66, 67, 69; Giovanni Mantese, *Memorie storiche della chiesa vicentina*, 2 vols. (Vicenza, 1952–59) no. IX; *ASVerona*, Ospedale Civico, no. 136; *ACVerona*, II-9–5v (AC 17 m3 n5).

75. *Reg. Volterra*, nos. 27, 29, 69, 76, 110, 116, 239, 322, 327, 336, 355, 571–73.

76. *Le più antiche carte dello archivio capitolare di Asti*, 1 nos. 16, 24, 26, 27, 42, 45, 48, 56, 66, 75, 87, 95, 112, 170, 187, 190, 191, 198; *Le carte dello archivio capitolare di Asti* nos. 1, 115, 171, 173.

77. Duchesne, *LP*, Chaps. 61, 63.

78. Duchesne, *LP*, Chaps. 73, 75, 76, 84, 85, 86.

reports that Theodore, the pontiff elected by one faction, "got to the patriarchate first and occupied its inner areas." The author's description of the "outer" parts held by the other contender, Paschal, make it clear that the papal residence at the Lateran is meant. Although the author of this entry uses both *episcopium* and *patriarchium* to describe the Lateran residence, only the latter term is used in the eighth- and early-ninth-century entries. Karl Jordan has attributed this change to the general influence of Greek popes.[79] But it seems more likely that the introduction of the term *patriarchium* is linked to Pope Sergius's dogged opposition to Emperor Justinian II's attempt to assert the equality of the patriarchate of Constantinople with the Roman see.[80]

Regardless of this clear change in the terminology of the papal residence, the authors of the *Liber Pontificalis* continued to use the term *episcopium* to identify the residences of other bishops. Pope John VII (705–707) is described as building an *episcopium* "for his own use" at the church of Santa Maria Antiqua, and the episcopal residences of the sees of Ravenna, Silva Candida, and Albano are identified as *episcopia*.[81] The See of Peter was clearly regarded by contemporaries as distinctive.

The usage of the term "palace" to describe the Lateran residence is clearly linked to the growing temporal claims of the papacy in Italy in the late eighth and early ninth centuries. Supported by their new allies, the Franks, the popes solidified their governance over what they called the "Republic of Saint Peter," a swath of territory in central Italy including Ravenna, the Pentapolis, and the duchies of Rome and Perugia. The famous forgery justifying this temporal power, the "Donation of Constantine" (or *Constitutum Constantini*), contains the first description of the papal residence as a *palatium*. The document explains how the earthly emperor lived in Constantinople since he should not reside where the "heavenly emperor" has his capital.[82] The dating of this fabrication has occasioned fierce debate, but it was most likely concocted in the late eighth century.[83] Beginning in the ninth century, the various authors of the *Liber Pontificalis* began, sporadically, to use the word *palatium* to refer to the Lateran residence. The first usage occurs in the very brief life of the extremely brief (forty-day) pontificate of Pope Valentine in 827.[84] Both *patriarchium* and *palatium* are used in the lives of popes Gregory IV (828–844), Leo IV (847–855), Nicholaus (858–867), and Stephen V

79. Jordan, "Die Entstehung der römischen Kurie," 99–100.

80. On the "Greek" popes of this era, see Schimmelpfennig, *The Papacy*, 58–64; on Sergius's resistance to Justinian, see Ullman, *The Growth of Papal Government in the Middle Ages*, 2nd corrected ed. (London, 1955; reprint, 1965), 42–43; and Franz Görres, "Justinian II und das römische Papsttum," *Byzantinische Zeitschrift* 17 (1908): 432–54, especially 450–51.

81. Duchesne, *LP*, Chaps. 88, 96.25, 97.76, 98.107.

82. Jordan, "Die Entstehung der römischen Kurie," 100; Schimmelpfennig, *The Papacy*, 83–84; *Monumenta Germaniae historica Fontes Iuris Germanici Antiqui, X. Constitutum Constantini*, ed. Horst Furhmann (Hannover, 1969; reprinted, 1984), 74, 84, 84 (references to Lateran as *palatium*, lines 121, 189, 219), 94–95 (on Constantinople and Rome, lines 271–76).

83. Thomas F. X. Noble, *The Republic of St. Peter: The Birth of the Papal State, 680–825* (Philadelphia, 1984), 134–37.

84. Duchesne, *LP*, 102.3, 5, 7–8.

(885–891).[85] The *vitae* of Sergius II (844–847), Benedict III (855–858), and Hadrian II (867–872) use only *patriarchium*.[86] The earliest example of a papal privilege redacted "in sacro palatio Lateranensi" dates from 813, and the term becomes common in papal correspondence and in the titles of Lateran officials over the ninth century.[87] From this point on, the papal residence is known as the *palatium Lateranense*.

85. Ibid., *patriarchium*, 103.4, 15, 35; 105.11; 107.6–7, 81; 112.1; and *palatium*, 103.36, 105.16, 50, 62; 107.48; 112.4–6. Leo IV also referred to the Lateran residence as the "palace" in a letter dated 853: *MGH Epist.*, 5, no. 23, 599.

86. Duchesne, *LP*, 104.5, 25; 106.5, 13, 17–18, 20; 108.1, 5, 7, 11, 23.

87. Jordan, "Die Entstehung der römischen Kurie," 101; *Regesto di Farfa*, 2: no. 270 (a placitum of 829 "in palatio lateranensi").

SELECTED BIBLIOGRAPHY

PRINTED PRIMARY SOURCES

General Collections:

Acta sanctorum quotquot toto orbe coluntur.
Edited by Jean Bolland, et al. Editio nova.
Paris and Rome: Victor Palmé, 1863–.

Affarosi, Camillo. *Memorie istoriche del
monastero di s. Prospero di Reggio.* 3 volumes.
Padua: G. B. Conzatti, 1733–46.

*Agnelli et Andreas Liber Pontificalis Ecclesiae
Ravennatis.* Edited by O. Holder Egger. In
*Monumenta Germaniae historica, Scriptores
rerum Langobardicarum et Italicarum saec.
VI–IX,* 265–391. Hannover: Hahn, 1878.

Andrieu, Michel. *Le Pontifical romain au moyen-
âge,* volume 1: *Le Pontifical romain du XIIe
siècle.* Studi e testi 86. Vatican City:
Biblioteca Apostolica Vaticana, 1938.

———. *Le Pontifical romain au moyen-âge,* volume
2: *Le Pontifical de la curie romaine au XIIIe
siècle.* Studi e testi 87. Vatican City:
Biblioteca Apostolica Vaticana, 1940.

———. *Le Pontifical romain au moyen-âge,* volume
3: *Le Pontifical de Guillaume Durand.* Studi e
testi 88. Vatican City: Biblioteca Apostolica
Vaticana, 1940.

Anselm of Lucca. *Collectio canonum una cum
collectione minore.* Edited by Fridericus
Thaner. 2 volumes. Oeniponte: Librariae
Academicae Wagnerianae, 1906–15.

Antiquitates Italicae medii aevi. Edited by
Lodovico Antonio Muratori. 6 volumes.
Milan: ex typographia Societatis palatinae,
1738–42.

Augustine of Hippo. *Sermones selecti
duodeviginti.* Edited by D. C. Lambot.
Brussells: In Aedibus Spectrum, 1950.

*Beroldus, sive ecclesiae Ambrosianae Mediolanensis
kalendarium et ordines saec. XII.* Edited by
Marcus Magistretti. Milan: Joseph
Giovanola, 1894.

Bonizo [of Sutri]. *Liber de vita christiana.*
Edited by Ernst Perels. Texte zur
Geschichte des römischen und kanonischen
Rechts im Mittelalter, Bd. I. Berlin:
Weidmannsche Buchhandlung, 1930.

Chrodegang of Metz. *Regula canonicorum.*
Edited by Wilhelm Schmitz. Hannover:
Hahn'sche Buchhandlung, 1889.

Chronica Parmensia a sec. XI. ad exitum sec. XIV.
Edited by Luigi Barbieri. Monumenta
historica ad provincias Parmensem et
Placentinam pertinentia, 3. Parma: ex
officina Petri Fiaccadorii, 1858.

Codice diplomatico longobardo. Edited by Luigi
Schiaparelli. 3 volumes. Fonti per la storia
d'Italia 62, 63, 64. Rome: Istituto storico
italiano / Tipografia del Senato, 1929–73.

Corpus Christianorum. Series Latina. Turnhout:
Brepols, 1953–.

Corpus Christianorum. Continuatio
Mediaevalis. Turnhout: Brepols, 1966–.

I diplomi di Berengario I. Edited by Luigi
Schiaparelli. Fonti per la storia d'Italia 35.
Rome: Forzani e c., tip. del Senato, 1903.

I diplomi di Guido e di Lamberto. Edited by
Luigi Schiaparelli. Fonti per la storia
d'Italia 36. Rome: Forzani e c., tip. del
Senato, 1906.

*I diplomi di Ugo e di Lotario, di Berengario II e di
Adalberto.* Edited by Luigi Schiaparelli.
Fonti per la storia d'Italia 38. Rome: Tip.
del Senato, 1924.

I diplomi italiani di Lodovico III e di Rodolfo II. Edited by Luigi Schiaparelli. Fonti per la storia d'Italia 37. Rome: Forzani e c., tip. del Senato, 1910.

Dykmans, Mark, S.J. *Le Pontifical romain révisé au Xve siècle.* studi e testi 311. Vatican City: Biblioteca Apostolica Vaticana, 1985.

Ennodius. *The Life of Saint Epiphanius.* Edited and translated by Genevieve Maria Cook. Washington, D.C.: Catholic University of America Press, 1942.

Fantuzzi, M. *Monumenti ravennati de'secoli di mezzo per la maggior parte inediti.* 6 volumes. Venice: Francesco Andreola, 1801-1804.

Gregory the Great. *Dialogues.* Edited by Adalbert de Vogüé. Sources chrétiennes 260. Paris: Cerf, 1979. English translation by Odo John Zimmerman OSB. *Fathers of the Church* 39. New York: Fathers of the Church, 1959.

Inventari altomedievali di terre, coloni e redditi. Edited by Andrea Castagnetti, Michele Luzzati, Gianfranco Pasquali, and Augusto Vasina. Fonti per la storia d'Italia 104. Rome: Istituto storico italiano, 1979.

Italia sacra. Edited by Ferdinando Ughelli. 2nd edition. 9 volumes. Venice: Sebastianus Coleti, 1717-22.

Jacobus a Voragine. *Legenda Aurea.* Edited by Th. Graesse. Wratislav: William Koebner, 1890. English translation, *The Golden Legend.* Translated by William Granger Ryan. 2 volumes. Princeton: Princeton University Press, 1993.

Le Liber Pontificalis. Edited by Louis Duchesne. 2 volumes. Paris: Ernest Thorin/École française D'Athènes et de Rome, 1886-1892. Reprinted with a third volume of commentary and indices edited by Cyrille Vogel. Paris: Boccard, 1955-57. English translation Raymond Davis: *The Book of Pontiffs (Liber Pontificalis).* Liverpool: University Press, 1989. *The Lives of the Eighth-Century Popes (Liber Pontificalis).* Liverpool: University Press, 1992. *The Lives of the Ninth-Century Popes (Liber Pontificalis).* Liverpool: University Press, 1995.

Liudprand of Cremona. *The Works of Liudprand of Cremona.* Trans. F. A. Wright. London: George Routledge & Sons, 1930.

Mitarelli, Johanne-Benedicto and Anselmo Costadoni. *Annales camaldulenses ordinis Sancti Benedicti.* 9 volumes. Venice: J. B. Pasquali, 1755-73.

Monumenta Germaniae historica, Auctores antiquissi morum. Berlin: Weidmannsche Verlagsbuchhandlung, 1879-1919.

Monumenta Germaniae historica, Diplomatum Karolinorum. Berlin: Weidmannsche Verlagsbuchhandlung, 1956–.

Monumenta Germaniae historica, Diplomatum regum et imperatorum Germaniae. Berlin: Weidmannsche Verlagsbuchhandlung, 1879–.

Monumenta Germaniae historica, Epistolae. Berlin: Weidmannsche Verlagsbuchhandlung, 1887–1939.

Monumenta Germaniae historica. Legum sectio III: Concilia. Hannover and Leipzig: Bibliopolius Hahnianus, 1893-.

Monumenta Germaniae historica. Legum sectio IV: Constitutiones et acta publica imperatorum et regum. 5 volumes. Hannover: Bibliopolius Hahnianus, 1893–.

Monumenta Germaniae historica. Libelli de lite imperatorum et pontificum saeculis XI et XII conscripti. 3 volumes. Hannover: Bibliopolius Hahnianus, 1891–97.

Monumenta Germaniae historica, Scriptores rerum Langobardicarum et Italicarum saec. VI–IX. Hannover: Hahn, 1878.

Monumenta Germaniae historica, Scriptorum. Hannover: Bibliopolius Hahnianius, 1826–. Reprinted, Stuttgart: Anton Hiersemann, New York: Kraus, 1903–.

Monumenta Germaniae historica, Scriptorum rerum Merovingicarum, tomus I. Hannover: Hahn, 1885.

The Ordinal of the Papal Court from Innocent III to Boniface VIII and Related Documents. Edited by Stephen J. P. Van Dijk and completed by Joan Hazelden Walker. Spicilegium Friburgense 22. Fribourg: Fribourg University Press, 1975

Otto of Freising. *Gesta Frederici I Imperatoris. Monumenta Germaniae historica, Scriptores rerum Germanicarum,* volume 7. Berlin: Weidmannsche Buchhandlung, 1930.

Papsturkunden in Italien: Reiseberichte zur Italia Pontificia. Edited by Paul F. Kehr. 6 volumes. Acta Romanorum Pontificum

1–6. Vatican City: Biblioteca Apostolica Vaticana, 1977.

Patrologiae cursus completus. Series Latina. Edited by J. P. Migne. 221 volumes. Paris: Garnier, 1844–64.

Paulinus of Milan. *Vita sancti Ambrosii*. Edited by A. Bastiaensen, *Vita di Cipriani. Vita di Ambrogio. Vita di Agostino*. 2nd edition. Milan: Mondadori, 1981. English translation by F. R. Hoare, *The Western Fathers*. New York: Sheed and Ward, 1954.

I placiti del «regnum Italiae». Edited by Cesare Manaresi. 3 volumes. Fonti per la storia d'Italia 92, 96, 97. Rome: Tipografia del Senato, 1955–60.

Ratherius of Verona. *Die Briefe des Bishofs Rather von Verona*. Edited by Fritz Weigle. Weimar, 1949. Reprinted in the series *Monumenta Germaniae historica, Die Deutschen Geschichtsquellen des Mittelalters 500–1500*. Volume 1. Munich: Monumenta Germaniae historica, 1977.

———. *The Complete Works of Rather of Verona*. Translated by Peter L. D. Reid. Medieval and Renaissance Texts and Studies 76. Binghamton, N.Y.: Medieval and Renaissance Texts and Studies, 1991.

———. *Praeloqviorvm libri VI—Phrenesis*. Edited by Peter L. D. Reid. Corpus Christianorum, Continuatio Mediaeualis 46A. Turnhout: Brepols, 1984.

———. *Opera minora*. Edited by Peter L. D. Reid. Corpus Christianorum, Continuatio Mediaeualis 46. Turnhout: Brepols, 1976.

———. "Urkunden und Akten zur Geschichte Rathers in Verona." Edited by Fritz Weigle. *Quellen und Forschungen aus italienischen Archiven und Bibliotheken* 29 (1938–39): 1–40.

Regesta Pontificum Romanorum. Edited by Philipp Jaffé. 2nd edition corrected by W. Wattenbach, edited by S. Loewenfeld, F. Kaltenbrunner, and P. Ewald. 2 volumes. Leipzig: Veit, 1885–88.

Regesta Pontificum Romanorum. Italia Pontificia. Edited by Paul F. Kehr. 10 volumes. Berlin: Weidmannos, 1906–.

Rerum Italicarum scriptores. Edited by Lodovico Antonio Muratori. 25 volumes. Milan: typographia Societatis palatinae, 1723–51.

Sacrorum conciliorum nova et amplissima collectio. Edited by J. D. Mansi. 53 volumes. Florence and Venice: Antonius Zata, 1759–98.

Salimbene de Adam. *Cronica*. Edited by Giuseppe Scalia. 2 volumes. Bari: Laterza, 1966. English translation by Joseph L. Baird. Binghamton, N.Y.: Medieval & Renaissance Texts & Studies, 1986.

Schimmelpfennig, Bernhard. *Die Zeremonienbücher der römischen Kirche im Mittelalter*. Tübingen: Max Niemeyer, 1973.

Sulpicius Severus. *Vita sancti Martini*. Edited by Jacques Fontaine. Sources chrétienne 130. Paris: Cerf, 1967. English translation by F. R. Hoare, *The Western Fathers*. New York: Sheed and Ward, 1954.

Tolosano, Master. *Chronicon Faventinum*. Edited by Giuseppe Rossini. *RIS* 28. Bologna: Nicola Zanichelli, 1939. This is a reprint of Venice 1771 edition originally published as *Ad scriptores rerum Italicarum cl. Muratorii. Accessiones historicae Faventinae . . . D. Johannis—Benedicti Mittarelli*.

Versus de Verona. Versum de Mediolano civitate. Edited by Giovanni Battista Pighi. studi pubblicati dall'Istituto di filologia classica dell'Università. degli studi di Bologna, Facoltà. di lettere e filosofia 7. Bologna: Zanichelli, 1960.

Charter Collections:

AREZZO

Documenti per la storia della città di Arezzo nel medio evo. Edited by Ubaldo Pasqui. 2 volumes. Vol. 1: Florence: G. P. Vieussex; Arezzo: U. Bellotti, 1899; Vol. 2: Florence: R. Deputazione di Storia Patria, 1916.

ASTI

Le carte dello archivio capitolare di Asti (830, 948, 1111-1237). Edited by F. Gabotto and N. Gabiani. Biblioteca della Società storica subalpina 37. Pinerolo: Chiantore-Mascarelli, 1907.

Le più antiche carte dello archivio capitolare di

Asti. Edited by Ferdinando Gabotto. Biblioteca della Società storica subalpina 28. Pinerolo: Chiantore-Mascarelli, 1904.

BERGAMO

Lupo, Mario. *Codex diplomaticus civitatis et ecclesiae Bergomatis*. 2 volumes. Bergamo: Vincentius Antoine, 1784–99.

Le pergamene degli archivi di Bergamo a. 740–1000. Edited by Mariarosa Cortesi. Bergamo: Edizioni Bolis, 1988.

BOLOGNA

"Le carte bolognesi del secolo decimo." Edited by Giorgio Cencetti. In *Notariato medievale bolognese* 1: 1–132. 2 volumes. Rome: Consiglio Nazionale del Notariato, 1977.

"Le carte del secolo XI dell'Archivio di S. Giovanni in Monte e S. Vittore." Edited by Giorgio Cencetti. In *Notariato medievale bolognese* 1: 133–82. 2 volumes. Rome: Consiglio Nazionale del Notariato, 1977.

Savioli, Lodovico Vittorio. *Annali bolognesi*. 3 volumes in 6. Bassano: Remondini, 1784–95.

BRESCIA

"Documenti—Le pergamene." Transcriptions by Leonardo Mazzoldi. *I Quaderni dell'Abbazia* 1 (1983): 59–77 and 2 (1984): 55–79.

Gradenigo, Giovanni Girolamo. *Brixia sacra. Pontificum Brixianorum series commentario historico illustrata*. Brescia: Bossini, 1755.

Odorici, Federico. *Storie bresciane*. 11 volumes. Brescia: Pietro di Lor. Gilberti, 1953–65.

Le pergamene del monastero di S. Giulia di Brescia ora di proprietà Bettoni-Lechi, 1043–1590: Regesti. Edited by Rosa Zilioli Faden. Monumenta Brixiae historica fontes 7. Brescia: Ateneo di Brescia Accademia di scienze, lettere e arti, 1984.

COMO

Carte di San Fedele in Como. Edited by D. Santo Monti. Como: Bertolini Nani e C., 1913.

CREMONA

Le carte cremonesi dei secoli VIII–XII. Edited by Ettore Falconi. 4 volumes. Ministero per i beni culturali e ambientali, Biblioteca statale di Cremona, Fonti e sussidi I / 1–4. Cremona: Linograf S.N.C., 1979–88.

FERRARA

Le carte ferraresi più importanti anteriori al 1117. Edited by I. Marzola. Vatican City: Libreria Editrice Vaticana, 1983.

IESI

Carte diplomatiche iesine. Edited by Antonio Gianandrea. In *Collezione di documenti storici antichi inediti ed editi rari delle città e terre marchigiane*, Volume 3. Ancona: Mengarelli, 1884.

IMOLA

Chartularium Imolense. Edited by S. Gaddoni and G. Zaccherini. 2 volumes. Imola: Soc. Typ. Iulii Unganiae, 1912.

IVREA

Le carte dello archivio vescovile d'Ivrea fino al 1313. Edited by Ferdinando Gabotto. 2 volumes. Biblioteca della Società storica subalpina 5–6. Pinerolo: Chiantore-Mascarelli, 1900.

LODI

Codice diplomatico laudense. Edited by Cesare Vignati. Biblioteca Historica Italica 2–3. Milan: Gaetano Brigola e Compagno, 1879; Fratelli Duomolard, 1883.

LUCCA

[Archivio Arcivescovile di Lucca]. *Carte del secolo XI dal 1018 al 1031*. Edited by Giuseppe Ghilarducci. Lucca: Maria Pacini Fazzi, 1990.

[Archivio Arcivescovile di Lucca]. *Carte dell'XI secolo dal 1031 al 1043*. Edited by Lorenzo Angellini. Lucca: Maria Pacini Fazzi, 1987.

[Archivio Arcivescovile di Lucca]. *Carte del secolo XI dell'archivio arcivescovile di Lucca dal 1044 al 1055*. Edited by Giuseppe Ghilarducci. Lucca: Edizioni S. Marco, 1995.

Inventari del vescovato della cattedrale e di altre

chiese di Lucca. Edited by Pietro Guidi
and Enrico Pellegrinetti. Rome:
Tipografia Poliglotta Vaticana, 1921.

*Memorie e documenti per servire alla storia di
Lucca*. 16 volumes. Lucca: [n.p.],
1813–1933.

Regesto del capitolo di Lucca. Edited by
Pietro Guidi and Ovidio Parenti. 3
volumes. Rome: Istituto storico
italiano, 1933.

MANTUA

*L'archivio capitolare della cattedrale di
Mantova fino alla caduta dei Bonacolsi*.
Edited by Pietro Torelli. Pubblicazioni
della R. Accademia Virgiliana di
Mantova, Serie I, Monumenta 3.
Verona: A. Mondadori, 1924.

Regesto mantovano. Edited by Pietro Torelli.
Regesta chartarum Italiae 12. Rome:
Ermanno Loescher, 1914.

MILAN

*Le carte del monastero di Santa Maria di
Morimondo I (1010–1170)*. Edited by
Michele Ansani. Spoleto: Centro
italiano di studi sull'alto medioevo,
1992.

*Gli atti del comune di Milano fino all'anno
MCCXVI*. Edited by Cesare Manaresi.
Milan: Capriolo & Massimino, 1919.

*Gli atti privati milanesi e comaschi del secolo
XI*. Edited by C. Manaresi, G. Vittani,
and C. Santoro. 4 volumes. Milan:
Ulrico Hoepli / Castello Sforzesco,
1933–69.

*Le pergamene della canonica di S. Ambrogio nel
secolo XII (1152–1178)*. Edited by Anna
Maria Ambrosiani. Milan: Vita e
Pensiero, 1974.

*Le pergamene del secolo XII del monastero di S.
Margherita di Milano*. Edited by Luisa
Zagna. Milan: Università degli studi,
1984.

*Regesto delle pergamene dell'archivio
arcivescovile di Milano*. Edited by A.
Palestra. Milan: Il Sole, 1961.

*Regesto di S. Maria di Monte Velate sino
all'anno 1200. Regestum chartarum
Italiae 22*. Rome: Istituto storico italiano
per il medioevo, 1937.

MODENA

Regesto della chiesa cattedrale di Modena.
Edited by Emilio Paolo Vicini. 2
volumes. Regesta chartarum Italiae 16
and 21. Rome: Maglione, 1931–36.

Registrum privilegiorum comunis Mutinae.
Edited by L. Simeoni and E. P. Vicini. 2
volumes bound in one. Reggio-Emilia:
Tipografia Moderna Umberto Costi / R.
Deputazione di storia patria per
L'Emilia e la Romagna, Sez. di Modena,
1940.

NOVARA

*Le carte dello archivio capitolare di Santa
Maria di Novara*. Edited by F. Gabotto,
et al. 3 volumes. Pinerolo and Turin:
Parzini / Cattaneo, 1913–24.

OSIMO

Carte diplomatiche osimane. Edited by Giosuè
Cecconi. In *Collezione di documenti storici
antichi inediti ed editi rari delle città e terre
marchigiane*, volume 4. Ancona:
Tipografia del Commercio, 1878.

PADUA

Codice diplomatico padovano. Edited by
Andrea Gloria. 3 volumes. Venice:
Deputazione di storia patria per le
Venezie, 1877–81.

PARMA

"Le carte degli archivi parmensi dei secoli
X–XI." Edited by Giovanni Drei.
Archivio storico per le province parmensi ns
22bis (1922): 535–612 [901–20]; 23
(1923): 225–353 [921–68]; 24 (1924):
221–95 [969–1000]; 25 (1925): 227–334
[1001–32]; 26 (1926): 135–239
[1032–55]; 28 (1928): 109–273
[1055–1100].

Le carte degli archivi parmensi del sec. XII.
Edited by Giovanni Drei. Parma:
L'Archivio di Stato, 1950.

*Codice diplomatico parmense. Volume primo,
secolo VIIII*. Edited by Umberto Benassi.
Parma: R. Deputazione di storia patria
per le province parmensi, 1910.

PIACENZA

*Le carte più antiche di S. Antonino di Piacenza
(secoli VIII e IX)*. Edited by Ettore
Falconi. Parma: Luigi Battei, 1959.

*Le carte private della cattedrale di Piacenza I
(784–848)*. Edited by Paola Galetti.
Fonti e studi, serie prima, IX. Parma:
Deputazione di storia patria per le
province parmensi, 1978.

Il registrum magnum del comune di Piacenza.
Edited by Ettore Falconi and Roberta
Peveri. 4 volumes. Milan: Giuffrè, 1984.

PISTOIA

*Regesta chartarum Pistoriensium. Canonica di
S. Zenone, secolo XI.* Edited by Natale
Rauty. Pistoia: Societa pistoiese di storia
patria, 1985.

*Regesta chartarum Pistoriensium. Enti
ecclesiastici e spedali, secoli XI e XII.* Edited
by Natale Rauty, Pilo Turi, and Vanna
Vignoli. Pistoia: Società pistoiese di
storia patria, 1979.

*Regesta chartarum Pistoriensium. Vescovado,
secoli XI e XII.* Edited by Natale Rauty.
Pistoia: Società pistoiese di storia patria,
1974.

RAVENNA

*Le carte del monastero di S. Andrea Maggiore
di Ravenna, I (896–1000).* Edited by
Giovanni Muzzioli. Storia e Letteratura,
Raccolta di studi e testi 86. Rome:
Edizioni di Storia e Letteratura, 1987.

*Codice Bavaro; Codex traditionum ecclesiae
Ravennatis.* Edited by Ettore Baldetti
and Alberto Polverari. Deputazione di
storia patria per le marche, studi e testi
13. Ancona: Savini-Mercuri, 1983.

*Monumenti ravennati de' secoli di mezzo per la
maggior parte inediti.* Edited by Marco
Fantuzzi. 2 volumes. Venice: Francesco
Andreola, 1801–02.

*Die nichtliterarischen lateinischen Papyri
italiens aus der Zeit 445–700.* Edited by
Jan-Olof Tjäder. 3 volumes. Lund: C.
W. K. Gleerup, 1954–.

*Regesto della chiesa di Ravenna; Le carte
dell'archivio estense.* 2 volumes. Edited by
V. Federici and G. Buzzi. Regesta
chartarum Italiae 7, 15. Rome: Ermanno
Loescher, 1911–31.

Regesto di S. Apollinare Nuovo. Edited by
Vincenzo Federici. Regesta chartarum
Italiae 3. Rome: Ermanno Loescher,
1907.

REGGIO

Le carte degli archivi reggiani (1051–1060).
Edited by Pietro Torelli and F. S. Gatta.
Biblioteca della R. Deputazione di storia
patria dell'Emilia e della Romagna,
Sezione di Modena n. 2. Reggio-Emilia:
Tipografia Moderna U. Costi, 1938.

"Le carte degli archivi reggiani
(1061–1066)." In *R. Deputazione di storia
patria per l'Emilia e la Romagna—Sezione
di Modena e Reggio—studi e documenti* 2
(1938): 46–64, 239–86; 3 (1939): 51–64,
113–29, 239–50.

Le carte degli archivi reggiani fino al 1050.
Edited by Pietro Torelli. Reggio-Emilia:
Cooperativa Lavoranti Tipografi, 1921.

*Edizione dei documenti degli archivi di Reggio
Emilia dal 1081 al 1090.* Transcribed by
Miranda Valli. Tesi di Laurea (rel.
Ettore Falconi), Università degli studi di
Parma, Facoltà di magistero, a.a.
1973–74.

*Edizione dei documenti degli archivi di Reggio
Emilia dal 1100 al 1106.* Transcribed by
Anna Messori. Tesi di Laurea (rel.
Ettore Falconi), Università degli studi di
Parma, Facoltà di magistero, a.a.
1974–75.

*Edizione dei documenti diplomatici degli archivi
di Reggio Emilia dal 1091 al 1099.*
Transcribed by Valeria Pastore. Tesi di
Laurea (rel. Ettore Falconi), Università
degli studi di Parma, Facoltà di
magistero, a.a. 1976–77.

*Edizione dei documenti diplomatici degli archivi
di Reggio Emilia dal 1107 al 1115.*
Transcribed by Erminio Magnani. Tesi
di Laurea (rel. Ettore Falconi),
Università degli studi di Parma, Facoltà
di magistero, a.a. 1976–77.

*Edizione diplomatica delle pergamene degli
archivi di Reggio Emilia dal 1067 al 1075.*
Transcribed by Loretta Marmiroli. Tesi
di Laurea (rel. Ettore Falconi),
Università degli studi di Parma, Facoltà
di magistero, a.a. 1969–70.

*Edizione diplomatica dei documenti degli
archivi di Reggio Emilia dal 1076 al 1080.*
Transcribed by Rossana Patroncini. Tesi
di Laurea (rel. Ettore Falconi),

Università degli studi di Parma, Facoltà di magistero, a.a. 1969–70.

Liber grossus antiquus communis Regii. Edited by F. S. Gatta. 6 volumes. Reggio Emilia & Modena, 1944–62.

Milani, Francesco. "Repertorio in regesto delle «scritture» conservate nell'archivio capitolare del duomo di Reggio Emilia." In *Presiedere alla carità. Studi in onore di S. E. Mons. Gilberto Baroni Vescovo di Reggio Emilia-Guastalla nel 750 compleanno*, 443–641. Edited by Enrico Mazza, Daniele Gianotti. Genoa: Marietti, 1988.

RIMINI

Antoni, Cecilia and Nicola Matteini. [Edizione informatica delle pergamene del archivio capitolare di Rimini]. Rimini: Biblioteca del Seminario di Rimini, 1994.

Tonini, Luigi. *Rimini dal principio dell'era volgare all'anno MCC, ossia della storia civile e sacra riminese*. Rimini: Tipi Malvolti ed Ercolani, 1856.

TORTONA

Le carte dello archivio capitolare di Tortona. Edited by F. Gabotto and V. Legé. Biblioteca della Società storica subalpina 29. Pinerolo: Chiantore-Mascarelli, 1905.

TRENT

Huter, Franz. *Tiroler Urkundenbuch. I. Abteilung: Die Urkunden zur Geschichte des deutschen Etschlandes un des Vintschgaus. I. Band: Bis zum Jahre 1200.*

Innsbruck: Landesmuseum Ferdinandem, 1937.

Papaleoni, Giuseppe. "Le più antiche carte delle pievi di Bono e di Condino nel Trentino (1000–1350)." *Archivio storico italiano* ser. 5, 7 (1891): 1–66, 225–66.

Regestum ecclesiae Tridentinae I. Regesto dei documenti dell'archivio capitolare di Trento dal 1182 al 1350. Regesta chartarum Italiae 27. Rome: Istituto storico italiano per il medio evo, 1939.

Santifaller, Leo. *Urkunden und Forschungen zur Geschichte des Trientner Domkapitels im Mittelalter. I. Urkunden zur Geschichte des Trientner Domkapitels 1147–1500.* Vienna: Universum, 1948.

TREVISO

Antichi documenti della diocesi di Treviso 905–1199. Edited by Antonio Sartoretto. Treviso: Tipografia Editrice Trevigiana, 1979.

VERONA

Le carte del capitolo della cattedrale di Verona I (1101–1151). Edited by Emanuela Lanza. Rome: Viella, 1998.

Codice diplomatico veronese. Edited by Vittorio Fainelli. 2 volumes. Venice: Deputazione di storia patria per le Venezie, 1940–63.

VOLTERRA

Regestum Volterranum. Regesten der Urkunden von Volterra (778–1303). Edited by Fedor Schneider. Rome: Ermanno Loescher, 1907.

SECONDARY SOURCES

Ackerman, J. S. "Sources of the Renaissance Villa." In *Studies in Western Art: Acts of the 20th International Congress of the History of Art II.* Princeton: Princeton University Press, 1963.

Ambienti di dimore medievali a Verona. Edited by Francesco Doglioni. Catalogo della mostra, Verona, Castelvecchio luglio-settembre 1987. Venice: Cluva, 1987.

Andenna, Giancarlo. "Honor et ornamentum civitatis. Trasformazioni urbane a Novara tra XIII e XVI secolo." In *Museo novarese.*

Documenti studi e progetti per un a nuova immagine delle collezioni civiche. Edited by Maria Laura Gavazzoli Tomea. Novara: Comune / Istituto Geografico de Agostini, 1987.

Andreani, Aldo. *I palazzi del comune di Mantova. Assaggi—rilievi—progetti e restauri.* Pubblicazioni della R. Accademia Virgiliana di Mantova, serie I, Monumenta 5. Mantua: Tipografia industriale mantovana, 1942.

Andrews, David. "Medieval Domestic Architecture in Northern Lazio." In *Medieval*

Lazio: Studies in Architecture, Painting and Ceramics, 1–121. BAR International Series 125. Oxford: BAR, 1982.

Andrews, David and Denys Pringle. "Lo scavo dell'area sud del Convento di San Silvestro a Genova." *Archeologia medievale* 4 (1977): 47–99.

Angellini, Luigi. "Scoperte e restauri di edifici medievali di Bergamo alta." *Palladio* IV / 1 (1940): 35–43.

Artioli, Nerio. "L'origine della cattedrale di Reggio Emilia." *Ravennatensia* 6 (1974–75): 211–36.

———. "Guida bibliografica della cattedrale e del battistero di Reggio Emilia." *Bollettino storico reggiano* 10 (1977): 13–25.

Auer, Leopold. "Die baierischen Pfalzen in ottonisch-frühsalischer Zeit." *Francia* 4 (1976): 173–91.

Baldini, Gianni. "Reggio nell'Emilia: Duomo, vescovado, S. Michele e battistero. Ricerche e testimonianze." *Atti e memorie della Deputazione di storia patria per le antiche provincie modenesi* ser. 11, 9 (1987): 59–95.

Banzola, Maria Ortensia. "Il palazzo del vescovado," *Parma nell'arte* 14 (1982): 25–51.

Barletti, Emanuele. *Il palazzo arcivescovile di Firenze vicende architettoniche dal 1533 al 1895*. Florence: Arti Grafiche «Il Torchio», 1989.

Barsali, Isa Belli. "La topografia di Lucca nei secoli VIII-XI." In *Atti del quinto congresso internazionale di studi sull'alto medioevo*, Lucca—3–7 ottobre 1971, 461–554. Spoleto: Centro italiano di studi sull'alto medioevo, 1973.

Bavant, Bernard. "Cadre de vie et habitat urbain en italie centrale byzantine (VIe–VIIe siècles)." *Mélanges de L'École française de Rome moyen âge—temps modernes* 101 (1989): 465–532.

Becatti, Giovanni. *Case ostiensi del tardo impero*. Rome: Libreria dello Stato, 1949.

Bek, Lise. "*Questiones Convivales*: The Idea of the Triclinium and the Staging of Convivial Ceremony from Rome to Byzantium." *Analecta Romana Instituti Danici* 12 (1983): 81–107.

Il bel San Giovanni e Santa Maria del Fiore: Il centro religiose di Firenze dal tardo antico al rinascimento. Florence: Le Lettere, 1996.

Belting, Hans. "Die beiden Palastaulen Leos III. im Lateran und die Entstehung einer päpstlichen Programmkunst." *Frühmittelalterliche studien* 12 (1978): 55–83.

Benericetti, Ruggero. *Il pontificale di Ravenna. studio critico*. Faenza: Seminario «Pio XII», 1994.

Bermond Montanari, G. "Ravenna—1980— Lo scavo della Banca Popolare. Relazione preliminare." *Felix Ravenna* 127–30 (1984–85): 21–36.

Bertacchi, Luisa. "Contributo allo studio dei palazzi episcopali paleocristiani: I casi di Aquileia, Parenzo e Salona." *Aquileia nostra* 56 (1985): 361–412.

Berti, Giuliano. *Sull'antico duomo di Ravenna e il battistero e l'episcopio e il tricolo*. Ravenna: Tipografia Calderini, 1880.

Besta, Enrico. "Per la storia del comune di Como." *Archivio storico lombardo* 58 (1931): 403–24.

Bezzecchi, Maurizio. "Vescovo e comune a Reggio Emilia nel XII secolo." *Strenna— Pio istituto artigianelli* 1 (1982): 168–73.

Biscaro, Girolamo. "Le temporalità del vescovo di Treviso dal sec. IX al XIII." *Archivio veneto*, ser. 5, 18 (1936): 1–72.

Blair, John. "The 12th-Century Bishop's Palace at Hereford." *Medieval Archaeology* 31 (1987): 59–72.

Blumenthal, Uta-Renate. *The Investiture Controversy: Church and Monarchy from the Ninth to the Twelfth Century*. Philadelphia: University of Pennsylvania Press, 1988.

Bocchi, Francesca. "Per la storia della chiesa di Ferrara nel secolo X: Il vescovo Martino (936–967)." *RSCI* 31 (1977): 157–81.

———. *Istituzioni e società a Ferrara in età precomunale: prime richerche*. Atti e memorie ser. 3 volume 26. Ferrara: Deputazione provinciale ferrarese di storia patria, 1979.

Bognetti, Gian Piero. "Problemi di metodo e oggetti di studio nella storia delle città italiane dell'alto medioevo." In *La città nell'alto medioevo*, 59–87. Settimane di studio del Centro italiano di studi sull'alto medioevo 6. Spoleto: Centro italiano di studi sull'alto medioevo, 1959.

Böker, Hans J. "The Bishop's Chapel of Hereford Cathedral and the Question of Architectural Copies in the Middle Ages." *Gesta* 37 / 1 (1998): 44–54.

Bordone, Renato. *Città e territorio nell'alto medioevo. La società astigiana dal dominio dei franchi all'affermazione comunale.* Deputazione subalpina di storia patria, Biblioteca storica subalpina 200. Turin: Palazzo Carignano, 1980.

Borghi, P. "Studio sul perimetro della Modena leodoiniana." *Studi e Documenti* 2 (1943): 78–89.

Boskovits, Miklós. *I pittori bergamaschi dal XIII al XIX secolo, vol. I: Le origini.* Bergamo: Bolis / Banca Popolare di Bergamo, 1992.

Boyd, Catherine E. *Tithes and Parishes in Medieval Italy.* Ithaca: Cornell University Press, 1952.

Braunfels, Wolfgang. *Mittelalterliche Stadtbaukunst in der Toskana.* Berlin: Verlag Gebr.Mann, 1953.

——. "Tre domande a proposito del problema «vescovo e città nell'alto medioevo»." In *Il romanico pistoiese nei suoi rapporti con l'arte romanica dell'occidente,* 117–42. Atti del I Convegno internazionale di studi medioevali di storia e d'arte. 27 Settembre—3 Ottobre 1964 Pistoia—Montecatini Terme. Pistoia: Ente Provinciale per il Turismo / Centro di studi storici Pistoia, 1966.

——. *Urban Design in Western Europe. Regime and Architecture, 900–1900.* Translated by Kenneth J. Northcott. Chicago: University of Chicago Press, 1988.

Brentano, Robert. *A New World in a Small Place: Church and Religion in the Diocese of Rieti, 1188–1378.* Berkeley and Los Angeles: University of California Press, 1994.

Brogiolo, Gian Pietro. "Brescia." In *Archeologia urbana in Lombardia. Valutazione dei depositi archeologici dei vincoli,* 48–91. Modena: Panini, [1985].

——. "Brescia: Building Transformations in a Lombard City." In *The Birth of Europe: Archaeology and Social Development in the First Millennium AD,* 156–65. Edited by Klaus Randsborg. Analecta Romana Instituti Danici Supplementum 16. Rome: L'Erma di Bretschneider, 1989.

Brühl, Carlrichard. " 'Palatium' e 'Civitas' in Italia dall'epoca tardo-antica fino all'epoca degli Svevi." In *I problemi della civiltà comunale, Atti del Congresso storico internazionale per l'VIIIo centenario della prima Lega Lombarda (Bergamo, 4-8 settembre 1967),* 157-165. Edited by Cosimo Damiano Fonseca. Milan: Comune di Bergamo, Cassa di Risparmio delle Provincie Lombarde, 1971.

——. "Königs-, Bischofs- und Stadtpfalz in den Städten des 'Regnum Italiae' von 9. bis zum 13 Jahrhundert." In *Historische Forschungen für Walter Schlesinger,* 400–19. Edited by Helmut Beumann. Cologne and Vienna: Böhlau Verlag, 1974.

——. *Palatium und Civitas: Studien zur Profantopographie spätantiker Civitates vom 3. bis zum 13. Jahrhundert.* 3 volumes. Köln / Vienna: Böhlau Verlag, 1975–90.

Brunati, Giuseppe. *Vita e gesta di santi bresciani.* 2 volumes. Brescia: Tipografia Venturini, 1854–55.

Bullough, D. A. "Urban Change in Early Medieval Italy: The Example of Pavia." *Papers of the British School at Rome* 34 (1966): 82–130.

Bumke, Joachim. *Courtly Culture: Literature and Society in the High Middle Ages.* Translated by Thomas Dunlap. Berkeley and Los Angeles: University of California Press, 1991.

Calderini, Cate. "Il palazzo di Liutprando a Corteolona." In *Contributi dell'Istituto di archeologia,* 5, 174–203. Edited by Michelangelo Cagiano de Azevedo. Milan: Vita e Pensiero, 1975.

Cantù, Cesare. *Storia della città a della diocesi di Como.* 2 volumes. Florence: Felice Le Monnier, 1856.

Caravita, Renzo. *Rinaldo da Concorrezzo Arcivescovo di Ravenna (1303–1321) al tempo di Dante.* Firenze: Leo S. Olschki, 1964.

Casagrande, Gloria. "Il ritrovamento del testo completo del «Polittico delle Malefatte»—anno c.a. 1040." In *Reggiolo medievale,* 101–32. Atti e memorie del convegno di studi matildici, Reggiolo, 9 aprile 1978.

Edited by Gino Badini. Reggio-Emilia: Bizzocchi, 1979.

Le case del capitolo canonicale presso il duomo di Verona. Ricerca storica con una proposta di intervento. Edited by Pierpaolo Brugnoli, Gian Paolo Marchi, Romualdo Cambruzzi, and Sandro Casali. Verona: Istituto di Credito Fondiario delle Venezie, 1979.

Cassinelli, Bruno, Luigi Pagnoni, and Graziella Colmuto Zanella. *Il duomo di Bergamo.* Bergamo: Edizioni Bolis, 1991.

Castagnetti, Andrea. *Società e politica a Ferrara dall'età postcarolingia alla signoria estense (secoli X-XIII).* Bologna: Pàtron Editore, 1985.

Cattaneo, Enrico. "Galdino della Sala Cardinale Arcivescovo di Milano." In *Contributi dell'Istituto di storia medioevale: Raccolta di studi in memoria di Sergio Mochi Onory,* 2: 356-83. Pubblicazioni dell'Università cattolica del sacro cuore, Contributi ser. 3, scienze storiche 15. Milan: Vita e Pensiero, 1972.

La cattedrale di Verona nelle sue vicende edilizie dal secolo IV al secolo XVI. Edited by Pierpaolo Brugnoli. Verona: EBS, 1987.

Le cattedrali di Brescia. Brescia: Grafo, 1987.

Cavalcabò, Agostino. "Le vicende dei nomi delle contrade di Cremona." *Bollettino storico cremonese* 3 (1933): 34-141.

Ceccarelli, Giampiero. *Il museo diocesano di Spoleto.* Spoleto: Dharba / Accademia Spoletina, 1993.

Cencetti, Giorgio. "Note di diplomatica vescovile bolognese dei secoli XI-XIII." In *Scritti di paleografia e diplomatica in onore di Vincenzo Federici,* 159-223. Florence: Leo S. Olschki, 1944.

Cerati, Guia. *Per un biografia di Aldo vescovo di Piacenza 1096-1121.* Tesi di Laurea (rel. Piero Zerbi), Università cattolica del sacro cuore, Facoltà di lettere e filosofia, a.a. 1978-79.

Cerrato, Luigi. *Notizie sui resti archeologici e sui monumenti antichi della zona imolese e dei comuni limitrofi.* Atti dell'Associazione per Imola storico-artistica 2. Imola: Paolo Galeati, 1947.

Clark, John, Stuart Hall, Tony Jefferson, and Brian Roberts. "Subcultures, cultures and class." *Cultural Studies* 7 / 8 (1975): 9-79.

Clarke, John R.. *The Houses of Roman Italy, 100 BC-AD 250: Ritual, Space, and Decoration.* Berkeley and Los Angeles: University of California Press, 1991.

Constable, Giles. *The Reformation of the Twelfth Century.* Cambridge: Cambridge University Press, 1996.

Contus, Laura. "Edilizia medievale a Viterbo: una casa con "profferlo" nel quartiere San Pellegrino." *Storia della città* 52 (1990): 109-14.

Corbetta, M. L. "Il vescovo Litifredo" *Novarien* 12 (1982): 9-41.

Cracco, Giorgio. "Ancora sulla «Sainteté en occident» di André Vauchez (con un appendice sul processo Cacciafronte del 1223-1224)," *Studi medievali* ser. 3, 26 (1985): 889-905.

———. "Religione, chiesa, pietà." In *Storia di Vicenza II: L'età medievale,* 359-425. Vicenza: Accademia Olimpica, Neri Pozza, 1988.

Cremona: La cattedrale. Cinisello Balsamo (Milan): Amilcare Pizzi / Cassa Rurale ed Artigiana di Casalmorano, 1989.

Crépin-Leblond, Thierry. "Une Demeure épiscopale du XIIe siècle: l'exemple de Beauvais." *Bulletin archéologique* ns 20-21 (1984-85): 7-49.

D'Alatri, Mariano. *L'inquisizione francescana nell'Italia centrale nel secolo XIII.* Rome: Istituto Storico dei Frati Minori Cappuccini, 1954.

———. "Il vescovo e il «negotium fidei» nei secoli XII-XIII." In *Eretici e inquisitori,* 1: 113-25. 2 volumes. Rome: Collegio San Lorenzo da Brindisi / Istituto Storico dei Cappuccini, 1986.

Dal Forno, Federico. *Case e palazzi di Verona.* Verona: Banca Popolare di Verona, 1973.

D'Ambrosio, Laura Polo and Anna Tagliabue. "Un ciclo bergamasco di primo duecento: Gli affreschi dell'aula della curia." *Arte cristiana* ns. 77 (1989): 269-82.

Dameron, George. *Episcopal Power and Florentine Society, 1000-1320.* Cambridge: Harvard University Press, 1991.

Davari, Stefano. *Notizie storiche topografiche*

della città di Mantova. Mantua: Stab. Tip. della cagazzetta di L. Rossi, 1903. Also in *Archivio storico Lombardo*, ser. 3, 7 (1897): 1–249.

——. *I palazzi dell'antico comune di Mantova e gli incendi da essi subiti*. Mantua: Adalberto Sartori editore, 1974.

de Azevedo, Michelangelo Cagiano. "Laubia." *Studi medievali* 10 / 2 (1969): 431–63.

——. "Le case descritte dal Codex traditionum ecclesiae Ravennatis." *Rendiconti dell'Accademia nazionale dei Lincei. Classe di scienze morali, storiche e filologiche* 27 (1972): 159–81.

de Blaauw, Sible. "Architecture and Liturgy in Late Antiquity and the Middle Ages." *Archiv für Liturgiewissenschaft* 33 (1991): 1–34.

De Carli, Giulio. *La città del concilio. Volume primo: Le pietre medievali*. Trent: TEMI, 1962.

de Francovich, Géza. *Il Palatium di Teodorico a Ravenna e la cosidetta "architettura di potenza." Problemi d'interpretazione di raffigurazioni architettoniche nell'arte tardoantica e altomedioevale*. Rome: De Luca Editore, 1970.

Dehio, G. and G. von Bezold. *Die kirchliche Baukunst des Abendlandes*. 2 volumes and plates. Stuttgart: J. G. Cotta'schen, 1884–1901.

Deichmann, Friedrich Wilhelm. *Ravenna Hauptstadt des spätantiken Abendlandes*. 3 volumes. Wiesbaden: Franz Steiner, 1969–89.

Del Bello, Sergio. *Indice toponomastico altomedievale del territorio di Bergamo. Secoli VII–IX*. Bergamo: Biblioteca Civica di Bergamo, 1986.

Deliyannis, Deborah Mauskopf. "Agnellus of Ravenna and Iconoclasm: Theology and Politics in a Ninth-Century Historical Text." *Speculum* 71 (1996): 559–76.

De Marinis, R., U. Tochetti Pollini, and G. P. Brogiolo. "La città in Lombardia. La sua nascita e la sua evoluzione." In *Archeologia urbana in Lombardia. Valutazione dei depositi archeologici dei vincoli*, 49–53. Modena: Panini, [1985].

Denti, Giannina. *Storia di Cremona*. Cremona: Editrice Turris, 1985.

Dictionary of the Middle Ages. 13 volumes. Edited by Joseph R. Strayer. New York: Scribner, 1982.

Dictionnaire de droit canonique. 7 volumes. Paris: Librarie Letouzey et Ané, 1935-65.

Dictionnaire de spiritualité ascétique et mystique, doctrine et histoire. Paris: Beauchesne, 1937–95.

Diepenbach, Wilhelm Albert. *"Palatium" in spätrömischer und fränkischer Zeit*. Phil. diss., Hessischen Ludwigs-Universität, Gießen. Mainz: Oscar Schneider, 1921.

Dining in a Classical Context. Edited by William J. Slater. Anne Arbor: University of Michigan Press, 1991.

Diocesi di Como. Edited by Adriano Caprioli, Antonio Rimoldi, and Luciano Vaccaro. Storia religiosa della Lombardia 4. Brescia / Varese: «La Scuola», 1986.

La Diocesi di Como; L'Arcidiocesi di Gorizia; L'amministrazione apostolica ticinese, poi diocesi di Lugano; L'arcidiocesi di Milano. Edited by Patrick Braun and Hans-Jörg Gilomen. Helvetica Sacra, sez. I, volume 6. Basil and Frankfort: Helbing and Lichtenhahn, 1989.

Dizionario biografico degli italiani. Rome: Istituto della enciclopedia italiana, 1960–.

Dolbeau, François. "La vita di Sant'Ubaldo, vescovo di Gubbio, attribuita a Giordano di Città del Castello." *Bollettino della Deputazione di storia patria per l'Umbria* 74 (1977): 81–116.

Dölger, Franz Joseph. " 'Kirche' als Name für den christlichen Kultbau," In *Antike und Chrisentum*, 161–95. Kultur- und religionsgeschichtliche studien, 6. Münster: Aschendorff, 1976.

D'Ossat, Guglielmo De Angelis. "Sulla distrutta aula dei *quinque accubita* a Ravenna." *Corsi di cultura sull'arte ravennate e bizantina* 20 (1973): 263–73.

Il duomo di Piacenza (1122–1972). Atti del Convegno di studi storici in occasione dell'8500 anniversario della fondazione della cattedrale di Piacenza. Piacenza: Deputazione di storia patria di Piacenza, 1975.

Duval, Noël. "Existe-t-il une «structure palatiale» propre à l'antiquité tardive?" In *Le Système palatial en orient, en Grèce et à Rome*, 463–90. Actes du Colloque de Strasbourg 19–22 juin 1985. Edited by E. Lévy. Strasbourg: EJB, 1987.

——. "L'Évêque et la cattédrale en Afrique du Nord." In *Actes du XIe Congrès international d'archéologie chrétienne—Lyon, Vienne, Grenoble, Genève et Aoste (21–28 septembre 1986)*, 1: 345–403. 3 volumes. Rome: École française de Rome; Vatican City: Pontificio Istituto di Archeologia Cristiana, 1989.

Duval, Noël, Paul-Albert Février, and Jean Lassus. "Groupes épiscopaux de Syrie et d'Afrique du Nord." In *Apamée de Syrie: Bilan des recherches archéologiques*, 233–44. Edited by Janine and Jean Ch. Balty. Brussel: Centre belge de recherches archéologiques a Apamée de Syrie, 1972.

Ellis, Simon P. "The End of the Roman House." *American Journal of Archeology* 92 (1988): 565–76.

Elsner, Jas. *Art and the Roman Viewer: The Transformation of Roman Art from the Pagan World to Christianity*. Cambridge: Cambridge University Press, 1995.

Elze, Reinhard. "«Sic transit gloria mundi»: La morte del papa nel medioevo." *Annali dell'Istituto storico italo-germanico in Trento* 3 (1977): 23–41.

Enciclopedia dell'arte medievale. Rome: Istituto della Enciclopedia Italiana, 1991-.

L'evoluzione delle città italiane nell'XI secolo. Edited by Renato Bordone and Jörg Jarnut. Annali dell'Istituto storico italo-germanico Quaderno 25. Bologna: Mulino, 1988.

Fappani, Antonio and Francesco Trovati. *I vescovi di Brescia*. Brescia: Edizioni del Moretto / Tipolitografia Artigiana, 1982.

Farioli, Raffaella. *Aggiornamento dell'opera di Émile Bertaux sotto la direzione di Adriano Prandi*. Appended to Émile Bertaux, *L'Art dans l'Italie méridionale* as volume 4. Rome: École française de Rome; Paris: Boccard, 1978.

Fasoli, Gina. "Sui vescovi bolognesi fino al sec. XII. Possessi e rapporti con i cittadini." *Atti e memorie della R. Deputazione di storia patria per le provincie di Romagna* ser. 4, 25 (1935): 9–27.

——. "I conti e il comitato di Imola (secc. X–XIII)," *Atti e memorie della Deputazione di storia patria per l'Emilia e la Romagna* 8 (1942–43): 120–92.

——. "Per la storia di Vicenza dal IX al XIII secolo, conti-vescovi, vescovi-conti." *Archivio veneto* ser. 5, 36–37 (1945): 208–41.

——. "La coscienza civica nelle «Laudes civitatum»." In *La coscienza cittadina nei comuni italiani del duecento*. Convegni del Centro di studi sulla spiritualità medievale 11. Todi: Accademia Tudertina, 1972.

Faulkner, P. A. "Some Medieval Archiepiscopal Palaces." *The Archeological Journal* 127 (1970): 130–46.

Fedalto, Giorgio. "Le origini della diocesi di Venezia." In *Le origini della chiesa di Venezia*, 123–42. Edited by Franco Tonon. Venice: Edizioni studium Cattolico Veneziano, 1987.

Ferrali, Sabatino. *L'apostolo S. Jacopo il Maggiore e il suo culto a Pistoia*. Pistoia: Opera dei Santi Giovanni e Zeno, Fabbriceria della Cattedrale, 1979.

Fliche, Augustin. *La Réforme grégorienne*. 3 volumes. Spicilegium sacrum Lovaniense, Études et documents 6, 9, 16. Louvain: Spicilegium sacrum Lovanensis, and Paris: E. Champion, 1924–37.

Fonseca, Cosimo Damiano. "«Ecclesia matrix» e «Conventus civium»: l'ideologia della cattedrale nell'età comunale." In *La pace di Costanza 1183: Un difficile equilibrio di poteri fra società italiana ed impero*, Milano-Piacenza, 27–30 aprile 1983, 135–49. Bologna: Cappelli, 1984.

Fonseca, Cosimo Damiano and Cinzio Violante. "Cattedrale e città in Italia dall'VIII al XIII secolo." In *Chiesa e città: Contributi della Commissione italiana di storia ecclesiastica comparata aderente alla Commission internationale d'histoire ecclésiastique comparée al XVII Congresso internazionale di scienze storiche (Madrid, 26 agosto-2 settembre 1990)*, 7–43. Galatina: Congedo, 1990.

Foote, David. *The Bishopric of Orvieto: The Formation of Political and Religious Culture in a Medieval Italian Commune.* Ph.D. diss., University of California Davis, 1998.

Forlati, Fernando. *Il palazzo dei trecento di Treviso.* Venice: Istituto Tipgrafico Editoriale, 1952.

Fornasari, Giuseppe. "S. Anselmo e il problema della «caritas»." In *Medioevo riformato del secolo XI. Pier Damiani e Gregorio VII,* 477–90. Naples: Liguori, 1996.

Franceschini, Adriano. "Curie episcopali ferraresi nella traspadana (sec. X-XIV)" *Ravennatensia* 5 (1972–73): 299–354.

———. "Il duomo e la piazza nella città medievale." In *Storia illustrata di Ferrara,* 81–96. Edited by Francesca Bocchi. San Marino: AIEP Editore, 1987.

Frigerio, Federico. *Il duomo di Como e il broletto.* Como: Cesare Nani, 1950.

Frigerio, Federico and Giovanni Baserga. "Il palazzo vescovile di Como." *Rivista archeologica dell'antica provincia e diocesi di Como* 125–26 (1944): 9–104.

Gambaro, L. and C. Lambert. "Lo scavo della cattedrale di San Lorenzo a Genova e i centri episcopali di Liguria." *Archeologia medievale* 14 (1987): 199–254.

Gambara, Lodovico, Marco Pellegri, and Mario de Grazia. *Palazzi e casate di Parma.* Parma: La Nazionale, 1971.

Gardelles, Jacques. "Les Palais l'Europe occidentale chrétienne du Xe au XIIe siècle." *Cahiers de civilisation médiévale Xe–XIIe siècles* 19 (1976): 115–34.

Garzella, Gabriella. *Pisa com'era: Topografia e insediamento dall'impianto tardoantico alla città murata del secolo XII.* Naples: Liguori, 1990.

Gasparotto, Cesira. *Padova ecclesiastica 1239. Note topografico-storiche.* Fonti e ricerche di storia ecclesiastica padovana I. Padua: Istituto per la storia ecclesiastica padovana, 1967.

Gavazzoli Tomea, Maria Laura. "Le pitture duecentesche ritrovate nel Broletto di Milano, documento di un nuovo volgare pittorico nell'Italia padana." *Arte medievale* ser. 2, 4 (1990): 55–70.

———. "Considerazioni sulle pitture medievali della curia episcopi di Novara." *Arte medievale* ser. II, 9 (1995): 69–83.

Gelichi, Sauro. "Castelli vescovili ed episcopi fortificati in Emilia-Romagna: Il castello di Gotefredo presso Cittanova e il *castrum S. Cassiani* a Imola." *Archeologia medievale* 16 (1989): 171–90.

Gem, Richard. "The Bishop's Chapel at Hereford: The Roles of Patron and Craftsman." In *Art and Patronage in the English Romanesque,* 87–96. Edited by Sarah Macready and F. H. Thompson. Occasional Papers (New Series) 8. London: Society of Antiquaries of London, 1986.

Gerola, Giuseppe. "Il ripristino della cappella di S. Andrea nel palazzo vescovile di Ravenna." *Felix Ravenna* 41 (1932): 71–132.

Gianani, Faustino. *Scritti sulle chiese romaniche pavesi.* Pavia: Mario Ponzio, 1984.

Giese, Wolfgang. "Die Bautatigkeit von Bischofen und Abten des 10. Bis 12. Jahrhundert." *Deutsches Archiv für Erforschung des Mittelalters* 38 (1982): 344–438.

Gini, Pietro. "La diocesi di Como nel patriarcato di Aquileia (607–1751)." *Archivio storico della diocesi di Como* 1 (1987): 255–66.

Ginzburg, Carlo. "Saccheggi rituali: Premesse a una ricerca in corso." *Quaderni storici* n.s. 65 (1987): 615–36.

Giovannucci Vigi, Berenice. *Ferrara: Chiese, palazzi, musei.* Bologna: Nuova Alfa editoriale, 1991.

Gloria, Andrea. *Intorno al salone di Padova.* Padua: Tipografia Gio. Batta. Randi, 1879.

Gobbi, Grazia and Paolo Sica. *Rimini.* Rome and Bari: Laterza, 1982.

Goldthwaite, Richard A. "The Florentine Palace as Domestic Architecture." *American Historical Review* 4 (1972): 977–1012.

———. *Wealth and the Demand for Art in Italy, 1300–1600.* Baltimore and London: Johns Hopkins University Press, 1993.

Golfieri, Ennio. "Topografia medioevale delle

aree intorno al duomo di Faenza,"
Ravennatensia 6 (1977): 25–42.

Golinelli, Paolo. *Culto dei santi e vita cittadina a Reggio Emilia (secoli IX-XII)*. Deputazione di storia patria per le antiche provincie modenesi, Biblioteca—Nuova Serie N. 53. Modena: Aedes Muratoriana, 1980.

——. *Indiscreta Sanctitas: Studi sui rapporti tra culti, poteri e società nel pieno medioevo*, 197–98. Istituto storico italiano per il medio evo, Studi storici Fasc. Rome: dall'Istituto, 1988.

——. "Negotiosus in causa ecclesiae: Santi e santità nello scontro tra impero e papato da Gregorio VII ad Urbano II." In *Les Fonctions des saints dans le monde occidental (IIIe–XIIIe siècle)*, 259–84. Actes du colloque organisé par l'École française de Rome avec le concours de l'Université de Rome «La Sapienza», Rome, 27–29 octobre 1988. Rome: École française de Rome, 1991.

——. "Strutture organizzative e vita religiosa nell'età del particolarismo." In *Storia dell'Italia religiosa, I: L'antichità e il medioevo*, 155–62. Edited by André Vauchez. Rome and Bari: Laterza, 1993.

——. *Città e culto dei santi nel medioevo italiano*. 2nd edition.Bologna: CLUEB, 1996.

Groppali, Alessandro and Francesco Bartoli. *Le origini del comune di Cremona*. Cremona: Giulio Mandelli, 1898.

Grundmann, Herbert. *Religiöse Bewegungen im Mittelalter*. 2nd edition. Darmstadt: Wissenschaftliche Buchgesellschaft, 1961. Translated by Steven Rowan as *Religious Movements in the Middle Ages: the Historical Links between Heresy, the Mendicant Orders, and the Women's Religious Movement in the Twelfth and Thirteenth Century, with the Historical Foundations of German Mysticism*. Notre Dame: University of Notre Dame Press, 1995.

Gualazzini, Ugo. " 'Infra terminos matricis ecclesiae' Ricerche sulla genesi di una cattedrale lombarda nell'alto medioevo." *Archivio storico lombardo* 95 (1968): 5–49.

Guidobaldi, Federico. "L'edilizia abitativa unifamiliare nella Roma tardoantica." In *Società romana e impero tardoantico, vol. II:* *Roma politica economia paesaggio urbano*, 165–237. Edited by Andrea Giardina. Rome and Bari: Laterza, 1986.

Guidoni, Enrico. *La città dal medioevo al rinascimento*. Rome and Bari: Laterza, 1981.

Guillou, Andre. "L'Habitat nell'Italia bizantine: Esarcato, Sicilia, Catepanato (VI–XI secolo)." In *Atti del Colloquio internazionale di archeologia medievale (Palermo-Erice, 20–22 settembre 1974)*, 140–54. Palermo: Istituto di Storia Medievale, 1976.

Gurrieri, Francesco. *La piazza del duomo a Pistoia*. Bergamo: Bolis, 1995.

Gy, Pierre-Marie. "La Papauté et le droit liturgique aux XIIe et XIIIe siècles." In *The Religious Roles of the Papacy: Ideals and Realities 1150–1300*, 229–45. Edited by Christopher Ryan. Toronto: Pontifical Institute of Mediaeval Studies, 1989.

Hacker-Sück, Inge. "La Sainte-Chapelle de Paris et les chapelles palatines du moyen âge en France." *Cahiers archeologiques* 13 (1972): 215–57.

Härtel, Reinhard. "Il progetto di ricerca e di edizione Urkundenbuch des patriarchats Aquileia (Codice diplomatico del patriarcato d'Aquileia)." *Memorie storiche forogiuliese* 64 (1984): 177–86.

Hartmann, Wilifried. "Verso il centralismo papale." In *Il secolo XI: Una svolta?*, 99–130. Annali dell'Istituto storico italo-germanico, Quaderno 35. Bologna: il Mulino, 1993.

Heger, Hedwig. *Das Lebenszeugnis Walthers von der Vogelweide: Dei Reiserechnungen des Passauer Bischofs Wolfger von Erla*. Vienna: A. Schendl, 1970.

Héliot, Pierre. "Nouvelles remarques sur les palais épiscopaux et princiers de l'époque romane en France." *Francia* 4 (1976): 193–212.

Hessel, Alfred. *Storia della città di Bologna dal 1116 al 1280*. Edited by Gina Fasoli. Bologna: Alfa, 1975.

Hlawitschka, Eduard. "Die Diptychen von Novara und die Chronologie der Bischöfe dieser Stadt vom 9.-11. Jahrhundert." *Quellen und Forschungen aus italienischen Archiven und Bibliotheken* 52 (1972): 767–80.

Hudson, Peter J. "La dinamica dell'insediamento urbano nell'area del cortile del tribunale di Verona. L'età medievale." *Archeologia medievale* 12 (1985): 281–302.

Hyde, J. K. *Society and Politics in Medieval Italy: The Evolution of the Civil Life, 1000–1350.* London: Macmillan, 1973.

Istituzioni, società e potere nella marca trevigiana e veronese (Secoli XIII–XIV). Sulle tracce di G. B. Verci. Atti del Convegno, Treviso 25–27 sett. 1986. Edited by Gherardo Ortalli and Michael Knapton. Studi storici 199–200. Rome: Istituto storico italiano per il medio evo, 1988.

Jaeger, C. Stephen. *The Origins of Courtliness: Civilizing Trends and the Formation of Courtly Ideals 939–1210.* Philadelphia: University of Pennsylvania Press, 1985.

Jarnut, Jörg. *Bergamo 568–1098. Verfassungs-, Sozial- und Wirtschaftsgeschichte in einer lombardischen Stadt im Mittelalter.* Vierteljahrschrift für Sozial- und Wirtschaftsgeschichte: Beihefte Nr. 67. Wiesbaden: Franz Steiner, 1979.

Jones, Charles W. *Saint Nicholas of Myra, Bari and Manhattan: Biography of a Legend.* Chicago and London: University of Chicago Press, 1978.

Jones, Philip. *The Italian City-State: From Commune to Signoria.* Oxford: Clarendon Press, 1997.

Jordan, Karl. "Die Entstehung der römischen Kurie." *Zeitschrift der Savigny-Stiftung für Rechtsgeschichte, Kanonistische Abteilung* 28 (1939): 97–152.

Keller, Hagen. *Adelsherrschaft und städtische Gesellschaft in Oberitalien 9. Bis 12. Jahrhundert.* Tübingen: Max Niemeyer, 1979.

Krautheimer, Richard. *Early Christian and Byzantine Architecture.* Baltimore: Penguin, 1965.

———. *Rome: Profile of a City, 312–1308.* Princeton: Princeton University Press, 1980.

Labriola, Ada. "Gli affreschi della cappella di San Niccolò nell'antico palazzo dei vescovi a Pistoia." *Arte cristiana* ns 76 (1988): 247–66.

Ladner, Gerhard. "I mosaici e gli affreschi ecclesiastico-politici nell'antico palazzo lateranense." *Rivista di archeologia cristiana* 12 (1935): 265–92.

Ladurie, Emmanuel Le Roy. *Montaillou, village occitan de 1294 à 1324.* Paris: Gallimard, 1975. English translation by Barbara Bray as *Montaillou, the Promised Land of Error.* New York: Vintage, 1979.

Lambert, Malcolm. *Medieval Heresy.* 2nd edition. Oxford: Basil Blackwell, 1992.

Lamoreaux, John C. "Episcopal Courts in Late Antiquity." *Journal of Early Christian Studies* 3 (1995): 143–67.

Lansing, Carol. *The Florentine Magnates: Lineage and Faction in a Medieval Commune.* Princeton: Princeton University Press, 1991.

———. *Power and Purity: Cathar Heresy in Medieval Italy.* Oxford: Oxford University Press, 1998.

Lanzoni, Francesco. *Storia ecclesiastica e agiografia faentina dal XI al XV secolo.* Edited by Giovanni Lucchesi. Vatican City: Biblioteca Apostolica Vaticana, 1969.

La Rocca, Cristina. " 'Dark Ages' a Verona. Edilizia privata, aree aperte e strutture pubbliche in una città dell'Italia settentrionale." *Archeologia medievale* 13 (1986): 31–78. Reprinted with updated addenda in *Paesaggi urbani dell'Italia padana nei secoli VIII–XIV.*

Lauer, Philippe. *Le Palais de Latran. Étude historique et archéologique.* Paris: Ernest Leroux, 1911.

———. "Le poeme de Baudri de Bourgueil adressé a Adèle fille de Guillaume le Conquérant et la date de la tapisserie de Bayeux." In *Mélanges d'histoire offerts a M. Charles Bémont,* 43–58. Paris: Librairie Félix Alcan, 1913.

Lavin, Irving. "The House of the Lord: Aspects of the Role of Palace Triclinia in the Architecture of Late Antiquity and the Early Middle Ages." *Art Bulletin* 44 (1962): 1–27.

Lechi, Fausto. *Le dimore bresciane in cinque secoli di storia.* 7 volumes. Brescia: Edizioni di Storia Bresciana, 1973–79.

Le Goff, Jacques. "Culture cléricale et traditions folkloriques dans la civilisation mérovingienne." *Annales* 22 (1967): 780–91.

Lizier, Augusto. *Storia del comune di Treviso*. Treviso: Tipografia Editrice Trevigiana, 1979.

Lizzi, Rita. "Ambrose's Contemporaries and the Christianization of Northern Italy." *Journal of Roman Studies* 80 (1990): 154–73.

Lodi, i palazzi. Cortili—portali—facciate. Lodi: Edizioni Lodigraf, 1988.

Lopreato, Paola. "Lo scavo dell'episcopio di Grado." In *Aquileia e le venezie nell'alto medioevo*, 325–33. Antichità altoadriatiche 32. Udine: Arti Grafiche Friulane, 1988.

Macci, Loris and Valeria Orgera. *Architettura e civiltà delle torri. Torri e familie nella Firenze medievale*. Florence: EDIFIR, 1994.

Magni, Mariaclotilde. *Architettura romanica comasca*. Milan: Ceschina, 1960.

Maioli, Maria Grazia. "Ravenna, lo scavo della Banca Popolare I «Bagni del clero»." In *Flumen Aquaeductus. Nuove scoperte archeologiche dagli scavi per l'acquedotto della Romagna*, 71–80. Edited by Luciana Prati. Bologna: Nuova Alfa Editoriale, 1988.

Malaspina, Mariella. "Gli episcopia a le residenze ecclesiastiche nella 'pars orientalis' dell'impero romano." In *Contributi dell'Istituto di archeologia 5*, 29–173. Edited by Michelangelo Cagiano de Azevedo. Milan: Vita e Pensiero, 1975.

Manaresi, Cesare. "Alle origini del potere dei vescovi sul territorio esterno delle città." *Bullettino dell'Istituto storico italiano per il medio evo e Archivio muratoriano* 58 (1944): 221–334.

Mancini, Girolamo. *Cortona nel medio evo*. Florence, 1897; reprinted Rome: Multigrafica, 1969.

Manselli, Raoul. *Il secolo XII: Religione popolare ed eresia*. Rome: Jouvence, 1983.

Mantese, Giovanni. "Gli antichi castelli dei vescovi di Vicenza." In *La diocesi di Vicenza. Pagine di storia*, 175–222. Vicenza: G. Rumor, 1943.

———. *Memorie storiche della chiesa vicentina*. 2 volumes. Vicenza: Scuola Tip. Istituto S. Gaetano, 1952–59.

Manzato, Eugenio. *Treviso, città d'arte*. Treviso: Matteo Editore, 1982.

Marani, Ercolano. "Una ricostruzione del duomo di Mantova nell'età romanica," *Bollettino storico mantovano* 7 (1957): 161–85.

———. "Vie e piazze di Mantova: Piazza Broletto." *Civiltà mantovana* 3 (1968): 139–99.

———. "Vie e piazze di Mantova (Analisi di un centro storico); Canonica San Pietro." *Civiltà Mantovana* 7 (1973): 234–48.

———. "L'antico centro episcopale di Mantova e il battistero urbano," *Civiltà mantovana* ns 1 (1983): 21–45.

Marchesan, Angelo. *Treviso medievale*. 2 volumes. Treviso: Tipografia Funzionari Comunali, 1923–24; reprinted Bologna: Atesa, 1990.

Martimort, Aimé-Georges. *Les "Ordines," les ordinaires et les cérémoniaux*. Typologie des sources du moyen âge occidental fasc. 56. Brepols: Turnhout, 1991.

Martindale, Andrew. "Painting for Pleasure—Some Lost Fifteenth Century Secular Decorations of Northern Italy." In *The Vanishing Past. Studies of Medieval Art, Liturgy and Metrology Presented to Christopher Hohler*, 109–31. Edited by Alan Borg and Andrew Martindale. [Oxford]: BAR International Series III, 1981.

———. "Heroes, Ancestors, Relatives and the Birth of the Portrait." In *Painting the Palace: Studies in the History of Medieval Secular Painting*, 75–111. London: Pindar Press, 1995.

Matilde, Mantova e il palazzi del borgo. I ritrovati affreschi del palazzo della ragione e del palazzo dell'abate. Edited by Aldo Cicinelli, et al. Mantua: Sintesi, 1995.

Mazzi, Angelo. "I «confines domi et palatii» in Bergamo." *Archivio storico lombardo* 19 (1903): 5–33 and 20 (1903): 326–67.

———. "Appunti sulle notizie riguardanti il ristabilimento degli antichi palazzi comunali di Bergamo." *Bollettino della civica biblioteca di Bergamo* 14 (1920): 1–28.

Mazzotti, Marco. "Considerazioni storico-archivistiche sulla parte più antica del fondo pergamenaceo dell'archivio capitolare di Faenza," *Studi romagnoli* 41 (1990): 113–39.

McKay, A. G. *Houses, Villas and Palaces in the Roman World*. Ithaca: Cornell University Press, 1975.

Meiggs, Russell. *Roman Ostia*. Oxford: Clarendon Press, 1973.

Meluzzi, Luciano. *I vescovi e gli arcivescovi di Bologna*. Collana storico-ecclesiastica 3. Bologna: [n.p.], 1975.

Merlo, Grado Giovanni. *Eretici ed eresie medievali*. Bologna: Il Mulino, 1989.

Miller, Maureen C. "The Development of the Archiepiscopal Residence in Ravenna, 300–1300." *Felix Ravenna* 141–44 (1991–92): 145–73.

———. *The Formation of a Medieval Church: Ecclesiastical Change in Verona, 950–1150*. Ithaca: Cornell University Press, 1993.

———. "From Episcopal to Communal Palaces: Places and Power in Northern Italy (1000–1250)." *Journal of the Society of Architectural Historians* 54:2 (1995): 175–85.

———. "Vescovi, palazzi e lo sviluppo dei centri civici nelle città dell'Italia settentrionale, 1000–1250." In *Albertano da Brescia: Alle origini del razionalismo economico, dell'umanesimo civile, della grande Europa*, 27–41. Edited by Franco Spinelli. Brescia: Grafo, 1996.

———. "Il «Palazzo della Città di Modena»: Di chi era questo 'palazzo'?" *Atti e memorie della Deputazione di storia patria per le antiche provincie modenesi* ser. XI, 21 (1999): 3–12.

Milo, Yoram. "Dissonance between Papal and Local Reform Interests in Pre-Gregorian Tuscany." *Studi medievali* ser. 3, 20 (1979): 69–86.

Modena: Vicende e protagonisti. Edited by Giordano Bertuzzi. 3 volumes. Bologna: Edizioni Edison, 1971.

Mollat, Michel. *The Poor in the Middle Ages*. Translated by Arthur Goldhammer. New Haven and London: Yale University Press, 1986.

Montal, Costanza Segre. "La pittura medievale in Piemonte e Valle d'Aosta." In *La pittura in Italia. L'altomedioevo, 33–46*. Edited by Carlo Bertelli. Milan: Electa, 1994.

Monti, Maurizio. *Storia di Como*. 2 volumes.

Como: C. Pietro Ostinelli, 1829; reprinted [n.p.] Arnaldo Forni Editore, 1975.

Montorsi, William. *Cremona: Dalla città quadrata a cittanova*. Deputazione di storia patria per le antiche provincie modenesi, Biblioteca ns. 58. Modena: Aedes Muratoriana, 1981.

Moore, R. I. *The Formation of a Persecuting Society: Power and Deviance in Western Europe, 950–1250*. Oxford: Basil Blackwell, 1987.

Mor, Carlo Guido. "La fortuna di Grado nell'altomedioevo." In *Aquileia e l'alto adriatico: 1, Aquileia e Grado*, 299–315. Antichità altoadriatiche 1. Udine: Arti Grafiche Friulane, 1972.

Mortet, Victor. "Hugue de Fouilloi, Pierre le Chantre, Alexandre Neckam et les critiques dirigées au douzième siècle contre le luxe des constructions." In *Mélanges d'histoire offerts a M. Charles Bémont*, 105–37. Paris: Librairie Félix Alcan, 1913.

Moschetti, Andrea. "Principale palacium communis Padue." *Bollettino del museo civico di Padova* 25 (1932): 143–92.

Müller-Weiner, Wolfgang. "Riflessioni sulle caratteristiche dei palazzi episcopali." *Felix Ravenna* 125–26 (1983): 103–45.

———. "Bischofsresidenzen des 4.-7. Jhs. im östlichen Mittelmeer-Raum." In *Actes du XIe Congrès international d'archéologie chrétienne—Lyon, Vienne, Grenoble, Genève et Aoste (21–28 septembre 1986)*, 1: 653–57, 697–709. 3 volumes. Rome: École française de Rome; Vatican City: Pontificio Istituto di Archeologia Cristiana, 1989.

Mumford, Lewis. *The City in History*. New York: Harcourt, Brace, and World Inc., 1961.

Nabuco, Joaquim. "La liturgie papale et les origines du cérémonial des évêques." In *Miscellanea liturgica in honorem L. Cuniberti Mohlberg*, 1: 283–300. 2 volumes. Rome: Edizioni Liturgiche, 1948.

Namias, Angelo. *Storia di Modena*. 2 volumes. Modena: Angelo Namias, 1894; reprinted, Bologna: Forni Editore, 1969.

Nasalli Rocca, Emilio. "Sui poteri comitali del vescovo di Piacenza." *Rivista storica italiana* 49 [ser. 4, vol. 3] (1932): 1–20.

Nella rinascita del broletto: Il comune di Pavia. Milan / Rome: Bestetti e Tumminelli, 1928.

Netto, G. and Campagner, A. *Il duomo e la canonica di San Pietro in Treviso fino al XV secolo. Ricerche.* Treviso: Marton, 1956.

Niermeyer, J. F. *Mediae Latinitatis Lexicon Minus.* Leiden: E. J. Brill, 1976.

Nironi, Vittorio. "I palazzi reggiani del comune e del capitano del popolo dal secolo XII agli inizi del XIV." *Bollettino storico reggiano* 47 (1980): 23–35.

——. *Il palazzo del comune di Reggio Emilia.* 2nd edition. Reggio-Emilia: Bizzocchi editore, 1981.

Noble, Thomas F. X. *The Republic of St. Peter: The Birth of the Papal State, 680–825.* Philadelphia: University of Pennsylvania Press, 1984.

North, William L. *Exegesis and the Formation of a Clerical Elite, 1049–1123.* Ph.D. diss., University of California, Berkeley, 1998.

Novelli, Silvana Casartelli. "Le fabbriche della cattedrale di Torino dall'età paleocristiana all'alto medioevo." *Studi medievali* ser. 3, 11 / 2 (1970): 617–58.

Nussdorfer, Laurie. "The Vacant See: Ritual and Protest in Early Modern Rome." *Sixteenth Century Journal* 18 (1987): 173–89.

Occhipinti, Elisa. "Immagini di città. Le *Laudes civitatum* e la rappresentazione dei centri urbani nell'Italia settentrionale." *Società e storia* 14 (1991):23–52.

Onory, S. Mochi. *Ricerche sui poteri civili dei vescovi nelle città umbre durante l'alto medioevo.* Rome: Rivista di storia del diritto italiano, 1930.

L'oratorio di San Siro in Novara: Arte, storia, agiografia tra XII e XIV secolo. Novara: Rotary Club di Novara / Istituto Geografico de Agostini, 1988.

Orioli, Georgio. "Cronotassi dei vescovi di Ravenna." *Felix Ravenna* 127–30 (1984–85): 323–32.

Orioli, Raniero. "Le correnti spirituali nel regno d'Italia." *Bullettino dell'Istituto italiano per il medio evo e Archivio muratoriano* 96 (1990): 283–302.

Orselli, Alba Maria. *L'idea e il culto del santo patrono cittadino nella letteratura latina cristiana.* Bologna: Zanichelli, 1965. Reprinted in *L'immaginario religioso della città medievale*, 5–182. Ravenna: Mario Lapucci-Edizioni del Girasole, 1985.

Orsini, Giustino Renato. "La giurisdizione spirituale e temporale del vescovo di Como." *Archivio storico lombardo* 81–82 (1954–55): 131–91.

Ortalli, Gherardo. "Comune e vescovo a Ferrara nel sec. XII: dai «falsi ferraresi» agli statuti del 1173." *Bullettino dell'Istituto storico italiano per il medio evo e Archivio muratoriano* 82 (1970): 271–328.

Osheim, Duane J. *An Italian Lordship: The Bishopric of Lucca in the Late Middle Ages.* Berkeley and Los Angeles: University of California Press, 1977.

——. "The First Consuls at Lucca: 10 July 1119." *Actum Luce* 7 (1978): 37–39.

Oswald, Friedrich. *Vorromanische Kirchenbauten: Katalog der Denkmäler bis zum Ausgang der Ottonen.* Revised edition. 2 volumes. Munich: Prestel-Verlag, 1990–91.

Ottolenghi, Luisa. "La cappella arcivescovile in Ravenna." *Felix Ravenna* ser. 3, 21 / 72 (1956): 5–32.

Padova, basiliche e chiese. Edited by Claudio Bellinati and Lionello Puppi. Vicenza: Neri Pozza Editore, 1975.

Padova, case e palazzi. Edited by Lionello Puppi and Fulvio Zuliani. Vicenza: Neri Pozza, 1977.

Padova: I rilievi del centro storico. Edited by Gaetano Croce; text by Roberto Castelli. Padua: Editrice "La Garangola," 1989.

Paesaggi urbani dell'Italia padana nei secoli VIII–XIV. Bologna: Capelli, 1988.

Palazzo, Eric. *Histoire des livres liturgiques: Le moyen âge des origines au XIIIe siècle.* Paris: Beauchesne, 1993.

Il palazzo apostolico lateranense. Edited by Carlo Pietrangeli. Florence: Nardini, 1991.

Il palazzo comunale di Modena: Le sedi, la città, il contado. Edited by Gabriella Guandalini. Modena: Edizioni Panini, 1985.

Panazza, Gaetano. *L'arte medioevale nel territorio bresciano.* Bergamo: Istituto italiano d'arti grafiche, 1942.

———. "Appunti per la storia dei palazzi comunali di Brescia e Pavia." *Archivio storico lombardo* ser. 9, 4 (1964–65): 181–203.

Papi, Anna Benvenuti. *Pastori di popolo: Storie e leggende di vescovi e di città nell'Italia medievale.* Florence: Arnaud, 1988.

Paratici, Carlo. *Il duomo e il gotico di Piacenza nella storia e nell'arte.* Piacenza: Mario Casarola, 1926.

Parma, la città storica. Edited by Vincenzo Banzola. Parma: Artegrafica Silva, 1978.

Pásztor, Edith. "La «vita» anonima di Anselmo di Lucca. Una rilettura," In *Sant'Anselmo vescovo di Lucca (1073–1086) nel quadro delle trasformazioni sociali e della riforma ecclesiastica,* 208–29. Edited by Cinzio Violante. Rome: Istituto storico italiano per il medio evo, 1992.

Patzak, Bernhard. *Palast und Villa in Toscana: Versuch einer Entwicklungsgeschichte.* Leipzig: Verlag von Klinkhardt & Biermann, 1912.

Paul, Jürgen. *Die mittelalterlichen Kommunalpaläste in Italien.* Inaugural-Dissertation zur Erlangung der Dokterwürde der Hohen Philosophischen Fakultät der Albert-Ludwigs-Universität zu Freiburg I. Br. [Cologne]: Universität zu Köln, 1963.

Pauler, R. *Das «regnum Italiae» in ottonischer Zeit: Markgrafen, Grafen und Bischöfe als politische Kräfte.* Tübingen: Niermeyer, 1982.

Payer, Hans Conrad. *Stadt und Stadtpatron im mittelalterlichen Italien.* Zürich: Europa, 1955.

Pelicelli, Nestore. *Il vescovado di Parma.* Parma: Officina Grafica Mario Fresching, 1922.

———. *I vescovi della chiesa parmense.* Parma: Officina Grafica Fresching, 1936.

Pensa, Pietro. "Dall'età carolingia all'affermarsi delle signorie." In *Diocesi d Como,* 46–53. Brescia: Varese, 1986.

Peressin, Mario. *La diocesi di Concordia-Pordenone nella Patria del Fruili (sviluppo storico-giuridico).* Vicenza: Edizioni L.I.E.F., 1980.

Petrucci, Enzo. "Attraverso i poteri civili dei vescovi nel medioevo." *RSCI* 34 (1980): 518–45.

Picard, Jean-Charles. *Le Souvenir des évêques. Sépultures, listes episcopales et culte des évêques en Italie du Nord des origines au Xe siècle.* Rome: École française de Rome, 1988.

———. "La Fonction des salles de réception dans le groupe épiscopal de Genève." *Rivista di archeologia cristiana* 65 (1989): 87–104.

———. "Le Modèle épiscopal dans deux vies du Xe siècle: S. Innocentius de Tortona et S. Prosper de Reggio Emilia." In *Les Fonctions des saints dans le monde occidental (IIIe–XIIIe siècle): actes du colloque organisé par l'École française de Rome avec le concours de l'Université de Rome «La Sapienza» Rome, 27–29 octobre 1988,* 371–84. Rome: École française de Rome, 1991.

Pinetti, Angelo. "Cronistoria artistica di Santa Maria Maggiore." *Bergomum* 20 (1926): 139–56.

Pistoni, Giuseppe. *Il palazzo arcivescovile di Modena.* Deputazione di storia patria per le antiche provincie modenesi, Biblioteca nuova seria 33. Modena: Aedes Muratoriana, 1976.

Pittura murale in Italia dal tardo duecento ai primi del quattrocento. Edited by Mina Gregori. Bergamo: Bolis / Istituto Bancario San Paolo di Torino, 1995.

Piva, Paolo. *Le cattedrali lombarde. Ricerche sulle "cattedrali doppie" da Sant'Ambrogio all'età romanica.* Quistello (MN): Edizioni Ceschi, 1990.

Porter, Arthur Kingsley. *Lombard Architecture.* 4 volumes. New Haven: Yale University Press, 1917.

I poteri temporali dei vescovi in Italia e in Germania nel medioevo. Edited by Carlo Guido Mor and Heinrich Schmidinger. Annali dell'Istituto storico italo-germanico, Quaderno 3. Bologna: Il Mulino, 1979.

Quintavalle, Arturo Carlo. *La cattedrale di Parma.* Parma: Università di Parma / Istituto di Storia dell'Arte, 1974.

Racine, Pierre. *Plaisance du Xème a la fin du XIIIème siècle: Essai d'histoire urbaine.* Thèse présentée devant l'Université de Paris I, le 5 mars 1977. 3 volumes. Paris: Diffusion Librairie Honore Champion; Lille: Atelier

Reproduction des Thèses Université de Lille III, 1980.

———. "Les Palais publics dans les communes italiennes (XII–XIIIe siècles)." In *Le Paysage urbaine au moyen-âge*, 133–53. Actes du XIe Congrès des historiens médiévistes de l'enseignement supérieur. Lyon: Presses universitaires, 1981.

———. "Évêque et cité dans le royaume d'Italie," *Cahiers de civilisation médievale* 27 (1984): 129–39.

Radke, Gary M. *Viterbo: Profile of a Thirteenth-Century Papal Palace*. Cambridge: Cambridge University Press, 1996.

Rando, Daniela. "Vescovo e istituzioni ecclesiastiche a Trento nei secoli XI-XIII. Prime ricerche." *Atti della Accademia rovertana degli Agiati* ser. 6, 26 (1986): 5–28.

Rasmo, Nicolò. *Pitture murali in Alto Adige*. Bolzano: Cassa di Risparmio della Provincia di Bolzano, 1973.

Rauty, Natale. "Rapporti tra vescovo e città a Pistoia nell'alto medioevo." *Bullettino storico pistoiese* 80 (1978): 108–130.

———. *L'antico palazzo dei vescovi a Pistoia. I, Storia e restauro*; and *II.1, Indagini archeologici* and *II.2, I documenti archeologici*, edited by Guido Vannini. Florence: Leo S. Olschki Editore, 1981-85.

Redi, Fabio. "Centri fondati e rifondazioni di quartieri urbani nel medioevo: Dati e problemi sulle tipologie edilizie nella Toscana occidentale." *Storia della città* 52 (1989): 65–70.

Reggiori, Ferdinando. *Dieci battisteri lombardi, minori, dal secolo V al secolo XII*. Rome: La Libreria dello Stato, 1935.

Renoux, Annie. "Les Fondements architecturaux du pouvoir princier en France (fin IXe–début XIIIe siècle)." In *Les Princes et le pouvoir au moyen âge*, 167–94. Paris: Publications de la Sorbonne, 1993.

———. "Palais épiscopaux des diocèse de Normandie, du Mans et d'Angers (Xie–XIIIe siècles)." In *Les Évêques normands du XIe siècle*, 173–204. Edited by Pierre Bouet and François Neveux. Caen: Presses Universitaires de Caen, 1995.

Reynolds, Roger. "Liturgical Scholarship at the Time of the Investiture Controversy: Past Research and Future Opportunities." In idem, *Law and Liturgy in the Latin Church, 5th–12th Centuries*, 109–24. Aldershot: Variorum, 1994.

Riccardi, Tommaso. *Storia dei vescovi vicentini*. Vicenza: Per Gio: Batista Vendramini Mosca, 1786.

Ricci, Corrado. "Il vivaio dell'arcivescovado di Ravenna," *Bollettino d'arte* 13 (1919): 33–36.

Riché, Pierre. "Le Représentations du palais dans les textes littéraires du haut moyen age." *Francia* 4 (1976): 161–71.

Righi, Renato Eugenio. "L'antica casa (o palazzo) del comune di Bologna. Secolo XII." *Strenna storica bolognese* 11 (1961): 407–21.

Rippe, Gerard. "Commune urbaine et féodalité en Italie au nord: L'exemple de Padove (Xe siècle—1237)." *Mélanges de L'École française de Rome moyen âge—temps moderns* 91 (1979): 659–97.

Rivani, Giuseppe. "I palazzi-castelli. Aspetti e singolarità dell'architettura bolognese nel periodo romanico." *Strenna storica bolognese* 15 (1965): 213–30.

Roberti, Mario Mirabella. "Gli edifici della sede episcopale di Aquileia." In *Aquileia e l'alto adriatico: 1, Aquileia e Grado*, 153–65. Antichità altoadriatiche 1. Udine: Arti Grafiche Friulane, 1972.

Robolini, Giuseppe. *Notizie appartenente alla storia della sua patria*. 7 volumes. Pavia: Fusi, 1823–36.

Rocchi, Giuseppe. *Como e la basilica di S. Fedele nella storia del medio evo*. Milan: La Rete, 1973.

Rodolico, N. and G. Marchini. *I palazzi del popolo nei comuni toscani del medio evo*. Milan: Electa, 1962.

Roggiani, Fermo. *Il palazzo arcivescovile di Milano*. Milan: Artigrafiche Vaj, 1986.

Rölker, Roland. *Adel und Kommune in Modena: Herrschaft und Administration im 12. und 13. Jahrhundert*. Europäische Hochschulschriften, Reihe 3, bd. 604. Frankfurt am Main: Peter Lang, 1994.

Rombaldi, Odoardo. "Il comune di Reggio Emilia e i feudatari nel secolo XII." *Atti e memorie della Deputazione di storia patria per le antiche provincie modenesi* ser. 11, 3 (1963): 258–77.

———. "Castra e curtes del Reggiano nel sec. XI." In *Studi Matildici II*, Atti e memorie del II convegno di studi Matildici, Modena-Reggio E., 1–3 maggio 1970, 327–60. Modena: Aedes Muratoriana, 1971.

———. "Canonica sanctae Mariae de civitate Reggio." *Atti e memorie della Deputazione di storia patria per le antiche provincie modenesi*, ser. 10, 10 (1975): 259–78.

———. *Il monastero di San Prospero di Reggio Emilia*. Modena: Banco S. Geminiano e S. Prospero, 1982.

Rondinini, Gigliola Soldi. "Problemi di storia della città medioevale." *Libri & documenti: Archivio storico civico e biblioteca trivulziana* 7 (1981): 11–18.

Ronzani, Mauro. "La 'Chiesa del Comune' nelle città dell'Italia centro-settentrionale (secoli XII–XIV)." *Società e storia* 6 (1983): 499–534.

Rosenwein, Barbara H. *To Be the Neighbor of Saint Peter: The Social Meaning of Cluny's Property, 909–1049*. Ithaca: Cornell University Press, 1989.

———. *Negotiating Space: Power, Restraint, and Privileges of Immunity in Early Medieval Europe*. Ithaca: Cornell University Press, 1999.

Rossi, Simona. *Arduino vescovo di Piacenza (1121–1147)*. Tesi di Laurea (rel. Annamaria Ambrosioni), Università cattolica del sacro Cuore, Facoltà di lettere e di filosofia, a.a. 1990–91.

Russell, Robert Douglass. *Vox Civitatis: Aspects of Thirteenth-Century Communal Architecture in Lombardy*. Ph.D. diss., Princeton University, 1988.

———. "Il palazzo della ragione di Bergamo riconsiderato." *Archivio storico bergamasco* 20 (1991): 7–34.

Saccani, G. "Cronotassi dei vescovi di Reggio-Emilia." In *Per il giubileo episcopale di S. Ecc. Rev.ma Mons. Vincenzo Manicardi*, 1–140. Reggio-Emilia, 1898; reprinted with corrections, Reggio-Emilia: Stabilimento tipo-litografico degli Artigianelli, 1902.

Saller, Richard P. "*Familia, Domus*, and the Roman Conception of the Family." *Phoenix* 37 (1984): 336–55.

Salmi, Mario. *L'abbazia di Pomposa*. 2nd edition. Milan: A. Pizzi, 1966.

Samaritani, Antonio. "Vita religiosa tra istituzione e società a Ferrara prima e dopo il mille (secc. IX–XII inc.)," *Analecta Pomposiana. Studi di storia religiosa delle diocesi di Ferrara e Comacchio. Studi vari*. 10 (1985): 15–108.

Sambin, Paolo. *L'ordinamento parrochiale di Padova nel medioevo*. Pubblicazioni della Facoltà di lettere e filosofia 20. Padua: Cedam, 1941.

Sancta Sanctorum. Milan: Electa, 1995.

Sandonà, Mario. *Il problema del palazzo pretorio di Trento con referimento ai lavori di restauro intrapresi nel marzo 1954 dalla locale sovraintendenza alle antichità e belle arti*. Trent: Tipografia Aor, 1955.

Sandonnini, T. "Del palazzo comunale di Modena." *Atti e memorie della R. Deputazione di storia patria per le antiche provincie modnesi* ser. 4, 8–9 (1897–99): 93–133.

Santa Maria della Scala. Archeologia e edilizia sulla piazza dello spedale. Edited by Enrica Boldrini and Roberto Parenti. Florence: Edizioni All'Insegna del Giglio, 1991.

Il Sant'Andrea di Mantova e Leon Battista Alberti. Atti del convegno di studi organizzato dalla città di Mantova con la collaborazione dell'Accademia Virgiliana nel quinto centenario della basilica di Sant'Andrea e della morte dell'Alberti (1472–1972). Mantova 25–26 aprile 1972. Mantua: Citem, 1974.

Sauer, Joseph. *Symbolik des Kirchengebäudes und seiner Ausstattung in der Auffassung des Mittelalters*. Münster: Mehren u. Hobbeling, 1964.

Savigni, Raffaele. "La signoria vescovile lucchese tra XI e XII secolo: Consolidamento patrimoniale e primi rapporti con la classe dirigente cittadina." *Aevum* 66 (1993): 333–67.

Saxer, Victor. "Domus ecclesiae—οικος Της Εκκλησιας in den frühchristlichen literarischen Texten." *Römische*

Quartalschrift für christliche Altertumskunde und Kirchengeschichte 83 (1988): 167–79.

Schimmelpfennig, Bernard. *The Papacy.* Translated by James Sievert. New York: Columbia University Press, 1992.

Schmölzer, Hans. *Die Fresken des Castello del Buon Consiglio in Trient und ihre Meister.* Innsbruck: Verlag der Wagner'schen Universitäts-Buchhandlung, 1901.

Schulz, Juergen. "The Communal Buildings of Parma." *Mitteilungen des Kunsthistorischen Institutes in Florenz* 26 (1987): 279–323.

Schumann, Reinhold. *Authority and the Commune, Parma 833–1133 (Impero e comune, Parma 833–1133).* Fonti e studi, Serie seconda 8. Parma: Deputazione di storia patria per le province parmensi, 1973.

Schupp, Volker. "Kritisch Anmerkungen zur Rezeption des deutschen Artusromans anhand von Hartmanns 'Iwein.' Theorie—Text—Bildmaterial." *Frühmittelalterliche studien* 9 (1975): 405–42.

Sergi, Giuseppe. "Vescovi, monasteri, aristocrazia militare." In *Storia d'Italia. Annali 9: La Chiesa e il potere politico dal medioevo al'età contemporanea,* 74–98. Edited by Giorgio Chittolini and Giovanni Miccoli. Turin: Einaudi, 1986.

Settia, Aldo A. *Castelli e villaggi nell'Italia padana: Popolamento, potere, e sicurezza fra IX e XII secolo.* Naples: Liguori, 1984.

Simeoni, Luigi. *Verona. Guida storico-artistica.* Verona: C. A. Baroni, 1909.

———. "I Vescovi Eriberto e Dodone e le origini del comune di Modena," *Atti e memorie della R. Deputazione di storia patria per le antiche provincie modenesi* ser. 8, 2 (1949): 77–96.

Simonini, Augusto. *La chiesa ravennate: Splendore e tramonto di una metropoli.* Faenza: F.lli Lega, 1964.

———. *Autocefalia ed esarcato in Italia.* Ravenna: A. Longo, 1969.

Solmi, Arrigo. *L'amministrazione finanziaria del regno italico nell'alto medio evo.* Pavia: Tip. Cooperative, 1932.

Sot, Michel. *Gesta episcoporum Gesta abbatum.* Typologie des sources du moyen âge occidental fasc. 37. Turnhout: Brepols, 1981.

Starn, Randolph and Loren Partridge. *Arts of Power. Three Halls of State in Italy, 1300–1600.* The New Historicism: Studies in Cultural Poetics 19. Berkeley and Los Angeles: University of California Press, 1992.

Storchi, Claudia Storti. *Diritto e istituzioni a Bergamo dal comune alla signoria.* Milan: Dott. A. Giuffrè, 1984.

Storia di Brescia. Edited by Giovanni Treccani degli Alfieri. 5 volumes. Brescia: Morcelliana, 1963–64.

Storia di Ferrara. 5 volumes. Ferrara: Gabriele Corbo, 1987.

Storia d'Italia. Edited by Giuseppe Galasso. Turin: Utet, 1980–.

Storia di Piacenza, II: Dal vescovo conte alla signoria (996–1313). Piacenza: Cassa di Risparmio di Piacenza, 1984.

Storia illustrata di Modena. Edited by Paolo Golinelli and Giuliano Muzzioli. 3 volumes. Milan: Nuova Editoriale Aiep, 1990–1991.

Storia illustrata di Rimini. Edited by Piero Meldini, Angelo Turchini. 4 volumes. Milan: Nuova Editoriale Aiep., 1990.

Stroll, Mary. *Symbols as Power: The Papacy following the Investiture Contest.* Leiden: E. J. Brill, 1991.

Swoboda, Karl M. "The Problem of the Iconography of Late Antique and Early Mediaeval Palaces." *Journal of the Society of Architectural Historians* 20 (1961): 78–89.

Sznura, Frank. *L'espansione urbana di Firenze del dugento.* Florence: La Nuova Italia, 1975.

Tabacco, Giovanni. "Vescovi e monasteri." In *Il monachesimo e la riforma ecclesiastica (1049–1122),* 105–23. Atti della quarta Settimana internazionale di studio, Mendola 23–29 agosto 1968. Milan: Vita e Pensiero, 1971.

———. "Il volto ecclesiastico del potere nell'età carolingia." In *Storia d'Italia. Annali 9: La chiesa e il potere politico dal medioevo al'età contemporanea,* 7–41. Edited by Giorgio Chittolini and Giovanni Miccoli. Turin: Einaudi, 1986.

———. *The Struggle for Power in Medieval Italy: Structures of Political Rule.* Translated by Rosalind Brown Jensen. Cambridge: Cambridge University Press, 1989.

——. "Chiesa e eresia nell'orizzonte giuridico e politico della monarchia papale." In *Spiritualità e cultura nel medioevo*, 151–56. Naples: Liguori, 1993.

Tabarelli, Gian Maria. *Palazzi pubblici d'Italia. Nascita e trasformazione del palazzo pubblico in Italia fino al XVI secolo.* Busto Arsizio: Bramante Editrice, 1978.

Tatti, Luigi. *Gli annali sacri della città di Como.* 3 volumes, plus appendix. I. Como: Nicolò Caprani, 1663. II. Milan: Gio. Battista Ferrario, 1683. III. Milan: Carlo Giuseppe Gallo, 1734. Appendix. Milan: Carlo Giuseppe Gallo, 1735.

Tellenbach, Gerd. *The Church in Western Europe from the Tenth to the Early Twelfth Century.* Translated by Timothy Reuter. Cambridge: Cambridge University Press, 1993.

Testi, Laudedeo. "Il palazzo vescovile di Parma e i suoi restauri," *Aurea Parma* 4 (1920): 325–35.

Testini, P., G. Cantino Wataghin, and L. Pani Ermini. "La cattedrale in Italia." In *Actes du XIe Congrès international d'archéologie chrétienne—Lyon, Vienne, Grenoble, Genève et Aoste (21–28 septembre 1986)*, 1: 5–229. 3 volumes. Rome: École française de Rome; Vatican City: Pontificio Istituto di Archeologia Cristiana, 1989.

Testi Rasponi, Alessandro. "Un'antica cronaca episcopale ravennate." *Felix Ravenna* 3 (1911): 123–29.

Thébert, Yvon. "Private Life and Domestic Architecture in Roman Africa." In *A History of Private Life*. Edited by Philippe Ariès and Georges Duby. Volume 1: *A History of Private Life From Pagan Rome to Byzantium*, 313–409. Edited by Paul Veyne and translated by Arthur Goldhammer. Cambridge: Belknap Press of Harvard University Press, 1987.

Theseider, E. Dupré. "Gli eretici nel mondo comunale italiano." In *Mondo cittadino e movimenti ereticali nel medio evo*, 233–59. Bologna: Pàtron, 1978.

Thompson, Michael. *The Medieval Hall: The Basis of Secular Domestic Life 600–1600 AD.* Aldershot, England and Brookfield, Vt.: Scolar Press, 1995.

——. *Medieval Bishops' Houses in England and Wales.* Aldershot, England and Brookfield, Vt.: Ashgate, 1998.

Tiraboschi, Girolamo. *Memorie storiche modenesi col codice diplomatico.* 5 volumes. Modena: Società tipografica, 1793–95.

Tirelli, Vito. "Il «palatium» a Lucca fino al sec. XIII." In *Il palazzo pubblico di Lucca: Architetture opere d'arte destinazioni*, Atti del Convegno, Lucca 27–28 ottobre 1979. Edited by Isa Belli Barsali. Lucca: Maria Pacini Fazzi, 1980.

Toesca, Pietro. *La pittura e la miniatura in Lombardia.* Milan: Ulrico Hoepli, 1912.

Tognato, Francesca Lomastro. *L'eresia a Vicenza nel duecento: Dati, problemi e fonti.* Vicenza: Istituto per le ricerche di storia sociale e di storia religiosa, 1988.

Tonduzzi, Giulio Cesare. *Historie di Faenza.* Historiae urbium et regionum italiae rariores 55. Faenza: Gioseffo Zarafagli, 1665; reprinted, Bologna: Forni, 1969.

Topografia urbana e vita cittadina nell'alto medioevo in Occidente. Spoleto: Centro italiano di studi sull'alto medioevo, 1974.

Torre, Alessandro. "Lavori fatti dall'Arcivescovo Simone nell'arcivescovado (1223)." *Felix Ravenna* 36 (1930): 14–16.

La torre e il palazzo abbaziale di San Zeno: Il recupero degli spazi e degli affreschi. Verona: Banca Popolare di Verona, 1992.

Toscano, Bruno. "Cattedrale e città: studio di un esempio." In *Topografia urbana e vita cittadina nell'alto medioevo in occidente*, 2: 711–42. 2 volumes. Spoleto: Centro italiano di studi sull'alto medioevo, 1974.

Toubert, Pierre. *Les Structures du Latium médiéval: Le Latium méridional et la Sabine du IX a siècle à la fine du XIIe siècle.* 2 volumes. Rome: École française de Rome, 1973.

Trexler, Richard C. *The Spiritual Power: Republican Florence under Interdict.* Leiden: E. J. Brill, 1974.

Trovabene, Giordana and Serrazanetti, Gloria. "Il duomo nel tessuto urbanistico." In *Lanfranco e Wiligelmo: Il duomo di Modena*, 265–274. Modena: Panini, 1984.

Turchini, Angelo. "La canonica riminese fra XI e XIV secolo," *Ravennatensia* 5 (1972–73): 211–62.

———, ed. *Rimini medievale: Contributi per la storia della città*. Rimini: Bruno Ghibi Editore, 1992.

Ullmann, Walter. *The Growth of Papal Government in the Middle Ages*. London: Methuen, 1955; reprinted 1965.

Vaccari, Pietro. *Pavia nell'alto medioevo e nell'età comunale*. Pavia: "Tipografica Ticinese" di C. Busca, 1956.

Vasina, Augusto. "Società ed economia a Faenza dopo il mille." In *Parliamo della nostra città: atti del convegno, Faenza 21–23–38–30 ottobre 1976*, 101–9. Faenza: Comune di Faenza, 1977.

———. "Il «Breviarium» nella storia della chiesa Ravennate." In *Richerche e studi sul «Breviarium ecclesiae Ravennatis» (Codice Bavaro)*, 9–32. Studi storici fasc. 148–49. Rome: Istituto storico italiano per il medio evo, 1985.

Vauchez, André. *La Sainteté en occident aux derniers siècles du moyen âge d'après les procès de canonisation et les documents hagiographiques*. Rome: École française de Rome, 1981.

Verzone, Paolo. "Il palazzo arcivescovile e l'oratorio di S. Andrea di Ravenna." *Corso di cultura sull'arte ravennate e bizantina* 13 (1966): 445–54.

———. "La distruzione dei palazzi imperiali di Roma e di Ravenna e la ristrutturazione del palazzo lateranense nel IX secolo nei rapporti con quello di Constantinopoli." In Istituto nazionale di archeologia e storia dell'arte, *Roma e l'età carolingia*, 39–54. Atti delle giornate di studio 3–8 maggio 1976, Istituto di storia dell'arte dell'Università di Roma. Rome: Multigrafica Editrice, 1976.

Vezzoli, Giovanni. *Il duomo nuovo e il duomo vecchio di Brescia. Guida alle cattedrali.* Brescia: Società per la storia della chiesa a Brescia, 1980.

Vicini, Emilio Paolo. "I confini della parrocchia del duomo nel secolo XIV." In *Atti e memorie della R. Deputazione di storia patria per le antiche provincie modenesi* ser. 7, 3–4 (1924–27): 65–147.

———. "Serie dei consoli modenesi." *Atti e memorie della reale Accademia di scienze lettere ed arti di Modena* ser. 4, 4 (1933–34): 55–99.

Violante, Cinzio. *La società milanese nell'età precomunale*. Roma and Bari: Laterza, 1981.

Violante, Cinzio and Cosimo Damiano Fonseca. "Ubicazione e dedicazione delle cattedrali dalle origini al periodo romanico nelle città dell'Italia centro-settentrionale." In *Il romanico pistoiese nei suoi rapporti con l'arte romanica dell'occidente*, 303–46. Atti del I convegno internazionale di studi medioevali di storia e d'arte. 27 Settembre—3 Ottobre 1964 Pistoia—Montecatini Terme. Pistoia: Ente Provinciale per il Turismo / Centro di studi storici Pistoia, 1966.

Viollet-Le-Duc, E. *Dictionnaire raisonné de l'architecture française du XIe au XVIe siècle*. 10 volumes. Paris: B. Bance, 1858–68.

Vismara, Guilio. "La giurisdizione civile dei vescovi nel mondo antico." In *La giustizia nell'alto medioevo (secoli V-VIII)*, 225–57. Settimane di studio del Centro italiano di studi sull'alto medioevo. Spoleto: Centro italiano di studi sull'alto medioevo, 1995.

La vita comune del clero nei secoli XI e XII. 2 volumes. Atti della Settimana di studio, Mendola, settembre 1959. Milan: Vita e Pensiero, 1962.

Vodola, Elisabeth. *Excommunication in the Middle Ages*. Berkeley and Los Angeles: University of California Press, 1986.

———. "Sovereignty and Tabu: Evolution of the Sanction against Communication with Excommunicates. Part 1: Gregory VII." In *The Church and Sovereignty c. 590–1918: Essays in Honor of Michael Wilks*, 35–55. Edited by Diana Wood. Oxford: Basil Blackwell, 1991.

Vogel, Cyrille. "Buße und Exkommunikation in der Alten Kirche und im Mittelalter: Ein historischer Überblick." *Concilium* 107 (1975): 446–52.

Volpe, Giaocchino. *Movimenti religiosi e sette ereticali nella società medievale italiana (secoli XI–XIV)*. Florence: Vallecchi, 1926.

Voltini, Giorgio. *S. Lorenzo in Cremona: Strutture, reperti e fasi costruttive dal X al XIII secolo*. Cremona: Turris, 1987.

Von Simson, Otto G. *Sacred Fortress: Byzantine Art and Statecraft in Ravenna*. Chicago: University of Chicago Press, 1948.

Waley, Daniel. *Mediaeval Orvieto: The Political History of an Italian City-State 1157–1334*. Cambridge: Cambridge University Press, 1952.

——. *The Italian City-Republics*. 3rd edition. New York: Longman, 1988.

Wallace-Hadrill, Andrew. *Houses and Society in Pompeii and Herculaneum*. Princeton: Princeton University Press, 1994.

Walter, Christopher. "Papal Political Imagery in the Medieval Lateran Palace." *Cahiers archéologiques* 20 (1970): 155–76, and 21 (1971): 109–36.

Ward-Perkins, Bryan. "Two Byzantine Houses at Luni." *Papers of the British School at Rome* 49 (1981): 91–98.

——. "La città altomedievale." *Archeologia medievale* 10 (1983): 111–24.

——. *From Classical Antiquity to the Middle Ages: Urban Public Building in Northern and Central Italy AD 300–850*. Oxford: Oxford University Press, 1984.

Webb, Diana. *Patrons and Defenders*. London: Tauris Academic Studies, 1996.

Weber, Simone. "Le residenze dei vescovi di Trento." *Studi trentino* anno V, fasc. I (1924): 1–15.

Wharton, Annabel Jane. "Ritual and Reconstructed Meaning: The Neonian Baptistery in Ravenna." *Art Bulletin* 69 (1987): 358–75.

——. *Refiguring the Post Classical City: Dura Europos, Jerash, Jerusalem and Ravenna*. Cambridge: Cambridge University Press, 1995.

White, L. Michael. *Building God's House in the Roman World: Architectural Adaptation among Pagans, Jews, and Christians*. Baltimore: Johns Hopkins University Press, 1990.

Wickham, Chris. *Early Medieval Italy: Central Power and Local Society 400–1000*. Totowa, N.J.: Barnes and Noble, 1981.

Wieruszowski, Helene. "Art and the Commune in the Time of Dante." *Speculum* 19 (1944): 14–33. Also in Helene Wieruszowski, *Politics and Culture in Medieval Spain and Italy*, Storia e letteratura, Raccolta di studi e testi 121, 475–502. Rome: Edizioni di Storia e Letteratura, 1971.

Winkelmann, Wilhelm. "Die Königspfalz und die Bischofspfalz des 11. und 12. Jahrhunderts in Paderborn." *Frühmittelalterliche studien* 4 (1970): 398–415.

Yegül, Fikret. *Baths and Bathing in Classical Antiquity*. New York: The Architectural History Foundation; Cambridge, Mass.: MIT Press, 1992.

Zanini, Laura. "L'impianto urbano e le case medievali di Priverno." *Storia della città* 52 (1989): 121–26.

Zanocco, R. "Luogo e vicende del palazzo vescovile di Padova nel medioevo." *Bollettino diocesano di Padova* 12 (1927): 593–603.

——. "Il palazzo vescovile attuale nella storia e nell'arte (1309–1567)." *Bollettino diocesano di Padova* 13 (1928): 175–92, 243–58, 334–42.

Zerbi, Piero. "Il vescovo comense Rainaldo: Un momento nei rapporti tra Como, la chiesa e l'impero nel secolo XI." In *Atti dei convegni celebrativi del centenario 1878–1978*, 23–43. Como: Ed. Società storica comense, 1979.

Zirardini, Antonio. *Degli antichi edifizi sacri di Ravenna—Libro postumo*. Ravenna: Claudio Zirardini, 1908–9.

Zizzo, Giuseppina. "S. Maria Maggiore di Bergamo «cappella della città»: La basilica bergamasca nei secoli XII e XIII." *Archivio storico bergomasco* 3 (1982): 207–29.

Zovatto, Paolo L. "Il significato della basilica doppia: L'esempio di Aquileia." *RSCI* 18 (1964): 357–93.

INDEX/GLOSSARY

Most individuals and buildings will be found here under their city. The page numbers immediately following a city refer to the see and its episcopal palace. Architectural and other terms are defined briefly in parentheses after the entry and, where possible, dates are given for bishops and rulers. The following abbreviations are used: b = bishop, c = cathedral, C. = century, cp = communal palace, ec = episcopal chapel, ip = imperial palace, n = note, pp = papal palace, sb = saint and bishop.

Accubita (Roman dining couches), 23
Ad abolendam (papal bull, 1184), 164–65
Anagni: sb Peter (d. 1105), 216–17, 219, 232, 241–42
Andreas Agnellus, 17n, 22–24, 51–53, 56–57, 62, 78, 81, 265
Angera, 203–6
Apostles, 50, 181–82, 192, 220, 233–36, 238
Apses (vaulted, semi-circular wall recesses), 20, 24, 27–28, 30, 36, 41, 44–45, 51, 57, 59, 64, 148, 171, 181, 185, 229, 232–34, 249–50
Aquileia, 19–22, 34–35, 45, 150, 171, 237
Arcades (range of counter-thrusting arches raised on columns or piers), 117–18
Architect, 100
Archives. *See* Treasuries
Arezzo, 92, 100, 254–55, 269–70
Arians (adherents of fourth-century Trinitarian heresy that denied the divinity of Christ, emphasizing instead his humanity), 57, 113, 219–22
Asti, 134, 139n, 263, 274
Asylum, 47–49
Atrium (open-roofed courtyard), 14, 40–43
Augustine of Hippo, 19–20, 50, 80, 129, 203, 242, 262
Aula/aule. See Halls

Baptisteries, 14, 23, 28, 34, 45, 87, 93, 111, 143, 226–28

Barrel Vault (semi-circular arched ceiling extending in a straight line), 28, 30
Basilica (oblong building, usually colonnaded, with apse opposite its entrance), 19, 40, 44–45, 47, 51
Baths, 23, 28, 31–33, 37, 44, 45, 74
Bedrooms (*cubicula, camerae dormitoriae*), 14, 37, 40–41, 59, 74, 77
Bergamo, 81–82, 84, 90, 104, 129, 137, 184–201, 263, 268, 272–73; cp, 117, 119–20; ec S. Croce, 105, 189, 218–19, 225–26, 247n, 251–52
Bifores (arched windows, further subdivided into two arched openings), 98, 108–9, 114. *See also* Windows
Bishops: burial places of, 128–29, 134–34; character of lordship, 2–3, 5, 55–56, 78–80, 83–84, 107–8, 114–15, 123–24, 140–45, 206, 241, 249, 253; households of, 56, 83, 244, 247, 249; representation of power, 27, 50, 168–69, 197–201; sanctity and spirituality of, 125–26, 129–33, 135–36, 238; social backgrounds of, 115; vassals of, 143–44; wills of, 83–85. *See also* Hagiography; Martyrdom
Bologna, 92, 264, 269, 271; cp, 119–20; ip, 140
Bolzano, 218
Brescia, 93, 128–29, 137–38, 142, 167–68, 237, 267, 273; cp, 117, 120, 205; sb Filastrius (4th c.), 129

Bulla Regia (House of the Hunt), 44–45
Byzantines, 8, 22, 70, 74, 76, 79, 174, 266

Caminata/caminate (heated rooms), 60, 63–64, 77
Canons. *See* Clergy: of cathedral
Carolingian Franks, 2, 61, 63, 78–79, 81–82, 266. *See also* Charlemagne
Casa/case a schiera (row houses), 111–15
Cathedra (throne), 17, 39, 48
Cathedrals, 45, 86, 113, 126–29, 132–33, 143, 222–23; bishops' relation to, 14–15, 17, 56, 66, 80, 83–85; location of, 17–18, 137–39, 126–29; rebuilding of, 88, 142–48, 152, 174–80, 216
Cesena, 135–36, 265; sb Maurus (892?-955), 135–36, 143, 179, 239, 268
Chapels, 15, 28–30, 37, 57, 100, 105–7, 152, 216–52, 256; at Aachen, 224, 230; Sainte-Chapelle, 224
Charlemagne, king (774–814) and emperor (800–814), 2, 79, 172, 181, 224, 254
Clergy: of cathedral, 14, 56, 80–85, 93, 133, 136, 185, 223, 241–46, 248–49; celibacy of, 3–4, 165, 245; culture of, 4, 15, 123–24, 172–215, 205, 228
Codice Bavaro (collection of Ravennate leases), 74, 76, 172
Como, 66–69, 79–80, 91–92, 97–98, 101, 108, 110, 117–18, 129, 134, 145–46, 173, 201–2, 268, 271; b Alberic (1010–28), 66–67; cp, 117–18, 120; ec S. Michele, 106, 218, 226–27, 228–29, 232, 247n
Communes: consuls of, 88, 120, 143–44, 158–59, 166, 168, 208; early meeting places of, 15, 87, 96–97, 115, 120, 152; emergence of, 2, 5, 86–89, 96–97, 123, 126, 141–45; and the holy, 152, 227–28; tensions with bishops, 125, 163, 199–201, 208, 222–23, 253. *See also* Palaces: communal
Constantine, emperor (307–37), 19, 51, 181, 235
Constantinople, 24, 233, 275
Construction, financing of, 98–100
Contado (countryside surrounding city), 104, 200, 205
Cortona, 254–55
Courtly culture, 172–73, 208–15, 240
Courtyards, 74, 76. *See also* Atrium; Peristyle courtyards

Cremona, 18, 62–63, 84, 88–89, 93–95, 133–34, 137–40, 263, 267–69, 272; b Lando (880–91), 62; b Landulfus (1004–30), 89; b Sicard (1185–1215), 243; cp, 117, 120; ec, 218, 232; ip, 140
Cross vault (arched ceiling formed by the right angle intersection of two barrel vaults), 28, 225

Decoration: exterior, 156–57, 224; interior, 24–30, 31, 34, 53, 78, 181–206. *See also* Frescos; Mosaics
Dining rooms (*triclinia, mensa*), 14, 23–27, 30, 33–34, 37, 40–41, 47, 59, 81, 111
Domestic architecture: medieval, 72–78, 110–13, 126, 140–41, 154–56, 172–73; Roman, 14, 17, 40–44, 51, 72–73
Double chapels (two small oratories, one on top of the other, usually connected through a central opening), 229–32, 249

Emperors, 7, 140, 245; episcopal relations with, 79, 84, 130, 144–45, 175, 181–82. *See also* Charlemagne; Constantine; Frederick Barbarossa; Henry IV; Palaces: royal/imperial
Ennodius, 32, 130–31, 182
Entrances, 148–56, 168
Excommunication, 253–56

Facade (front of a building), 111–15, 117, 146
Faenza, 18, 92, 137, 153, 218, 265, 273; ec SS. Giovanni e Paolo/S. Ordinazione, 105, 232–33
Feasting, 210–13
Ferrara, 93, 134, 142, 181, 265, 270–71; cp, 120; ec S. Tomaso, 218, 233
Floors: mosaic, 34–36, 45–47; wooden, 69–70, 74
Florence, 18, 20–21, 88n, 92–93, 105, 139, 153n, 228, 255, 263, 269–70; cp, 119–20; sb Podius (989–1002), 132
Fortification, 61–62, 64–65, 67–68, 71–72, 76–77, 80, 97–98, 107, 132–33, 144
Forum, 18, 75–76, 184, 186
Frederick Barbarossa, emperor (1155–90), 89, 118, 126, 145, 158–59, 199, 202, 237
Frescos: at Angera, 203–5; at Bergamo (Aula della Curia), 189–201, 252; in communal palaces, 205; at Como, 201–2; in Lateran, 181–82; at Novara, 182–84; at Parma, 201; at Pistoia, 202–3, 235–36; at Spoleto, 202

Gardens, 30, 74, 76

Genealogy: secular, 205; spiritual, 31, 52–53, 182–83, 205, 236–37

Genoa, 61, 66–68, 80, 83

Gesta Episcoporum, 17, 53, 62, 265; of Naples, 34, 51, 62. *See also* Andreas Agnellus; *Liber Pontificalis* (Rome)

Ghibelline (pro-imperial), 154, 165, 205, 255

Grado, 17n, 20–21, 33–35, 46–47, 129, 150, 171; Patriarch Elia (571–87), 46, 48, 52

Gregory the Great, pope (590–604), 16, 39; *Dialogues* of, 30, 32, 81, 211, 263

Groin vault. *See* Cross vault

Gubbio, 158–59; sb Rodolphus, 136n, 211, 239; sb Ubaldus (1129–60), 136, 157–61, 236

Guelph (pro-papal), 154, 166, 255

Hagiography: episcopal, 16, 19, 125, 129–33, 135–37, 157–63, 211, 216–17, 236, 239, 240–41

Halls, 34, 36–37, 71, 100–104, 107, 111, 117, 144, 172–215, 224, 249; *aule*, 14, 47, 59; communal, 117, 205; *sale/camere* 63–64, 74, 77–78; *salutatoria/secretaria*, 38–39, 47; triconch, 30–31, 47, 51, 59

Heating: by braziers, 70; by hearths, 63–64; by hypocaust, 34

Henry IV, king (1056–1106) and emperor (1084–1106), 2, 5, 140, 254

Herculaneum, 42

Heresy, 5, 161–69, 253, 256, 268

Hippo Regius, 20, 23; sb Augustine (396–430), 19, 50, 80, 129, 203, 242, 262

Inscriptions, 32, 34, 46, 48, 52–53

Interdict, 125, 253–56

Invasions, 61–62, 64, 66, 129–31

Investiture conflict, 2, 4–5, 86, 89, 95, 181–82, 216, 268–69. *See also* Reform

Ivrea, 18, 93n, 134, 218, 273

Kitchens, 30, 74, 76

Laubia. See Loggia

Laudes Civitatum, 126–38, 168

Liber Pontificalis (Ravenna). *See* Andreas Agnellus

Liber Pontificalis (Rome), 17n, 33, 37, 40, 44, 51, 59–62, 265, 274–76

Linguistic Change, 13–14, 49–50, 54, 59–60, 89–96, 142, 261–76

Liturgy, 175–79, 242–49

Lodi, 134, 218, 237, 267, 274

Loggia (*laubia*, covered gallery or room open on at least one side), 63, 71–72, 77–78

Lombards, 2, 61, 70, 74, 127, 141

Lucca, 84, 88n, 97, 218, 263–64, 269, 271; sb Anselm (1073–86), 240–41, 243; ducal residence at, 77; ip, 140

Luitprand of Cremona, 66, 78

Magyars. *See* Invasions

Mantua, 77, 91, 95, 268–70; cp, 119–20, 205; ip, 140

Martyrdom, 125, 132, 157–60, 220, 235–36

Mary, Blessed Virgin, 134, 184, 192, 201–2

Mendicants, 114, 180, 210

Milan, 19, 22, 64, 77, 126–29, 133–35, 137, 182–83, 203–6, 236, 263–65, 269, 273; ip, 95, 140; sb Galdinus della Sala (1166–76), 157, 160, 162–63, 179

Modena, 83, 88, 91, 93–94, 97, 133, 137, 264, 267–70; ec, 218, 241; cp, 120; sb Geminianus (4th C.), 133–34

Monasteries and monasticism, 134–36, 140, 157, 240–41, 262

Mosaics, 43; at Aquileia, 34–36, 45–46; at Grado, 46–48; at Naples, 34, 57; at Ravenna, 24–30, 31, 219–22; at Rome, 34, 59, 181

Naples, 17n, 20–21, 33–34, 88n; b Paul III (794–819), 57; b Stephen II (766–94), 57, 59–60; b Vincentius (554–78), 34, 52

Nicholas, Saint, Bishop of Myra (4th C.), 233–36, 238, 248–49, 256

Nicolaitism. *See* Clergy: celibacy of

Nonorthogonal (not right-angled) spaces, 51

Novara, 18, 134, 153, 182–84, 263, 273; b Boniface (1172–94), 115, 236–38, 241; cp, 117, 120; ec S. Siro, 236–40, 247n, 248, 250, 252

Orvieto, 88n, 134, 165–66, 202, 218, 241; pp, 107, 154

Ostia, 42–43, 61

Paderborn, 174–75, 249

Padua, 91–92, 119, 129, 134, 137, 153n, 182, 264, 268–70; cp, 117, 120; ec S. Marco, 218, 242

Paintings, mural, 182–83; at Novara, 237–39

Palaces: communal, 97, 115–20, 141–42, 168, 185–87, 205–6, 208; papal, 107, 154; royal/imperial, 77–78, 90, 95, 115–16, 126, 140, 173–74, 249. *See also* Rome (Lateran)

Papacy, 4, 154–56, 237, 245–49, 258–59; of Gregory IV (828–44), 59–61, 254; of Gregory VII (1073–85), 2–3, 5, 254; of Hadrian (772–95), 58–59, 61; of Hilary (461–68), 33; of John VII (705–7), 36; of Leo III (795–816), 24, 59, 181; of Leo IV (847–55), 61; of Lucius III (1181–85), 103–4, 164; of Sylvester II (999–1003), 244; of Zacharias (741–52), 33–34, 40

Parenzo, 20–21, 36–37, 150, 157–58, 171

Parma, 9–10, 18, 62, 83, 88–92, 97–98, 101, 104–5, 108, 117, 129, 142–46, 153, 168, 170–71, 173–81, 189, 201, 264, 268–70; b Aicardus (1062–69), 145; b Bernard II (1169–94), 101, 104–5, 111, 115, 145, 175, 177; b Cadalus (1045–71), 95, 97–98, 100, 175; b Grazia (1224–36), 105, 108, 111, 115, 145, 175–80, 188–89, 209–10; b Obizzo (d. 1224), 170, 212; b Ugo (1027–44), 92, 97–98, 160, 175; c S. Maria, 86–88, 111, 120, 133, 174; cp, 111, 120; ec, 106, 218–19; ip, 95; sb Bernard of the Uberti (1104–33), 89, 136, 145

Patrons: in late antiquity, 17, 40–50; saints, 133–34, 201

Paulinus of Nola, 16, 37

Pavia, 18–19, 63–64, 77, 85, 91, 129, 135, 137, 263, 272; cp, 116, 125; ip, 140; sb Lanfranc (1180–98), 125, 145, 155, 157–60, 162, 168, 179, 211, 236, 257–58; sb Epiphanius (467–96), 32, 130–31; sb Syrus (4th C.), 129, 134, 183, 236–38

Peace of Constance (1183), 89, 95, 126, 145, 164–65, 168, 199, 238

Pelicelli, Nestore, 9–10

Pensile (hanging) Apse, 231–34

Peristyle (surrounded by columns) Courtyards, 42–44, 51

Peter, Saint, 25–27, 57, 128, 181–82, 235, 237

Peter Damian (1007–72), 135–36, 179, 211, 235, 239, 257, 268

Piacenza, 18, 62–63, 88, 90–92, 93n, 116, 129, 133–34, 145, 148, 149, 166–67, 263–64, 268, 272; b Tedaldus (1167–92), 115; cp, 116–17

Piazza (plaza), 5, 15, 107, 111–20, 145–57, 168, 224, 256

Pisa, 88n, 119, 134, 139n, 141

Pistoia, 68–71, 79–80, 90–91, 100–101, 105, 108, 110, 113–14, 117, 148–52, 173, 202–3, 264, 272; b Ildebrand (1105–31), 90–91, 222; cp, 120; ec S. Niccolò, 106, 218, 222–24, 229–30, 232–35, 247n, 248–49, 256

Po River/Valley, 7, 18, 94–95, 267

Podestà (governor or chief executive), 10, 145, 166–67, 200, 255

Pompeii, 41–43

Poor, 160–69, 171, 210–13, 257–59

Portico (covered entryway with outer supporting columns), 58–59, 68, 74, 76, 78, 104, 111–14, 117, 146, 168

Profferlo (staircase parallel to facade), 154–56, 224

Ravenna, 18, 20–33, 51, 56–58, 80, 91, 113–14, 119–20, 128–29, 135, 152–53, 171–72, 182, 210, 244, 265–66, 272, 275; b Maximian (546–54), 31–32, 182, 233; b Neon (458), 23, 26, 52; b Peter II (494–520), 27, 36, 219–22; b Valerianus (787–810), 57, 113; b Victor (537–44), 31, 52; ec S. Andrea, 28, 105, 217, 219–22, 233, 249; ip, 95, 140; *Liber Pontificalis* (see Andreas Agnellus); sb Ursus (d 396), 23, 44

Reform, 3–4, 15, 95, 100, 107, 123–24, 126, 134–35, 143, 168, 179, 228, 233, 238, 241–42, 245, 249, 253–56, 269

Reggio Emilia, 63–65, 78–80, 83–84, 104, 129–33, 208–10, 264, 267, 269, 271; b Nicholas (1211–43), 208–9; b Peter (900–15), 64; b Teuzo (979–1030), 129–32; cp, 120; sb Prosper, 129–32, 134

Rieti, 210, 266; pp, 107, 154

Rimini, 18, 76, 139n, 265, 271; cp, 120

Rome, Lateran, 18, 24, 33–34, 37, 40, 47, 51, 58–61, 104, 107–8, 110, 154, 171, 181–82, 217, 246, 274–76; ec. S. Lorenzo/Sancta Sanctorum, 59, 181, 232, 244, 247n, 248n; ec. S. Michele, 59; ec S. Niccolò, 232–35, 247n; ec S. Silvestro, 40, 248n; ip 140; other churches, 19, 33, 36, 44, 61

Sacking of Episcopal Palaces, 257–58

Sacristies, 38, 47, 232–33, 248n–49n

Saints. See Hagiography; *specific saints*

Sala/sale. See Halls

Salimbene de Adam (1221–87), 86–89, 111, 170, 181, 208–15

Salutationes (Roman social ritual in which clients visit their patron), 40–42, 45

Segni, 180–81; b Bruno (1079–1123), 180–81, 211

Shops, 105

Siena, 19, 88n, 134, 263

Simony, 4, 164, 245, 268

Solarium (balcony or terrace), 57, 59–60, 63, 68–69, 71–72, 77–78

Spoleto, 147–48, 153, 202, 265

Staircases, 66, 68–69, 76–77, 105, 107, 113–14, 148–51, 153–56, 168, 256. *See also Profferlo*

Towers, 14, 57–58, 60–62, 65–66, 68, 70–71, 76, 97–98, 107, 144, 172

Treasuries, 38–39, 222

Trent, 83, 269, 271; sb Adelpretus (1156–77), 157; sb Vigilius (380–405), 19, 134

Treviso, 98n, 119, 218, 273; cp, 120

Triclinia (Roman formal dining rooms). *See* Dining rooms

Triconch (having three apses). *See* Halls

Trifores (arched windows further subdivided into three arched openings), 108, 114, 258

Turin, 139n, 141; b Maximus (5th C.), 19

Tympanum (arch-enclosed space over window or doorway), 108, 110

Urban civil architecture, 114–20, 146

Urban development, 110, 119–21, 125–26, 137–39

Verona, 18, 54–55, 77, 83–85, 91–92n, 97, 103–4, 108, 110, 128–29, 133–34, 139n, 145, 156, 182–83, 237, 263, 273; b Adelard (1188–1214), 104, 115, 145; b Omnebonus (1157–85), 103, 106, 110, 115, 145, 156; b Ratherius (931–34, 946–47, 961–68), 54–56, 77, 83–85, 141, 267; b Tebaldus (1135–57), 91–92n, 115; comital residence, 141; cp, 120; ec S. Zeno, 106, 218, 241; ip, 140

Vestries (*vestiaria*). *See* Sacristes

Vicedominus (episcopal official for overseeing temporalities of see), 84, 143

Vicenza, 90, 218, 274; b John Cacciafronte (1179–84), 136, 157, 159–61, 179, 211, 236, 244

Viterbo, pp, 154, 207

Vivarium, 30, 58

Volterra, 264, 267, 274

Wells, 71, 75, 76

Windows, 71, 73–74, 107–8, 113–14, 146, 168, 171, 224, 246. *See also* Bifores; Trifores

William Durand, Bishop of Mende (1285–96), 246–47